LOGIC

An Introduction

LOGIC

An Introduction

LIONEL RUBY
Professor of Philosophy
Roosevelt College

J. B. LIPPINCOTT COMPANY
Chicago · Philadelphia · New York

TO MY MOTHER

To My Mother

Preface

In that delightful 17th-century comedy, *The Bourgeois Gentleman,* Moliere describes Monsieur Jourdain's quest for an education. Jourdain, an unlettered nouveau riche, has employed several tutors to impart culture to him. In the first lesson, the instructor in philosophy endeavors to teach him the difference between prose and verse. Prose, the instructor informs him, is what one normally speaks. Astonished and delighted, our simple friend hurries off to tell his wife that he has had the distinction of speaking prose all his life without being aware of his own powers. In a similar fashion, the average person would probably also be amazed, if not delighted, to learn that he has been reasoning in syllogisms all his life, without being aware of his logical powers.

There are several types of mental activity that are classified under the general head of "thinking," such as daydreaming or reverie, remembering, reaching decisions, and so on, but the science called "logic" is concerned with the type of thinking known as "inference." Inference is a mental activity in which we say, "This is so because that is so," or "This is so; therefore, that is so." Inference, in other words, is present whenever we assert that a given statement is true because another is. Whenever we furnish evidence for our beliefs, whenever we answer the challenging question "Why?" with a "Because" and state our reasons or evidence for believing as we do, we engage in the "logical type" of thinking. We have been logicians all our lives without knowing it.

But though all of us, like M. Jourdain, speak in prose, we may do so well or badly. Similarly, though all of us draw inferences, our evidence may or may not be sufficient to justify our conclusions. It is perhaps unnecessary to call the reader's attention to the fact that he is well acquainted with persons who reason unsoundly. The distinction between sound and unsound inference is a familiar one. And it is this distinction which is the central theme of logic defined as the science of valid inference. Logic is the study of the principles that determine whether inferences are justified or unjustified. This does not mean that the logician is in possession of a secret lore, or that he has a vested interest in certain special principles called "logical," but only that he seeks to clarify what all of us are doing whenever we engage in reasoning.

Some popular criticisms, confusions, and misunderstandings of logic and the use of logical principles call for comment. We find an attitude of hostility toward logic in the following statement by the Chinese writer, Lin Yutang:

> Humanized thinking is just reasonable thinking. The logical man is always self-righteous and therefore inhuman and therefore wrong, while the reasonable man suspects that perhaps he is wrong and is therefore always right. (*The Importance of Living,* The John Day Co., 1937.)

Mr. Lin objects to self-righteous individuals who regard themselves as infallible. This is truly an undesirable characteristic and logicians will join with Mr. Lin in deploring this attitude. Few persons, perhaps, are so vividly aware as logicians of the difficulties in attempting to demonstrate that any factual proposition is true. And it is to be hoped that the logical individual will, above other men, never forget that perhaps *he* is wrong and the *other man* right. The reader may also be assured at this point that logicians are only human.

A misunderstanding which we shall call the "fear of logic" is based upon the assumption that logic tends to falsify experience in some mysterious manner. This "logophobia" is expressed in the following remarks from a speech delivered in the House of Commons by Austen Chamberlain, British Foreign Minister in the years following World War I:

> I profoundly distrust logic when applied to politics, and all English history justifies me. [Ministerial cheers] . . . Instinct and experience alike teach us that human nature is not logical,

that it is unwise to treat political institutions as instruments of logic, and that it is in wisely refraining from pressing conclusions to their logical end that the path of peaceful development and reform is really found.*

When Mr. Chamberlain speaks of logic he evidently has in mind a type of thinking which stupidly applies rigid principles to situations in which such principles are inapplicable. But such thinking, far from being "logical," is simply illogical. The logician who seeks to understand the world in which he lives will not refuse to recognize the "stubborn, irreducible facts" of political realities. Politics is not the same thing as mathematics, and anyone who treats human beings as if they were nothing but abstract symbols is following no logical law in doing so. But it is just as unreasonable to condemn "logic" for such bad thinking as it would be to condemn the science of arithmetic because bookkeepers make errors in addition. The question which the logician asks is: "Have we the evidence which is adequate to prove our conclusions?" It is the logician's task to point out the principles of proof which are employed in answering that question.

Comment is also required on Mr. Chamberlain's remark that "human nature is not logical." If this is so, then perhaps logic is irrelevant in human affairs. Aristotle, on the other hand, tells us that man is "the rational animal." Aristotle did not of course mean that human beings always reason correctly. The fact that he sharply criticized the writings of his philosophical predecessors is sufficient proof of this. He meant only that human beings possess the capacity for logical thinking, recognizing at the same time the wide gap between capacity and performance. Though we agree with Aristotle, Mr. Chamberlain's remark will be acceptable if it is interpreted to mean that we are emotional as well as reasoning creatures. Human nature is both logical and non-logical, in different respects. The non-logical factors call for further discussion.

Strong feelings and emotions, as is well known, make it difficult to think clearly. Prejudice and bias are responsible for distortions in our perceptions of facts. Wishes beget beliefs, for "the wish is father to the thought," often regardless of the evi-

* Quoted in L. S. Stebbing, *Thinking to Some Purpose*, Penguin Books, p. 8.

dence. And it is indeed hard to be consistent in applying the same standards to others as to ourselves, as is illustrated by the amusing "inflections" of the adverb "firm," in "I am firm; you are stubborn; he is a pigheaded fool." An English newspaper that asked its readers for other examples of this sort of thing received the following among many others:

"I am righteously indignant; you are annoyed; he is making a fuss about nothing."
"I am sparkling; you are unusually talkative; he is drunk."
"I am beautiful; you have quite good-looking features; she isn't bad-looking, if you like that type."

Modern psychology emphasizes the role of emotion in human behavior. Studies in the psychology of crowds and in mass behavior reveal the ineffectiveness of the appeal to reason in many situations. The studies in "psychodynamics," which use the methods of psychoanalysis in explaining individual and cultural phenomena, reveal the influence of the so-called "unconscious" factors in human behavior. From these and like studies there emerges a picture of the human mind as a kind of dark Dostoevskeian cavern in whose labyrinthine gloom strange and irrational visions brood. We shall acknowledge our debt to the psychologists and social scientists who have revealed the hitherto unsuspected irrationalities in man's nature. Nevertheless, Aristotle was right in saying that man is *capable* of rationality, and insofar as we seek rational consistency in our thoughts, or verifiable knowledge (in the science of psychodynamics as well as in other fields) logic is relevant.

It is perhaps unnecessary to add that logic is not the whole of life. Not only are we sometimes illogical, but large areas of experience are also *non*-logical or *non*-rational. An experience of joy or sorrow is neither logical nor illogical; it is simply an experience. There are areas in which logical analysis may be inappropriate, as in writing lyrical love verses. And certainly logic does not supply the dynamic energies necessary for action. But to the extent that we are interested in acquiring verifiable knowledge, we must concern ourselves with the criteria of proof and the adequacy of evidence, and it is here that logical principles are appropriate.

A word now as to the general plan and contents of this book. There are three parts, each of which discusses an indispensable aspect of the enterprise of rational thinking. The careful thinker will be interested in language, the instrument of thinking; in the soundness of his arguments; and in the truth of his assertions. Part One is concerned with linguistic and semantical problems; in Part Two we shall discuss the principles of valid inference or sound reasoning; and in Part Three we shall examine the methods employed by the sciences of nature and society, seeking to determine the methods whereby these disciplines attempt to furnish us with logically justifiable beliefs. In the classroom approximately 20 per cent of the time might be devoted to Part One, about 50 per cent to Part Two, and 30 per cent to the last part.

In the narrow sense of the term "logic" (defined as the study of valid inference), only Part Two is concerned with logic. But logic is interpreted more broadly throughout, as the study of valid inference *and* its applications in the search for truth. To this end we shall study the nature of language as a preliminary to the study of validity, since we must understand exactly what is being said before we can analyze reasoning, and in Part Three we shall study the problem of applying the rules of inference to the subject matter of the sciences. This third part, which discusses scientific methods, is concerned with the field usually called "inductive logic."

Our discussion of valid inference, or deductive logic, is largely based upon the so-called "classical tradition" in logic that began with Aristotle. Though this logic was developed in the Middle Ages, it remained largely unmodified until the 19th century. The prestige of the classical logic was once so great that it was believed that it represented the science of logic in its final form. Modern logic has shown that the older logic was incomplete in that it does not cover all of the logical forms that can be investigated by a more generalized "symbolic" logic. The newer logic has also shown that the whole of logic may be systematized as a rigorous formal science in "mathematical" form. The logical tradition remains unbroken, however, since the older logic has been incorporated into the new. We shall note some of the newer developments insofar as they extend, and require clarification of, the classical doctrine. Our emphasis, however, will be on logic as a part of general education, and on the use of logical principles in the clarification and analysis of everyday discourse.

The author wishes to thank many friends, including colleagues and former students, for their helpful comments and criticisms. In particular he is greately indebted to Professors A. C. Benjamin of the University of Missouri, Millard S. Everett and Wayne A. R. Leys of Roosevelt College, Douglas N. Morgan of Northwestern University, and Warner A. Wick of the University of Chicago for their very valuable suggestions and criticisms. Special thanks are due also to Mrs. Louise Landes for stylistic criticisms, to Mrs. Elizabeth Bianchi for several useful suggestions, and to Miss Virginia Briska for typing the stencils in the experimental edition. The author's indebtedness to other writers is too great to be detailed, but mention should at least be made of the works by Cohen and Nagel, Frye and Levi, and Castell.

Specific acknowledgment is made in the text to the works from which quotations are drawn. The following authors and publishers gave their kind permission to quote excerpts from their publications: Appleton-Century-Crofts, Inc.; *The Chicago Daily News; The Chicago Sun-Times; The Chicago Tribune;* The Clarendon Press; Coward-McCann, Inc.; Felix Frankfurter; Ginn and Company; Harcourt, Brace and Company, Inc.; Harper and Brothers; Harper's Magazine; Henry Holt and Company, Inc.; Houghton Mifflin Company; Alfred Korzybski and the Non-Aristotelian Library Publishing Co.; Little, Brown and Company; Liveright Publishing Corporation; The Macmillan Company; *New Republic;* Prentice-Hall, Inc.; G. P. Putnam's Sons; American Association for the Advancement of Science, Charles Scribner's Sons; Simon and Schuster, Inc.; Time, Inc.; Whittlesey House; and the Yale University Press.

LIONEL RUBY

Preface to the Second Edition

This revision was undertaken with three main purposes in mind: to make the exposition clearer and thus to make the book more efficient as a teaching instrument, to replace illustrations that had become "dated" or which were of doubtful pedagogical value with new examples of more enduring interest, and to add a discussion of some of the techniques of symbolic logic. The discussion of symbolic logic will be found in Chapter 13. An appendix explaining the use of the Venn diagrams for testing syllogisms has also been added.

With some few exceptions this is a revision rather than a re-writing of the original book. Though there is scarcely a page on which there has not been some alteration; though sentences, paragraphs, and in some cases entire pages have been re-written; though the order of the sections or exercises has occasionally been revised, nevertheless the only extensive re-writing occurred in the final chapter. I have tried to point up the logical elements in discussions of values and to soften the somewhat polemical tone of the first writing. Other important changes: the former Chapter 13, on Dilemmas, is now the final section in Chapter 12, and much of the discussion and exercise material on Complex Propositions in the old edition is now incorporated into the new chapter on Symbolic Logic.

Among less important changes I may note the elimination of truth-functional symbols in the discussion of Compound Propositions in Chapter 12. These symbols are used for the first time in Chapter 13. I have also substituted the expression "negated conjunction" for "disjunction." Since many writers use the latter term for what I call "alternation," this change will eliminate some of the confusion of students when they read other texts in logic. I still prefer the name "alternation" for alternations!

I wish to thank Professors Douglas N. Morgan and Warner A. Wick for their generous help in contributing criticisms and suggestions for the improvement of the original draft of Chapter 13. I also wish to thank my wife for catching many obscurities in exposition.

LIONEL RUBY

CONTENTS

Part One

Language and Logic

Chapter 1

Disputes: Verbal and Otherwise

Section I: A Few Examples

1. Scene: A college dormitory at 1:00 A.M.

A "bull session" is in full swing. Bill and Jim are arguing a frequently debated question: Are all men created equal?

BILL: I tell you that men aren't equal. People who say that men are created equal just don't know what they are talking about. Use your own eyes! Do you *see* the equality of mankind? Don't we see that everyone is different from everyone else? Don't people differ in their abilities and in their physical, mental, and moral endowments? Don't intelligence tests show that some individuals are near-geniuses and others are non-geniuses? In my opinion Thomas Jefferson uttered preposterous nonsense in the Declaration of Independence when he wrote, and I quote, "We hold this truth to be self-evident, that all men are created equal." This so-called truth is not evident to me, so it can't be self-evident! In my opinion this so-called truth is actually a falsehood.

JIM: I am sorry, Bill, but you are the one who doesn't know what he is talking about. Men *are* equal, and I agree completely with Jefferson. The equality of mankind is the foundation of our democracy. No man has the right to special privileges from which others are excluded because of their race, religion, or color. Every person is entitled to equal opportunities, and no one should suffer discrimination because he belongs to a minority group. The equality of mankind is the basis of our legal system, which tells us that all men are equal before the law. Do you deny that? Are you in favor of racial and religious discrimination?

BILL: No, Jim, I don't believe in racial and religious per-

3

secution or discrimination. But I repeat once more: men aren't equal. Why, most people don't even have the intelligence to distinguish honest men from crooks, especially in elections, and that's why we have so much corruption and inefficiency in our government. Your equality is a myth . . .

2. Another night

TOM: Russia is certainly not a democracy, no matter how long and often Russians may claim it to be so. In Russia there are no opposition parties, and no man dares to oppose the edicts of the ruling class. There are no guarantees against arbitrary arrest, and anyone may be held without trial if he criticizes the government. I believe it is impossible to have democracy unless you have capitalism and free enterprise, for when the state controls a man's job it has the power of life and death over him, and his freedom has disappeared. His actions and his thoughts must then be subservient to the state.

JACK: And I say that Russia is a democracy. In Russia every man is guaranteed a job and is free from the worst of all fears, namely, economic insecurity. There is no such thing as involuntary unemployment in Russia. And Russia recognizes the principle of equality for all races and religions and for the sexes. Women have equal rights with men in economic, political, and spiritual activities. Russia is a democratic country.

TOM: Russia is not democratic since there is no freedom, not even "economic freedom." There are no free labor unions, since labor unions are not permitted to strike for higher wages or for better working conditions. Striking is considered an act of treason against the state. You can't have democracy when union leaders are stooges of the party and its bosses. There is no involuntary unemployment in Russia, true, but this is because the state assigns jobs to the workers, who must take the jobs whether or not they like the work or the wages . . .

The disputes you have just read are examples of a type of discussion which is all too common. Disputes of this type are futile and frustrating. The argument gets nowhere, no one ever convinces anyone else, and the dispute proceeds endlessly if continued in the vein described, until the disputants give up because of mutual exhaustion. They will then part company, each experiencing a sense of profound pity or contempt for the other, and each thinking that "there are none so blind as those who will not see."

Disputes of this type are usually called "verbal disputes," or "verbal disagreements." Such "disputes," as we shall see, may not be *actual* disagreements, the disagreement being such only in *appearance*. Before we attempt to analyze them, however, we shall examine a "real" disagreement.

3. A real disagreement

BEN: If we wish to eliminate strikes and lockouts in the United States, then we ought to require the arbitration of all labor disputes. The Australians have had compulsory arbitration for a great many years, and they have reduced strikes to a minimum.

SIDNEY: On the contrary. *The 1939 Year-Book of Labour Statistics,* published by the International Labour Office, shows that for the decade 1929–1939 Australia was the world's third highest nation in the average number of days lost each year because of strikes and lockouts. In Australia they lost 61 days per 100 employees; in the United States only 36 days were lost.

BEN: Your statistics are out-dated. For the three year period 1951 to 1953, the figures are 40 days lost in Australia as compared with 80 lost in the United States. For 1954 to 1956, the figures are 37 for them and 56 for us.

In Dispute 3 the parties are in actual disagreement. They are in disagreement over whether the compulsory arbitration of labor disputes has or has not been successful in eliminating strikes in Australia, and they are in disagreement over whether or not compulsory arbitration would eliminate strikes in the United States. It is not our concern here to determine whether one of these parties is right, the other wrong. The point is that they are engaged in a genuine dispute.

Let us now return to our examples of verbal disputes. In Dispute 1 Bill and Jim *appear* to be in disagreement over the proposition that all men are equal. Bill says that men are not equal; Jim says that they are. But we soon find that Bill and Jim have used the word "equal" in different senses. By "equal" Bill means similarity in physical and mental attributes; by "equal"

Jim means that all men are entitled to justice, that is, to the same privileges and opportunities. Though each has used the same word, each means something quite different from what the other means.

Bill and Jim believe that they are in disagreement over certain facts, but actually they may not be. Each may be right in what he affirms, and wrong only in claiming that he necessarily disagrees with the other. For Bill and Jim defined the word "equal" in different ways, and if we now translate what Bill and Jim *said* into what they *mean,* we shall find that their "dispute" may be summarized in the following manner:

BILL: Human beings are not possessed of the same physical and mental qualities.

JIM: You are wrong, Bill. All men are entitled to justice.

BILL: And I assert that men do not have the same physical and mental qualities.

In other words, Bill and Jim are not necessarily in disagreement on any issue whatsoever. They think that they are in such disagreement only because they overlook the fact that the innocent word "equal" has been used in more than one sense. When this is pointed out to the disputants they will probably abandon their original dispute at once. They may then go on to discuss some other related question, but they will not continue a type of discussion which can never get beyond its starting point.

We see, then, that some disagreements are such in appearance only. Dispute 3 was a real or actual disagreement concerning certain facts, but Dispute 1 was a dispute only in appearance. Our discussion indicates that we must distinguish between real (or genuine) and merely apparent disputes. In a *real* dispute the parties actually disagree; in an *apparent* dispute they think they are in disagreement but actually are not, or may not be. A *verbal dispute* is an *apparent* dispute in this sense, for in such disputes the possible actual agreement of the parties is concealed by the fact that *they use a key word in more than one sense.* In such disputes the parties believe that they are in actual disagreement concerning some specific issue, but they may be in entire agreement over the facts and differ only in the manner in which they use the key term. When a key term is used in more than one sense the parties may be in agreement, or they may be in disagreement, but the difference in the usage of the key term prevents them from knowing that they are in agreement, or, if in disagreement, from knowing the precise issue over which they differ.

In Dispute 2, the term "democracy" is obviously used in two different senses. Tom is actually saying that the Russian people lack certain freedoms. Jack asserts that there is no economic insecurity in Russia. This is what they really mean in asserting that Russia is or is not a democracy. There is thus no actual disagreement in the propositions asserted by Tom and Jack. But of course to point out these things to disputants will not automatically settle all their differences. When a verbal dispute has been eliminated, the participants become aware of the fact that they have been using the key word in different senses, and there may be nothing further to discuss. But they may also not regard this difference in senses as legitimate, and they may go on to discuss how a word should or should not be used. They may question the allegations of facts as stated by their opponents. Or they may claim that their opponents are not using the key word in its commonly accepted sense. The main point is that there may be no actual disagreement in positions *as originally stated.*

The same type of analysis is often applicable when *agreements,* rather than disagreements, are verbal rather than actual. An agreement may also be such in appearance only, because of the different senses in which words are used. Such agreements are *verbal agreements.* For example, the United States, Great Britain, and the U.S.S.R. agreed at the Yalta and Potsdam "summit" conferences that democratic governments would be established through free elections in Poland and elsewhere. The words "democracy" and "free" were not precisely defined, and it soon became apparent that the parties had entirely different notions as to what the words meant. They were in fundamental disagreement concerning policy, but their disagreement was concealed by their acceptance of words which they interpreted differently.

Another example: Grey says "I agree" when Brown argues that God exists. But when Brown uses the word "God" he means the personal God of the Jewish-Christian tradition, while Grey accepts John Dewey's definition of God as "the natural forces and conditions—including man and human association—that

promote the growth of the ideal and that further its realization."
Dewey's God is not a supernatural God, but rather a name for
certain natural conditions. The Jewish-Christian conception of
God is quite different. Brown and Grey have thus confused an
agreement in words with an agreement concerning facts. They
were in actual disagreement and in apparent agreement. Their
agreement was only in the use of the same word. They were
actually talking about different things, almost as if one person
were to say, "I believe that X is the best candidate," and for the
other to answer, "Yes, I agree that Z is the best candidate."
Brown might have been horrified if he knew just what it was to
which Grey was agreeing. It is, in general, easier to become religious by definition than by conversion.

We may define a verbal agreement as an agreement which
is such in appearance only, in which the possible actual disagreement of the parties is veiled by the fact that a key term is used
in different senses.

We shall now state a basic principle of all intelligent discourse: In order to agree or disagree with another person both
parties must be in agreement with respect to all of the key terms
used in their discussion. Paradoxically, it is impossible to disagree with another person without agreeing with him (on the
meanings of the terms). Otherwise our discussions move at cross-
purposes and there is no meeting of minds.

The basis of all verbal agreements and disagreements lies in
the ambiguity of words. An ambiguous word is one which may
have more than one meaning, so that it is capable of being understood in more than one sense. These variant meanings give
us the equivalents of several different words which happen to
be spelled in the same manner. A "spade," meaning a garden
implement, has only a remote connection with a "spade," meaning a suit in a deck of cards. These are the equivalents of two
different words spelled in the same manner. Now, if we imagine
a conversation during a bridge game, during which one of the
players (a suburbanite who likes to garden) remarks that he has
"three spades" (meaning garden implements) and his partner
contradicts him with "You can't have any; the spades have all
been played," we would have the basis for a verbal dispute
similar to those we have already examined. The two disputants
would be talking about altogether different things. (It is perhaps

unnecessary to call the reader's attention to the unwritten law among bridge players which makes it a heinous crime to make such remarks during a bridge game.)

A possible misunderstanding should be cleared up at this point. We cannot define a verbal dispute as a "dispute over words." A "dispute about words" may be a real dispute, as in the following:

PAUL: When most persons mention the word "religion" they refer to membership in some church and to the belief in a personal God.

JOE: I disagree. I believe that most persons use the word "religion" to signify that some person or persons have a whole-hearted devotion to certain social ideals and objectives.

This is a real dispute as to the manner in which most persons use the word "religion." Paul and Joe are in disagreement concerning word usage. Similarly, if Paul argued that religion really means "belief in a personal God," and Joe denied this, this would also be a real dispute, for Paul and Joe would be in genuine disagreement. A real dispute may also occur over the correctness of a "value judgment," i.e., over whether something is good or bad. The sole determining element is this: Are the parties in actual or merely apparent disagreement?

A verbal dispute, then, is not a genuine dispute *in the terms in which the dispute is formulated,* for when the parties use a key word in two different senses they are talking about different things. They must use this key word in the same sense before they can determine whether they are in agreement or disagreement. They may differ over the way in which the key word ought to be used, and this will be a genuine disagreement, but this is not the way in which the issue presents itself in a verbal dispute. A verbal dispute, then, is a merely apparent dispute in its original formulation, but it is a merely apparent dispute of a special variety: one in which the parties use a key word in different senses. In a verbal dispute the parties believe that their statements cannot both be correct, whereas actually they may be. Each may be correct in accordance with the sense in which he employs the key term. But in a real dispute the parties cannot both be correct. *Only one* of them can be right, though of course both may be wrong.

Section II: The Analysis of Disputes

In our study of logic we shall learn the principles of correct reasoning, but we shall also learn how to apply these principles to examples. Theory without practice is almost useless in a subject such as this. We shall, accordingly, apply the principles we have just learned to the analysis of some examples. Practice will make the reader adept at the analysis of disputes. He will then be better able to recognize verbal disputes when they occur in his everyday conversations and may thus avoid falling into the traps to which such disputes expose the unwary. And, if it is not too risky an undertaking, the reader may also be able to help others avoid the futile types of disputes.

Every dispute should be examined in terms of the 5-step analysis which we shall now state. The first three steps should be applied to *all* disputes in order to determine whether they are verbal or non-verbal. If the third step is answered in the affirmative, then the dispute is a verbal one, and the remaining steps should then be worked out to show that there may be no actual disagreement.

1. What is the point in disagreement, or the issue in dispute?
2. State the sentences expressing the essential positions asserted by the disputants.
3. Do the parties use a key term in different senses so that there is no "meeting of minds"? If so, state the ambiguous term.
4. State the different senses in which each disputant employs the ambiguous term.
5. Restate the essential sentences as asserted by the disputants in Step 2 above, except that you must now replace the ambiguous term in each of these sentences by the variant definitions of this term as found in Step 4. The ambiguous term must not appear in these restated sentences.

We shall illustrate this method of analysis by applying it to Dispute 2, page 4.

The results of the analysis will be as follows:

1. Is Russia a democracy?
2. Tom: Russia is not a democracy.
   Jack: Russia is a democracy.
3. "Democracy" is used in different senses by the disputants.

4. TOM: Democracy means a government which guarantees freedom to all individuals.

JACK: Democracy means a system in which all men have economic security.

5. TOM: Russia is not a country in which the government guarantees freedom to all men.

JACK: Russia is a country in which all men have economic security.

Note that the sentences as stated in Steps 2 and 5 should be *identical* except with respect to the key term and its definitions. The key term is used in Step 2; its definitions are stated in Step 5.

The analysis indicates that the parties are not necessarily in genuine disagreement, so far as they have stated their positions. The dispute should, therefore, be abandoned in its original form. When the parties find that their original "dispute" has vanished, one of several things may happen. They may then find that they are in essential agreement with each other, each granting that democracy may be properly defined in the two senses. They may say, "We see that the word 'democracy' may be used in different senses, in one of which our question would be answered affirmatively, in the other negatively. Our original question should therefore be answered 'yes' or 'no,' depending upon what one means by 'democracy.' " But the disappearance of the original dispute may also initiate new disputes. Tom may accuse Jack of "misusing" the term democracy, and they may then discuss the question as to whether democracy may properly be defined as Jack defined it. Or Jack may accuse Tom of the same error. In any case, if the parties cannot agree on what they mean by "democracy," it is futile to discuss the question as to whether or not Russia is a "something-we-know-not-what."

Disputes may also arise over statements of fact made by the parties. Is it true that men and women enjoy freedom in the democracies? Is it true that Russia guarantees economic security to all? It is obvious that the possibilities of new verbal disputes also lurk in these questions. What do "freedom" and "economic security" mean? Our analysis of verbal disputes does not dispose of all problems, but it does eliminate a dispute in which the parties themselves do not know what, if anything, is at issue between them.

A warning is necessary at this point. We have emphasized the importance of "defining one's terms." But let us not use this method of analysis for the purpose of quibbling. Let us not be hypercritical where such criticism is unimportant, i.e., where it is reasonable to suppose that the parties use their words in substantially the same ways. When words are sufficiently understood for the purposes of a given discussion, then it is a waste of time to argue over definitions. But an awareness of the linguistic problems of argumentative discourse is always necessary, and most of us err in being too uncritical.

Exercises

A. In the following group, distinguish the real disagreements from those which are merely apparent. Which of the merely apparent disputes are "verbal"? Which are non-verbal? Check your answers by asking yourself the question: Can both of the parties be right? If they can, then there is no real dispute.

    1. BLACK: The earth has been in existence for only 100 million years.

    BLUE: And I contend that the earth is at least 5 billion years old.

    2. ROY: When I say it's propaganda, I mean it's a pack of lies, for that is what propaganda means.

    RAY: You are mistaken. Propaganda really means any act of influencing or persuading another person to some predetermined end.

    3. HARRY: George Washington was the first president.

    HENRY (who is slightly deaf): You are mistaken. John Adams was the second president.

    4. SAM: Picasso is a great artist because of his profound sense of form, space, and light.

    SEYMOUR: In my opinion, his sense of form, space, and light is superficial, rather than profound; so he is not a great artist.

    5. SAM: I like Picasso's paintings.

    SEYMOUR: I don't. I think they're terrible!

    6. ED: Monogamy is the ideal form of marriage relationship.

    ERNEST: I believe that polygyny is the ideal form.

7. MILDRED: The American people approve of monogamy.
   MYRTLE: The Moslems approve of polygyny.
8. GEORGE: The correct spelling is l-a-b-o-r.
   GODFREY: And I say that the correct spelling is l-a-b-o-u-r.
   (Would it make any difference if Godfrey were an Englishman?)
9. ETHEL: The junior Senator from Alaska is a propagandist.
   MARCIA: He is not.
   (Ethel and Marcia may be engaging in a verbal dispute, but then again they may not be. Explain.)

B. In the following exercises, analyze each dispute in terms of the 5-step analysis. Also note whether you think that the parties would abandon their disputes after the analysis is completed or whether they would be likely to disagree over some other question.

1. WALTER: Senator X is a liberal, for he believes in freedom. He supports our system of free enterprise and opposes the extension of bureaucratic regulation of business. He is opposed to all attempts to limit the freedoms of speech, press, and assembly. He stands four-square against totalitarian systems and wishes to keep us from moving in that direction.
   WARREN: And I deny that he is a liberal. He voted against federal aid to education, which indicates that he is not concerned over the welfare of the common man.

2. JOE: A tree which falls in an uninhabited forest does not make a sound when it crashes to the earth. There is no one there to hear any sound, and when no one can hear a sound, the sound does not exist.
   AL: There certainly is a sound when the tree crashes in an uninhabited forest. The crash of the tree sets up longitudinal wave motions in a transmitting medium, the air. These longitudinal waves are present in the atmosphere whether or not anyone is present, and so there is sound present.
   JOE: But no one's auditory nerve is affected. No sensation is produced through the organs of hearing, and no one can have the mental experience of hearing if no one is in the forest. So you are mistaken in saying that there can be sound in an uninhabited forest.

3. JOHN: I believe that the Western Powers were wholly justified in shooting the Nazi leaders at the close of World War II. But I believe that it was wrong to try them for the violation of international law, for the simple reason that they

could not have been guilty of violating something which did not exist. It was wrong to condemn them for violating international law, for there is no such thing. Law exists only when a governing body enjoys complete power over the persons within its jurisdiction and issues commands to those persons. Such commands are backed up by "physical sanctions," the power to enforce the commands by physical force. There is no world government, so international law is nonexistent.

PHILIP: And I believe that the Nazis were properly tried for having violated international law. They did violate that law, for they violated the moral, social, and political codes which govern the conduct of nations. International law has existed for a long time. There have been international courts and tribunals; there are treaties which are binding on the nations which sign them. The Nazis violated the moral codes of mankind. They were guilty of deliberate and premeditated murder, and so they were properly tried and properly executed.

4. STACE: The Nazis were guilty of morally monstrous deeds. They violated the basic principles of all moral systems. These principles require that we should be just to our fellow men and that we should respect the integrity and dignity of our fellow human creatures.

SUMNER: But morality is relative to the approval of a particular group. The mores can make anything right, and so if the German community or group approved of the Nazis' conduct, then the Nazis acted quite morally. Of course, *we* don't approve of their conduct; *we* don't choose to behave that way, and people who acted like the Nazis would act immorally in the United States.

5. The Chicago Art Institute recently presented a show devoted to abstract and surrealist art. Differences of opinion were rife among the spectators. Jane, for example, said that the paintings were great works of art, for they expressed the mechanical dynamism of our contemporary industrial world and the psychological frustrations which accompany living at high speed. John, on the other hand, said that this "modernistic stuff" could not be great art, for these paintings did not depict anything recognizable in the real world, nor, he added, do they express noble thoughts and feelings.

6. During the 1930's, estimating the number of persons unemployed in the United States became a popular pastime

Chapter 2

The Meaning of "Meaning"

Section I: Semantics and Logic

In the first chapter we noted the importance of the linguistic aspects of reasoning. We saw how inattention to the meanings of terms may result in a failure to communicate. We saw how unawareness of the pitfalls into which language may lead us will sometimes result in a verbal dispute. When we engage in such disputes we confuse disagreements over the meaning of words with disagreements over the manner in which such words are applied to a particular situation, but we do not know that this is what we are doing.

Our analysis of disputes raised a number of problems and questions concerning language usage. Some of these questions, and others which may have occurred to the reader, are the following:

1. Does each word have a correct meaning? Does a word *really* mean one thing and not some other thing, so that some senses in which a word is used are legitimate, others illegitimate?
2. If we answer the above questions in the affirmative, how are the correct meanings determined? Does the etymology of a word give us its correct meaning?
3. May an individual define a word to suit himself?
4. What is the meaning of ambiguity and how does it arise?
5. What is a good definition?

The answers to these questions all involve the problem of *meaning,* the basic problem in the relationship between language and reasoning. This problem will occupy our attention in the remainder of Part One. We shall be concerned with the influence of language on thinking and reasoning, in order that

for statisticians. These estimates often varied wid
one occasion the National Association of Manufa
asserted that there were only 3 million unemploye
CIO claimed that there were 7 million unemploye
suming that the disputants made their estimates o
basis of statistics gathered by competent sources of inf
tion, how do you account for this difference in figures
plain why this dispute may have been a purely verbal
and analyze accordingly.

we may know what we are doing when we use words in discourse. Knowledge of the principles of meaning will also enable us to eliminate some of the obstacles to clear thinking arising from the improper use of language and help us to avoid falling prey to various kinds of linguistic confusions.

The relationship of language to thinking is much closer than is commonly suspected, and linguistic investigations may yield surprising results. For example, the children in an underprivileged neighborhood did very poorly in an intelligence test which contained questions such as, "A hand is to an arm as a foot is to a ———." It was later discovered that "is to" was an unfamiliar concept to these children. When "goes with" was substituted for "is to," their I.Q.'s immediately increased. Similarly, a public opinion poll phrases its questions in a specific manner. Phrased in a different way, the "public opinion" sought for might reveal quite different results.

The general study of meaning, in particular the study of the meanings of words in their relationship to the things for which they stand, is called "semantics." The term "semantics," derived from the Greek word *sema,* which means "sign," was introduced into modern usage by the French linguist Michel Bréal, in his *Essai de Sémantique,* published in 1897. "Semantics," however, is but a new name for a type of linguistic investigation which is almost as old as philosophy itself, though only in recent years has this subject emerged as a full-fledged discipline. Today it refers to a vast and complex field of investigation, into which our present discussion will offer only a few glimpses. It is also important to note that the interests of writers on semantics are very diverse. Thus we find that some writers are primarily interested in the anthropological aspects of language and in the origin of language (Malinowski, Whorff, Koffka, Köhler). A number of logicians are interested in the analysis of systems of signs (Carnap, Morris). A third group is interested in the psychological analysis of meaning (Ogden, Richards, Walpole). Finally, we note a group of writers who call themselves "General Semanticists" (Korzybski, Hayakawa, Stuart Chase). These writers believe that semantics may be usefully employed as a therapeutic agent for the elimination of social maladjustments and personal neuroses. But all writers on semantics have in common a concern with the problem of meaning. We turn now to the nature of this problem.

Section II: Signs and Symbols

To say that words have meaning is to say that they refer to something other than themselves. To "refer to something other than itself" is to function as a *sign*. Thus all words are signs, and all meaning-situations are sign-situations.

A sign-situation involves three aspects: The sign, such as a word, which in itself is simply a noise or a mark on paper; the thing signified, or referred to, which we shall call "the referent"; and persons or interpreters who refer to or who are referred to the referent. Thus a sign is something which refers to something for someone.* This three-fold aspect of sign-situations may be shown in a "triangle of reference," viz:

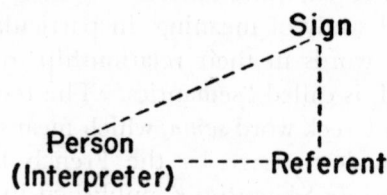

Signs may be divided into two major types, natural and conventional. A natural sign is an event in our experience which

* The expression "refers to something" requires a qualification and a cautionary remark. Some signs are exceptions to the rule, for some words have no referents. Examples are such words as "and," "or," "not," "all," "some," etc., which serve certain logical functions, and ejaculations such as "ouch," "wow," and "yippee," which merely express feelings without designating referents. But the rule will hold for all other types of words, and we shall ignore this qualification in the following discussion.

Though we shall speak of referents as "things," for simplicity's sake, the reader should note that referents are not necessarily physical objects in the external world, i.e., things which can be seen and touched. They may be events, activities, relations, conditions, and so on. We must therefore reject such views as those of Stuart Chase, as expressed in his *Tyranny of Words,* that words have meaning only when they refer to "something real enough to be kicked." Referents may be abstractions, such as "energy"; or feelings, such as those of pleasure and pain; or creatures of man's imagination, such as dragons and other mythical monsters. The words "centaur" and "mermaid" have referents, though none such exist in the physical world of space and time. We do not confuse the referents of the world of the imagination with the referents of the real world when we know what we are doing.

refers to some other event because our experience has taught us that the two events are associated or connected in some fashion. Thus, a Kansan sees a dark cloud on the horizon, and he interprets what he sees as the sign of an approaching tornado. The cloud is a natural sign of the tornado. A conventional sign, which we shall call a "symbol," is an artificial construct made by human beings for the purpose of referring to something. A symbol is a sign which is deliberately employed in order to convey a meaning. Symbols become part of a language when human beings agree that they shall "stand for" given referents. Symbols are signs, but not all signs are symbols.

One or two details may be noted before we leave these definitions. Some objects may combine the functions of natural and conventional signs. Thus, a thermometer which indicates that the temperature is 100° F. on a July afternoon combines both types. The movement of the mercury is a natural sign of heat, but the fact that the degree of heat is called "100° Fahrenheit" is established by convention. It should also be obvious that many symbols are nonverbal. A yellow line drawn on your side of a highway symbolizes "Do not pass here." Road-markers, numbers, diagrams, codes, shorthand systems, gestures, or even the use of lanterns in the "Ride of Paul Revere" ("one if by land and two if by sea") are all symbols. We should also note that though symbols refer to things other than themselves, they may also be interesting for their own sakes. A theme song on a radio program is a symbol of a certain type of entertainment, but the theme music may also be enjoyed for its own sake. Word-symbols may of course also possess aesthetic qualities, as in poetic expressions.

Section III: Communication

Successful communication occurs only when a speaker and hearer make the same connections between symbols and the things which they are intended to signify. The hearer must be referred to the referent to which the speaker wishes to direct his attention. The typical form of the process of successful communication may be illustrated by the following diagram, which combines the triangles of reference for both the speaker and the hearer:

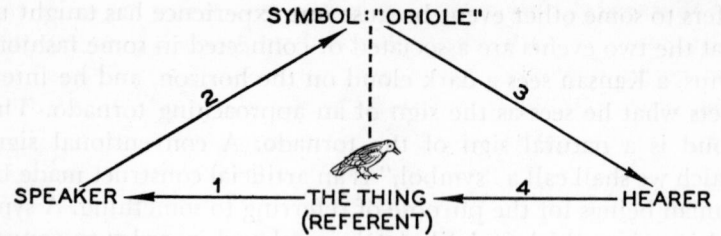

Arrow 1 represents the situation in which the speaker thinks of something before he has found the word he wishes to use. (The word and the referent may also come to the speaker's mind simultaneously.)

Arrow 2 represents the finding of the word to stand for the thing. (The connection between the word and the thing is indicated by the broken line.)

Arrow 3 indicates the word coming to the attention of the hearer.

Arorw 4 indicates that the hearer's mind is referred to the referent.

The diagram indicates that the hearer has correctly interpreted the symbols used by the speaker. Communicator and communicatee have the same terms in mind. But this happy consummation is not always attained, as we have already noted in our discussion of verbal disputes. Failures in communication occur when the symbol refers to different referents for the speaker and hearer. Let us symbolize these different referents by R_1 and R_2. The triangles of reference will then appear as follows:

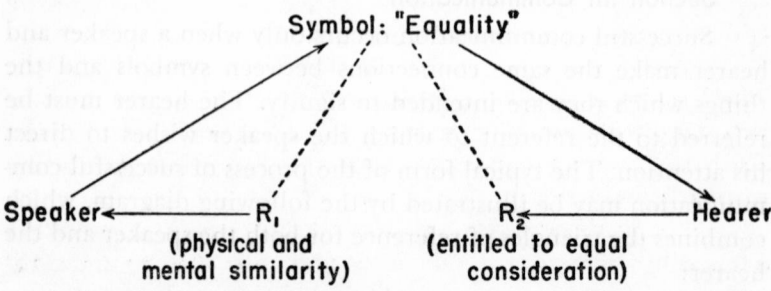

Successful communication occurs only when the reference is the same for both the speaker and the hearer. But note that the symbol may refer the hearer's mind to much more than the ostensible referent. It may indicate fine shades of subtle meanings, reveal the personality of the speaker, and so on.

Section IV: The Arbitrariness of Meanings

A symbol is a sign the meaning of which has been conventionally agreed upon. A symbol, such as a word, designates a referent by agreement or convention. Human decisions are thus required in order to establish the meaning of symbols, and such decisions are arbitrary ones, since "arbitrary" means "resting on a judgment which is not fixed by rule or law." This means that any object may be given any name which we choose to confer upon it. Names arise as a result of human agreements, or stipulations. This is illustrated in its purest form by the procedure whereby new words are coined today, as when chemists invent a new name for a new element. The procedure is wholly conventional and proceeds in something like the following manner: "Let us call this new element 'argon'." This is a stipulation entered into by mutual consent. This naming activity is arbitrary in the sense that any other name might have been given to this element, such as "aeron," a name earlier suggested.

No generation ever makes up its living vocabulary as a whole in this manner, since we inherit most of our words from our linguistic tradition, and certainly language did not originate by such conscious stipulations. "We can hardly suppose," as Bertrand Russell said in *The Analysis of Mind,* "that a parliament of speechless elders met together and agreed to call a cow a cow and a wolf a wolf." Many names come into being by unconscious and unnoticed affirmations in usage, and they come to be accepted in the same manner. In such cases the stipulation may be said to be implicit, but in order that a word may retain its meaning there must be constant and renewed acts of affirmation. These go on daily when we reaffirm (implicitly) that "house" will stand for an architectural edifice of a certain sort. We are at liberty, however, subject to certain limitations, to change the word at any time.

Though all symbols result from human decisions, note that a few symbols resemble their referents, so that their relationship to their referents is not a *merely* arbitrary one. We refer to *onomatopoetic* words, which sound like their referents, i.e., words such as "bow-wow," "buzz," "boom," "crack"; and to *iconic* signs, which look like their referents. Examples of iconic signs are diagrams, maps, and sketches. Nevertheless these signs are also symbolic by convention and agreement.

The conventional or arbitrary nature of symbols has not always been recognized. At one time it was believed that words have a "natural" relation to their referents, i.e., that the relationship was grounded "in the nature of things." We shall call this view the "natural theory." In Plato's dialogue, *Cratylus*, Socrates asserts that there is a natural connection between words and things. He believed that the gods call things by names which are naturally correct, but that human beings often erroneously call things by wrong names. The Garden of Eden incident, in which God asked Adam to name all things, is a variant of the natural theory, for Adam, as God's agent, would presumably give things their "right" names. Hebrew would then be regarded as the natural language. The natural consequence of such a view is that all other languages are incorrect, and this indeed is the assumption which underlies the story of the Tower of Babel, concerning the supposed origin of the multitude of languages. The babelization of tongues is described as a punishment for man's presumption in seeking to reach too high. Inventions of new international languages such as Esperanto and Basic English may be regarded as efforts to remove these consequences of sin.

The natural theory was aptly criticized by the English philosopher John Locke, in his *Essay on the Human Understanding*, with the remark that if names were natural, all human beings should speak the same language. The natural theory was also rejected by Aristotle. "By a noun," said Aristotle, "we mean a sound significant by convention . . . nothing is by nature a noun or name—it is only so when it becomes a symbol." *(De Interpretatione.)* This is the view which we accept.

Names are thus neither right nor wrong in a logical sense—they simply are what they are. Words may be appropriate or inappropriate according to aesthetic standards; they may be in accordance with customary usage or not, but the criteria of truth and falsity are not applicable to the names we use for referents. This is not to deny the great importance of aesthetic and customary standards, especially the latter. There *is* a significant sense in which words may be said to be "right" or "wrong." A student of botany is expected to be able to identify flowers by name, and if he is unable to identify members of the Polemoniaceae family correctly he may fail to receive credit in the course. Communication requires that we use words in their customary senses. Failure to know the "right name" in this sense is usually due to ignorance. We must learn the conventionally-agreed-upon names of things.

Nevertheless, words *are* the results of stipulations, and it follows that writers or speakers may present their own individual stipulations for the meanings of any words. When Mr. Hugh Walpole, in his *Semantics,* tells us that whenever he uses the word "interpret," he will mean "to be affected by," he has violated no rule of language or logic. But writers should exercise some restraints in exercising their freedom to stipulate their own meanings if they desire successful communication with an audience. Mr. Walpole's stipulation is an unusual one, for it requires, as he says, that we speak of a window "interpreting" a stone when the stone breaks the window. The novelty of this usage may result in a blockage of communication for many readers. But the "freedom to stipulate" sometimes enriches the language when novel usages win general acceptance.

The courts also place certain restraints upon individual stipulations. It would be no defence in a suit for libel to plead that when you called Jones a "swindler," you had previously stipulated that whenever you used the word "swindler" you should be understood to mean "native-born citizen." Custom also places limitations on our complete freedom to stipulate meanings. A young man who informed a young lady that he would mean "Darling" whenever he called her "Monster" might have difficulty in securing her affection. We may also note that many writers conceal their novel stipulations and thus mislead their hearers or readers. When the Japanese conquered a large part of Asia during the thirties, they stated that they were setting up a "Greater East Asia Co-prosperity Sphere." "Co-prosperity" was used in a highly novel sense, without notice as to what the Japanese had in mind. In contemporary political discussions, words like "democracy" and "freedom" are also used in novel senses by many writers.

In this section we have noted the arbitrary and conventional character of all symbols. Symbols are the results of stipulations, conventions, and agreements. Names are not "natural." Thus, several types of answers are possible to the question "Why is a certain thing called by its name?" We may answer that we call it by that name because it is customary to do so, or because we choose to, or because that name appears appropriate to us. The procedure of conferring proper or personal names on children is typical of the naming procedure.

A boy is called "John." This is an arbitrary act in the sense that we might have called him by any other name. The parents' reasons for calling him "John" rather than some other name are wholly external to the naming activity as such. His parents may have wished to give him his father's name or to honor a biblical hero, but these are "external" reasons. The fact that a new-found planet is called Pluto rather than Mickey Mouse, because it is customary to name planets after Greek divinities, is simply an aesthetic reason of appropriateness. The naming process is an arbitrary matter.

The reader may now raise the question: Does the etymology of a word determine its meaning? And is this not a nonconventional and nonarbitrary determination of meaning? But the fact that the English language obtained many of its words from Romance, Germanic, and Greek roots does not argue against the theory that the relationship between a symbol and referent is an arbitrary one. "House," for example, is derived from Germanic roots, i.e., *Haus;* and *Haus* in turn was derived from an earlier language; but somewhere in the past the begetting of these words was the result of the arbitrary naming activity. When we call a self-moving vehicle an automobile, from the Greek root *autos* (self) and the Latin *mobilis* (movable), it may appear that the choice is not a wholly arbitrary one. But the ancients (or their predecessors) had no such reasons of appropriateness when they used *autos* and *mobilis* for these referents. Etymologies do not affect the arbitrary nature of the naming process.

Section V: Etymologies

The subject of etymologies, briefly touched on at the end of the last section, deserves further attention. Etymology is a branch of philology which deals with the derivation of words and traces them back to their immediate or remote sources, thus giving us the history of individual words. Etymologies often throw important light on the meanings of words and sometimes reveal significant meanings not previously noted or understood. But though it is always interesting and generally useful and instructive to know the roots and origins of the words in our intellectual currency, the source of a word does not determine its present meaning. Linguistic changes and customs control in these matters, so that etymologies are logically irrelevant with respect to the present meanings of words. If human beings agree to use a certain word to symbolize a given referent, the inconsistency of the present usage with the original meaning is irrelevant. Thus the word "democracy," in its original sense, meant government directly by the people. Today the word has been extended in its meaning, and has a customary application to representative forms of government. If this is the referent of the term today, then the narrow etymological meaning is no longer the only meaning. The former meaning has not necessarily been superseded by the new meaning; a new meaning has been added to the former one.

Most etymologies are genuinely enlightening in clarifying the meanings of words, and the study of the roots of words is always fascinating. To cite some examples, the word "philanthropist" is derived from two Greek roots: *philein,* to love, and *anthropos,* man. A philanthropist is a "lover of mankind." Similarly we have "philosopher," which combines *philein* and *sophia* (wisdom). *Sophia* is the root of sophisticated and sophistry, words in which knowledge, rather than wisdom is emphasized. Sophomore combines *sophos* (wise) and *moros,* a Greek word meaning fool. This derivation reveals a penetrating insight.

Some etymologies are merely interesting without being useful. It is interesting to know that the beverage "gin" got its name from its origin in Geneva, Switzerland, but that the homonym "gin" in Whitney's "cotton gin" was an abbreviation of "engine."

Etymologies may also be misleading. Many words have meanings today which bear no significant relationship to their root words. Examples are "knave," from the German *Knabe,* or boy; "spinster," which originally meant "one who spins";

"assassin," an eater of hashish; and "orchestra," which originally meant the dancing place in a Greek theater. Or, consider the use of the word "barbarian." Its most important sense today refers to cruel and savage people. The word comes from the Greek, where all foreigners were called barbarians, without exception. The word originated among the Greeks to designate the languages of foreigners, which, they said, sounded like "bar-bar-bar." The word "barbarian" also carried a connotation of contempt, since the Greeks considered themselves to be a superior people. But our use of "barbarian" today dates from its application to the "foreigners" who overran the Roman Empire, committing many acts of vandalism and horror in the process. The point of this illustration is that the "real" meaning of barbarian is not "foreigner," though this is the word from which it is derived.

The last examples point to a very important truth, namely, that etymologies do not give us the "real" meanings of words. Words mean what we agree that they shall mean, since all symbols are established by "conventions" or agreements. Barbarian does not *really* mean foreigner, though that is the word from which it is derived. The present meaning of the word "etymology" itself is a case in point. The derivation of the word is found in two Greek words: *etymos,* true, and *logos,* which means "word" or "law." The earlier etymologists accepted the natural theory, and held that the true meanings of words could be traced through their shapes. But modern linguists mean by etymology the history of words, in which we simply trace words back to their roots, or at least as far back as possible.

Our conclusion is that etymologies are interesting, useful, instructive and enlightening, but that they are logically irrelevant in the sense that they do not determine what the meaning of any word is today. Etymology could give us the "true" meanings of words only if there were an original "natural" language from which all other languages had been derived. But we have rejected the notion of such a natural language. At best, then, etymologies can take us back to the original words, but if these original words have no etymologies of their own, then they came into being by actual or implied acts of stipulation. Words mean what we decide that they shall mean, or what custom decides. As Humpty-Dumpty sagely remarked in *Through the*

Looking Glass, "The question is, Which is to be master . . . ?"
We or the words?

Section VI: Growth and Change in Language

We have been discussing some of the formal aspects of
semantics, and we have learned that meanings are the results of
affirmations. In the next section we shall presently discuss some
of the linguistic errors which result from a failure to recognize
the correct principles of symbolism, but first we shall examine
some of the historical aspects of language growth and change
so that the reader may be able to place the theoretical aspects
of the subject within the perspective of living language.

Languages are not "made"—they grow. They are not manu-
factured as complete wholes except in artificial languages such
as Esperanto, and even this international language is based upon
familiar Latin roots. The origin of language is a subject
shrouded in mystery, a subject of which nothing certain is
known. There are, of course, many theories as to how languages
originated, but these are merely speculations. As examples of
such theories, some of which have received amusing nicknames,
we may cite the following: The "Bow-wow," or "Ding-dong"
theory holds that the first words were onomatopoetic, or imita-
tions of the sounds of nature. The "Pooh-pooh" theory (for the
expression indicating contemptuous indifference) holds that the
first words were expressions of strong emotion. The "Yo-he-ho"
theory, that words originated in work activities for the purpose
of expediting such work, is illustrated by the singing of the
Volga boatmen as they pull on their ropes. But as noted, these
theories must be regarded as nothing more than suggestive
guesswork.

The researches of anthropologists into the languages of
primitive peoples have uncovered linguistic elements which may
have been *stages* in the growth of language. One such element is
a type of verbal usage called the "holophrase," in which a single
word stands for a complete sentence or thought. A single word
may stand for "There are fish in the stream," but the language
in which this word appears may contain no word for "fish" as
such. This suggests that language may have begun with words
for complete activities or experiences rather than with words
for individual objects. Thus the whole appeared before the

parts; sentences before the parts of speech. A single word combined the functions of both subject and predicate.

A later stage in the development of language may thus involve a breaking down of the holophrastic sentence into its parts. Specific names will be given to things, to their qualities, to activities, and to relations. Further development then goes on in two directions, towards the process of analysis, or breaking a thing down into its parts, and towards synthesis, which involves the process of building up a whole from its parts. Classes are broken down into subclasses (analysis), and individual things are joined together into classes of things (synthesis).

Language and thought are of course indissolubly united in these developments. Language develops with thought, and thought develops with language. Whether thinking is possible without language is a question we need not discuss here, but it is certain that thought would be extremely limited without language. And it is thinking which finds distinctions among things which were formerly thought to be alike, and which finds resemblances among things which were formerly thought to be different. Language reflects these developments in thinking by adding new words to the vocabulary as new distinctions and generalizations appear, and words, in turn, help thought in making further distinctions and classifications.

Different languages reveal different stages in the developments toward analysis and synthesis. When we find a word which covers a very large group of things and find no words for important distinctions within the group, this may indicate that the process of analysis has not been carried through, or it may mean that the distinctions were not considered important enough to warrant new names. Thus, among the Hopi Indians, the same word stands for "He is running" and "He was running." The modern Slavic languages have the single word "finger" to signify both fingers and toes as these words are used in the English language. We have carried the process of analysis into the general class of digits of the hands and feet. The failure to distinguish these digits by different words may indicate that the distinction was not considered of sufficient importance to require separate names. On the other hand, the failure to carry the process of synthesis far enough is found in some primitive languages, such as the Tasmanian, which have words that designate the species within a genus without having words for the genus itself. Thus the Tasmanian has names for different types of trees, but no name for "tree" as such. In such cases further synthesis may be required. (The absence of a synthesizing word does not necessarily mean that the similarities were unnoticed.) A contrary fault is found in persons who look at all trees as if they were simply "trees," without being able to distinguish one variety from another.

Languages which make fine discriminations may reveal lack of generalizing power, and languages which have general words may lack discriminating ones. The most developed languages are those which are richest in words designating both discrimination and generalization. These words, however, are invented only after thought has done its job of noting distinctions and similarities.

Human interest is responsible for these developments in language. Frequently, interest in certain generalizations or distinctions disappears, and words then fall into disuse. This frequently happens in cases where the discriminating process has been carried too far for general interest. An English journal, *Tid-Bits,* once noted the fine distinctions made by previous generations with respect to the dismemberment of flesh and fowl at the dining table. Where we use the single word "carve," they "allayed" a pheasant, "disfigured" a peacock, "spoiled" a hen, "tranched" a sturgeon, and so on. Words designating different types of collections of living things, depending upon the type of creature involved, also seem to be losing out in general speech. Thus we have such words as "herd" of cattle, "flock" of sheep, "pack" of wolves, a "shoal" of fish, "covey" of partridges, "bevy" of larks, etc. These distinctions may become of lesser importance to city-dwellers, but this would mean a loss of richness in the language.

Thus far we have noted some of the general factors in the growth and change of language. We shall now note some more specific types of change, change being omnipresent in language, which is a living, dynamic thing. Old words take on new meanings, and new words are invented for familiar referents. Custom is king in these matters, but custom supersedes custom. Thus the meanings of words are narrowed, extended, or completely changed through use. "Paper" once referred only to papyrus,

but now refers to many other substances. Its meaning has been
extended. "Surgeon," on the other hand, has had its meaning
limited in sense, since it once referred to anyone who worked
with his hands. Words may also change their forms without
change of meaning, as in changes in spelling.

We also find new languages growing out of old ones. Thus
the "Romance" group of languages (French, Italian, Spanish,
Portuguese, Romanian) developed out of Latin in western Europe, and similarly all of the European languages, as well as the
Hindu Sanskrit, probably developed out of a common mother
tongue. Similarities such as those found in the English
"mother," Greek *meter,* Latin *mater,* Russian *mat,* and the
Sanskrit *mata;* or among the English "two," the Greek and Latin
duo, the Russian *dva,* and the Sanskrit *dvau* make a common
origin probable. Their common "progenitor" language is assumed to be the "Indo-European" root language, though no
historical evidences of this language have been found. This
Indo-European language is a hypothetical construct. It is worthy
of mention here that the so-called "Aryan race" is the supposed
race of people who spoke this hypothetical root language. Nothing whatsoever is known concerning the characteristics of this
race, if indeed there was such a race, though many pages have
been written concerning the glorious "blood-qualities" of this
people.

Why do languages change in these ways? Linguists have
noted such reasons as mishearing, misunderstanding, defective
memory, imperfect speech organs, laziness, the desire to be
distinctive in one's utterance, the need to express new ideas,
and the desires for clarity, euphony, and economy. We may also
note the influence of foreign languages on each other. Gradual
and unnoticed changes develop in time into very large modifications of the original language.

Change is not all, of course, for language customs do endure
—sometimes over very long periods of time. There are also
various ways in which we attempt to stop the flow of change in
usage. The dictionary, for example, attempts to fix the definitions of words, but even such "fixed" definitions give way to new
usages, and many dictionary definitions become obsolete in
time. Dictionary definitions are written by scholars who are
specialists in their respective fields, and these scholars tell us

how words are used in terms of the prevailing customary usage. The writer of a dictionary definition is a historian rather than a law-giver, a judge rather than a legislator. Dictionaries do not lay down laws of usage which command us to use words in certain ways. The usefulness of the dictionary lies in its giving us information as to the commonly accepted senses of words in order to facilitate successful communication.

A word is also required here as to the authoritativeness of dictionary definitions. We must always remember that a few very important words have no universally accepted meanings, and there is thus no genuine custom which we can follow. The word "propaganda" is a case in point. There are almost as many definitions of propaganda as there are individuals who define the word. Words like "truth," "morality," and "beauty" are words which have been defined and redefined for the past 2,000 years and the search for adequate definitions of these terms is not yet concluded. Obviously the dictionary cannot solve these problems, for no one has as yet solved them. In a discussion concerning the meaning of "beauty" the dictionary can do no more than help to initiate discussion; it cannot settle the matter.

It is because of the changing meanings of words in daily use that scientific and professional terminologies are invented. Ordinary words become ambiguous by acquiring new meanings, and science requires precise and unambiguous terms so that misunderstanding of referents will be reduced to a minimum. Technical vocabularies are accordingly invented, as in the biological sciences, where Latin names for diseases, plants, and animals are used. Latin terminology is also a great convenience for international communication. Since these words are not in daily usage, custom cannot modify them. Considerations of this sort led Professor Spearman, the English psychologist, to propose abandoning the word "intelligence" in psychology and to employ as a substitute the symbol "G-factor" for the referent which many psychologists have in mind when they employ the term. Instead of speaking of an individual's "intelligence quotient," one would speak of his "G-factor quotient." The ambiguity of the term as presently used would thus be eliminated.

The practice of inventing new vocabularies, however, also has some disadvantages, particularly in the social sciences, where unique terminologies make scientific writings unintelligible to the uninitiated. There is also the danger that the invention of a professional vocabulary for items of common experience may result in a pretentiousness of diction that may conceal a barrenness of thought, as in the professional report that "clinical observations and statistical correlations reveal that pre-adolescents exhibit multiform tendencies and predispositions toward variant and differential patterns of behavior." What is meant here is that it has been observed that young children do not all act in the same manner. A different type of professionally obscure language is found in the writings of some philosophers, such as in those of Heidegger, the contemporary German existentialist philosopher. It is said that his German readers must have his German writings translated into German before they can understand him.

We have emphasized the element of change in language, but again, we must remember that the great body of words is relatively permanent and unchanging. Language is like a tree; its leaves change with the seasons, but its roots are relatively stable. Shakespeare used many words which have become obsolete, but the great body of his vocabulary has the same meaning today as it had in the sixteenth century.

Section VII: Some Errors of Symbolism

In this section we shall note some of the important errors which result from the failure to understand and apply the principles of symbolism studied in this chapter. Our list is not exhaustive, of course, and we shall also have occasion to note other types of errors of symbolism in later chapters. The discussion of the four errors noted in this section will also help to clarify the meaning and implications of the principles of symbolic usage.

1. The magical power of words

This error results from the failure to note that words are mere "noises" which acquire meaning through their association with referents. It is a primitive superstition that the "name" has a mysterious power or magical potency. Primitives believe that words have a causal or magical influence over events. This superstition lies behind the "abracadabra" of the medicine man, the "Open Sesame" which caused the cave door to open for Ali

Baba, and the practice of tribesmen who change their names after being cursed, so that they may escape the evil which has become attached to their names, and thus to themselves. It is common practice for primitives to burn the name of their enemy even after his body has been destroyed. J. G. Frazer, in *The Golden Bough,* reports that the Malagasy soldier refuses to eat kidneys, for the word for kidney in his language is the same as the word for "shot"; thus he believes that he will be shot if he eats kidneys.

Another form of verbal magic is found in the belief that some words are so holy and sacred that they must never be uttered by man. Among the ancient Hebrews the name of God, "Yahweh" or "Jehovah" was "unnamable," and its actual utterance was forbidden in both speech and prayer. God could be spoken of only by the use of the substitute word or surrogate "Adonai," meaning "The Lord." Hades, the Greek god of the world below, was called Pluto (the giver of wealth) in ordinary conversation because people feared to pronounce the dreaded name of Hades. The prewar Japanese believed that the name of their emperor was sacred. A peasant, in ignorance of the emperor's name, named his son "Hirohito" and committed hara-kiri when he discovered his error.

Words have no causal influence on events; they can bring neither luck nor disaster through the airwaves set up when they are spoken. But from primitive times until today superstitious beliefs abound. We "knock on wood" after noting our good fortune; the dice player pleads with the dice and uses such endearing expressions as "Little Joe" and "Big Dick" to influence the bounce; the bettor on horses believes in the magical potency of the name. All these exemplify the belief in the magical power of words to influence events.

We may note, finally, the use of *euphemisms,* i.e., the use of an agreeable expression for a disagreeable event. We avoid mentioning the word "death," and say "passed on," "went to his reward," "departed," "sleeping," and so on. These circumlocutions are used to transform evil into good. It is as if our refusal to mention the awesome word would somehow obviate the disaster itself. Euphemisms, however, may also be used in nonmagical ways, as noted below.

2. Words as guarantees of existence or value

We often overlook the fact that the referent of a word may be a creation of human imagination. This error has two aspects. We may assume that the existence of a word guarantees the existence of a corresponding thing in space and time. But proof must be offered for the existence of facts; the mere utterance of the word is insufficient. The existence of the word "Devil" does not guarantee the existence of an actual Lucifer or Beelzebub waiting for those who fail to take out the appropriate fire insurance. When we speak of the "State" or "consciousness" as *things* separate and apart from the "entities-in-relation" to which these terms refer, we commit the same error in the form known as *hypostatization* or *reification*.

A second aspect of this error is the assumption that "good" words guarantee the existence of good things and "bad" words guarantee bad things. The manner in which propaganda organizations and advertisers use the emotional associations attached to value words in order to manipulate their audiences requires little comment. Orators and demagogues use attractive or unattractive names in order to mislead us. The proverb says that "we give a dog a bad name and then hang him." Men stand condemned in the public eye merely because they have been called "Reds," "communists," "reactionaries," or "fascists." Similarly, organizations confer "good" names upon themselves in order to mislead the public. A magazine fostering race prejudice was called *The Galilean* and it was published by The Fellowship Press. A communist-front organization which supports aggression by communist nations and opposes defensive measures by anticommunists nations may call itself "The People's Committee for Peace." The use of a "good" name does not guarantee the existence of a good thing.

Euphemisms may also illustrate the use of words as guarantees of facts, as in the use of "tourist" for "third class" on ocean liners or on Russian trains, where "third class" has been changed to "third category," since the Russians have abolished all class distinctions. The use of euphemisms, however, is not necessarily an error of symbolism. Social conventions may dictate the avoidance of words with disagreeable associations, and the substitution of a pleasant term for an unpleasant one may sometimes give us a more realistic description of a situation, as when a Home for Incurables changed its name to Institution for Chronic Diseases. The new name gave the patients a more hopeful attitude, and it is also more in the spirit of medical science, which may some day find cures for diseases now considered incurable.

But in no case, of course, does the name actually guarantee either the existence or the value characteristics, good or bad, of the referent to which it refers. A rose, as Juliet remarked, would smell as sweet though called by any other name.

3. The "real" connection between words and things

All meanings are arbitrary. Failure to recognize (or denial of) this arbitrariness results in a third semantical error. This error occurs when we think of words as "really belonging" to certain referents, as if there were some indissoluble or "real connection" between them. The error occurs in certain typical forms.

A "young lady" now famous among writers on semantics approached an astronomer shortly after the planet Pluto was discovered, and asked him how it was that the astronomers knew that the newly discovered planet was *really* Pluto and not some other planet. The error lies in the assumption that names "belong" to certain things and to no others. This type of error is also the source of much humor. Thus Gracie Allen asks a male acquaintance whom she had just met to call her "Gracie." To his remonstrance that he hardly knows her, she responds, "Why, just as soon as I was born my mother called me Gracie, and she didn't know me at all."

The belief that some words "really mean" some referents, or that certain things "must" be called by certain names, assumes that the thing could not be called by any other name. To say "Pigs are so-called because they are such dirty animals" illustrates this point. But names seem to belong to things only because they have become associated with these things; the connection is always an arbitrary one.

A variant of this error is found in the belief that communism *really* means one of its definitions, as when it is said that Russia is *really* not a communist state. Or that the form of government in the United States is *really* that of a republic, so that it is *wrong* to call the United States a democracy. But all names are arbitrary designations for their referents, and if the American people wish to emphasize certain aspects of their government which are called democratic, there is no linguistic law which forbids them from doing so. Custom is supreme in determining the usage of words. No thing can once and for all pre-empt the use of any name for itself.

As previously pointed out, the expression "Things should be called by their right names" does have a legitimate meaning, if we do not interpret "right" names as "real" names. For success in communication, words should be used in their customary meanings. If most people think of a "free" society when the word "democracy" is used, then it is improper for a speaker to call a totalitarian state a democracy merely because he chooses to do so or because he has a peculiar and private undisclosed definition of the term in his mind. The use of words in this manner is dishonest if there is a deliberate intent to mislead people into thinking that the speaker has *their* referent in mind when *he* actually has another. This subject will be discussed more thoroughly in the chapter on "definition."

It may be helpful to distinguish the error of "real connection" from the error of "words as guarantees of existence." In the latter error we mistakenly believe that the existence of a word guarantees the existence of the thing to which it refers ("We have the word 'dragon'; therefore, dragons exist now or once existed"). In the former error we find that a word is used to refer to a certain referent and assert that this word and no other can be used to designate this referent, on the ground that the association is a nonarbitrary one.

It is one thing to say that the king of the underworld *must* be called the devil, because that is his right name; it is a different error when we say that the existence of the word "devil" is in itself proof that there is a king of the underworld.

4. The use of words without referents

Human beings sometimes use words without thinking of the referents to which they refer. This type of evil is sometimes encouraged by educational systems in which students repeat words and formulas without understanding their meaning. Justice O .W. Holmes had this type of error in mind when he admonished us to "think things, not words." In general, it is good educational practice for students (or readers generally) to translate what they read into their own words in order to be sure that they are avoiding this evil, for "one's own words" usually have clear referents.

George Orwell, the English critic, in *Modern English Writings*, describes this vice as involving the use of "meaningless words." "In art criticism," he writes, "words like romantic, plastic, values, human, dead, sentimental, natural, vitality" are "strictly meaningless, in the sense that they not only do not point to any discoverable object but are hardly expected to do so by the reader." Mr. Orwell exaggerates, but his remarks call attention to a serious fault in the type of writing to which he refers. One may also question the use of the expression "meaningless words," on the ground that a word without meaning (such as "higher-gloob") is, strictly speaking, not a word at all. Mr. Orwell means that writers often use words without having any definite referents in mind.

What we refer to by this error, then, is *not* the use of meaningless expressions, such as are found in the following amusing example of "double-talk" (from the work of the master in this field, David Ross):

> We have a lot of fun, and do you know, the entrain does not findle the boller, either. After all, who am I to shrake the leavings? I am a mere bildring. My life is neither frenner or planrate. The pen is the outgrabe of the mome, the hordling always does the gets.

No words are meaningless in themselves, but words are often used without meaning when the writer or speaker uses them without having referents in mind. But the reader should be cautioned against making this charge against a writer, for the unintelligibility of a piece of discourse may be due to his own inadequate vocabulary. "No cenobites are troglodytes" contains words unfamiliar to many persons who speak the English language, but it is unexceptionable as a meaningful sentence.

Confusions also abound with respect to the use of "abstract" words, i.e., words of wide generality such as the words cited by Mr. Orwell. Stuart Chase, for example, often speaks of abstractions as if they were necessarily meaningless because their refer-

ents are not "real enough to be kicked." As examples, he cites
such words as "capitalism," "fascism," "communism," and
"democracy." But these words have meaning, however they may
be used by careless writers and however ambiguous they may be.
One should take the trouble to find out exactly what a writer
means when he uses these words, though it is undoubtedly true
that many persons use them without having any specific referents in mind. When Max Weber writes in his *Sociology of
Religion,* "We shall examine the influence of religious ideas on
the development of an economic spirit or the ethos (ethics) of
an economic system," his language is highly abstract, but he
means something by these words. Such highly abstract language
may be undesirable in terms of "good style," but that is another
matter.

Our point is that we should be sure that we have referents
in mind when we use words. The reader may ask himself, for
example, just what he has in mind when he uses expressions
such as "God is Love" or "Love your enemies." And what
specific referents are referred to when it is said that "Capitalism
exploits the working class"? The hearer of this statement may
suspect that the speaker has no referents in his mind. It then
becomes appropriate to ask that the words be translated into
concrete language in order to make the ideas clear. The ultimate
test of meaning lies in the "cash value" of the words used, i.e., in
the actual existences to which they refer.

Exercises

The following exercises should be analyzed and discussed in
terms of the material covered in the relevant sections of the chapter.
Since these exercises are designed to test the student's comprehension of the text, the relevant principles should be mentioned in connection with the student's analyses.

A. *Signs and Symbols*

Classify the following signs as natural or conventional:
a. A chemist dips litmus paper into his test tube. He interprets the sign, red, or the sign, blue, as meaning acid or
   base.

b. During the invasion of France in 1940 the Nazis put weird wailing sirens on their Stuka bombers in order to terrify the Allied soldiers.

c. A work of abstract art which we do not "understand."

B. *The Arbitrariness of Meanings*

1. Humpty-Dumpty said: "There's glory for you." "I don't know what you mean by 'glory,'" Alice said. Humpty-Dumpty smiled contemptuously. "Of course you don't—till I tell you. I meant, There's a nice knock-down argument for you." "But 'glory' doesn't mean 'a nice knock-down argument,'" Alice objected. "When I use a word," Humpty-Dumpty said in a rather scornful tone, "it means just what I choose it to mean, neither more nor less." "The question is," said Alice, "whether you *can* make words mean so many different things." "The question is," said Humpty-Dumpty, "which is to be master—that's all." (Lewis Carroll, *Through the Looking Glass,* Ch. VI.)

2. The Book of Genesis (II, 19–20): "And out of the ground the Lord God formed every beast of the field, and every fowl of the air. And brought them unto Adam to see what he would call them, and whatsoever Adam called every living creature, that was the name thereof. And Adam gave names to all cattle and to the fowl of the air, and to every beast of the field." Mark Twain wrote that one of these animals gave Adam great difficulty and he appealed to Eve for help: "What name shall I give to this animal?" "Call it a horse," answered Eve. "But why a horse?" "Well," said Eve, "it looks like a horse, doesn't it?"

3. Parson Thwackum, in Henry Fielding's *Tom Jones:* "Religion is not manifold because there are various sects and heresies in the world. When I mention religion, I mean the Christian religion; and not only the Christian religion, but the Protestant religion, and not only the Protestant religion, but the Church of England."

4. Our own conclusion is that, if by autocracy is meant government without prior discussion and debate, either by public opinion or in private session, the government of the USSR is, in that sense, actually less of an autocracy than many a parliamentary cabinet. (Beatrice and Sidney Webb, *Soviet Communism: A New Civilization?* Scribner's, 1936, p. 479.)

5. "I believe in democracy, but in a democracy which is made

up of 100 per cent white, Protestant, and native-born American citizens."

C. Etymologies

1. Look up the etymologies of the following words and state whether you consider their etymologies useful or misleading:

   a. propaganda   d. gentile   g. liberal
   b. varsity   e. bolshevik   h. radical
   c. polite   f. pagan   i. conservative

2. Comment on Jespersen's remark that "we get no further at all towards understanding what a tragedy is when we are informed that the word must once have meant 'goat song.'"

D. Growth and Change in Language

George Orwell translates the following passage from *Ecclesiastes* into what he calls "Modern English of the worst sort":

Ecclesiastes: "I returned, and saw under the sun, that the race is not to the swift, nor the battle to the strong, neither yet bread to the wise, nor yet riches to men of understanding, nor yet favor to men of skill; but time and chance happeneth to them all."

Modern English: "Objective consideration of contemporary phenomena compels the conclusion that success or failure in competitive activities exhibits no tendency to be commensurate with innate capacity, but that a considerable amount of the unpredictable must invariably be taken into account." ("Politics and the English Language," *New Republic,* June 17, 1946.)

E. The Errors of Symbolism

Check the following for possible errors of symbolism. Note whether the error involves the Magical Use of Language, Words as Guarantees of Existence or Value, the "Real Connection" between Words and Things, or the use of Words Without Referents. Explain your answers. One of each of these errors will be found in the first four examples.

1. The French call it *"pain,"* the English call it "bread," but its real name is *"brod."*

2. An Arab was being cursed by a compatriot. He threw himself on the ground in order that the curse-words might fly harmlessly over his head.

3. You ask, do I favor the "right to work" law which is being debated in the State legislature? Of course I do. The "right

to work" sounds very good to me. I can't see why anyone would be against the right to work.

4. "For Portsymasser and Purtsymessus and Pertsymiss and Partsymasters, like a prance of findigos, with a shillto shallto slipny stripny." (James Joyce, *Finnegans Wake*.)

5. The Divine is properly so-called.

6. Speak of the Devil and he's sure to appear.

7. In Norway many people believe in trolls. Children say that trolls must exist, for otherwise how could people paint pictures of them?

8. "Mother, when I was born, how did you know that I was Charlie and not some other little boy?"

9. The following answers are given by children:
"Could the moon have been called 'sun' and the sun 'moon'?"—*No.*—"Why not?"—*Because the sun makes it warm, and the moon gives light.*
Roc (6½) admits that God might have changed the names: "Would they have been right or wrong?"—*Wrong.*—"Why?"—*Because the moon must be the moon and not the sun, and the sun must be the sun.*
"But if everyone had called the sun 'moon' and the moon 'sun,' would we have known it was wrong?"—*Yes, because the sun is always bigger, it always stays like it is and so does the moon.*
"Why is the sun called what it is?"—*Because it behaves as if it was the sun.* (Jean Piaget, *The Child's Conception of the World*, Harcourt, Brace, 1929, pp. 81–4.)

10. In the fourth inning of a baseball game between the Chicago Cubs and the Cincinnati Reds, the first Cincinnati player made a hit. The narrator, Bert Wilson, announced, "Fans, that was the Reds' first hit, but you will note that I did not mention the fact that the Reds had made no hits in the first three innings. If I had, and the next man had made a hit, hundreds of fans would have written protesting letters to me telling me to keep my big mouth shut."

11. A gelding is a horse which has ceased to be entire.

12. Wilfrid Lay, an English writer, was pleading for greater frankness in sex discussion in families. He advocated that parents should not stress concealment of the body in the home; in fact, he urged, "parents should sometimes appear before their children in *puribus naturalibus.*"

13. The United States is not a "great democracy," for our forefathers established a great republic. A democracy is a

country where the people rule directly, not through their elected representatives.

14. It is improper to call the "American Revolution" a *revolution,* because the word really means a fundamental change in the basic social, economic, and political institutions of a country. There have really been few real revolutions in the history of mankind, such as were the French Revolution of 1789 and the Russian Revolution of 1917.

15. From Lewis Carroll's "Jabberwocky":
     'Twas brillig, and the slithy toves
     Did gyre and gimble in the wabe:
     All mimsy were the borogroves,
     And the mome raths outgrabe.

16. Wherefore, be it resolved: To resolve every universally considerate wish evoking critical-concept into a reasonably efficacious resistance-eliminating inanimate-device of time-saving-calculability and contiguous-service time-synchronization, that may be factorable from "possibility" to "probability," thus intent to streamline man's competitive-volition, unknown to him, into a scientifically designed direction-of-least-resistance, upon the occasion of his each and every initial-dislodgment from habit-inertia. (R. Buckminster Fuller, *Nine Chains to the Moon,* J. B. Lippincott Co., 1938.)

17. During World War II, a bill before the Illinois legislature proposed that no liquor could be called "whiskey" if it contained more than 50 per cent neutral spirits. A spokesman for the liquor industry stated that stocks of whiskey in Illinois were already low, and that if the bill were passed stocks of whiskey would immediately decrease by 75 per cent.

18. The word "God" has meaning; therefore it refers to something. But the word as we use it refers to nothing else than a supernatural being; therefore, the supernatural being, God, exists.

19. Abraham Lincoln once asked an audience, "If I call the tail of a horse a leg, how many legs will the horse then have?" "Five," they responded. "No," answered Lincoln, "calling a horse's tail a leg doesn't make it one." (Did Lincoln's audience commit an error of symbolism? Did Lincoln also commit a semantical error? Discuss.)

20. Herbert Spencer's definition of evolution: "A continuous change from indefinite, incoherent homogeneity to definite

coherent heterogeneity of structure and function, through successive differentiations and integrations."

21. Spencer's definition was parodied by Kirkman, as follows: "Evolution: A change from a nohowish, untalkaboutable, all-alikeness to a somehowish, and in general talkaboutable not-all-alikeness by continuous somethingelseifications and sticktogetherations."

22. In 1937, when Hitler and Mussolini were in power, Stuart Chase collected a hundred responses from various persons as to their reactions to the word "fascism." He asked those questioned to tell him what kind of picture came into their heads when they heard the term. A few of the answers mentioned by Chase were:

Schoolteacher: A dictator suppressing all opposition.
Governess: Obtaining one's desires by sacrifice of human lives.
Lawyer: A state where the individual has no rights, hope, or future.
College student: Hitler and Mussolini.
Schoolboy: War. Concentration camps. Bad treatment of workers. Something that's got to be licked.
Author: I can only answer in cuss words.
Elevator starter: I never heard of it.

Chase then quotes the following definition of fascism by Harold Laski:

"I suggest the conclusion that Fascism is nothing but monopoly capitalism imposing its will on the masses which it has deliberately transformed into slaves. The ownership of the instruments of production remains in private hands."

Chase states that the "student of semantics" will react to this definition as follows:

Meaning in the form of a row of abstractions does not satisfy him. He finds three high-order terms equated and an inference applied to one or all of them: private property = capitalism = fascism. He is immediately suspicious of the identification of three timeless, spaceless, descriptionless entities. He never saw an "ism" imposing its will. He asks what are the referents for "private ownership," "monopoly capitalism" and "fascism." He wonders what is meant by "capitalism imposing its will on the masses," re-

membering that this is a stock phrase in socialist propaganda . . . "Ownership of the instruments of production"
troubles him as another stock phrase. He recalls how Berle
and Means in their *Modern Corporation and Private Property* show that many legal "owners" of large corporations
have nothing to say about their property . . . "Private
hands" worries him more. He knows that whatever titles
private persons may hold to property in Germany or Italy,
the Government jolly well tells them when, where, and
how much to let go of.

He is not disposed to argue with Mr. Laski, because
the apparent meaning has faded into a series of semantic
blanks. Laski is not necessarily wrong; he is saying nothing
worth listening to.

But should one not be afraid of fascism and fight
against it? The student of semantics is not afraid of evil
spirits and takes no steps to fight them . . . If the armies of
Mussolini or Hitler invade his country, he is prepared to
fight. But he refuses to shiver and shake at a word. (Stuart
Chase, *The Tyranny of Words,* Harcourt, Brace, 1938,
pp. 188–93.)

Discuss the following:
a. Of which error of symbolism is Laski guilty, according
   to Chase?
b. What is Chase's attitude toward abstractions, such as
   "fascism"?

Chapter 3

Ambiguity

Section I: The Meaning of Ambiguity

There are many obstacles in the path of successful communication, but ambiguity is undoubtedly the worst offender. An ambiguous word is one that may be understood in more than one sense. Thus a symbol may be interpreted differently by speaker and hearer; communicators and communicatees are at cross-purposes and there is no meeting of minds.

Most of the words in any language have more than one referent. This is in many ways a boon rather than an evil, for the range of possible meanings in any limited number of words is greatly increased. Our vocabularies are enlarged when one word has different meanings in different contexts; the single word then becomes the equivalent of many different words. In many cases the differences in referents may be on a "large" scale, as when the word "secretary" refers in turn to "a person who attends to correspondence," "an executive officer in the government," "a writing desk," and "a South African bird with long legs." There are many other words in which the differences in the referents are of a more subtle nature, the shifts in meaning being less obvious, as in the different ways in which the word "man" is used in the following contexts:

All *men* are mortal.
The child is father to the *man.*
Those were the days when *men* were *men.*
What a piece of work is *man!* How infinite in capacity!
The football team is under*manned.*

Successful communication occurs only when the reader correctly interprets the symbols used by the writer. In our discus-

45

sion of the "triangle of reference" we showed how this occurs. When the communication is successful then the communicator and the communicatee have their minds referred to the same referents; they have the same *terms* in mind. They have "come to terms." But ambiguous words are obstacles to such happy consummations; communication is frustrated. We have already noted examples of such frustration in our discussion of the manner in which ambiguous words like "democracy," "equality," and "law" may lead to verbal disagreements. When such failures of communication occur, the speaker and the hearer have different referents in mind.

But note that ambiguity is an evil only when it results in these frustrations of communication. In scientific discourse, where the aim is to achieve clear and precise reference, ambiguity is an unmitigated evil. But there are other fields of thought in which ambiguity may have certain desirable effects. This is the case in poetry, where ambiguity may sometimes contribute to the poetic effect by suggesting a rich aura of implied meanings: "Life is a tale told by an idiot, full of sound and fury, signifying nothing"; "Faith is the substance of things hoped for; the evidence of things not seen." In this manner poetry approximates the effects produced by music, which, among all of the arts, is certainly the most expressively ambiguous. One of the great charms of music lies in the ambiguity with which it expresses moods, so that each hearer may interpret the musical score in his own way. Ambiguity also has more mundane uses. Diplomatic language has developed the art of saying things ambiguously so that failure to agree will be masked by "face-saving" language. Finally, the ambiguous aspects of words are exploited as a rich source of humor. Gagsters and punsters thrive on the double-meanings of words. Our primary interest, of course, is to learn how to avoid ambiguity in scientific discourse.

Ambiguity is the direct opposite of synonymity (the use of synonymous words). An ambiguous word refers to several referents; in synonymity a single referent is referred to by several different words. "Spade" refers to at least two referents: a playing card and a garden implement. Fool, lout, simpleton, oaf, dunderhead, ninny, nincompoop, addle-pate, and dope, all refer to the same referent, or to substantially the same referent, since few synonymous words are absolutely identical in meaning. The difference between ambiguity and synonymity may be revealed schematically:

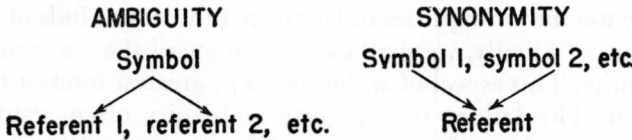

AMBIGUITY   SYNONYMITY

Symbol   Symbol 1, symbol 2, etc.

Referent 1, referent 2, etc.   Referent

Section II: The Analysis of Ambiguity

Though many words have more than one meaning, the context of surrounding circumstances will usually clarify the sense in which the word is used. The initial ambiguity is often completely eliminated by the context. We shall be primarily concerned with examples in which the ambiguity is not eliminated by the context, with a resulting blockage of communication. In the verbal disagreements studied in Chapter 1 we saw examples of ambiguity that were not clarified by the context, at least not for the persons participating in the discussions. In this chapter we shall examine the different ways in which ambiguity may result in the failure of communication.

When two or more interpretations of an author's language are possible, the reader does not know what is in the author's mind. We should be clear as to the task of the logician in analyzing instances of ambiguity. The logician cannot eliminate ambiguity; his primary task is to call attention to the fact that ambiguity occurs and to show the different ways in which it occurs. The logician can also help to make the reader sensitive to ambiguities in places where ambiguity might be unsuspected. The logician can also advise the reader to find out what was in the author's mind before the reader interprets ambiguous language. The reader's task here may be likened to that of a judge whose task is to decide what the legislature meant by the ambiguous language in a law. The court will investigate the circumstances in which the law was passed, the remarks of legislators concerning the intent of the law, and so on. In other words, the context will be studied for light on the probable meaning of the words.

We shall examine the manner in which ambiguity occurs in the use of words, phrases, and sentences. Ambiguity, as we know, is a fruitful source of humor, and we shall note some of the entertaining aspects of its various forms. Humorists deliberately use the ambiguities of language in various kinds of jokes and "gags." Finally, we shall examine some of the "fallacies" of ambiguity. This aspect of ambiguity is of greatest interest to the logician. The failure to recognize ambiguity often results in misinterpretations of meanings and in erroneous inferences.

Section III: The Types of Ambiguity

1. Simple ambiguity

By *simple* ambiguity we shall mean the fact that single words or phrases may refer to more than one referent, even after we have examined their contexts. Verbal disagreements are based upon this type of ambiguity. Any statement containing a word which is ambiguous in its context exemplifies this vice: "The early Christians were communists." Since the word "communist" has more than one referent in this context, ambiguity exists. "Communist$_1$" means one who favors a system of social organization in which goods are held in common; "communist$_2$" means an advocate of "the dictatorship of the proletariat." Before we affirm or deny the truth of a statement we should find out what the writer means. Questions may also involve simple ambiguity, as in "Do you believe in God?" "God" means different things to different persons, and a yes-or-no answer is inappropriate until we learn what referent the questioner has in mind. Spinoza, for example, defined God as "everything which exists." Spinoza was a deeply religious man whose pantheistic philosophy was permeated with devotion to God. The Catholic Church, however, has condemned his pantheism as equivalent to atheism.

Simple ambiguity is closely related to "vagueness," but should be distinguished from it. An ambiguous word has several distinct referents; a vague word lacks precision and definiteness in its reference. Thus, the question, "Has there been any progress during the past 2,000 years?" involves the use of the vague word "progress." The reader spontaneously responds to such a question with his own questions: "Progress in what sense? In spiritual growth? In the advancement of the common man? In a material sense?" The word "progress" is vague rather than ambiguous, for in each case it means "advancement toward a definite goal," but the question does not specify the goal involved.

Vagueness, rather than ambiguity, will also be found in the following incident. In the summer of 1947 General Eisenhower was reported to have said that "the United States Army is a 'poor second' to that of Russia." Congressman Short asked, "In what sense?" In quantity? In quality? The United States Army has never been equal to the Russian army in size either in war or peace. Here too, "poor second" is not ambiguous, since it means "far behind the first," but its meaning is not precise.

Questions containing vague words cannot be answered without further clarification of their meaning. We should also note how careful thinking may result in the discovery that "clear" words are actually vague. Thus, the question "Is this building moving?" may appear to be clear. But we must ask: "In relation to which frame of reference?" In relation to the sun, this building is moving at a speed of eighteen miles per second. In relation to the earth, however, it is stationary.

Simple ambiguity has two forms, written and oral. The phonetic sound "teers" may stand for two different words: "tiers" and "tears." An amusing example of oral ambiguity based on this sound is found in the following:

> A reporter was describing a scene at the House of Commons to another reporter. "There, on the floor of the house, stood the Prime Minister speaking," he said, "back of him were the members of the Cabinet, in front of him sat the members of the Opposition, and in tiers around him sat the other members of the House."
> The second reporter was very young and very earnest. "Not really *tears*," he exclaimed. "Poor chaps!" (Albert Levi and Albert Frye, *Rational Belief,* Harcourt, Brace, 1941, p. 108.)

Simple ambiguity lies at the basis of much humor, especially in puns, as in Wordsworth's remark, "If I had a mind to, I could write like Shakespeare."

2. Amphiboly

"I shall lose no time in reading your manuscript," the noted critic wrote to the aspiring young author. Should the author have been pleased with this message? Would the critic read his manuscript soon or never?

The critic's remark is an example of an amphibolous sentence. Its meaning is ambiguous though no *word* in the sentence is ambiguous. The ambiguity results from the way in which the words are put together in the sentence.

Amphiboly refers to the fact that the meaning of a sentence may be ambiguous, not because any of its words are ambiguous, but because the grammatical construction of the sentence permits several interpretations as to its meaning. The amphibolous sentence is capable of being understood in more than one sense. This may result in a failure in communication. A sentence combines words in order to express a thought. The referents have a certain relationship in the mind of the speaker. The grammatical construction of the sentence may fail to direct the hearer's mind to the relationship referred to by the speaker. The logician calls the reader's attention to these factors. The grammarian seeks to teach writers how to make themselves clear.

Vivid examples of amphiboly are found in humorous exaggerations of this fault. Thus, the following account was reportedly given by a newspaper reporter, with reference to the departure of the famous prewar dirigible from the Lakehurst airport: "The Graf Zeppelin was leaving the Lakehurst airport. Among the last to enter was Mrs. Smith, lone woman passenger. Slowly her huge nose was turned into the wind. Then, like some huge beast, she crawled along the grass . . ."

Grammarians have noted a type of error similar to amphiboly in the error called "the dangling participle," as in "Zooming along under her own power, Jane was fascinated by the spectacle of the glider before her." The participle "zooming" seems to refer to Jane. The words are unambiguous, but ambiguity results from the manner in which they are put together.

A famous historical source of amphiboly is found in the Delphic oracle, in ancient Greece. The oracle was certainly the most astute diplomat who ever lived and also the Nostradamus

of its time, except that, unlike Nostradamus, the oracular pronouncements were right 100 per cent of the time. This success
was due to the use of amphiboly. The oracle was consulted on
the eve of great undertakings, in order to obtain its "inspired"
predictions as to success or failure. The oracle always retained its
reputation for infallibility because of the manner in which it
made its pronouncements: "Apollo says that the Greeks the
Persians shall subdue." Cyrus, the Persian King, sent messengers
to the oracle for a prophecy concerning a projected war. The
messengers were informed that "the King yet lives that Cyrus
shall depose." The variant interpretations of these statements
are obvious.

Amphibolous sentences of the type just noted may be called
completely amphibolous in that the reader does not know how
to interpret them correctly. In most cases, though two or more
interpretations are possible, it will generally appear that one
interpretation is more reasonable than the others, either from
the context or the customs of speech. Thus, when a law court
is presented with an amphibolous document, the "reasonable"
interpretation will be applied. For example, a licensing agreement between the holder of a patent and the manufacturer provided that the manufacturer would pay the patentee "50¢ a unit
for producing 5,000 units or less, and 30¢ a unit for all units of
an output of over 5,000 units." The manufacturer claimed that
when the output exceeded 5,000 units he was obligated to pay
30¢ per unit for *all* units produced. The court ruled that the
agreement meant "50¢ for the first 5,000 units and 30¢ for all
units in excess of 5,000." Otherwise the patentee would receive
less royalties for a production of 6,000 units than he would
receive for 4,000.

It is impossible to state whether a sentence is true or false
until we understand its meaning. An amphibolous sentence
must be given a definite interpretation before we can judge it as
true or false. For example, a man says, "All women are not
fickle." By this he may mean either that "some women are not
fickle" or that "no women are fickle." If the speaker is available
we should question him to determine what he meant. If he is
not available, how shall we interpret the statement?

Note that the sentence takes the "All . . . are not . . ."
formation. The logician adopts a rule of interpretation here,

stating that all such statements shall be read as if they meant "*Not all* women are fickle" or "Some women are not fickle," unless he has clear evidence from the context or elsewhere that the speaker meant "No women are fickle." In the sentence "All human beings are not perfect" the speaker probably means "No human beings are perfect," but in "All Russians are not communists" he probably means "Some Russians are not communists."

Other types of amphiboly that require interpretation are such sentences as "All agree with me who are not ignorant of the facts." This may mean either "All who agree with me are persons who are not ignorant of the facts" or it may mean "All who are not ignorant of the facts agree with me." The speaker may mean either one, but in the absence of further evidence, the grammarian will adopt the latter interpretation as the more likely one.

3. Ambiguity in emphasis

A unit of discourse may make different kinds of sense depending upon which of its parts we accent or emphasize. We should always seek to give writings the emphasis which the author intended them to have, but when the writing is ambiguous in this respect, the reader may be unable to determine where the proper emphasis lies. The full and complete meaning of a sentence may even require that we hear it spoken. Thus the invitation "I hope that you will come to dinner" may accent "I," "you," or "dinner" when it is spoken. When you leave, you say, "The dinner was very good." You may accent "dinner." It is for this reason that classroom instruction is superior to mere reading for most students, since the instructor gives oral emphasis to the most important words.

Ambiguity of emphasis occurs when a reader does not know which parts of a writing deserve chief emphasis. Troublesome cases of this sort occur when a writer presents somewhat conflicting points of view, as in Book V of Plato's *Republic,* concerning the nature and status of women in his ideal state. The reader will find "equalitarian" remarks such as, "The only difference between men and women consists in the fact that women bear and that men beget children," and "The differences between men and women do not justify different types of education for the two sexes. Women as well as men, should be trained to qualify as rulers of the state." But elsewhere Plato says that "women are inferior to men in all pursuits followed by each." Again, that "men and women possess the same qualities and differ only in their comparative strength and weakness." Does Plato believe that women are essentially the same as men, or does he hold that the weaker sex is the inferior sex? No one can answer this question with certainty.

When summaries are made of writings, ambiguity of emphasis may create similar difficulties. The summarizer should emphasize the most important elements. When excerpts and quotes are given they should be truly representative of the author's meaning. Summaries, however, open the door to many errors of carelessness or deliberate misinterpretation, to be discussed further under the "fallacies of ambiguity." Book reviewers are often accused of "not having read the whole book" when the author thinks that his position has been misinterpreted. The reviewer's misinterpretation, however, may be due in whole or in part to the author's failure to make his points clear. Or the author may state somewhat conflicting positions, as in the selections from Plato's *Republic*.

A different type of problem concerning emphasis or "accent" occurs in problems of punctuation. Literary scholars seek to interpret Shakespeare's meanings accurately, but there are variant readings of many of the plays. The Folio and the Second Quarto editions, the oldest sources, differ in many important respects. Consider the different possible readings of Hamlet's speech to Guildenstern (II, 2, 315). The Neilson and Hill version of the speech, based upon the Quarto version, is stated as follows:

> What a piece of work is a man! How noble in reason! How infinite in faculty! in form and moving! How express and admirable in action! How like an angel in apprehension! How like a god!

The Everyman's edition, following the Folio version, prints the lines as follows:

> What a piece of work is man! How noble in reason! how infinite in faculty! In form and moving how express and admi-

rable! in action how like an angel! in apprehension how like a god!

4. The ambiguity of significance

By this type we refer to statements whose semantical meaning may be clear, but whose factual significance is not. A statement may contain no ambiguous words, its sentence structure may convey an unambiguous meaning, and it may contain no ambiguities of emphasis. But its significance may be "ambiguous." As an illustration, consider the statement that there were 454 deaths due to traffic accidents in the United States during the Thanksgiving holiday weekend last year. The significance of such a statement is ambiguous in many respects. An isolated fact means something, of course. We all deplore the large number of deaths reported. But its full significance would require knowing whether the number was higher or lower than the number killed during the previous year's holiday weekend, and whether the figures for a non-holiday weekend are higher or lower.

It should be apparent that alertness to this kind of "ambiguity" is almost synonymous with the scientific attitude. Every statement whatsoever will have different kinds of significance depending upon its context or surrounding circumstances. It should also be obvious that this kind of "ambiguity" is not a genuinely semantical problem. We deal with it here only because it concerns a kind of uncertainty to which readers should be alerted, and because ambiguity in its broadest sense refers to doubtfulness or uncertainty.

Many other examples of such ambiguous isolated statements come to mind. "There are 3 million unemployed in the United States." Up or down since last month? In comparison with last year? What is the normal number of unemployed even in periods of "full employment"? Many statements are ambiguous to the uninitiated though not to the well-informed. "You have 5 billion germs in your mouth." What is the significance of that fact to a non-physiologist? In all the examples cited we find statements whose referential meaning is unambiguous, but whose significance is subject to varying interpretations.

The significance of many statements is ambiguous until we

answer the questions: "Who said it?" and "under what circumstances?" In the fall of 1947 a United States Congressman said, "We will be at war with Russia in one month." Who was the speaker? A responsible or an irresponsible talker? When we listen to criticism of the foreign or domestic policies of the federal administration, we should of course judge these criticisms on their own merits, but we should also be concerned with the background of the critic. Is he a member of the opposition party? Is he blindly partisan? In the absence of coercive evidence we will give greater or lesser weight to criticism depending upon the stature of the critic. If the speaker is thought to be impartial, greater weight will be given to his criticism. In a law court great weight is given to statements which are called "admissions against one's own interest."

Another important distinction concerns the question as to whether a statement is being made in jest or in earnest. "Smile when you call me that" is a type of comment which emphasizes the ambiguity of significance. Persons whose humor is "dry" often make ironical or sarcastic statements that should not be interpreted literally.

An amusing example of the ambiguity of significance occurred when the late Heywood Broun, a wit among drama critics, once wrote that a certain actor, *J*, was "the world's worst 'actor.'" Broun was sued for libel and acquitted. Sometime later, *J* appeared in another play, and Broun, reporting the performance, wrote: "Mr. *J* was not up to his usual standard last night."

Section IV: The Fallacies of Ambiguity

Thus far we have noted four different types of ambiguity. When confronted with ambiguities we are not certain as to how we should interpret (1) single words or phrases, (2) the sense of a sentence, (3) the emphases or accents desired by the writer or speaker, or (4) the significance of a statement. The careful reader will be alert to the presence of these uncertainties. He will ask the appropriate questions in order to get information that will help to interpret the statements correctly.

A *fallacy* of ambiguity is a distortion of meaning or an error of reasoning based upon an incorrect interpretation of an ambiguous word or phrase. These errors of reasoning usually occur in *use* (by the writer). Distortions of meaning, on the other hand, occur in *interpretation* (by the reader).

Note that the presence of ambiguity is not, in itself, an "error." If a friend tells us that he shot a secretary (meaning a bird) on his last safari to Africa, we may or may not be aware of the ambiguity of the word "secretary." If we jump to the conclusion that he shot a beautiful female of the human species, this would be an error resulting from our faulty interpretation of the ambiguous word. We shall now examine two major fallacies arising from the various types of ambiguity: equivocation and accent.

1. Equivocation

The fallacy of equivocation is an error of use, rather than of interpretation, i.e., it is committed by writers and speakers rather than readers and listeners. It occurs when a writer (or speaker) uses an ambiguous word (or root or phrase) in more than one sense in a given unit of discourse, such equivocal use resulting in an unjustified inference. Some examples: A speaker says: "I am sure that communists really believe in God. It is generally agreed that for its followers communism is a religion, and religious people believe in God." The term "religion" is used in two different senses. Communism is a religion in the sense that its followers show an ardent devotion and fidelity to its tenets, but it is not a religion in the traditional sense of "conviction of the existence of a Supreme Being." The failure to distinguish these meanings resulted in an unjustified inference.

Our second example involves the ambiguous term "law." In its legal sense law means a rule regulating human conduct established by an appropriate governing body. In science, a law refers to the uniform behavior of natural events, i.e., to an order or pattern in nature that is regarded as unvarying under the given conditions. An example is the law of gravitation. It is impossible to "violate" such a law, nor can it have exceptions, for if there is an exception the behavior is not uniform and there is no law. A convenient way of distinguishing the two senses of law is to say that a law of nature is a *description* (of nature); a legal or civil law is a *prescription*, a command. Now suppose one were to argue as follows:

Science has discovered many laws of nature. This is proof that there is a God, for a law implies the existence of a lawgiver, and God is the great Lawgiver of the universe.

The term "law" is used equivocally in this argument. Law in the sense of an order or command implies the existence of a lawgiver or commander, but law in the sense of a description does not.

Equivocation may of course be used deliberately for the purposes of wit and humor. "Your argument is sound, nothing but sound." Thus Benjamin Franklin's pun, "If we don't hang together, we'll hang separately." Or the absurd syllogism, "Some dogs have shaggy ears. My dog has shaggy ears. Therefore, my dog is *some* dog."

Note that equivocation can occur only if the ambiguous term is used at least twice in the same unit of discourse. When an ambiguous word is used only once, this is simple ambiguity. It goes without saying that equivocation should be avoided in our discussions. A word should be used in the same sense throughout a unit of discourse. If we do not use our words consistently there can be no communication or reasoning.

2. Accent

The fallacy of "accent" is an error which results from giving an obviously improper accent or emphasis to the words in a sentence or to the ideas in a unit of discourse.

Such improper accenting or distortion of meaning may be done deliberately, in order to deceive, but usually occurs where there is ambiguity of emphasis. Misinterpretations may then occur because of careless writing or careless interpretation. We shall note three typical ways in which the fallacy occurs:

a. The incorrect emphasis of the words in a sentence

The commandment says, "Thou shalt not bear false witness against thy neighbor."

If one were to stress the word "neighbor," implying that it is permissible to bear false witness against those who are not our neighbors, this would be an obvious misinterpretation.

b. The incorrect interpretation of amphibolous sentences

If one were to interpret the example given earlier (p. 50) as meaning that *Jane* was zooming along under her own power, the amphibolous sentence would be misinterpreted.

c. Incorrect summaries

When a summary is made of an author's statements, it should represent his most important thoughts. When a unit of discourse is improperly summarized, the fault may lie, of course, with the author, whose meaning was not clear. On the other hand, the summarizer may distort the author's meaning either carelessly or with the intent to deceive. We shall now examine some of the forms in which this type of accent occurs.

The reader should always be on the alert when excerpts from a writing are presented. Dishonest examples of "excerpt-lifting" abound. A dramatic critic writes that he "liked all of the play except the lines, the acting, and the scenery." He is quoted as having said that "he liked all of it." Ironical remarks are open to this kind of misinterpretation. A schoolteacher tells her civics class that "communism is the best type of government if you care nothing for your liberty or your material welfare." She is quoted as having said that "communism is the best type of government." Unwitting errors of the same sort occur when a student fails to distinguish between a lecturer's own views and those which he quotes, or even between a speaker's own views and those which he attacks.

The careful thinker will always be on his guard against quotations taken out of their context and he will ask, "Let's have the whole of that quotation." This does not mean that quotations are improper, but only that quotations should be fair and accurate representations of the meaning of the author.

Newspaper headlines purportedly summarize the news, but may distort the meaning by improper emphasis. The "headline reader" is thereby misled. "Let me write the headlines," an editor once said, "and I care not who writes the news." Advertisements may achieve similar results by the use of large case type in bold letters. The "come-on" elements will be presented in large letters, and the less attractive ones will be minimized by the use of small type. A famous example is one that was used by Barnum to advertise the first Canadian concert of the Belgian violinist, Ysaye. It read,

THEIR EXCELLENCIES,
THE PRINCE AND PRINCESS OF BELGIUM
have been asked whether they
WILL ATTEND THE CONCERT OF YSAYE,
WORLD'S GREATEST VIOLINIST

A form of summary called "special pleading" or "stacking the cards" is perhaps of greatest importance in this connection. Speakers emphasize only those elements in a report which suit their purposes and omit the rest. This may be permissible practice for debaters and lawyers who seek to win a case, but it is not in the spirit of the seeker after truth. Thus, in the days when India was struggling for its independence, rioting was frequent. A pro-Indian spokesman on a radio panel was denouncing the British for their callous disregard of elementary decency and reported an incident in the House of Commons in which the Conservative members of parliament "stood up and cheered" when informed that the British Army in India had killed 500 Indians. His audience was profoundly shocked by this report. But another speaker on the same program then read from the full Parliamentary report of the incident. This report stated that many British soldiers had been killed during the rioting, that about 500 Indians had been killed, and the report ended with the Prime Minister's declaration that the government intended to preserve law and order at all costs. (Cheers from Conservative benches.)

Accent, of course, is sometimes a fruitful source of humor when the incorrect interpretation of accent or emphasis is deliberate. Thus, Humpty-Dumpty says to Alice: "They gave it me—for an unbirthday present." "I beg your pardon?" Alice said with a puzzled air. "I'm not offended," said Humpty-Dumpty.

Another: "Would you—be good enough"—Alice panted out, after running a little farther, "to stop a minute—just to get one's breath again?" "I'm *good* enough," the King said, "only I'm not strong enough. You see, a minute goes by so fearfully quick. You might as well try to catch a bandersnatch!"

Exercises

I The Four Types of Ambiguity

A. Simple Ambiguity

1. Find seven different senses of the words "right," "good," and "fast."
2. Find the important ambiguous words in the following questions. Show how each question might be answered "Yes" and "No" and thus lead to verbal disputes.
   a. Were the early Christians communists?
   b. Do conservative senators vote right?
   c. Will Hitler be regarded as a great historical figure by future historians?
   d. Is there "rock and roll" music in this room now?
   e. Is the inside of a ripe watermelon red before it is opened?
3. Identify the ambiguous terms in the following, and state two senses in which these terms may be understood:
   a. John just broke a record.
   b. I have two diamonds, two spades, eight clubs, and one heart.
   c. A cub reporter was assigned to report a social gathering. "Among the most beautiful young ladies present," he wrote, "was our genial mayor, J. S. Zipf." When asked to explain, he insisted, "Well, that's where he was."
   d. "Beauty is truth, truth beauty,"——that is all
      Ye know on earth, and all ye need to know. (Keats)
   e. Here the Red Queen began again. "Can you answer useful questions?" she said. "How is bread made?"
      "I know that!" Alice cried eagerly. "You take some flour—"
      "Where do you pick the flower?" the White Queen asked. "In a garden or in the hedges?"
      "Well, it isn't picked at all," Alice explained, "it's ground—."
      "How many acres of ground?" asked the White Queen. "You mustn't leave out so many things." (Lewis Carroll, *Through the Looking Glass,* Chapter IX.)
      (Which special type of simple ambiguity is found in this item?)
4. In the following examples is the "word-trouble" vagueness or ambiguity? Explain your answers. (If it is ambiguity, point out two meanings of the ambiguous term.)

    a. Even in the summertime one should not use too much salt.

    b. A statute provides that no vehicles shall be allowed in a public park.

    c. Rent control is inconsistent with the American way of doing things.

    d. Socialism is not a democratic type of political system.

    e. Is semantics a science?

    f. Thomas Jefferson hoped the United States would have a rebellion every twenty years.

    g. Bishop Gore: "Christianity has not failed; it has never been tried."
Graham Wallas: "A religion that can exist for 1900 years without being tried has failed."

    h. The trouble with common sense is that it is so uncommon.

5. Criticize the following in terms of the necessity for successful communication:

A speaker at a meeting of philosophers stated that he had found that every philosopher who uses the words God and Religion means something different from what other philosophers mean. But, he argued, this was quite proper, since every person who uses these words actually does mean something different from what other people mean.

B. *Amphiboly*

Point out at least two different interpretations of the amphibolous sentences below and note which interpretation seems most reasonable to you. The first example indicates the general method of analysis.

1. Some years ago, a *Chicago Daily News* sportswriter wrote that Jim Jeffries, in Hollywood to make a movie, was asked, "I say, Jeff, do you think you could whip Joe Louis?" "Son," answered Jim slowly, "I've whipped better men than Joe Louis." "And right here," said the writer, "came the argument. Did the old boilermaker mean that he had whipped better men than Joe Louis IS or than he HAS whipped?"

2. "Hercules the dragon will slay."

3. Wanted: Young girls to sew lace trimmings on the eleventh floor.

4. After the general watched the lion perform, he was taken

to the city hall and fed twenty-five pounds of meat before a large crowd.

5. While we were eating a young man the son of the proprietor came in.
6. Serve the meat when thoroughly stewed.
7. Newspaper headlines:

U. S. MISSIONARY   HALT WORK ON
HELD BY REDS IN   FILM TO HONOR
MOSCOW SAFE   U. S. WAR HEROES

8. How much is 3 times 2 plus 4?
9. All men are not evil.
10. "Where never is heard a discouraging word, and the skies are not cloudy all day."
11. All are prejudiced who know only one side of the facts.
12. An insurance policy read, "This policy shall be incontestable on no grounds other than non-payment of premiums."
13. In a lease given by White to Smith, Robinson guaranteed that Smith would fulfill his obligations, in the following document: "I hereby bind myself to White for the true and faithful performance of the agreement on the part of Smith in case Smith should die within three years I agree to pay up to that time and deliver the property to White as above stated."
14. From Kant's *Fundamental Principles of the Metaphysic of Morals:*

In this manner, then, results a harmony like that which a certain satirical poem depicts as existing between a married couple bent on going to ruin, "O, marvellous harmony, what he wishes, she wishes also"; or like . . . the pledge of Francis I to the Emperor Charles V, "What my brother Charles wishes, that I wish also (viz. Milan)."

C. Ambiguity in Emphasis

Note the manner in which the following items may take on different meanings when we accent different words, by punctuation or otherwise:

1. Last summer Susan went to a pretty little girl's camp.
2. Nothing is too good for you.
3. From the collegiate magazine, *Ohio State Sundial* (quoted in *Time*, Nov. 11, 1946.):
    HE: I suppose you dance?
    SHE: Oh, yes, I love to.
    HE: Great! That's better than dancing.

4. Woman without her man is a beast. (Hint: Try using an exclamation mark after "woman.")

5. In an English class, the teacher was explaining the use of the past perfect tense in "had had." An exercise was given to John and Jim involving the use of "had" and "had had." The result: "John where Jim had had had had had had had had had had the teacher's approval." Interpret the sentence by supplying the proper punctuation marks in order to give it sense. (Hint: Use a semicolon in the sentence.

6. The Elizabethan translators of the Bible always italicized words which the translators added to the text in order to make the text clear. In I Kings, 13:27 we find the following: "And he spake unto his sons, saying, Saddle me the ass. And they saddled *him*."

D. *The Ambiguity of Significance*

Disregard any possible semantic ambiguities in the following, and note two different interpretations of the significance of the statements.

1. A sea captain and his first mate alternated in writing the happenings of each day in the ship's log. One day the mate drank too much, and the next day he found the entry, "The mate was drunk today." He was very much annoyed, but the captain justified the entry on the ground that the entry was true. The next day the captain (who was a sober man) opened the log and found the mate's revenge in the notation, "The captain was not drunk today."

2. Department store sales in dollars are two per cent higher than last year during the same month.

3. The United States has a stronger military establishment today than it had in 1953.

4. You will find that congressmen from the farm states pay more attention to the demands of their constituents than they do to the broader problems of the general welfare.

II The Fallacies of Ambiguity

A. *Equivocation*

1. In the following examples, find the term which is used in two different senses, and state the two meanings:
   a. Business is business.

   b. Those were the days when men were men.
   c. Lawyers tell us that the common law has two branches: the criminal law and the civil (noncriminal law), and yet they frequently distinguish the common law from the civil law.
   d. "In the United States we have political freedom; in Russia they have economic freedom. Since both kinds of freedom are desirable, the United States should move toward Russia's economic freedom, and Russia should move toward our political freedom."
   e. Love, as in tennis, means absolutely nothing.

2. In the following, explain how the fallacious conclusion is based on the use of a term in more than one sense:
   a. Since tall basketball players are tall men, it must follow that good basketball players are good men.
   b. A poor man does not have the right to compel his rich brother to help him financially, so he shouldn't feel that he has any right to such help.
   c. A crust of bread is better than nothing. Do you also agree that nothing is better than true love? Then you must agree that a crust of bread is better than true love.
   d. No news is good news. Strikes and lockouts are no news. Therefore, strikes and lockouts are good news.
   e. The maintenance of a nuisance is, of course, a crime. Now, Junior is a little "nuisance." Therefore, his maintenance is a small crime. (How many terms are used equivocally in this one? Explain.)
   f. Improbable events happen almost every day. But what happens almost every day is a very probable event. Then improbable events must be very probable events.

B. *The Fallacy of Accent*

1. A whiskey is widely advertised under the name BONNIE ANGUS, A BLEND. The law requires that the label state an analysis of the contents. This reads: "ALL THE WHISKIES IN THIS BOTTLE ARE AT LEAST 5 YEARS OLD. 28% whiskey, 72% neutral spirits."
2. Plato said that women are always inferior to men.
3. In an article entitled "The Ethical Teachings of Jesus," which appeared in the *Outlook*, in 1910, Dr. Lyman Abbott, pastor and publicist, argued as follows to prove that Christianity is not hostile to the rich man:

My radical friend declares that the teachings of Jesus are not practicable, that we cannot carry them out in life, and that we do not pretend to do so. Jesus, he reminds us, said, "Lay not up for yourselves treasures upon earth"; and Christians do universally lay up for themselves treasures upon earth; every man that owns a house and lot, or a share of stock in a corporation, or a life insurance policy, or money in a savings bank, has laid up for himself treasures upon earth. But Jesus did not say, "Lay not up for yourselves treasures upon earth." He said, "Lay not up for yourselves treasures upon earth *where moth and rust doth corrupt and where thieves break through and steal.*" And no sensible American does. Moth and rust do not get at Mr. Rockefeller's oil wells, nor at the Sugar Trust's sugar, and thieves do not often break through and steal a railway or an insurance company or a savings bank. What Jesus condemned was hoarding wealth. (Reported by Upton Sinclair in *The Profits of Religion.*)

4. A newspaper headline:

ATOMIC WAR
unlikely says senator

5. The professor made the following comment on a student's thesis: "Your thesis is both good and original. Unfortunately, the good things in it are not original and the original things are not good." If the student were an expert excerpt-lifter, how might he commit the fallacy of accent?

Chapter 4

The Uses of Language

Section I: Neutral, Emotive, and Directive Words

In Chapter 2 we examined the manner in which words act as symbols for referents. The types of referents symbolized by words are things, ideas, states of mind, emotions, relations, attributes of things, and activities. When words act as symbols for referents, we say that symbols are used in a "cognitive" or "referential" manner. Words are used in this manner whenever we wish to communicate information to others. But the communication of information is only one of the purposes for which human beings use language. Language is also used to evoke emotional attitudes and feelings and to direct the activities of others.

With rare exceptions all words symbolize referents in the "cognitive" manner. But in addition to such references the speaker may wish to express his own emotional attitudes, to arouse the emotional attitudes of others and to get others to act in a certain way. We shall therefore speak of the three uses or purposes of language: the informational use, the expressive use, and the directive (or practical) use. (The expressive use has two aspects, the expression of the feelings of the speaker and the evocation of feelings in the hearer.)

Words thus have three functions. They are symbols which point to referents. But they may do more than that. "To close" refers to an activity. But when the verb is used in its imperative sense, as in "Close the window," it calls forth activity on the part of others and becomes a "directive" word as well as a referential one. Similarly, some words may stir emotional attitudes in the hearer. The word "kiss," for example. This word is a symbol for an activity, the act of osculation, whereby two persons salute each other mutually by the touching of the lips. But in addition to its referential function, the word may stir an emotional attitude in the reader. When words have the purely (or almost purely) cognitive or intellectual function, we shall call them neutral symbols. When they stir emotional attitudes we shall call them emotive symbols. Directives form a third group.

Whether a word has a neutral or emotive significance to a hearer (or speaker) depends upon the past experiences of the individual. The word "moon" has a neutral meaning to an astronomer, an emotive meaning to a lover. "Sex" has a neutral meaning to a biologist, an emotive meaning to an adolescent. The distinction is a relative one, depending upon the particular experiences of the individual. A word may be neutral to an individual in one context, emotive in another; neutral at one time and emotive at a later time. "Bread" was a neutral word for Frenchmen before 1940; an emotive word in 1945. These individual associations with words are the basis for the "word-association" tests used by criminologists in crime detection. Words associated with the crime will arouse emotional responses in the guilty person, whereas they will be neutral to the innocent.

Thus words are "neutral" or "emotive" depending upon the effects which they have on us, not because of characteristics inherent in the words themselves. Nevertheless, since there are large areas of experience shared by most human beings within a group, we can reasonably presuppose that *some* words will tend to arouse emotional responses in the hearers. "Pencil" and "paper" are neutral words to most persons, but words such as "God," "atheist," "love," "Red," and "Fascist" will be emotive. These emotive words arouse attitudes of "for" and "against," approval or disapproval.

The importance of context should also be emphasized. When a political scientist writes that "Caesar aspired to be dictator" or "Mussolini was the dictator of Italy," the word "dictator" has a primarily neutral significance, though emotional overtones may not be altogether absent. But when a well-known Chicago newspaper constantly referred to Franklin Delano Roosevelt as a "dictator," the word had a primarily emotive significance. The newspaper sought to arouse the feelings of fear and hatred in the reader. In order to know whether a word has a neutral or an emotive significance for a speaker, we must know something about his background, intention, and purposes.

Section II: The Three Purposes of Discourse

There are three major uses or purposes of language: the informational, expressive, and directive. We speak in order to inform others ("The diameter of Betelgeuse, the largest star, is 300 times that of the sun." "Jane left for Florida yesterday.") We speak to express our feelings ("Great!" "Bravo!" "The dirty dog!") or to affect the feelings of others, as in tales of horror, or in poetic lines such as "Comes the blind Fury with the abhorred shears, and slits the thin-spun life." Finally, we speak in order to influence the actions of others. ("Do unto others as you would have others do unto you." "Release that woman!") All of these uses are indispensable in communication. Man is a rational animal, but a large part of his speech and thought is concerned with nonrational matters. In our social relations we greet people with conventional expressions, we tell anecdotes to amuse our friends, and we state our feelings of approval and disapproval for a host of things and activities.

It is doubtful whether any person uses language in a manner which exemplifies only one of the purposes noted. Our purposes usually are mixed. Consider the sentence, "Capitalism is a horrible conspiracy to exploit the workers and to grind the faces of the poor." Assuming that the speaker sincerely means what he says, we shall find all of the uses of language in this unit of discourse. The speaker wishes to inform his hearers that capitalism has certain effects on the lives of human beings. (His language is, of course, ill-adapted to its informative purpose.) The sentence is also expressive. We detect that the speaker is emotionally moved by the "crimes" of capitalism; his sentence is a kind of agonized cry. The words are also intended to affect the feelings of the hearer so that he will sympathize with the victims. Finally, the speaker has a directive purpose in mind. He wishes to move the hearer emotionally so that the hearer will do something about the plight of the workers and the poor.

With this reminder that all the uses of language may be found in a single unit of discourse, we turn to a detailed examination of the purposes of discourse. Though language is mixed, the mixture is made up of distinguishable elements.

1. The informative purpose of discourse

The desire to inform others concerning facts, i.e., that something is or is not the case, is obviously a major purpose of communication. Little comment will be required, except to note the types of words which best fulfill this function of discourse. If it is one's purpose to inform others concerning facts, neutral words * will be most appropriate, since emotive words * may arouse the reader's emotions and interfere with his understanding of the facts. Emotion tends to distort the judgment; it is also a highly individual factor, and emotive words may affect different hearers in different ways. In the ideal type of scientific discourse, then, emotive words will be eliminated insofar as this is possible. It would be impossible, however, to dispense with all words having emotional significance for readers of books on contemporary political issues, for many key words will inevitably arouse emotions in some readers. Vague emotive terms such as "reactionary" should be avoided, and words like "communism" should of course be used with great caution. But since some persons *are* communists, it is merely a matter of pure information to call them such, even though the word is also an emotive one for many readers.

The speaker who desires to inform will also avoid "question-begging" epithets, i.e., words which prejudge facts, or take disputed conclusions for granted. An example of this occurs when we refer to an accused person as "that criminal" before he has been proved guilty. Good informative language will be made up of statements which are readily verifiable. This point is constantly applied in courts of law. If a witness states that an injured man "has not walked normally since the accident," an objection will be raised to the use of the word "normal." The witness should describe the facts, the exact manner in which the injured man walks. "Not normal" prejudges the issue; testimony should describe facts on which the jury may base its own judgments.

2. The expressive purpose of language

Language may be used to express one's own feelings or to affect the feelings of others, or both. Emotive words are often

* That is, words that would be typically considered as such.

appropriate in this use of language, but we should bear in mind that the types of words used are not reliable indicators of the purpose of the speaker. The fact that a speaker uses emotive words does not prove that he is expressing his own feelings or that he desires to affect the feelings of others; contrariwise, he may use neutral words when he wishes to stir emotion. We are presently concerned with the *purpose* we call expressive, and not with emotive words as such.

a. The desire to express one's own feelings

We use language in spontaneous expressions of feeling, as in "Ouch!" "Damn!" or the groan of the patient in the dentist's chair. Profanity furnishes many examples of this use of language, from its mild damns to its roaring expletives. Astonishment is spontaneously expressed in words like "Bro-ther!" Frequently the use of language in this manner appears to be without the intent to communicate anything to others. But when we say "How terrible!" or "How perfectly divine!" we not only express our own feelings, but we also indicate that the referent has a certain valuable or disvaluable quality. We thus communicate some information, even though very little.

We may also note a type of expression which appears to be "talk for talk's sake," a kind of perpetual motion of the larynx. Some people may talk just to "let off steam" or "to get a load off their chests." Such expression of feelings has a practical value in acting as a safety valve for pent-up emotions. The Catholic confessional and the session in the office of the psychiatrist may make use of this type of expression for therapeutic purposes.

The presence of the "self-expressive" purpose of language is not always obvious. Poetry is often written for self-expressive purposes, and so also are many sentences written by critics of poetry, as in the rhapsody:

> Each poet, from Homer to our own day, has been to some extent and at some point, the voice of the movement and energy of poetry; in him poetry has for the moment become visible, audible, incarnate, and his extant poems are the record left of that partial and transitory incarnation. (Mackail, *Lectures on Poetry*.)

The writer is expressing his feelings in these remarks, in addition to whatever other purposes we may find. Frequently, too, we find writers who fall in love with words and use them because of the emotional satisfaction derived from their use. Goethe, in discussing free will, said, "The word 'freedom' sounds so beautiful, that we cannot do without it, even though it should designate an error."

b. The desire to affect the feelings of others

Various motives are included within this aspect of expressiveness. We may seek sympathy from the hearer or desire that he share in our gladness. We may seek to stir his emotions as a means to a practical end, with an ultimate directive purpose in mind. This very important use of expressive language will be more fully dealt with under the "directive" purpose. Another very important use of this aspect of expressive language is the "poetic use," which we shall use in a broad sense as referring to the creation of literary works for artistic purposes. The poet's primary purpose is to convey an experience to the reader. It is not the poet's primary aim to instruct us through the communication of information or to move us emotionally so that we will act, but to affect our feelings, attitudes, intelligence, and imagination in such a manner that we will live through an enriching experience as an end in itself.

We must remember that the purposes of discourse are never pure and rarely simple. The poet may also communicate information, and he may also arouse our desire to correct social maladjustments, as in Steinbeck's *Grapes of Wrath*. But unless he succeeds in what we have called the poetic function of language, his work will be a tract, and not a poem.

We must repeat again that though some words are most appropriate for a particular purpose of language, this is not a "one-to-one" relationship; that is, types of words and the purposes of discourse are not correlated as a button is correlated with a buttonhole. The poet does not necessarily use a "poetic" language. In the past, of course, academicians sometimes promulgated rules concerning the kinds of words they considered admissible in poetry. To cite one example, in France, during the 1820's, only "noble" words were considered appropriate in poetry. Lytton Strachey *(Landmarks in French Literature)* states that the use of the common word *mouchoir* (handkerchief) actually produced a riot in Paris during a performance of *Othello*. But the idea is still prevalent that poetry uses only emotive words. Consider, for example, the following experiment by Thouless (*How to Think Straight,* Simon & Schuster, 1939). Thouless took the lines from Keats' "Eve of St. Agnes,"

> Full on this casement shone the wintry moon,
> And threw warm gules on Madeline's fair breast,

and rewrote them, substituting neutral words for the emotive ones, to read,

> Full on this window shone the wintry moon,
> Making red marks on Jane's uncolored chest.

Thouless triumphantly noted that the poetic effect disappeared. But his lines are a parody and do not prove that poetry cannot be written except in emotive language. The poet seeks to evoke feelings and attitudes and will thus make liberal use of emotive words, but such words are not necessary to create poetic effects. It is simply not true that poetry *must* use "poetic" words. Robert Frost writes poems containing an unusual amount of neutral words, as in the first lines of "The Death of the Hired Man" (*Complete Poems of Robert Frost,* Henry Holt and Company, 1949):

> Mary sat musing on the lamp flame at the table
> Waiting for Warren. When she heard his step,
> She ran on tiptoe down the darkened passage
> To meet him in the doorway with the news
> And put him on his guard. "Silas is back."

The poet aims at an effect in the mind of the reader. If he achieves his aim he has created a poem.

3. The directive purpose of language

The directive purpose refers to a speaker's desire to arouse others to action. To this end he may use the type of words we have called "directives," such as verbs in the imperative mode. Thus: "Vote for Zipf!" "Live dangerously!" "Workers of the world, unite!" But the directive purpose may be present without the use of such directives, or "motivators." Frequently, the speaker who wishes to gets others to act will choose to accomplish his purpose in a more subtle manner, for fear that a direct appeal may cause suspicion or resentment. Every parent has used the method of suggestion rather than direct appeal to get action from a small child: "Now, you wouldn't want . . . would you?" But the readiest manner in which speakers get individuals to act without the use of directive words is through an appeal to the emotions. Psychologically, a very close connection is found between our emotions and our tendencies to act, since all emotions tend to seek fulfillment in action. Love and hate make us want to do something. Our resentment against injustice or what we conceive to be injustice stimulates us to take up arms against it. The speaker who wishes action will thus seek to stir emotions as an indirect means of achieving his purpose.

A classical example of the manner in which emotive language is used to stir action is found in Mark Antony's funeral oration in Shakespeare's *Julius Caesar*. Here are a few lines from the oration:

> If you have tears, prepare to shed them now.
> You all do know this mantle: I remember
> The first time ever Caesar put it on;
> 'Twas on a summer's evening, in his tent,
> That day he overcame the Nervii:
> Look, in this place ran Cassius' dagger through:
> See what a rent the envious Casca made:
> Through this the well-beloved Brutus stabb'd;
> And as he pluck'd his cursed steel away,
> Mark how the blood of Caesar follow'd it,
> As rushing out of doors, to be resolved
> If Brutus so unkindly knock'd, or no;
> For Brutus, as you know, was Caesar's angel:
> Judge, O you Gods, how dearly Caesar loved him!
> This was the most unkindest cut of all.

The Roman mob finally leaves Antony, resolved to wreak their vengeance on the traitors who stabbed their beloved Caesar, whom they had previously suspected of the desire to become a dictator over them.

Emotive words and the expressive use of language are thus well adapted to stirring emotion which results in action. But neutral words and the informative use of language may also stir emotional attitudes which lead to action. A prospectus which states that "thousands of your fellow-Americans are making thousands of dollars each year raising minks" will stir the emotion of cupidity and lead to investment of one's savings. "The X nation is mobilizing its troops" is informative, but will stir action. The lack of correlation between the language used and the purposes of the speaker may be illustrated by examining the sentence: "Here comes a lion." A circus attendant might use the words to convey information; uttered by a child, the words might express delighted rapture; but if the lion had just escaped from its cage, the words would direct us to take cover.

The importance of emotion-stirring words in directing action is implicitly assumed in *The Fine Art of Propaganda* (Harcourt, Brace & Co., 1937), by The Institute for Propaganda Analysis. The writers attempted to classify the devices and techniques of the propagandist, who seeks to influence the actions of others. Among the emotion-stirring devices listed were the following:

Name calling. The use of "bad names" attached to individuals or groups, such as "Red," "Fascist," "radical," and "reactionary." These words usually stir emotions of dislike and hatred and result in action against those so referred to.

Glittering generalities. The use of "virtue words" or phrases such as "the American Way," "our Christian civilization," "the family is the bulwark of the nation," and "Uncle Sam." When these honorific slogans are attached to individuals and groups, we tend to act favorably toward them.

Testimonials. The fact that "important people" approve of a program will stir the attitude of reverence and imitation. Contrariwise, the fact that "bad people" are for or against a program will stir feelings of aversion and result in action contrary to theirs.

Plain folks. The speaker talks to us as if he were one of us common people, "just an ordinary Joe," even as you and I. We trust him; he has aroused the sentiment of "belonging." We act as he suggests.

Band wagon. "Everybody else is with us, why not you?" Man is a gregarious animal and hates to be apart from the crowd. We hop on the band wagon.

Ceremonial language is another form of directive language. Greetings such as "Nice day," "Foul weather, isn't it?" or "Pleased to meet you" are not necessarily spoken to convey information. Social intercourse requires the use of language rituals, and we utter ceremonial phrases in order to establish a friendly attitude in the person spoken to. Feelings of communion are stirred, leading to the type of action desired.

We may note finally that directive language may be used in order to *prevent* action. This is often accomplished by the deliberate use of neutral words. Just as emotive words may arouse an emotional attitude toward "neutral" events, so "neutral" language may create an attitude of indifference toward events which would normally stir strong feelings within us. Apologists for foul deeds customarily use this type of language. They tell us not to believe in "atrocity" stories, which, they claim, are "nothing but propaganda." But the atrocities may really exist, and the reader may thus fall a victim to "propaganda against propaganda."

Section III: Appropriate and Inappropriate Language

We have distinguished the uses of language and have noted that most discourse is mixed. Each type of usage is a legitimate one—in its proper place. Poetry, eloquence, ringing calls to action, and eulogies have their honored and legitimate places in discourse, and no sensible person will wish to disparage the use of emotive words in these fields. As logicians, however, it is important that we should know what we are doing and it is at least equally important to know what others are doing when they speak to us. We shall now examine some "misuses" of language, by which we mean the use of inappropriate language within the specific context. When we are interested in receiving information, we want facts and not an emotional harangue. To use emotive language in a scientific discourse is a misuse of language, as would be a technical explanation of chlorophyll in a poem about daffodils.

When a biologist reads a report of an experiment, he

wishes the unvarnished truth, facts without emotional colora-
tion. When the same biologist attends a rally of his political
party he is willing that his emotions should be stirred with respect to social programs and ideals. Action requires emotional
motivation, for purely thinking beings would probably make no
distinctions between good and evil. When the biologist opens
his morning newspaper and reads about a recent strike, about
conditions in Europe, or a discussion of election issues, does he
desire information or emotional stimulation? Obviously, in
order to act intelligently, he must know what the facts are. A
newspaper editor may quite legitimately express his own opinions about national policies, but he should not write his editorials in the news columns. The same considerations hold when
we listen to a political speech. The political speaker is quite
naturally a partisan for a point of view. But if he is worth listening to, if he expects to convince men of good will who want to
make intelligent decisions, he should present facts on which to
base such decisions. But the actual state of affairs is well described in the following:

> Overstatement, understatement, half-truths, distorted logic,
> innuendo, and sheer intellectual dishonesty characterize the
> utterances of far too many of our public men. They bandy
> opprobrious terms about, in describing each other. This juve-
> nile penchant of many American public men serves, upon
> analysis, to demonstrate the contempt in which they hold the
> electorate. It is not sufficient, for their purposes, that the elec-
> torate be informed fully and correctly, and then permitted to
> draw its own conclusions . . . They seek to inflame rather than
> to inform. They seek to excite passion rather than reason. They
> appeal to fear instead of intelligence. And, in so doing, they
> evidence a contempt for the body politic and its ability to
> understand the issues of the day. (Milburn P. Akers, *Chi-
> cago Sun-Times.*)

As samples of inappropriate language let us examine the
two following news items:

> Renewing Republican demands for a congressional in-
> vestigation of our occupation program, Senator C today accused
> the administration of inflicting a "deliberate policy of mass
> starvation" upon Germany, without distinction as to age, guilt
> or innocence. The policies we have pursued, the senator as-

serted, have "degenerated into the callous and inhuman practices of the Nazis themselves." . . . Senator C attributed the
starvation policy to a "conspiratorial clique" of "vengeful
fanatics" in the administration who formulated the Morgen-
thau plan to impose a Carthaginian peace upon Germany.

The Virginia vigilantes tried to lynch labor in the House
again last week. For one bad moment it seemed that they might
get away with it. They didn't. But in the effort they identified
some of the men and forces willing to join their mob. The *New
York Times,* for instance, was right out in front holding the
rope . . . indeed, the daily press was almost all there. So was
Southern democracy . . . Representative Howard W. Smith,
Virginia banker and axe man for the Byrd machine, was, as
usual, the instigator.

The reader's reaction to these passages will of course be influenced by whether or not he considers the statements *true.*
Though it is easier to detect faults when we disagree with the
speaker, the candid reader will recognize, nevertheless, that both
of these selections use very intemperate language. Note the substitution of question-begging epithets, such as "starvation policy," "tried to lynch labor," etc., in place of the facts on which
the conclusions ought to be based. Note the emotionally toned
words: "degenerated," "vengeful fanatics," "lynch," "mob," and
"axe-man." These words are calculated to arouse fear and hatred
in the reader. There is very little information; the reader has
only a vague idea as to what events are taking place. An intelligent citizen demands facts on which to base his decisions and
attitudes. Even though one's sympathies are with labor, one
should object to such items as the second sample, for only
knowledge of the facts will enable one to successfully meet unfair criticisms of labor's position. These examples are flagrant
misuses of emotive language in situations in which statements of
fact are required.

An opposite type of inappropriateness that we touched on
earlier consists in writing in a detached, cool, objective, "scientific" manner to gloss over unpleasant facts. George Orwell has
noted some typical examples of the use of neutral words in such
writings:

Defenseless villages are bombarded from the air, the in-
habitants driven out into the countryside, the cattle machine-

gunned, the huts set on fire with incendiary bullets: this is called *pacification*. Millions of peasants are robbed of their farms and sent trudging along the roads with no more than they can carry: this is called *transfer of population* or *rectification of frontiers*. People are imprisoned for years without trial, or shot in the back of the neck or sent to die of scurvy in Arctic lumber camps: this is called *elimination of unreliable elements*. ("Politics and the English Language," *New Republic*, June 24, 1946.)

Section IV: The Logical and the Non-Logical Uses of Language

1. The truth values of sentences

The logician is interested in language with respect to its "truth-values," i.e., he is interested in statements insofar as they are true or false. A statement is true or false in the logical sense when it is capable of being verified or disproved by evidence. Not all statements are true or false in this sense, nor do speakers always seek to make "truth-value" statements. Many poetic utterances are obvious examples of statements to which the criteria of truth and falsity in a logical sense are irrelevant. The poet may use metaphorical language which has "poetic truth" (i.e., adequacy in terms of feelings and attitudes), but not literal truth. To examine every poetic utterance as if it were intended to be literally true is not only to grossly misinterpret the poet's purpose but is a common cause for the inability of many persons to appreciate and enjoy poetry.

Thus, when Wordsworth writes, "The river glideth of its own sweet will," his statement is not false; scientific truth is irrelevant. When Shelley writes of the skylark,

> Hail to thee, blithe spirit,
> Bird thou never wert,

"he did not really mean to deny that the lark belongs to the class *aves*," as it has been well remarked. When Macbeth said "Life is a tale told by an idiot, full of sound and fury, signifying nothing," his statement must not be interpreted literally, though it does contain a profound judgment concerning life and is, in a sense, verifiable. One should, therefore, not read poetry for a collection of informative sentences. One may find true statements in poetry, but the reader who picks up Wordsworth's "I Wandered Lonely as a Cloud" for botanical knowledge concerning daffodils would be sadly mistaking the poet's purpose. A poem is not a proposition, but an experience.

The logician is interested in language insofar as it states propositions, i.e., statements which are either true or false. The grammarian tells us that there are four types of sentences, declarative, interrogative, imperative, and exclamatory. Obviously, ordinary questions are neither true nor false, nor are imperatives, or commands. Thus, neither "Is the window open?" nor "Close the window" make statements which are true or false. Declarative and exclamatory sentences, on the other hand, *may* be propositions. Poetic utterances such as those quoted above are declarative sentences which are not propositions. A declarative sentence is a proposition when it states that something is or is not the case, in a manner verifiable by factual evidence. Exclamatory sentences such as "The Cubs won!" and "How rapidly he played that difficult passage!" are obviously sentences which make statements concerning facts, in addition to expressing the satisfaction and amazement of the speaker.

Questions and commands, we agree, are not propositions. But we must look beneath the surfaces of some questions and commands. For example, a "rhetorical question" is not intended as a genuine question but as a concealed statement. Thus when someone says, "What's the world coming to, anyway?," he is not requesting an answer but saying, "The world really is in bad shape."

Most interesting to the logician are the "complex questions." These are genuine questions, but they are like propositions in that they carry concealed assumptions that certain facts exist, i.e., that certain propositions are true (or false). For example, during a trial the prosecuting attorney snapped, "Tell me sir, have you stopped beating your wife? Answer yes or no!" This is a complex question because it contains the assumption that the witness *has* been beating his wife, and either a yes or no answer would acknowledge the truth of this assumption.

A complex question, of course, may be legitimate or illegitimate depending upon the nature of what it assumes. Thus, if the witness *had* been beating his wife, this would have been a legitimate complex question. We shall call a complex question "legitimate" when either (1) its fact-assumptions are true or (2) both speaker and hearer are willing to accept them as true. When the facts assumed are obviously true to everyone, as in "What reasons were primarily responsible for the admission of Alaska as the forty-ninth state?" we do not usually call the question complex, though it is. The question assumes that Alaska was admitted as the forty-ninth state.

The important thing, of course, is to be alert to complex questions when they make illegitimate assumptions. Such questions present traps into which the unwary may easily fall. When we are asked, "Why is it that labor leaders are so much less concerned with the general welfare than are the leaders of business?" the reader's tendency is to say, "You know, that never occurred to me. I wonder why it is so." He immediately puts his mind to work helping the questioner. But before we seek explanations of a fact, we should be sure that the fact exists. We should critically examine the truth or falsity of the assumptions concealed in questions.

Similarly, commands may contain concealed assumptions. In "Be careful" we assume that a dangerous situation exists. The apprentice who was asked to bring the journeymen a left-handed monkey wrench was victimized by an illegitimate command.

2. Ought Sentences and Evaluations

Difficult problems of interpretation arise when we seek to classify "ought" sentences and "evaluations" in terms of our distinction between the logical and the non-logical uses of language. Let us note the nature of these problems.

Ought sentences. Consider the sentence, "One ought never to tell a lie." Does this sentence convey information? Does it express the feelings of the speaker and affect those of the hearer? Is it a directive statement? Is it perhaps all three combined? The word "ought" requires close examination.

The word "ought" is used in at least three different senses, logical, conditional, and unconditional. Thus, in "If you worked out the addition correctly, you ought to have gotten the sum of 625," the word ought is used in a purely logical sense. In "If you want to keep in good physical shape, then you ought to keep regular hours," the word is used in a conditional manner, i.e., you are advised to keep regular hours on the condition that you want to keep in good physical shape. The third use is unconditional or categorical: One ought never to tell a lie. No condition is stated; the ought is stated without any ifs, ands, or buts.

Our example of a sentence containing the logical use of "ought" is one which clearly involves a proposition: The sum of these numbers is 625. This is an informative sentence. The example of the conditional "ought" is also easily translatable into a proposition: Keeping regular hours is a means toward keeping in good physical shape. This is an informative sentence which is often used with a directive purpose. It is the third use, the use of "ought" in an unconditional or categorical sense, that raises serious logical difficulties. What exactly does it mean? Can it be translated into a proposition?

"One ought never to tell a lie" may be interpreted as a command; if so, then it is not a proposition, for a command, as we have seen, is neither true nor false, as "Close the window." Perhaps it is a concealed type of conditional "ought" statement, and should be interpreted conditionally, even though the condition is not explicitly stated. Such an interpretation would give us something like: "One ought never to tell a lie if he wishes to have a good reputation" (or some other condition). This conditional "ought" could then be translated into a proposition. Or perhaps the unconditional "ought" sentence may simply express the emotions of the speaker, in particular that he hates lying and liars, and perhaps he also hopes that others will feel the way he does about lies. This translation tells us something about the speaker but does not yield a proposition.

Some ethical theorists would accept none of these translations. They tell us that categorical "ought" sentences are not really commands, not merely expressions of emotion, and that to translate them into conditional statements destroys their distinctively unconditional character. In other words, these sentences are unique in meaning. An adequate discussion of this problem, however, would take us beyond the scope of semantical analysis.

Sentences containing evaluations. By "evaluations" we mean statements which assert that something does or does not possess a specific kind of value. Our discussion will be limited, however, to moral and aesthetic values. We shall consider sentences which declare that persons are morally good or evil or that things are beautiful or ugly. Consider the sentence: "Picasso's paintings are great works of art." How shall we classify this sentence—as informative, expressive, or directive? Does the statement tell us something about Picasso's paintings or does it merely tell us something about the speaker? When Churchill, in one of his eloquent speeches, referred to Hitler and Mussolini as "those wicked men," was he giving us information about Hitler and Mussolini or about himself? Or about himself and them?

The problem, simply stated, is this: If evaluations give us information concerning the thing evaluated, then they are statements of fact and, like all statements of fact, will be true or false. On the other hand, if they are mere expressions of the feelings or emotions of the speaker, then they are simply forms of expressive language, and neither true nor false concerning the thing evaluated. Under the latter interpretation, the evaluations quoted above would be equivalent to the following sentences: "I like Picasso's paintings"; "I hate Hitler and Mussolini." We must also consider the possibility that evaluations contain concealed "oughts." Perhaps they mean "This is the way I feel about Picasso and Hitler, and you ought to feel as I do."

Evaluations, of course, often purport to be statements of fact. Most persons would regard the following as an example of a *false* evaluation: "The homes in the slums of Chicago are architecturally more beautiful than the homes of the movie stars in Beverly Hills." But if this is false, it is a "factual statement" of fact and not a mere expression of the feelings of the speaker. Our present interest in these sentences, however, lies in calling attention to the semantical problems involved in evaluations. The solution of these problems, if there is a solution, must be found in the sciences of ethics and aesthetics. Further discussion of these questions will also be found in Chapter 19.

Exercises

1. Explain the following diagrammatic summary of the types and purposes of language:

TYPES OF WORDS   PURPOSE OF USING THE TYPES

NEUTRAL WORDS ———————————> TO GIVE INFORMATION

EMOTIVE WORDS ——————————> ⎰ TO EXPRESS ONE'S OWN FEELINGS
                                       ⎱ TO AFFECT THE FEELINGS OF OTHERS

DIRECTIVE WORDS ————————————> TO GET ACTION (OR INACTION)

2. Identify what appear to you to be emotive words in the following. Are these words necessarily emotive in nature? Are they usually emotive? Are they emotive to the writer? Explain.
   a. "Our opponents are petty bourgeoisie, capitalists, fascists, hyenas, hangmen, cannibals, lackeys, flunkeys, mad dogs, white guards, and renegades." (From a communist pamphlet.)
   b. Mr. Winston Churchill, in his *A History of the English-Speaking Peoples,* makes frequent use of the following words: royal, throne, scepter, realm, banner, clarion.

3. Identify the emotive words or phrases in the following and translate them into "neutral" language:
   a. I have never seen such a stubborn fool.
   b. The starry-eyed, breast-beating world-savers, do-gooders, and global thinkers are ganging up on American patriots.

4. State the purpose or purposes which are probably fulfilled by the following:
   a. A thing of beauty is a joy forever.
   b. How do you do?
   c. Blessed are the meek.
   d. Hatred and happiness are not compatible.
   e. A man's best friend is his dog.
   f. "I think there must be something in the place," said Mrs. Nickleby, "for, soon after I was married, I went to Stratford with my poor dear Nickleby, in a post-chaise from Birmingham—was it a post-chaise though!" said Mrs. Nickleby considering; "Yes, it must have been a post-chaise, because I recollect remarking at the time that the driver had a green shade over his left eye . . ."

5. The following items are from James Harvey Robinson's *An Introduction to the History of Western Europe* (Ginn and Com-

pany, 1931). Show how each item illustrates a different function of discourse:

a. We must learn, above all, to study sympathetically institutions and beliefs that we are tempted at first to declare absurd and unreasonable. The aim of the historian is not to prove that a particular way of doing a thing is right or wrong as, for instance, entrusting the whole government to a king, or forbidding clergymen to marry. His object is to show how a certain system came to be introduced, what was thought of it, how it worked and how another plan gradually supplanted it.

b. Louis XIV exhibited as woeful a want of statesmanship in the treatment of his Protestant subjects, as in the prosecution of disastrous wars.

c. New Zealand, during the closing decade of the nineteenth century, became famous for its experiments in social reform.

6. In the following items what is the chief purpose of the discourse? If there is more than one purpose, is one subordinate to the others? Which type of words are most important in each selection? Do you consider the language used in each case appropriate for the speaker's purpose? Is there any sense in which you consider the language inappropriate?

a. We will answer their demand for a gold standard by saying to them: You shall not press down upon the brow of labor this crown of thorns, you shall not crucify mankind upon a cross of gold. (William Jennings Bryan)

b. I warn John L. Lewis and his communistic cohorts that no second carpetbag expedition into the Southland, under the red banner of Soviet Russia and concealed under the slogans of the CIO will be tolerated. If the minions of the CIO attempt to carry through the South their lawless plan of organization, if they attempt to demoralize our industry, to corrupt our colored citizens, to incite race hatred and race warfare, I warn him here and now that they will be met by the flower of Southern manhood, and they will reap the bitter fruits of their folly. (Speech in the U. S. House of Representatives, June, 1937.)

c. The things which will change "the world" are the great discoveries and inventions, the new reactions inside the social organism, and the changes in the earth itself on account of changes in the cosmical forces. These causes will make of it just what, in fidelity to them, it ought to be. The men will be carried along with it and be made by it. The utmost they can do with their cleverness will be to note and record their course as they are carried along, which is what we do now and is that which leads us to the vain fancy that we can make or guide the movement. That is why it is the greatest folly of which a man can be capable, to sit down with a slate and a pencil to plan out a new social world. (William Graham Sumner, "The Absurd Effort to Make the World Over," from the *Essays of William Graham Sumner,* Yale University Press.)

7. Rewrite the selection in Exercise 6b above, substituting neutral words and phrases for the emotive language used by the speaker.

8. The following "definitions" appeared under the title "Primer for New Voters," in Sidney J. Harris's column, *Strictly Personal.* Does the reader share Mr. Harris's indignation?

"Public servants"—officeholders who belong to your party.

"Bureaucrats"—officeholders who belong to the other party.

"Necessary expenditures for public welfare"—a padded payroll when your party is in office.

"Look at the record"—the partisan presentation of a mass of falsified statistics, half-truths, glittering generalities, and empty platitudes.

"Great statesmanship"—when your party has a strong leader.

"Political dictatorship"—when the other party has a strong leader.

"The Constitution"—a noble document that every politician is for, hardly any politician has read, and virtually no politician understands.

"Liberty and Justice"—what a candidate begins talking about when he is afraid to discuss his record.

"Will of the people"—the result of an election in which not more than 40 per cent of the voters go to the polls to elect a candidate they had no voice in choosing, after a campaign of insults and outright lies. (From *The Chicago Daily News,* Oct. 1, 1946.)

9. Which of the following items are propositions?
   a. Render unto Caesar the things which are Caesar's.
   b. What immortal hand or eye could frame thy fearful symmetry?
   c. No women are fickle.
   d. My darling!
   e. Much have I traveled in the realms of gold.
   f. We hold this truth to be self-evident: that all men are created equal.

10. Identify the complex questions (or commands) in the following. Where assumptions concerning facts are found, state whether you regard the assumptions as legitimate or illegitimate. In some cases you may wish to qualify your answer by noting the circumstances under which the assumptions may be regarded as legitimate.

   a. "Why did God become Man?" (This was the title of a book by the philosopher Anselm during the Middle Ages: *Cur Deus Homo?*)
   b. Is God omnipotent?
   c. Does God exist?
   d. Why did Grover Cleveland defeat Benjamin Harrison in the presidential election of 1888?
   e. Why did the United States declare war on Germany immediately after Pearl Harbor?
   f. Do human beings have the power of mental telepathy?
   g. Will the resurrection be in the flesh or in the spirit only?
   h. Have you given up your evil habits?
   i. How do you account for the great popular support for restrictions on unions?
   j. Explain why democracy has been successful in the United States.
   k. Explain why comic books are responsible for juvenile delinquency.
   l. How do you explain the fact of mental telepathy?

11. Do the following statements exemplify the logical or the non-logical use of language? Justify your answers.

   a. Woman's place is in the home.
   b. Many Americans think that it is sinful for cousins to marry.
   c. Cannibalism is morally wrong.
   d. Unemployment is the most important problem facing capitalism today.
   e. Dante is a greater poet than Edgar Guest.
   f. When the great spirit of Abraham Lincoln looks through the long corridor of time upon the party he founded, he sees that from the day of his passing on the torch until the last day of the Republican party in office, it held aloft the light of inalienable liberties of men. (Herbert Hoover)
   g. Comment on the following: In his *Philosophy and Logical Syntax,* R. Carnap writes that to say "Killing is evil" is the same as to say "Do not kill," i.e., it is a command in misleading grammatical form, the expression of a wish, and therefore neither true nor false.

12. Identify the three types of "ought" in the following, and indicate whether or not these sentences are translatable into propositions.
  a. Your car ought to run OK now.
  b. You ought to sleep more if you want to gain weight.
  c. I ought not to do unto others what I would not want them to do unto me.

Chapter 5

The Definition of "Definition"

Section I: The Importance of Definition

In Oscar Wilde's play, *Lady Windermere's Fan,* the Duchess says: "Do, as a concession to my poor wits, Lord Darlington, just explain to me what you really mean."

"I think I had better not, Duchess," answers the Lord. "Nowadays to be intelligible is to be found out."

When we define our terms we explain "what we really mean," with all the risks attendant thereto. But if we desire to avoid obfuscation and discussions which move at cross-purposes, we must give definite and precise meanings to our terms. A definition sets a term within its proper boundaries, and the injunction "Define your terms!" is of first importance.

Throughout the discussions in the previous chapters we have frequently noted the importance of definition. Our discussion of ambiguity in verbal disagreements revealed the importance of defining one's terms. Whether or not all men are equal depends upon what we mean by "equal." The answer is Yes or No, depending upon the senses in which the term is understood. To say that a word has different senses is to say that it may be defined in different ways. Similarly, diplomatic questions concerning whether or not a certain nation has fulfilled its international obligation under treaty to institute "free" and "democratic" governments in areas within its control will depend upon the definitions of these terms.

The most important question in many discussions is "What do you mean by ———?" For example, *Euglena,* a water organism, behaves like a plant under some conditions and like an animal in others. Is *Euglena* a plant or an animal? Neither? Both? Our answers will depend upon our definitions of plant and animal. Is *Forever Amber* an obscene novel? Exactly what do we mean by "obscene"? We can now appreciate the importance of Voltaire's famous remark, "Before I will discuss anything with you, you must define your terms."

The subject of definition is of very wide scope. We shall examine many of its aspects in the discussion which follows. But before we do so we must note two important distinctions among the ways in which words refer to their referents, i.e., in "extension" and "intension," and as "abstract" and "concrete." These distinctions are indispensable to an understanding of the nature or definition of definition, and we now turn to these distinctions.

Section II: Two Basic Distinctions

1. The extension and the intension of terms

The first distinction is that between the extension and intension of terms. We shall also employ synonyms for these terms: extension is synonymous with denotation; intension with connotation.

The term "human being" has meaning in two different ways. On the one hand it refers to all those creatures who are members of the family of mankind: Mark Antony, Cleopatra, Joe Kelly, Hi Ginsberg, and so on. "Human being" *means* the creatures we have mentioned. In one sense, then, a term means the objects to which it applies. This kind of meaning is called the "extensional" meaning. The extensional meaning of "football player" covers such individuals as Eckersall, Red Grange, Jay Berwanger, Sid Luckman, Otto Graham, and others. Observe also that general terms may either denote the individuals to which the term applies or they may denote subclasses of the general class. The general term "dog" refers to the subclasses, terriers, beagles, poodles, in its extensional meaning, as well as to the individuals, Fido and Rover. "Extensional meaning" covers both of these types.

But terms like "human being," "football player," and "dog" have meaning in a second sense: "human being" means "rational animal." This gives us the term's "intensional" meaning. A term, then, denotes the objects to which it is correctly applied (extensional meaning) and it connotes those characteristics possessed by the objects to which it applies (intensional meaning). Most dictionary definitions give us the intensional meanings of the words being defined.

We say that Julius Caesar is included in the extensional meaning of "man." Why? Because he has the characteristic of a man, such as animality, rationality, etc. It is the intensional meaning of "man" which determines the application of the term to Julius Caesar. "Man" means "rational animal" in its intensional sense, and it means Caesar as part of its extensional sense. Whenever we answer the question, "Why is X included under the extension of a term?" we think of the *characteristics* which an object must possess in order to be included within a certain class. The statement of these characteristics is the term's *intension*. The intension of the term "President of the United States" is "chief executive officer." The intension of "football player" is "athlete who plays in a game in which a large inflated ball is carried, thrown, and kicked, etc." The intension of a term, as we have noted, is what is usually called its definition. The extension, on the other hand, simply refers us to the set of objects to which the definition applies.

Let us now consider some of the ways in which extension and intension are related to each other. Examine the following terms: physical being, living being, animal, mammal, dog, spaniel. Note the varying quantities in the extensions of the terms as we move from left to right in the list. "Physical being" covers more objects than "living being," for "physical" covers inanimate as well as animate objects. The classes in our list are ordered in accordance with their relative sizes. The extensions get smaller as we go from left to right.

Now consider the intensional meanings of these terms. "Dog" connotes more, i.e., more characteristics, than does "mammal." A dog has all the characteristics which come under the definition of "mammal" plus those special characteristics which distinguish dogs from other mammals. Examining our list once again, we find that the terms at the right connote more than those at the left.

We see then the basis for an "inverse" correlation: in our list the extensions decrease from left to right, but the intensions increase from left to right. The intension and the extension of terms vary inversely. This is generally true, but the law of inverse correlation we just mentioned requires a qualification. The term "crow" has less intensional meaning than the term "crows not over five feet tall," i.e., it connotes fewer characteristics, but the extensional groups of the two terms are identical, since there are no crows over five feet tall. This means that there may sometimes be no decrease in extension accompanying increasing intension. But there is always decreasing intension with increasing extension. Our revised law: As extension increases, there is decreasing intension; as intension increases the extension will either decrease or remain the same.

One further point concerning extension. The smallest possible extension is one which refers to a single individual, which may be thought of as a class having only one member. The name "Trixie," for example, denotes a single individual, and this is the case for all proper names.

Extension and intension are thus intimately related, but they refer to objects in different ways—extension to a listing of the individuals who fall within its quantitative scope, intension to the qualities or characteristics of the individuals. When we are asked, Which is the larger class—dogs or cats? we think of the extension of each. When we are asked, Which is the friendlier animal? we think of the intensional aspect of the terms.

We shall now draw a distinction between two types of intension, *subjective* and *conventional*. By *subjective* intension we refer to the characteristics which may come to the mind of a *given* person when he thinks of "dogs." The subjective intension refers to the individual associations attached to a term in any given individual's mind. These associations will not be exactly the same for any two persons, nor indeed are they always the same for the same person. "Dog" arouses connotations in my mind which differ from those in yours, for our experiences with dogs have been different, and my associations may be different tomorrow from what they are today. To one man the dog is a friendly animal; to another he is dangerous. The *conventional* intension, on the other hand, refers to those characteristics which are considered necessary and sufficient for regarding an object as belonging within the extension of a term. A *definition* usually states the conventional intension of the term. The conventional intension states the elements which all dogs are known to have in common, and this type of intension does not vary from person to person. Thus, Peter may regard Rover with affection; John may regard him with aversion. Peter thinks of a friendly animal when he thinks of dogs; John, of an unfriendly animal. Their subjective intensions differ. But both agree that Rover is a dog, since the conventional intension of "dog" is the same for both. They do not disagree with respect to the essential characteristics which distinguish a dog from other animals. In other words, the *context* of our experiences with dogs influences our subjective intensions, which we may call the "marginal" associations aroused in our minds by a term, but it does not affect the conventional intension.

Another related distinction is that between logical and physical identity. When a bookkeeper adds up a balance, the word "dollar" means exactly the same thing every time it is used, for one dollar is logically identical with any other dollar. The conventional intension of "dollar" is *exactly* the same on each occasion of its use. Physically, however, no two objects in the world are identical. No two paper dollars are exactly the same physically. No two snow-flakes are exactly alike, and it is only the grossness of our vision which makes two grains of sand appear to be alike. No two fingerprints are alike physically. But when we say that the FBI took A's fingerprints and that they also took B's fingerprints, the use of the term "fingerprint" is logically identical on each occasion.

2. The abstract and the concrete

We think about things in different ways. We may think of dogs "in general," i.e., of the conventional intension of "dog." When we think of "triangularity," we think of those characteristics possessed by all triangles, whether they be large or small, colored blue or red, whether they be equilateral, isosceles, or scalene. We may think of "man" as a "rational animal." In all these cases we are thinking abstractly. On the other hand, we may be thinking of Rover, or of John, or of this triangle, △; these are examples of the concrete.

Words are not abstract or concrete because of something in the words themselves. "Humanity," "triangularity," "beauty," and "justice" are called abstract words because they refer to referents "abstractively," that is, we use them to refer to the general qualities possessed by a group of things. Words are abstract because of the way in which we use them; it is the word's designation which makes it abstract or concrete. The important distinction is between two ways of thinking. When we think of an individual object or situation in all of its fullness of individuality, we are thinking concretely. When I think of Abraham Lincoln, the fine day we had yesterday, or the fact that the roller on my typewriter is loose, I am thinking concretely. But when I think of the mortality of all men, or of the principle that the volume of a gas is related functionally to its temperature, I am thinking abstractly. Language is concrete when it refers to individual things which can be perceived by the senses; "abstract" language refers to those qualities or attributes which are possessed by the concrete objects within a certain class.

It should be obvious that a given word may be used in an abstract or in a concrete sense. "A pencil" refers to the general characteristics possessed by all pencils, and is an abstraction. "My red pencil" refers to a concrete entity. When I read Pascal's: "Man is but a reed, the weakest in nature, but a thinking reed," I think of man in an abstract way. But when someone tells me that he talked to a man on the bus, I understand "man" as referring to a specific person, i.e., a concrete entity.

The concrete and the abstract are correlative terms, i.e., these terms mutually involve each other. When we speak of the *abstractions* triangularity or humanity we refer to those characteristics which all *concrete* triangles or men have in common. Humanity or triangularity do not "exist" apart from individual men and triangles, but this does not mean that abstractions are "unreal." The abstractions refer to characteristics that are actually possessed by the concrete things. We call an object a "man" because he possesses the qualities to which the abstraction refers. We can think of those qualities, or attributes, or relations, apart from the specific individuals in whom they are "embodied," even though the qualities cannot "exist" apart from the concrete.

Exercises

1. Which items, among the following, are part of the conventional intension of "athlete"? In answering this question consider whether a dictionary would use any of these phrases in its defini-

tion of "athlete." Which items are part of your subjective intension when you think of "athlete"? Which items should be included within the extension of the term?

a. Jim Thorpe
b. football players
c. Joe Louis
d. jockeys
e. being a good runner
f. having competitive spirit
g. sound in wind and limb
h. having great physical strength
i. chess players
j. having sportsmanlike attitude
k. barflies
l. ping-pong players

2. Arrange the following terms in the order of extension, so that the term having the largest extension will be at the top of the list; the one with the smallest extension at the bottom:

a. quadrilateral
b. square
c. figure
d. rectangle
e. parallelogram
f. plane figure

Now arrange them with the term having the maximum intension at the top of the list, decreasing the intension as you go down.

3. Compare the extensions of "living human being" and "living human being with a heart," and explain why this requires a modification of the rule that "the extension and the intension of terms vary inversely."

4. H. W. B. Joseph: "The intension of the term 'baby' does not increase or decrease with fluctuations in the birth rate." Comment.

5. Distinguish the following terms as abstract and concrete: pencil, kettle, man, humanity, John X. Jones, the first man in line at the 1958 World Series.

6. Proper names may become common nouns, as "a Nero," "a Waterloo," "a Quisling." But do proper names as such possess connotation? Does "John F. Smith" connote anything?

7. Comment on the following items from Korzybski's *Science and Sanity* (The International Non-Aristotelian Library Publishing Co., 1948) in terms of the distinction between logical and physical identity:

a. Now, returning to the analysis of the object which we called "pencil," we observe that, in spite of all "similarities," this object is unique, is different from everything else, and has a *unique* relationship to the rest of the world. Hence, we should give the object a *unique name*. Fortunately, we have already become acquainted with the way mathematicians manufacture an endless array of individual names without unduly expanding the vocabulary. If we call the given object "pencil₁" we could call another similar object "pencil₂," etc. In this way, we produce individual names, and so cover the *differences*. By keeping the main root word "pencil," we keep the implications of daily life and also of *similarities*. (p. 381.)

b. And so individualizing (indexes) and temporal devices (dates) etc., should be used *conjointly*. Thus, obviously chair₁ ¹⁶⁰⁰ is not the "same" as chair₁ ¹⁹⁴⁰, nor is Smith₁ Monday the "same" as Smith₁ Tuesday. (p. xxxvi.)

8. S. I. Hayakawa, writes that "one of the premises upon which modern linguistic thought is based" is the premise that "no word ever has exactly the same meaning twice." He continues, "The extent to which this premise fits the facts can be demonstrated in a number of ways. First, if we accept the proposition that the contexts of an utterance determine its meaning, it becomes apparent that since no two contexts are ever *exactly* the same, no two meanings can ever be exactly the same. How can we 'fix the meaning' even for as common an expression as 'to believe in' when it can be used in such sentences as the following?

'I *believe in* you.' (I have confidence in you.)
'I *believe in* democracy.' (I accept the principles implied by the term democracy.)
'I *believe in* Santa Claus.' (It is my opinion that Santa Claus exists.)

"Secondly, we can take for example a word of 'simple' meaning like 'kettle.' But when John says 'kettle,' its intensional meanings to him are the common characteristics of all the kettles John remembers. When Peter says 'kettle,' however, its intensional meanings to him are the common characteristics of all the kettles he remembers. *No matter how small or how negligible the differences may be between John's 'kettle' and Peter's 'kettle,' there is some difference.*

"Finally, . . . if John says 'my typewriter' today, and again 'my typewriter' tomorrow, the extensional meaning is different in the two cases, because the typewriter is not *exactly* the same from one day to the next (nor from one minute to the next); slow processes of wear, change, and decay are going on constantly. Although we can say, then, that the differences in the meanings of a word on one occasion, on another occasion a minute later, and on still another occasion another minute later are *negligible* we cannot say that the meanings are exactly the same." (S. I. Hayakawa, *Language in Action,* Harcourt, Brace, and Co., 1941, pp. 49–50.)

Discuss this selection from Hayakawa in terms of the following:

    a. Does the ambiguity of "believe in" prove that this phrase never has the same meaning in different contexts? Compare "I believe in you" and "Jim believes in Joe."

    b. Does the "kettle" example take into account the distinction between subjective and conventional intension?

    c. Does the "typewriter" example take into account the distinction between logical and physical identity?

Section III: The Types of Definitions

There are several types of definitions, each appropriate for different needs and purposes, though all definitions seek to enlighten the hearer by clarifying the range of the application of a word. We shall consider three types of definitions: (1) word substitution, (2) explicating the extension or denotation of a word, and (3) explicating the conventional intension or connotation of a word. We shall call the latter type "analytical," since it analyzes an abstract concept. Each of these types gives us the range of application of the word, but in different ways, and each type is appropriate for certain purposes and inappropriate for others.

1. Definition by word-substitution

When we are engaged in working out crossword puzzles we are usually interested in this type of definition, i.e., one which provides us with synonymous terms. "Alar" is a four-letter word meaning "wing-shaped." There are many other occasions in which synonyms are all that we desire. Thus, a reader confronted with the sentence "No cenobites are troglodytes" would probably turn to the dictionary. He will learn that a cenobite is a member of a religious community, such as a monastery or convent. "Troglodyte" has the synonym "hermit." He is informed that two different words designate the same referent and that we may substitute one of these words for the other.

A synonymous definition has value in that it substitutes a familiar word for an unfamiliar one. The same result may be obtained by the use of a familiar antonym, or word of opposite meaning. Thus, the meaning of "atypical" is clarified when we learn that it means the opposite of "typical." Correlatives, or related terms which presuppose each other, such as husband and wife, may be used in a similar manner.

2. Extensive or denotative definition

Every student has had the experience of being called on to define a technical term in class and saying, "I can't define it, but I can give an example." Actually, giving an example is a form of definition, for it clarifies the meaning of a term by citing its extension or denotation.

Let us give some examples of extensive definitions: Fascism means the type of government which prevailed in Italy, Germany, and Japan during the thirties and which still prevails in Spain (1959); "A 'pun' refers to the manner in which the word 'hang' was used in Benjamin Franklin's warning." Note that these are extensive definitions of "extensive definition." An extensive definition presents an example or list of examples to which the term applies.

When an extensive definition is accompanied by a demonstrative gesture which specifies the referent by actually pointing to it, we have what is called definition "by demonstration," or "ostensive" definition. Examples: "*This* is an ocarina," "*That* is an aileron." We *point* to a specimen of the class of things denoted by the term and call it by its name. The "demonstrative" gesture may also occur in a figurative sense, as in "The sound which you will hear in a moment will be the tone of a bassoon." "The color 'violet' is the color which you will find at the extreme right end of the spectrum."

The demonstrative method of defining is an important pedagogical element in the educative process, for it is the method whereby a child learns many of the words in his early vocabulary. Helen Keller has vividly described the manner in which she first learned that the word "water" meant that which was flowing over her hands from a fountain. A great educative virtue of this method is its vividness. It eliminates the dangers of mere bookish knowledge or the vice of "thinking words, not things," to use a phrase of Justice O. W. Holmes, and thus prevents us from losing ourselves in abstractions. John Dewey, America's most important philosopher of education, has constantly emphasized the value of personal experience, in this direct sense or in an imaginative sense, in understanding new concepts.

But extensive definitions also have many weaknesses. They tell us nothing about the nature of the objects to which the term refers. Just what type of government existed in Germany and Italy during the thirties? This question must be answered before we can pretend to an understanding of the term "fascism." We should also note that an extensive definition presupposes at least some understanding of the intensional meaning of the term, since we could not identify Germany as an example of fascism unless we had some notion of what fascism means in its intensional sense.

More serious is the basic vagueness of an extensive definition. Suppose we point to the United States as an example of a "free-enterprise" system. Are our subsidies to businessmen and farmers part of what we are pointing to? A classic example of the vagueness of reference that may accompany the gesture of pointing is illustrated in the narrative of J. H. Weeks, in his *Among Congo Cannibals:*

> I remember on one occasion wanting the word for table. There were five or six boys standing around, and tapping the table with my forefinger, I asked, What is this? One boy said it was a *dodela,* another that it was an *etanda,* a third stated that it was *bokali,* a fourth that it was *elamba,* and the fifth said it was *meza.* These various words we wrote in our notebook and congratulated ourselves that we were working among a people who possessed so rich a language that they had five words for one article.

But later Weeks discovered that,

> One lad thought we wanted the word for tapping; another understood that we were seeking the word for the material of which the table was made; another had an idea that we required the word for hardness; another thought we wished a name for that which covered the table; and the last, not being able, perhaps, to think of anything else, gave us the word *meza,* table—the very word we were seeking.

There are of course many ways whereby we may eliminate some of these ambiguities. If Weeks had been able to ask, "What is the name for this article of furniture?" instead of "What is this?", the gesture of tapping would have been unambiguous.

In closing our discussion of extensive definition we shall consider very briefly, an interesting theoretical problem. It is this: Are some terms indefinable?

The English philosopher, G. E. Moore, in his *Principia*

Ethica, has argued that "good" is an indefinable term, comparable in its indefinability to such a term as "yellow." If the reader
is not aware of the difficulties presented by the attempt to define
a color quality in its sensuous sense, let him consider how he
would define "yellow" to a person who had been blind from
birth. But discussions concerning whether or not a given term is
indefinable may easily degenerate into verbal disputes unless we
recognize the ambiguity of the word "indefinable" and draw a
distinction between different kinds of definition. When it is
said that "yellow" is indefinable, what is usually meant is that
it is impossible to give this term an analytical definition, for
yellow is a simple quality, and only complex entities (which
have "parts") may be analyzed. But certainly "yellow" can be
defined extensively, i.e., by demonstration to a person with
normal vision by pointing to an example, and an extensive type
of definition may be given for the word "good" whatever our
conclusion may be with respect to the possibility of analyzing
this term.

3. Intensional, connotative, or analytical definition

Example: Democracy is a system of government in which
the people periodically elect their governing officials in free elections and which guarantees the ideals of freedom and equality.
Note how this definition differs from those previously discussed.
Here we are not given a synonymous term, or a demonstrative
gesture, or a mere list of democratic governments. We are
given the intensional or connotative meaning of the term, i.e.,
an analysis of the referent which we have in mind when we
speak of "democracy." Henceforth we shall use the term "analytical" for this type of definition. (We are not concerned as yet
with the adequacy of any particular example of this sort.)

Analytical definition is far and away the most useful of the
three types we are considering, and when we speak of "definition" we usually refer to this type of definition. For example, in
a discussion concerning the existence of God, one of the speakers
asks for a definition of the term. An analytical definition would
normally be expected, since it would be quite inadequate to
define by a synonym, such as "Deity," and an extensive definition is not feasible. Similarly, it is definition in the analytical

sense which is required when such vague or ambiguous terms as democracy, communism, art, or religion are used.

When we ask, "What is poetry?" we are not satisfied with the extensive definition: "Milton's *Paradise Lost* is an example of a poem." Nor is there a useful synonym of the word "poetry." What is desired is a clarification of the nature of the referent. It is only when the referent of a synonym is clearly understood that we are satisfied with a synonym for an unknown word. This was the case in our substitution of "hermit" for "troglodyte," where an analytical definition was not called for. But if the reader had been unfamiliar with the referent of the word "hermit," then this term might have required analysis.

In the next section we shall examine some of the criteria of an adequate analytical definition. But before turning to these criteria we shall examine the structure of an analytical definition. And henceforth we shall employ two new technical terms, *definiendum* and *definiens,* to designate the two formal parts of every definition. The *definiendum* is the word being defined; the *definiens* is the defining part of the definition. In a definition such as "Man is a rational animal," "man" is the definiendum; "rational animal," the definiens.

With respect to structure, the *definiens* of an analytical definition has two parts, which are usually called the *genus* and the *differentia.* In our definition of "man," "rational animal" is the definiens. "Animal" is the genus, and "rational" the differentia. Genus is used in a special sense, as meaning the *general class* of things to which the definiendum is assigned, and differentia refers to the *special characteristics* possessed by the definiendum. Thus, in our previous definition, we may say that "animal" is the genus, or general class to which man belongs, and that rationality is his differentia within the class of animals. If "man" were defined as "an animal," the definition would be incomplete, since no *differentia* is stated.

We should also note that the logician's distinction between genus and differentia is not an absolute one. For example, a whale is a marine mammal of fish-like form. But we might also define a whale as a marine or fish-like creature which is a mammal. Which term is called genus will depend upon the aspect which we wish to emphasize as appropriate to the purpose of the definition. But all analytical definitions tell us that something belongs to a general class of things and that it is distinguished from other members of its class by certain characteristics.

The manner in which the differentia distinguishes the definiendum from other things within the general class may take varied forms. Here again the purpose of the definition will be the controlling factor. In scientific definitions we find an emphasis on the manner in which things are produced, or the manner in which they produce certain results. Thus, a metal may be defined by a layman in terms of its qualities of hardness, heaviness, malleability, etc. But a chemist defines it as "any chemical element which combines with oxygen so as to form a base." (A base is a compound which combines with an acid so as to form a salt.) In contemporary physics concepts are defined in terms of operations. But we will find genus and differentia in all analytical definitions.

Exercises

A. Which types of definition are found in the following?
1. Labor unions are organizations such as the United Steelworkers, the Auto Workers, the Brotherhoods of Machinists, Teamsters, etc.
2. Capitalism is a system in which there are large accumulations of capital.
3. Erne means a sea-eagle.
4. The symbol < means "included in the class of."
5. Exercise 1 was an example of a denotative definition.
6. A sexagenarian is a person who is in his sixties.
7. Left means the opposite of right.
8. A parent is a person who brings children into this world.
9. A mule is an animal which is half horse and half donkey.
10. An explorer is a bum with an excuse.
B. In the following definitions, what is the definiendum? The definiens? Identify the genus and differentia in each definiens.
1. A lady is a woman of good breeding.
2. The soul is a psychic substance.
3. A good citizen is one who pays his debts and obeys the laws.
4. A lemur is a small mammal related to the monkeys. They are mostly nocturnal, with fox-like faces and soft fur, and are of about the size of a cat.
5. "The concept of length involves as much as, and nothing

more than, the set of operations by which length is determined [e.g., laying a measuring-rod along a straight line]."
(P. W. Bridgman, *The Logic of Modern Physics*.)

Section IV: The Criteria of an Adequate Analytical Definition

We shall now discuss the criteria, or "rules," to which an adequate *analytical* definition must conform. Five criteria will be considered:

1. The rule of equivalence.
2. The rule concerning essential characteristics.
3. The rule concerning clarity.
4. The rule against circularity.
5. The rule that definitions should be positive, not negative.

Most of our discussion will be devoted to the rule of equivalence; we shall give the other rules a less extended treatment.

1. The rule of equivalence

The definiens should be equivalent to and convertible with the definiendum: it should be neither too broad nor too narrow.

"A triangle is a plane figure having three (straight) sides" is a definition which satisfies the rule of equivalence. The definiens "plane figure having three sides," refers to exactly the same entities as are referred to by the definiendum "triangle." These referrals are identical or equivalent. Furthermore, the definition is convertible, by which we mean that it can be turned around or reversed in direction. We can say with equal truth: "A plane figure having three sides is a triangle."

Another way of checking equivalence or convertibility is to apply the "all" and "only" test. If our definition is an equivalent one, then we should be able to say that *all* triangles and *only* triangles are figures having three sides. We can, so the definition is an equivalent one.

When a definition fails to satisfy the requirement of equivalence, it will be either too broad or too narrow. A definition of a dog as a four-legged mammal would be too broad. By "too broad" we mean that the definiens covers too much ground, i.e., "four-legged mammal" applies to many animals other than dogs, such as cats, cows, horses, etc. No equivalence here. We can say that *all* dogs are four-legged mammals, but not that *only* dogs are such.

"Too narrow," on the other hand, means that the definiens fails to apply to each and every entity referred to by the definiendum. The definition of a triangle as a "plane figure having three equal sides" would be too narrow, for it fails to include isosceles and scalene triangles. Here again we find a failure to pass the *all* and *only* test. In this case *only* triangles are figures having three equal sides, but it is not true that *all* triangles have such sides.

When a definition fails to pass the "all" test, it is too narrow; when it fails to pass the "only" test, it is too broad. The definition of a Christian as "a person who accepts the doctrines of Jesus as stated exclusively in the New Testament, and without reliance on tradition" is too narrow, for we cannot say that *all* Christians are thus described. Catholics would be excluded from the ranks of Christians if we accepted this definition. On the other hand to define a Christian as "one who believes that God created the world and governs it" is too broad, for we cannot say that *only* Christians believe this. Jews and Moslems also share this belief.

Let us now work out more precisely what is meant by saying that an equivalent definition is convertible. Consider again the definition of man as a "rational animal." If this is an equivalent definition, we should be able to say that "all rational animals are men," in addition to being able to say that "all men are rational animals." * In an equivalent definition, each of these statements will be true. An equivalent definition is like a mathematical equation. If $2 + 2 = 4$, then $4 = 2 + 2$.

We shall now symbolize this test for equivalence. Let "W" stand for Word, i.e., the definiendum, or the word being defined. Let "D" stand for the definiens, or the defining part of the definition. We should be able to make the following true statements if the definition is equivalent:

All W's are D's. [All men (W's) are rational animals (D's).]

All D's are W's. [All rational animals (D's) are men (W's).]

In testing definitions, we should ask two questions: (1) Are all W's D's? (2) Are all D's W's? If the answer to both questions

---

* "All rational animals are men" has the same meaning as "only men are rational animals." The "all" and "only" test again.

is Yes, then the definition is an equivalent one. If the answer to the first question is No, then the definition is too narrow; if it is No to the second question, the definition is too broad.

Here are some additional illustrations of this testing procedure: "Democracy (W) is a system of government in which the chief executive is elected by the people (D)." We ask the first question: Are all W's D's? The answer is No, for England is a democracy in which the monarch, the chief executive, is not elected. This definition is too narrow. Another: "A triangle (W) is a plane figure (D)." This will fail to pass the second question (Are all D's W's?) for there are plane figures which are not triangles (squares, circles, etc.). This definition is thus too broad. The "too narrow" definition failed to cover all cases denoted by the definiendum, "democracy"; the latter describes all triangles, but too much else besides.

The following definition fails both tests: "Man (W) is an animal with hair on his chest (D)." This is not true of all men, and there are hairy-chested animals which are not men.

The rule of equivalence is the most important of the criteria of an adequate definition, and the vices of being too broad or too narrow are the Scylla and Charybdis on which most definitions founder. But equivalent definitions are not easily constructed, except, of course, in mathematics, where the notion of equivalence symbolized by "$\equiv$" is a familiar one. But when we deal with key words such as religion, beauty, art, and propaganda, we find that the quest for adequate definitions is neverending. As an example of the difficulties we encounter in these fields, consider the problem of defining "religion." It appears inadequate to define religion without some reference to belief in a God, but Confucianism and Buddhism do not involve such beliefs. It would be presumptuous indeed to say that creeds which hold the allegiance of almost a third of the human race are not religions. John Dewey, in *A Common Faith,* has argued that it is utterly impossible to find an adequate equivalent definition of religion. If this is so, then we must be satisfied with something less than perfection and must seek to clarify the range of the term as adequately as may be possible.

It should be obvious that an adequate definition cannot be constructed on the basis of rules, nor can a definition be checked for adequacy on the basis of rules alone. Familiarity with the subject matter is indispensable in order to apply the tests. One must know the facts concerning religion or political institutions in order to check definitions in those fields. *The rules merely tell us how to use our knowledge.*

2. The definiens should state the essential characteristics of the definiendum

By "essential characteristics" we refer to characteristics which are important in terms of the purposes for which the definition is required. "Essential" is thus used in a relativistic manner, since what may be essential for one purpose is not so for another. If we were interested in a definition of "man" in order to contrast men with the lower animals, it would not be satisfactory for most purposes to define man as "the animal who can fly a jet plane at supersonic speed," nor as "the animal capable of laughter," which is an equivalent definition, as the former is not. An unessential characteristic is usually referred to as an "accident."

In a political discussion concerning conservatism and radicalism, a definition of "conservative" may be requested. To define a conservative as "a man with good sense" may or may not be true of conservatives, but the definition would not state an essential characteristic for the purpose of the given discussion.

3. The definiens should clarify the nature of the definiendum

A definition should clarify the nature of the thing defined. It should inform and enlighten the person addressed. Typically, neutral or informative language, rather than "poetic," "literary," or expressive language, will be appropriate, and figurative terms will be avoided. "Sickness is Nature's protest against the misdirection of her forces" is a "poetic" type of definition and would be inappropriate in a scholarly essay in biology. A good definition will also avoid obscurity, i.e., the dark and non-transparent. (Is this a figurative definition of "obscurity"?)

The admonition against obscurity requires care in its application. That which is obscure to one person may not be so to another. To the uninformed all things are obscure. The type of audience addressed should be taken into account. Technical material that is obscure to the general public may be quite clear to the average college student. The test should be: Would a reasonably well-informed person in the audience being addressed find the definition obscure? If one cannot confidently answer this question in the affirmative, then he should not criticize the definition on this ground.

This discussion, of course, is relevant to definitions which aim at literal accuracy. We should not confuse this type of definition with those which aim at humor. The formulating of witty definitions is a popular pastime, and such definitions may give us penetrating insights as well as delightful humor, e.g., "A politician is a man who sits on a fence with his ear on the ground"; "Deliberation: the act of examining one's bread to determine on which side it is buttered," or Oscar Wilde's definition of a cynic: "One who knows the price of everything and the value of nothing." The reader may also recall Sydney Harris' "definitions" on page 85.

4. An analytic definition should avoid word-substitution

Word-substitution, as we have seen, is a legitimate form of definition for many purposes, but it is not satisfactory when we desire an analysis of the nature of the referent. The present rule has several aspects. The definiens should not repeat the definiendum, nor should it state synonyms, antonyms, or correlatives, of the definiendum. To commit these faults is to be guilty of "circularity."

a. Do not repeat the word being defined

Polonius informs the King and Queen of Hamlet's strange condition:

> Your noble son is mad;
> Mad call I it; for, to define true madness,
> What is't but to be nothing else but mad?

A rose is a rose and a spade is a spade, but these are not definitions. The same fault is found in a definition of literature as "writing which has a literary quality," or of democracy as "a system of government which uses democratic procedures." These require no comment. But note that the rule does not forbid the following type of definition: "A good citizen is a citizen who seeks to promote the common welfare." The repetition of "citizen" in the definiens is unexceptionable, since only the meaning of "good" in "good citizen" is in question. Note also that the purpose of the definition is always a controlling consideration. A definition of a Communist for legal purposes as "A person who holds a membership card in the Communist party" clarifies the nature of the referent for a given purpose.

b. *Do not use synonyms or antonyms or correlatives*

"A morally good man is one who acts virtuously" substitutes the synonym "virtuous" for "morally good." But if we were looking for clarification of the meaning of "morally good" so that we may know to what kinds of conduct it refers, it is not helpful to be told that we may substitute the term "virtuous" for "morally good." This immediately raises the question: But, what is virtue? Morally good action? Synonyms are not adequate substitutes for analysis.

To define "right conduct" as conduct which is "not wrongful" merely gives us an unhelpful antonym, mere word-substitution once again. Finally, as an example of the use of an unhelpful correlative term, consider the definition of "cause" as "that which has an effect." But nothing can be called a cause unless it has an effect, and an effect cannot be called such unless it had a cause. But what is the analytical meaning of these terms? This question is not answered.

5. A definition should be positive rather than negative

The reason for this rule should be obvious. "A man is a creature who does not breath through gills" is true, but of little help. This negative definition covers all plants, all land animals, all whales. A merely negative definition will be too broad unless it mentions everything in the universe which is not the thing being defined, and even this kind of completeness would give us no analysis of the term being defined.

Most negative definitions are not guilty of these absurdities, however. The term being defined will usually be contrasted with some closely related terms in the same "universe of discourse," as in the following: "A Protestant is a Christian who is not a Catholic." When we have a complete list of the items within a universe of discourse, as in knowing that there are just three types of triangles, we may formulate a precise negative definition of a scalene triangle by saying that it is neither isosceles nor equilateral.

Note, however, that there are some negative definitions which are quite satisfactory even as analytical definitions, as in defining a bachelor as "an adult male who is not married," or in defining parallel lines as "straight lines which do not intersect no matter how far extended."

In general, this rule should be taken as a warning that we should "accentuate the positive" and seek to avoid the pitfalls of most negative definitions. In any case, the controlling consideration in testing analytical definitions is this: Does the definiens give us an adequate analysis of the subject-matter?

Exercises

A. Check the following definitions for equivalence. Apply the two test questions to each and state whether the definition is equivalent, too narrow, too broad, or both too broad and too narrow. Remember that it is not possible to answer the test questions intelligently unless you have a good understanding of the relevant subject matter.
   1. Amnesia is a form of mental disease.
   2. A dog is a domesticated animal having four legs.
   3. A Moslem is a person who believes in one God.
   4. A Catholic is a person who believes in the divinity of Christ.
   5. Assuming that elementary and high school girls are not properly called "coeds," we may define a coed as a female student who attends a school of higher learning, such as a college or university.
   6. A circle is a figure whose radii are equal.
   7. Poetry is a form of literature written in metrical language.
   8. An alcoholic is a person who drinks large quantities of alcoholic beverages.
   9. A phonograph is a device for the recording and reproducing of sounds.
   10. A man is a featherless biped. (An ancient Greek once plucked a chicken in order to criticize this definition. Why?)
   11. Fascism means a totalitarian government in which a dictator rules.

12. Capitalism is a system of industrial organization which develops large scale production.

13. Propaganda means any attempt to influence the opinions of others.

14. A cause means the invariable antecedent of any event.

15. Check the following definitions of a "beautiful object":

    a. Something which possesses formal design and is pleasing to the eye or ear.

    b. Something which exhibits unity in variety.

    c. Something which causes a certain kind of mental state in the spectator, in which thought and emotion achieve a harmonious equilibrium.

    d. Pleasure regarded as the quality of a thing. (Santayana.)

B. Check the following definitions for violations of rules 2–5. Note that a definition may violate more than one rule, e.g., an antonymic definition. Also note whether you think the definition a satisfactory one despite the fact that a rule is violated. It may be helpful to apply these rules in the following order: (4) Does it contain synonyms, etc.? (5) Is the definition positive? (2) Does it state essential characteristics? (3) Is it obscure? (Use rules 2 and 3 only as "last resorts.") Be precise in explaining your answers. The first four examples illustrate each of the four rules:

1. Poison means something which has a toxic effect.

2. Tickling may be defined as "an intensely vivid complex of unsteady, ill-localized, and ill-analyzed sensations, with attention distributed over the immediate sensory contents and the concomitant sensations reflexly aroused."

3. A Republican is one who does not favor government controls to advance the economic welfare of the average man.

4. A human being is an animal who knows how to use chopsticks.

5. By "mental" we mean what is not physical.

6. A conspiracy is a collusion in machination.

7. A bald man is one who does not have a full head of hair.

8. A lady is a woman in whose presence a man behaves like a gentleman.

9. Peace means the absence of war.

10. A good man is one who always does the right thing.

11. Time is the moving image of eternity. (Plato.)

12. A communist means a person who is dissatisfied with everything.

13. Faith is the substance of things hoped for; the evidence of things not seen. (St. Paul.)

14. Life is that which distinguishes living from non-living things.
15. The du Pont Company formulated the following definition of nylon: "A generic term for any long-chain synthetic polymeric amide which has recurring amide groups as an integral part of the main polymer chain, and which is capable of being formed into a filament in which the structural elements are oriented in the direction of the axis."
16. A star is a stellar body seen in the heavens at night.
17. A moral man is one who does not lie, steal, or live intemperately.
18. A fanatic is a man who redoubles his efforts after he has forgotten his aim. (Santayana.)
19. Social dancing is a stilted form of perambulation slightly impeded by a semicooperative member of the opposite sex.
20. A crossword puzzle has been defined "an intensively rectangular and essentially heterogeneous concatenation of dissimilar verbal synonyms, i.e., similitudes, replete with internal inhibitions, yet promulgating extensive ratiocination and meticulously designed to promote fulminating vituperation, dispel hebetudinosity and develop speculative, contemplative, introspective, deliberative, and cogitative faculties."

Section V: Plato and the Rules of Definition

The criteria for an adequate definition were worked out by Plato (427–347 B.C.), and his dialogues are a rich mine of material in definition analysis. The following passages present a highly condensed version of his *Euthyphro,* in which the definition of piety is discussed. The selections are from a translation published by the Macmillan Company.

A word as to the background of the conversation. Euthyphro is on his way to the court to swear out a warrant against his father for murder. It appears that Euthyphro's father had become incensed against a drunken overseer who had killed a slave. The overseer was bound up hand and foot and thrown into a ditch. He died of exposure while awaiting a decision concerning his punishment. Euthyphro believes that his father is guilty of murder and that moral duty, or "piety," requires that he have his father prosecuted. In reading these passages, note the irony so characteristic of Socrates in his conversations with the self-opinionated. After reading this selection answer the questions at the end.

SOCRATES: Good heavens, Euthyphro! Surely the multitude are ignorant of what makes right. I take it that not everyone could rightly do what you are doing; only a man who was already well advanced in wisdom.

EUTHYPHRO: That is quite true, Socrates.

SOCRATES: Was the man whom your father killed a relative of yours? Nay, of course he was: You would never have prosecuted your father for the murder of a stranger?

EUTHYPHRO: You amuse me, Socrates. What difference does it make whether the murdered man was a relative or a stranger? The only question that you have to ask is, did the slayer slay justly or not? But my relatives are furious with me; so little do they know the divine law of piety and impiety.

SOCRATES: Tell me, then: what is piety and what is impiety?

EUTHYPHRO: Piety means prosecuting the wrongdoer who has committed murder or sacrilege or any other such crime.

SOCRATES: But many other actions are pious, are they not, Euthyphro?

EUTHYPHRO: Certainly.

SOCRATES: I did not ask you to tell me one or two of all the many pious actions that there are; I want to know what is the essential form of piety which makes all pious actions pious. [1]

EUTHYPHRO: Well, then, what is pleasing to the gods is pious, and what is not pleasing is impious.

SOCRATES: Beautiful, Euthyphro. Now you have given me the sort of answer that I wanted. Whether what you say is true, I do not know yet. But of course you will go on to prove the truth of it. . . . Now, the same action is pleasing to some gods, and displeasing to others; dear to Zeus, but hateful to Cronos. So the same action will be pious and impious at the same time? [2]

EUTHYPHRO: Well, I should say that piety is what all the gods love and that impiety is what they all hate. I think that the definition is right this time. [2a]

SOCRATES: We shall know that better in a little while, my good friend. Now consider this question. Do the gods love piety because it is pious, or is it pious because they love it?

EUTHYPHRO: They love it because it is pious; it is not pious because they love it.

SOCRATES: Then piety is not what is pleasing to the gods. Piety, and what is pleasing to the gods, are different things. My question, Euthyphro, was, What is piety? But it turns out that you have not explained to me the essence of piety; you have been content to mention an attribute which belongs to it, namely, that all the gods love it. [3]

EUTHYPHRO: But, Socrates, I really don't know how to explain to you what is in my mind. Whatever we put forward always somehow moves around in a circle, and will not stay where we place it. [4]

SOCRATES: I would rather that our definitions had remained firm and immovable than have all the wisdom of Daedalus and all the riches of Tantalus to boot. But I will do my best to help you to explain to me what piety is: for I think that you are indolent. Don't give in yet. Tell me; do you not think that all piety is just? [5]

EUTHYPHRO: I do.

SOCRATES: Well, then, is all justice pious too? Or while all piety is just, is a part only of justice pious, and the rest of it something else?

EUTHYPHRO: I do not follow you, Socrates.

SOCRATES: Yet you have the advantage over me in your youth no less than in your wisdom. But, as I say, the wealth of your wisdom makes you indolent. Exert yourself, my good friend: I am not asking you a difficult question. What I mean may be explained by this illustration: odd numbers are part of numbers, so that where you have the odd you must also have number, though where you have number, you do not necessarily have the odd. Now I think you follow me?

EUTHYPHRO: I do.

SOCRATES: Well, then, this is what I meant by the question which I asked you: is there always piety where there is justice? or, though there is always justice where there is piety, yet there is not always piety where there is justice, because piety is only part of justice? Shall we say this, or do you differ? [6]

EUTHYPHRO: No; I agree. I think that you are right.

SOCRATES: Now observe the next point. If piety is a part of justice, we must find out, I suppose, what part of justice it is. Now, if you had asked me, just now, for instance, what part of number is the odd, and what number is an odd number, I should have said that whatever number is not evenly divisible by two, is an odd number. Is it not so?

EUTHYPHRO: Yes.

SOCRATES: Then you see if you can explain to me what part of justice is piety.

EUTHYPHRO: Well, then, Socrates, I should say that piety is that part of justice which has to do with the attention which is due to the gods, and that what has to do with the attention which is due to man, is the remaining part of justice. [7]

SOCRATES: But what result is accomplished by our attention or service to the gods?

EUTHYPHRO: I think that nothing is dearer to them.

SOCRATES: Then piety means that which is dear to the gods? [8]

EUTHYPHRO: Most certainly.

SOCRATES: Do you not see that our definition has come around to where it was before? Surely you remember that we have already seen that piety, and what is pleasing to the gods, are quite different things. . . . Then we must begin again and inquire what is piety? Do not deem me unworthy; give your whole mind to the question, and this time tell me the truth. For if anyone knows it, it is you; it cannot be that you would ever have undertaken to prosecute your father for the murder of the overseer unless you had known exactly what piety is. You would have feared to risk the anger of the gods, in case you should be doing wrong. So tell me, my excellent Euthyphro, and do not conceal from me what you hold it to be.

EUTHYPHRO: Another time, then, Socrates. I am in a hurry now, and it is time for me to be off.

Exercises

The questions refer to the material immediately preceding the numbers in brackets.

1. Which type of definition did Euthyphro offer? Why is Socrates dissatisfied with his answer?
2. Why is the second definition more satisfactory to Socrates? How does he criticize it?
2a. How does Euthyphro amend the second definition?
3. Explain how Socrates demolishes the definition of piety as "that which is pleasing to the gods."
4. What is Euthyphro beginning to discover?
5. Note Socrates' new and more constructive approach. He is looking for the genus of "piety." Under which general class does he place it?
6. Are piety and justice equivalent to each other? If not, which is the larger class or genus?

7. In what way does Euthyphro attempt to state the diffentia of an analytical definition?
8. Why is Euthyphro guilty of "reasoning in a circle"?

Section VI: Truth and Falsity in Definitions

In our discussion of the criterion of equivalence in definitions, we made an assumption which was not explicitly stated; namely, that a definition could be true or false. Thus, in testing the definition "Man is a rational animal" we asked, "Is it true that all men are rational animals?" and, "Is it true that all rational animals are men?" Our interpretation, based upon the assumption that definitions may be true or false, is usually referred to as the "realistic" interpretation of definitions.

We must now consider a different theory of definition, one which holds that definitions are neither true nor false. This point of view is called "nominalistic." The nominalist draws a sharp distinction between definitions and factual propositions. "Germany and Russia signed a mutual assistance pact on August 23, 1939" is a factual proposition and is of course either true or false. But a definition, according to the nominalist, is nothing but a stipulation or declaration as to how a word will be used by the speaker and is thus neither true nor false: "Let 'G' factor stand for the ability to solve problems." This view is expressed by Whitehead and Russell, in their *Principia Mathematica* (Cambridge University Press, 1910, p. 11):

> A definition is a declaration that a certain newly-introduced symbol or combination of symbols is to mean the same as a certain other combination of symbols of which the meaning is already known . . . A definition is concerned wholly with symbols, not with what they symbolize. Moreover it is not true or false, being the expression of a volition, not of a proposition . . . Definitions are merely typographical conveniences.

The nominalistic point of view is also expressed by Frye and Levi, in their *Rational Belief*. These authors present a test to determine whether a given sentence is a factual proposition or a definition. Their test is: Can you substitute the word "means" for the word "is" in the sentence? If you can, they say, then the sentence is a definition, and neither true nor false. Examine the sentence, "The Eiffel Tower is taller than the Washington Monument." Since "means" cannot here be substituted for "is," the sentence is a factual proposition. But "Man is a rational animal" permits the substitution into "Man means a rational animal" and is thus neither true nor false.

According to the nominalistic interpretation, it is not *untrue* to define "man" as "any book with a blue cover, weighing more than two pounds." We can say only that this is not the customary meaning of the word "man" in the English language, or that such a definition would serve no useful purpose. Definitions, in other words, are classified as customary or uncustomary, useful or useless, but not as true or false. Definitions are regarded as nothing but stipulations as to how we shall use a given word, so that the definition "Man is a rational animal" may be translated into "Let the word 'man' stand for 'rational animal.' " An act of stipulating is like a command, or a directive, or other imperative types of statements, neither true or false.

The controversy between the realists and the nominalists over the truth values of definition often overlooks the fact that we may stipulate a definition of "definition" itself. In other words, not even the word "definition" has a "real" meaning. But, this point aside, when we examine the purposes for which definitions are required we shall find that the role of stipulation varies with the purposes of definition. Let us examine some of the situations in which definitions are called for:

(1) When a new technical term is introduced into a scientific discussion, a stipulative definition is appropriate, as in "Let 'G-factor' stand for 'the ability to solve problems.' " Similarly when a vague or ambiguous term is central to a discussion the speaker may stipulate that he will use the term in one and only one of its senses.

Such stipulative definitions are neither true nor false. In an earlier chapter we learned that words are affixed to referents by acts of affirmation which are logically arbitrary, that there are no "real" names of things and that the naming activity is neither true nor false. Definitions introduced as typographical conveniences, to save space and time, are also mere stipulations: "Let '$<$' mean the same as 'are included in the class of' "; "Let 'definiens' mean the same as 'the defining part of a definition.' "

In these stipulative definitions we are not concerned with truth or falsity or even with the customary meaning (if there is one) of the symbols being defined. The only question is: Are they useful for the intended purposes? Note also that the rule of equivalence in analytical definitions is inapplicable to such definitions. We do not think of asking whether the definition of "G-factor" as "problem-solving" is either too broad or too narrow for we are dealing with a command or stipulation rather than with a description which might be true or false.

(2) Sometimes a question arises as to whether a term is being used in its customary sense. Custom must be checked in such cases by referring to a standard dictionary or to the appropriate literature or speech habits. But it is inappropriate to speak of definitions as true or false in terms of custom. We should merely note whether the definition is customary or uncustomary.

(3) There are many theoretical discussions in which we desire a "true" definition. Let us suppose that we are discussing poets and poetry. A speaker says that there is very little poetry in Shakespeare's plays, but we discover that he defines poetry as meaning "verse with rhyming couplets." We object that this is not a correct definition of poetry, that it is too narrow. The speaker retorts that he stipulates that this is what he will mean whenever he uses the word. But we regard his definition as not only incorrect but as useless, since it is not even descriptive of what most people mean by poetry. This indicates that we are not satisfied with an arbitrary stipulation; we are seeking for an equivalent definition of the term.

Dictionaries give us the customary meanings of a term, but we may find these customary meanings unsatisfactory, as in the dictionary definition: "Poetry is language which expresses beautiful thoughts and feelings." This definition will not satisfy us if we regard T. S. Eliot as a poet, for he does not express "beautiful thoughts and feelings." We continue our search for a definition that will adequately describe the common characteristics in the writings of Homer, Dante, Shakespeare, Keats, Yeats, Eliot, and others. When we ask for a definition of poetry we want a description of the characteristics which are common and peculiar to these works; we wish to know the qualities which all poems have in common, but which are not possessed by other writings. In other words, we want an equivalent definition. The definition, "Poetry is language which expresses beautiful thoughts and feelings," does not describe its subject matter correctly. It is not an equivalent definition.

A definition, of course, gives the meaning of a symbol. We do not define a thing, such as a chair, but the word "chair," and we do not define a poem, but the word "poem." But "poem" refers to what is common among certain kinds of writings, and an adequate analysis of its meaning will state the characteristics common and peculiar to these writings, for these are what we have in mind whenever we use the word. An equivalent definition, then, is true insofar as it correctly describes what we have in mind when we seek to refer to these common and peculiar characteristics. A definition which purports to do this and fails will be a false definition.

(4) It is important to note, however, that even a realistic or descriptive definition involves a stipulation. Thus, an equivalent definition involves two aspects, stipulation and analysis. On the one hand, there must be the stipulation, explicit or implicit, that the word "poetry" will be the name for the works of Shakespeare, *et al.* The use of the word "poetry" for these works is of course a mere arbitrary stipulation, and thus neither true nor false. The second aspect, analysis, requires that the definiens contain a description of the common and peculiar characteristics of these writings. Similarly, the definition of man as "a rational animal" has these two aspects: (a) We stipulate that the name "man" will be used to designate beings such as those who go to ball-games, movies, dances, polling booths, and so on. We stipulate that the definiendum shall designate such referents as these. This stipulation is an arbitrary one. (b) We then analyze the nature of these referents who are arbitrarily called "men." The two aspects, which correspond to the extensional and intensional aspects of meaning, may be illustrated by a diagram:

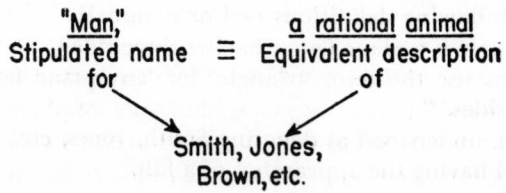

We might have called the referents Smith, Jones, and Brown, "palookas." Such "calling" would not be false, though it would be uncustomary. If we adopted this new name, then it would again be true to define "palookas" as "rational animals."

Definitions of words such as propaganda, love, religion, law, usually require realistic descriptions of the common and peculiar characteristics of the referents. When we use such words as these we have a vaguely apprehended notion as to the characteristics of the referents, and desire to refine our crude notions by careful analysis. Conflicts over the meanings of these words are not mere conflicts as to the customary usage of these terms, since custom differs from custom, and many writers misunderstand the nature of the referents involved. A good definition thus contributes to knowledge.

Exercises

1. Comment on the following, from Frye and Levi, *op. cit.*, p. 24: Note that of a definition we may ask, Is it meaningful? and Is it useful? but we cannot ask, Is it true? It is impossible to question the truth of a definition. *Definitions are neither true nor false,* simply because the test of truth or falsity is not applicable to them. A definition is merely the explicit resolution to use words in a certain manner. When Euclid says, "A scalene triangle is one having three unequal sides," he is to be understood as saying, "Henceforth I shall use the words scalene triangle *to mean* triangle with three unequal sides." There is no issue of truth or falsity here. *A definition is a linguistic convention.* It is *a stipulation,* to all intents and purposes a command, and is indeed to be treated as logically and analogous to an imperative statement. "Shut the door!" True or false? Neither, certainly. "Let the words scalene triangle have the meaning triangle with three unequal sides." True or false? The same.
2. Are the following definitions real or nominal?
   a. A triangle is a plane figure having three sides.
   b. "Let us use the term 'triangle' for 'any plane figure having three sides.'"
   c. A man, understood as denoting Smith, Jones, etc., is a marine animal having the appearance of a fish.

3. What stipulation is required to make the following a true definition? "A man is a creature that lives in water and breathes air through its gills."

4. Discuss the following problems in definition with reference to the nominalist-realist controversy. Do the definitions aim at stipulation or true description?

   a. Dr. Zilboorg says that present day psychiatry does not possess any satisfactory definition of mental illness or neurosis. To illustrate, he told a story: A psychiatrist was recently asked for a definition of a "well-adjusted person" (not even slightly peculiar). The definition: "A person who feels in harmony with himself and who is not in conflict with his environment." It sounded fine, but up popped a heckler. "Would you then consider an anti-Nazi working in the underground against Hitler a maladjusted person?" "Well," the psychiatrist hemmed, "I withdraw the latter part of my definition." Dr. Zilboorg withdrew the first half for him. Many persons in perfect harmony with themselves, he pointed out, are in "distinctly pathological states." (*Time*, Nov. 24, 1946.)

   b. Definition is of crucial importance in tariff problems. The Canadian tariff was higher on vegetables than on fruit. How should a shipment of rhubarb be taxed? The botanist defines a fruit as the matured seed-vessel of a flowering plant. Thus tomatoes are fruit, rather than vegetables. But most people would call a tomato a vegetable. The test adopted by the customs court was: Is it served with meat as a vegetable, or is it eaten as a dessert?

   c. Slander is defined in law as defamation of reputation by speech; libel as defamation in permanent form, capable of wide circulation, such as writings or drawings. How should a court rule on the question as to whether defamatory remarks made by a radio commentator are slander or libel?

Section VII: The Construction of Definitions

We have been concerned with the analysis and criticism of definitions. We shall now discuss the problem of *constructing* adequate analytical definitions. This is sometimes a very difficult task, particularly when there is controversy over the "proper" meaning of a word.

Let us assume that we require a definition of "art." We should first stipulate that the word will denote certain referents: "Let the word 'art' stand for productions in the fields of painting, sculpture, architecture, literature, and music." This stipulation clarifies the extension of the term and eliminates certain ambiguous usages of the word "art" as in "Medicine is an art rather than a science" or in Plato's references to the arts of cobbling and the training of horses. Our next task is to analyze the nature of the referents for which the word stands. We must seek for the characteristics which are common and peculiar to paintings, poems, etc., so that our definition will have the virtue of equivalence. We shall leave to the reader and the art critic the task of finding the common and peculiar characteristics of works of art and also the more difficult problem of defining "greatness" in works of art.

Let us now examine a somewhat different type of problem, that of defining the word "propaganda." If the reader will examine the definitions of this term in several dictionaries and in a dozen books dealing with public affairs, it is a safe guess that he will find as many definitions as there are writers. This is, of course, a highly unsatisfactory situation, for when a speaker uses the word we cannot know what the speaker is referring to, and communication breaks down. The multiplicity of definitions of this word is such a scandal that a public-spirited citizen in New York is reported to have offered a prize of $1,000 to anyone whose definition of the word would win general acceptance. It has also been seriously suggested that the use of the word be discontinued because of the extraordinary variety of its meanings.

When we examine the many definitions of "propaganda," however, we find that the word is used in two fundamentally different senses. In popular usage the word carries a derogatory connotation and refers to dishonest types of persuasion that seek to mislead the public. This meaning is rather widely accepted, for to call a speaker a "propagandist" is to tar him with the brush of opprobrium. On the other hand, we find a "neutral" definition of propaganda popular among some social scientists: "Propaganda is the expression of opinions or actions by individuals and groups deliberately designed to influence opinions or actions of other individuals or groups with reference to predetermined ends." (From *Propaganda Analysis,* by Clyde R. Miller.) Those who accept a variant of this latter definition tend to speak of *all* speakers as propagandists. They also recommend that we draw a distinction between bad and good propaganda, depending upon the aims of the propagandist. But neither of these definitions has won universal acceptance.

At this point the reader may ask, "Can we not arbitrarily stipulate *any* meaning for propaganda, and let the matter go at that?" As we have already noted, stipulation is not a merely arbitrary matter if we wish to define a word so that our definition will be "equivalent" to the referents denoted by it. Thus, some stipulations will be found satisfactory; others not. A stipulation that propaganda shall be understood to refer to "love poetry" will be wholly useless. When we think of "propaganda" we refer to certain kinds of activities that we apprehend only vaguely, and the search for a definition is the search for a description of these activities. Thus we reject some stipulations as inadequate and distinguish between definitions which describe our referents correctly and those which do not.

The attempt to construct an adequate definition of propaganda might proceed along the following lines: We begin with a stipulation that the word shall denote certain kinds of activities, such as wartime broadcasts by government agencies that seek to create a defeatist spirit in the enemy, to defame him, or to bolster the morale of one's own people. A poster designed to encourage the sale of war bonds during the last war is also a good example of the denotation of the term. This poster showed a picture of a marine lying on a foreign beachhead and asked the question, "Do you want our boys to die for the lack of guns?" followed by "Buy bonds!" The "Freedom Train," which sought to popularize knowledge of our civil liberties, in order to create affection for the democratic form of government, is another example.

If these examples are typical of the items properly included in the extension of the term "propaganda," then we must reject the two types of definitions noted above. Propaganda is not necessarily a dishonest type of persuasion which seeks to mislead the public. The "Freedom Train" did not mislead, and its purpose was a laudable one. The derogatory definition is thus too narrow. The neutral definition, on the other hand, is far too broad, for it covers *all* persuasive discourse, including the explanation of a formula in a class in mathematics, and even such expressions as "Please pass the salt" at the dinner table. It is worthy of note here that the Institute for Propaganda Analysis, which adopted the neutral definition cited above, also developed the classification of the tricks and devices of propaganda noted in Chapter 4. But it is surely inconsistent to define propaganda as equivalent to all persuasive discourse and then to speak of the special tricks and devices of the propagandist. Unless propaganda is in some sense evil, why should we be warned against its diabolical devices?

Let us now seek to analyze the referents denoted by our term. We begin by seeking for an adequate genus. Let us suggest the following: "A form of directive language used by groups desiring the public's support and action for the group's objectives." (These objectives may be political, economic, religious, and so on.) Our genus states that the propagandist desires action from his hearers. In this respect he differs from the educator, who is interested in communicating knowledge or truth in order to enlighten his audience.

We must now attempt to find the proper differentia. Here, too, the distinction we have drawn between the educator and the propagandist is the crucial one. The educator will seek to teach the truth and will not conceal relevant portions of the truth in order to influence his hearers in a given direction, but will present all of the relevant facts and permit his hearers to make up their own minds. He assumes that his hearers are rational beings who can think intelligently and who will act wisely when they know the evidence. The propagandist, on the other hand, seeks action, not truth. He wishes to mold his hearers' minds in a certain direction, regardless of the evidence. If the truth will serve his purpose, then he will tell the truth, but he has no real devotion to truth rather than to falsehood. And since action may be hindered by an appeal to thought, the propagandist will seek to inflame his hearers' emotions as the most effective prelude to action.

These considerations lead to the following definition: "Propaganda is directive language which seeks to get action for a group's objectives by the means best calculated to achieve action, usually by appealing to the emotions rather than to the intelligence of its audience and which disregards the truth when it appears convenient to do so."

This definition should be examined critically to determine whether it adequately states the characteristics which are both common and peculiar to propaganda. The reader should note that our definition appears to make all propaganda "bad," since it appears to be an intrinsically undesirable form of persuasion. This point must be clarified. A propagandist may of course have our good in mind, as was the case in the sale of war bonds during the war. The sale of these bonds was required in order to avoid inflationary tendencies which would have disrupted the economy and interfered with the effective prosecution of the war. But the government did not explain these facts to the people. The posters implied that the failure to buy bonds would mean that the soldiers would have no ammunition. The picture of a dead soldier was an emotional appeal which brought more action than would a reasoned argument against inflation. Since a rational appeal would presumably have brought no action, this propaganda may have been necessary, and few persons will object to its use. But when we give people propaganda instead of truth we treat them as children rather than as adults, unable to decide issues by a complete and truthful presentation of the relevant facts. Propaganda, then, is an intrinsically undesirable means of persuasion, but will be required so long as people lack the wisdom to choose wisely on the basis of rational considerations. In any case, those who have the wisdom to do so will always distinguish between the propagandist's appeals and his real purposes.

Before we leave the subject of definition, a warning is necessary. Stanley Baldwin, onetime Prime Minister of Great Britain, expressed an attitude of hostility toward the process of definition when he remarked, "Don't let us be too keen on definition . . . If we try to define the Constitution too much, we may split the Empire into fragments, and it will never come together again. Politically, if ever a saying was true, it is this: 'The letter killeth, and the spirit giveth life.'"

Susan Stebbing, in *Thinking to Some Purpose* (Penguin Books, p. 13), commented on this remark. She wrote,

> He supposes that the logician must demand a definition, and that the definition must set forth precisely determinable characteristics. But whosoever demands such a definition of that which lacks precisely determinable characteristics is being illogical. The mistake consists in demanding that a sharp line be

drawn concerning characteristics which are not in fact sharply distinguishable.

Logicians, in other words, will not commit the error against which Miss Stebbing warns. We must, of course, use a word in a determinative sense, for otherwise we would be guilty of using "words without referents," but we must not be too rigid in applying a term whose boundaries are not precisely delimited. We must take a similar attitude toward our definition of propaganda.

Exercises

1. Criticize the definitions of propaganda found in the following: Joe and Jim are listening to a famous radio commentator who is pontificating in his usual pontifical style. Jim says, "Oh, turn that guy off; that's just propaganda." Joe retorts brilliantly, "Whaddayamean, propaganda?" Jim answers, "Just a pack of lies." Joe: "My dear fellow, you have a sadly antiquated notion as to what propaganda is. Propaganda means any speech or action which has the purpose of influencing the actions of others. It follows that every public speaker is a propagandist. The only possible distinction we can make is whether or not we like the particular type of propaganda which is being dished out. If you like it, it is good propaganda so far as you are concerned; if you don't like it, it is bad."

2. Criticize: The only difference between "propaganda" and "education" really is in the point of view. The advocacy of what we believe in is education. The advocacy of what we don't believe in is propaganda. (Edward L. Bernays, *Crystallizing Public Opinion*, Liveright, 1923, p. 210.)

3. Construct an adequate analytical definition of a "big" word, such as "religion," "democracy," "socialism," "communism," or "fascism."

Deductive Logic

Chapter 6

Logic and Argument

Section I: Argument and Assertion

In Part Two we shall study the principles of valid reasoning, i.e., the principles which determine whether an argument is sound or unsound. Since the argument is the fundamental unit of reasoning, our first task is to understand the nature of argument.

The word "argument" is used in more than one sense. In popular speech "argument" often refers to a contest in reasoning, to a dispute, a wrangle, or a battle of ideas. Such arguments are contentious; each arguer tries to "win." In logic, however, the term argument refers to the basic unit of reasoning, and we define it as "a unit of discourse in which beliefs are supported by reasons."

An argument is a unit of discourse which seeks to prove that something is or is not the case. Here is an example: "You can't vote at the next election, for you aren't registered, and only those who are registered can vote." This argument undertakes to prove that you can't vote at the next election, and related reasons are presented in support of this point. Note that every argument contains two parts: (1) a point, or belief, or thesis, usually called the "conclusion" of the argument and (2) the supporting reasons, or evidence, usually called the "premises." The premises are the facts or assumptions on which the conclusion of the argument is based.

It is important to distinguish an argument from a "mere assertion." The French essayist Montaigne once said that "to philosophize is to learn how to die," i.e., that a wise man will not fear death. This is a mere assertion as it stands. But Montaigne weaves this assertion into the conclusion of an argument when he gives his reasons for his belief. The argument goes as follows:

"A wise man will not fear the loss of life, for it is foolishness to fear the loss of something one can never regret having lost." The conclusion is stated before the comma; the rest is the supporting reason or premise. The argument is the whole. A statement becomes a premise or conclusion by virtue of the role it plays in the argument.

An argument is discourse containing inference, in which we say "This is so because of that," or "This is so; therefore that is so." The student should seek to acquire facility in distinguishing the conclusion from the premises of arguments. There are two questions he should ask himself whenever he encounters argumentative discourse: (1) What is the writer's point, i.e., exactly what is he trying to prove or "put across"? (2) What reasons does he present to support his point? These questions concern only the structure of the argument and not its adequacy or inadequacy. Questions concerning the soundness of arguments will be discussed later.

An argument, then, has two parts, premises (or evidence) and conclusion. Note that the order of these parts is immaterial. The conclusion may be stated first, last, or it may be sandwiched between the evidence. The three possibilities follow:

1. Evidence stated first . . . *therefore* . . . conclusion.
2. Conclusion stated first . . . *because* . . . evidence.
3. Part of evidence . . . *therefore* conclusion . . . *because* remainder of evidence.

The following arguments are respective examples:

1. All men are mortal, and Socrates is a man; *therefore,* Socrates is mortal.
2. Socrates is mortal *because* all men are mortal, and Socrates is a man.
3. All men are mortal; *therefore,* Socrates is mortal *because* he is a man.

These forms state exactly the same argument, despite the difference in the arrangement of its parts. Most arguments contain *logical indicators,* i.e., words which signal that a part of the argument is premise or conclusion. "Because" and "therefore" are such indicators. These words have many synonyms. Synonyms for "therefore" are words like "so," "hence," "consequently," "thus," which always introduce the conclusion of the argument. This function may also be performed by phrases such as "which indicates that," "which shows that," "we may conclude that," "must be," and so on. Synonyms for "because" are words like "for," "since," or phrases like "in view of," or "for the reason that," etc. Remember that "because" and its synonyms always introduce a premise.

Some arguments contain no logical indicators, as in "We are headed for socialism. Congress just voted big subsidies for farmers." The speaker obviously intends the second sentence to be evidence for the first. The logical indicators may also indicate subsidiary elements rather than the main conclusion in an argument. But the student who is alert to the presence of the indicators will have little difficulty in distinguishing the premises and conclusion of an argument.

Exercises

Read the units of discourse stated below, and distinguish collections of mere assertions from arguments. Are beliefs alone stated, or are reasons given for the beliefs? Identify "logical indicators" where present. If the unit is an argument, analyze it into two parts, evidence and conclusion, and restate it with the conclusion first (Form 2 above).

1. All men are mortal and fallible, so some mortal beings are fallible.
2. Since only citizens can vote, John must be able to vote, for he is a citizen.
3. If a man is able to vote, then I know that he must be a citizen. John must be a citizen, for I know that he can vote.
4. Good sense is of all things the most equally distributed among men; for everybody thinks himself so abundantly provided with it that even those most difficult to please in all other matters do not commonly desire more of it than they already possess. (Descartes)
5. There are thousands of persons on the federal payroll who don't

earn their pay but who are kept on until they can retire. The commission studying this matter may recommend that these workers be let off with adequate severance pay.

6. All men are mortal and fallible. All men are sinners.

7. The following excerpts are from a speech delivered by General George Marshall, former Secretary of State and author of the Marshall Plan, in Chicago, Illinois, on November 18, 1947:

   (a) It seems evident that as regards European recovery, the enlightened self-interest of the United States coincides with the best interests of Europe itself and of all those who desire to see conflicts of whatever nature resolved, so that the world can devote its full attention and energy to the progressive improvement of the well-being of mankind. The place to begin that process is in Europe.

   (b) We recognize that our people will be called upon to share their goods still in short supply and will have to forego filling a portion of their own requirements until the greater needs of Europe have been met. This is a direct contradiction of the allegation that we are seeking to dump surplus foods in Europe in order to avoid the depressing effects of oversupply.

8. There is no race in the whole world that consists of families of uniform character. Every race embraces many diverse family lines. It is incorrect to assume that all the members of a racial group possess uniform characteristics because they are similar in some respects. All people who are blond and who have blue eyes have not the same characteristics and there is no reason to give inordinate weight to this single feature. (From "remarks" by Franz Boas in a pamphlet, 1934.)

9. The first condition of free government is government not by the arbitrary determination of the ruler, but by fixed rules of law, to which the ruler himself is subject. We draw the important inference that there is no essential antithesis between liberty and law. On the contrary, law is essential to liberty. (L. T. Hobhouse, *Liberalism,* Henry Holt.)

10. Human beings do not live "by bread alone"; they also need to dream, to have great hopes and aspirations. This is especially true of today's teenagers, who are so accustomed to modern luxuries that they no longer thrill to material possessions.

   Modern parents no longer have dreams. They now possess what they used to dream about. They have split-level ranch homes, picture windows, finny automobiles, and automatic dishwashers.

This is the reason why today's parents have so little influence over their teenagers.

Section II: The Law of Rationality and Evasions Thereof

We have distinguished arguments from mere assertions. An argument is discourse containing inference, in which we say, "This is so because of that." But the inference may be sound or unsound. In Part Two we will be concerned with the principles of sound reasoning. Before proceeding to the principles, however, let us consider the aim of logical thinking and the manner in which this aim may be frustrated.

Every person who is interested in logical thinking accepts what we shall call the "law of rationality," which may be stated as follows: *We ought to justify our conclusions by adequate evidence.* The meaning of adequacy will be explained in detail as we proceed. Let it suffice here to say that by "adequate evidence" we mean evidence which is good and sufficient in terms of the kind of proof which is required. There are occasions when we require conclusive proof, as in mathematics, and there are occasions when it is sufficient to establish the probability of a given conclusion, as in weather prediction. But in all cases the evidence must be adequate to its purpose.

Adequate evidence is evidence which is relevant to the conclusion to which it is directed. We need not define "evidence" or "relevant," since we may assume that these words will be generally understood by most persons. Unless the meaning of these words were understood by the reader of a book on logic prior to his reading the book, he would not be able to follow the author's reasoning. The reader must be warned, however, that "relevance" is not always easily determined. When we say that one fact is relevant to another, we mean that there is a connection of some kind between them. This connection is not always apparent. For example, a historian investigating the causes of the decline and fall of the Roman Empire must consider only matters relevant to his study. Should he study the history of the building of the Great Wall in China, and the practice of human sacrifice among the Aztecs? Both facts may appear irrelevant, but we find to our surprise that the first fact is relevant. For the Great Wall was built to keep the Huns out of China, and they turned west instead. In their travels for pillage and loot they finally came to the Roman Empire and had an important role in its destruction. But all of us understand what relevance means. When one fact is irrelevant with respect to another, then that fact, like "the flowers that bloom in the Spring," has "nothing to do with the case."

Though few, if any, will have the temerity or the foolishness to challenge the law of rationality, it is often evaded. Evasion usually occurs through carelessness, but it may also occur through design. In this section we shall note some of the typical ways in which the obligation to support beliefs by adequate evidence is evaded.

In every argument we find the assertion of a belief, which we shall call "P," (for "probandum," or proposition to be proved). Someone says that P is true. When we ask the speaker, "Why," or "What reasons do you have for believing that P is true?" we ask for evidence. We then expect adequate evidence to support his belief. This adequate evidence should be relevant to the question at issue, and it should be good and sufficient evidence. In the rest of this chapter we shall be concerned with the *evasion* of the requirement that evidence be furnished. The proverb says that we asked for bread and were given stones. Paraphrased, we shall find that we asked for evidence and received the Argumentum ad Misericordiam, or the Argumentum ad Hominem, or the Argumentum ad Verecundiam. We turn now to the evasions, seven of which will be considered.

1. The Appeal to Authority

This evasion has the following structure: Jones says that P is true. When asked, Why? he answers, "Because X says so." Now, P (the *probandum*) should be proved by adequate evidence, but the fact that X says it is true is not *evidence* for its truth. The citing of authority in this bald manner is an evasion of the law of rationality.

Now, to say that "the appeal to authority" is an evasion of the law of rationality is not to say that we are guilty of this evasion whenever we cite an authority for our beliefs. There is no doubt that sensible people must rely on authorities for many, if not most, of their important decisions and for the beliefs on which these decisions are based.

When a physician tells us that we need an operation we rely on his authority. We accept the authority of the weatherman that rain is probable. We have neither the time nor sufficient knowledge to investigate the evidence for all of our beliefs. The point, however, is this: No belief is true merely because someone says so. It is true because of the evidence in its behalf. When we trust an authority, we merely place credence in the fact that *he* has evidence. And if we wish to *know,* rather than merely to believe, we should inquire into the evidence on which his conclusions are based. For example, the reader believes that the earth is in motion. On what evidence?

In general, three questions should be kept in mind when considering the statements of an authority: Is the cited authority an authority in the specific field in which he has made his pronouncements? Does the authority have evidence to prove his statements? Do all qualified investigators agree on the general soundness of the type of proof offered? A great physicist may be an authority in the field of nuclear physics, but that does not qualify him to be dogmatic in the field of religion. A man may be very critical in one field and very uncritical in another. A theologian may be an authority in the field of theology, but he is not necessarily an authority on the question of the existence of God, since not all qualified investigators are agreed on the soundness of his methods of proof. On the other hand, we accept the statements of astronomers that the mean distance of the sun from the earth is close to 93 million miles, because they are authorities with respect to such matters, their evidence is available to all, and all qualified investigators agree on the soundness of their methods. We accept our physician's statement that we should take medicine for our ailments for similar reasons (or at least we believe these reasons to hold). But even the acceptance of competent authority is never a substitute for *proof.*

When the authorities are in conflict, i.e., when "the doctors disagree," two courses of action are open to us. If the problem is a purely theoretical one, and we are not required to take immediate action, we should suspend judgment. If action is required, we should accept the authority who appears to be most competent and trustworthy.

The appeal to authority is often called the "Argumentum

ad Verecundiam," a learned-sounding Latin phrase which means the "appeal to reverence." A revered authority or tradition is often regarded as infallible, so that anyone who disagrees is in some sense disloyal to that which ought to be revered. This type of appeal is sometimes employed with respect to the theory of evolution. We may be told that evolution cannot be true because it is contrary to the story in the Book of Genesis. But this question must be decided by those who have examined the available evidence, and the writers of that ancient book did not possess our present knowledge. Reverence is not a substitute for evidential proof. Reverence was also exhibited by the mediaeval professor who looked through Galileo's telescope, but who continued to teach the ancient astronomical ideas because he preferred to distrust the evidence of his senses rather than doubt the authority of Aristotle.

The fact that "everybody knows that this is so" is no proof. The masses of men have frequently been mistaken. They once thought that the earth was flat. They still believe that the speed of a falling object depends on its weight. The voice of the people is not necessarily the voice of God on all questions.

2. The Appeal to Emotion

The structure of this evasion: "The proposition 'P' is true." Why?—"Because I (or you) have strong feelings concerning it." But strong feelings do not constitute evidence for the truth of a proposition. The fact that people have emotional attachments to religious and political doctrines does not make the doctrines true.

The appeal to emotion takes two forms, one subjective or personal, and the other objective or social. In its *personal* form the appeal is to one's own emotions. A person is convinced of the truth of a proposition because he "cannot bear to think it untrue." If I feel so strongly about it, his argument goes, then it surely must be true. But wishes are fathers to thoughts, and this is an evasion of the law of rationality. The argument is usually not stated in this bald manner, but it is often found in a concealed form.

In the *objective* form the appeal is to the emotions of other persons, as when a speaker substitutes emotional appeals for evidence. In traditional logic this is called the "Argumentum ad

Populum," the appeal to the people, or, in less flattering terms, to the mob. The masses of men are often moved by emotion rather than by reason. Speakers inflame crowds of people with emotionally loaded language, rabble-rousing and prejudiced appeals, by spell-binding, "pulling the heart strings," and appeals to popular sentiment. But the truth is not always one with our emotions. Mark Antony's speech, part of which was quoted in Chapter 4, is an excellent example of the use of this evasion. It is Mark Antony's task to convince the mob that Caesar was not a dictator. His argument, reduced to its structural elements, goes as follows: If Caesar's wounds are pitiful to behold, then Caesar could not have aspired to be a dictator. If Caesar remembered you in his will, then he did not aspire, etc. Emotion overcomes reason, but again, no evidence.

Mark Antony's speech is also a good example of a special variety of the appeal to emotion called the "Argumentum ad Misericordiam," or the "appeal to pity." This appeal is used by attorneys for the defense who tell the jury that the prisoner at the bar has a wife and four small children. It was this type of argument which Socrates disdained to use in his speech defending himself to the Athenian jury, as reported in Plato's *Apology*. Finally, we note the "appeal to laughter." This means that we meet an opponent's arguments, not by evidence, but by a joke, to arouse laughter at his expense and to divert the attention of the hearers from the issue. But laughter, like loud talking, is never a substitute for evidence.

A warning is called for before we leave this evasaion. We have not said that all emotional appeals are inappropriate. When the facts are not in question and action is desired, an emotional appeal is appropriate, even indispensable. In the critical days of 1940 when England was threatened with invasion Prime Minister Winston Churchill's emotional eloquence inspired his people and spurred them to heroic efforts. What must be condemned is the substitution of emotion for proof when proof is required.

3. The Argumentum ad Hominem

The Latin title means "an argument directed to the man," to the man (speaker, writer), that is, instead of to the point at issue. For example, let us suppose that we disagree with what a speaker says. We may try to disprove what he says by presenting contrary evidence. But sometimes we don't bother to present the evidence. Instead, we try to disprove what the speaker says by attacking *him,* (verbally, of course).

This evasion is a form of *disproof,* rather than *proof.* It seeks to show that a certain proposition is false but substitutes an attack against the speaker for an attack against the proposition itself. Its structure: "P is false." "Why is P false?" "Because he who asserts P is a certain kind of person."

It may be instructive to contrast the "ad hominem" with the "appeal to authority." There is a sense in which these are opposites, for in the latter we say "P" must be true because X says it is. In the "ad hominem" we say "P" must be false because X is a certain kind of person. The ad hominem argument, in other words, has a negative purpose: to discredit a proposition by discrediting the speaker. It is an evasion of the law of rationality because it fails to provide relevant evidence against the proposition it seeks to disprove.*

To illustrate. A woman reads Schopenhauer's *Essay on Women,* aptly described by G. K. Chesterton as "that hideous essay." Schopenhauer writes:

> It is only the man whose intellect is clouded by his sexual impulses that could give the name of the fair sex to that undersized, narrow-shouldered, broad-hipped, and short-legged race: for the whole beauty of the sex is bound up with this impulse. Instead of calling them beautiful, there would be more warrant for describing women as the unaesthetic sex. Neither for music, nor for poetry, nor for fine art, have they really and truly any sense or susceptibility; it is a mere mockery if they make a pretense of it in order to assist their endeavor to please. Hence, as a result of this, they are incapable of taking a purely objective interest in anything.

And more of the same. He says that women are interested only in acquiring husbands, in dress, jewelry, and cosmetics. Now, practically all women and most men would disagree with

---

* Note that "ad hominem" is sometimes used in a different sense—for an argument based on an appeal to a person's private prejudices: "You, as a property owner, will surely oppose building a new high school, for this will mean higher taxes."

Schopenhauer. But how does the "typical" woman reader meet Schopenhauer's argument? By pointing out that his statements are untrue, or highly misleading in their selectivity? No. She attacks Schopenhauer himself, stating that he must have been a disappointed lover or that he must have had a very unhappy childhood to write such tripe. But this attack does not meet his argument. "Attacking the man" is an evasion of the law of rationality, and it is not a proper substitute for presenting evidence to refute his argument.

In general, the "ad hominem" takes the form of directing one's attack toward the speaker rather than to what he has said. The implied assumption is that his being a certain kind of person, or having a certain personal history, tends to make his statements false. Thus we answer an opponent by noting that he is a millionaire or a poor man, as the case may be, young or old, an employer or a member of a labor union. The popularity of the "psychoanalytic" method in recent years has made this method of approach a common one. Instead of meeting an opponent's arguments with evidence we seek to psychoanalyze him. If he says that a strong government is desirable, then we find that he is seeking a substitute for a "father-image." If he thinks a weak government is desirable, then he is in revolt against his father-image.

Note how this approach seems to discredit whatever view it seeks to "explain." In general, we employ this psychological approach only for views with which we disagree, for it seldom occurs to us to seek a psychological explanation, or any explanation at all, for what seems obvious to us. One who takes the psychological approach thus usually assumes the falsity of the view he seeks to explain. It is as if the speaker were to say, "Your ideas are so patently false that it is difficult to see how an intelligent man could assert such things. So there must be a psychological explanation." But if we believe that ideas are false, then we are duty-bound to present the evidence. A pejorative psychological analysis of the supposed psychological causes of a belief is no substitute for logical analysis. Indulging in "personalities" is irrelevant with respect to the logical force of ideas. Euclid's geometry stands or falls on its own merits, whether or not Euclid was a kind husband and father.

We should not confuse the ad hominem with an attack

against a man's character. If we say that Roe is a liar, or dishonest, or a spy, we have made allegations which may be false and slanderous, but the ad hominem does not occur unless we contend that Roe's *statements* must be *false* because Roe is a certain kind of person. This distinction should be borne in mind when considering a special variety of the ad hominem called "Poisoning the Wells." This figure of speech refers to the demand that we should suspect or ignore whatever some people may say on the ground that the truth cannot be in them. "Do not drink water from that well," it is said, "for the well is poisoned." In practice, this takes the form of an attack which seeks to discredit a witness, by alleging that he is a dishonest witness. This is sometimes a legitimate procedure, provided that we do not confuse this kind of an attack with a disproof of what the speaker says. This important distinction requires careful analysis.

We do *not* commit the ad hominem evasion when we attack a person's character, as when we say that he is a liar and should not be trusted. Thus in a law court a witness for the prosecution testifies that he observed the defendant in the act of committing the crime. The attorney for the defense then presents "character witnesses" who testify that the witness is a notorious liar who has been previously convicted of perjury. This evidence proves that the witness is untrustworthy, and that his testimony is of little worth with respect to its credibility. A jury will be reluctant to accept his statements at face value and will probably disregard his evidence. But liars sometimes tell the truth, and we should not confuse proof that a witness is untrustworthy, with proof that what the witness is now saying is false. We also discredit a speaker when we find that he has been paid to give his testimony, that he is an apologist for special interests or groups, that he is notoriously biased or prejudiced, or that he is insincere, and so on. If we know that a person is a communist, and as such would never find any fault with Russia, his statement that Russia is right in a particular international dispute would carry little weight. In the same manner we discount a Republican's attacks against a Democratic administration, and vice versa, because we feel that such criticisms are apt to be prejudiced. But in none of these examples have we proved that the speaker's statements are false.

We also seek to discredit a speaker when we accuse him of

being inconsistent, but this is not to prove his last statement false. For example, ex-Governor Arnall of Georgia once stated that he thought it inadvisable to outlaw the Communist Party. An opponent retorted, "But Governor, a year ago you favored outlawing this party." The Governor answered that he had reconsidered, and now believed it would be a mistake to suppress ideas with which he disagreed. The fact that the Governor was inconsistent did not prove that he was now wrong (or right). But when we find a person consistently inconsistent, then we lose respect for his mental quality and integrity, and in such cases he becomes a discredited witness. Though we may admire people who have sufficiently flexible minds to change their opinions with new evidence, we do not admire those whose opinions change, like weather vanes, with every shift in the winds of doctrine. But though an attack against a man's authority may be legitimate, we must never confuse this with an attack against the ideas he has expressed.

A similar distinction must be made when we read a history of ideas. When a historian gives us a sociological or a socio-political-economic interpretation of ideas, he "explains" how a particular thinker came to develop his system of thought. For example, Thomas Hobbes (1588–1679) advocated the principles of absolute monarchy in his *Leviathan*. It is highly enlightening to know that Hobbes was personally a rather timid man. Perhaps he desired the security which a strong king would give him. We may also learn that he wrote in a time of troubles, when the social situation was disorganized and chaotic and when men longed to escape the horrors of civil war. The historian may explain how the principle of absolute monarchy reflected the social needs of the time. But insofar as Hobbes presented a reasoned defense of his principle for *any* society, then his argument must be met with logical criticism as well as sociological interpretation.

The same considerations apply to John Locke's (1632–1704) defense of constitutional monarchy. Locke was an apologist for the reign of William and Mary, the constitutional monarchs who ascended the throne in 1689 at the invitation of the English Parliament. But Locke's argument for the advantages of representative government can also stand on its own feet. Edmund Burke (1729–1797) was a liberal in his early career.

The French Revolution aroused a horror of revolution in him and he became an extreme conservative, arguing that social reform was certain to cause more harm than good. But once again, our knowledge of the conditions which led him to this position do not in themselves invalidate the argument. It may be that Burke's psychological experiences gave him an insight which he had not previously had.

The value of the historical explanation of ideas is that it may call into question our unthinking acceptance of assumptions which appear to be eternally valid. The critical mind welcomes a questioning of first principles. "Truth" is a very complex matter in the field of political philosophy, and history reveals that most political ideas play a very practical role in organizing society under certain historical conditions. Nevertheless, political programs are also general techniques for achieving certain universal goals, and as such their validity transcends their immediate historical setting.

Before we leave this topic we shall note a popular type of defense against the ad hominem attack. We may defend ourselves against an ad hominem by our own ad hominem, directed against its proponent. This type of defense is called the "tu quoque," which means "You're another." An illustration: X, a forty-year-old professor argued in favor of the military draft in 1949. He stated that it was necessary for the defense of the nation. A student interposed, "You favor the draft because you are in the higher age bracket and are not in danger of being drafted." The professor responded with his own ad hominem in the form of the tu quoque, "By the same token, you are against the draft merely because you are afraid that you will be drafted." The question at issue in this discussion was: Is the draft necessary for the welfare of the country? The tu quoque settles nothing, but is a useful rhetorical device to expose the evasion called the ad hominem. Similarly, if we are told that we believe in the truth of P merely because we have been "conditioned" in a certain way, the proper retort is that our opponent considers P false merely because *he* has been conditioned in a different way. We shall usually find that those who use the ad hominem seldom realize that it may be applied to themselves. Thus, a Marxian sees the doctrines of classical economics as false, "since they are merely products of a special historical situation," but the Marxian economics is regarded as infallibly true and not as the mere product of a historical situation. But the critic may be hoisted with his own petard.

4. Argumentum ad Ignorantiam

This means the "appeal to ignorance." It has the structure: "P is true." Why? "Because you can't disprove it." This type of evasion often occurs in discussions which involve religious faith. Thus a man may argue that the Book of Genesis gives a literal account of the creation of the world. A skeptic may state that this account appears improbable to him, though he may also admit that he cannot disprove it. The religious protagonist then asserts, "You must now admit that it is true, for you cannot disprove it." This is the appeal to ignorance or inability to disprove. But inability to disprove is not equivalent to proof. Only evidence gives us proof. If we accepted this kind of substitute for evidence we should be required to believe that the Angel Gabriel visited the prophet Mohammed to inform him that God had decided that the Moslem religion was to supersede the Jewish and Christian religions. For how would you go about disproving this claim? We are not required to accept the improbable merely because we do not know how to disprove it. As cautious thinkers, we will withhold belief until we have positive evidence in favor of a proposition.

5. Begging the Question

This evasion, known in traditional logic as "Petitio Principii" consists in our pretending to prove something when actually we *assume* in the "proof" that which we are supposed to prove. "Why do I believe that Zilch is guilty? Because he is guilty." The evasion has the following logical structure: "P is true." Why? "Because P is true." The "evidence" here merely restates the conclusion. There is thus no independent relevant evidence whatsoever; we have merely assumed the truth of that which we are supposed to prove. The conclusion is used to establish itself.

This evasion is seldom stated in this bald form. The fact that we use the conclusion to establish itself is usually concealed in various ways. X argues that it is wrong for women to sit at bars. When asked, Why? he answers, "Because I know that it isn't right." The expression "wrong" and "not right" are equivalent to each other. "Arguing by definition" usually involves begging the question. Thus, X asserts that all Christians are virtuous men. Y then points to the example of Thwackum, who is a Christian, but no exemplar of virtue. "Ah," answers X, "Thwackum may attend his church regularly, but he is no Christian, since, if he were, then he would be a model of virtue." This is begging the question by definition, since X has *defined* a Christian as a virtuous man. Thus his statement "All Christians are virtuous men" was a mere statement of the tautologous remark that "All virtuous men are virtuous men." This is certainly true, but it is no proof that "Christians," in the sense of "being a member of a Christian church," are all virtuous men. The original proposition appeared to be a significant statement only because the implied tautology was concealed.

Question-begging may also occur independently of arguments. Statements may assume matters that ought to be proved, as in the use of "question-begging epithets" such as "stupid conservatism," or "wild-eyed radicalism," or in referring to a person on trial as "that criminal." Complex questions (Have you stopped beating your wife?) also "beg the question" by assuming that which ought to be proved.

Though we should not assume what needs to be proved, some assumptions are indispensable in any discussion. The careful thinker is one who tries to be aware of his assumptions. Few of us, however, are capable of exercising the care shown by a cautious man who was famous for never saying anything he was not sure of. While driving through the country with a friend they passed some sheep. "Those sheep seem to have been sheared recently," said his friend. "Yes," answered the cautious man, "at least on one side." Charles Lamb, the English essayist, was also a careful man. He is reported to have refused to admit that 2 plus 2 is 4 until he knew what use would be made of his admission.

"Reasoning in a circle" is a "drawn-out" form of begging the question. It contains intermediate steps. The conclusion is used to establish itself, but it is smuggled into a chain of reasons rather than into only one. A fairly complicated example: The founder of a new religion tells us that he is inspired, so that we may believe whatever he tells us (P). When challenged for proof he presents us with a book which states that he speaks in God's name (Q). "Why should we believe this book?" we ask. "Because it comes from God (R), he answers. "But how can we know this?" we persist. "Because you can take my word for it (S)." "And why should we take your word?" "Because I am inspired (P)." If we should now ask, "How can we know that you are?" the circle will start all over again.

The structure of this argument may be shown in schematic form:

Assertion that P is true. Proof: Because Q is true. (Question: How do we know Q is true?)

Proof that Q is true. Because R is true. (Question: How do we know R is true?)

Proof that R is true. Because S is true. (Question: How do we know that S is true?)

Proof that S is true. Because P is true. (But this is what we started out to prove!)

6. Diverting the Issue

The law of rationality requires that we furnish evidence for or against the proposition in issue and not for some other proposition. The evasion we call "diverting the issue" takes the following structure: P is true (or false) because I can prove R (where the truth of R is irrelevant to the truth of P). This evasion is seldom found in this obvious form, for usually R bears some superficial resemblance to P, and it may appear that we have proved P when we have proved R.

An example: In 1940, the "isolationist" chancellor of a leading American University argued against the proposal that the United States should send military aid to England during the early stage in the World War. He sought to prove his point by the rhetorical questions, "Do you think that a victory for the British Empire will result in the disappearance of all of the ills which afflict us here at home?" and "Are we to help the British Empire every time it goes to war?" His argument boils down to the following: We should not help England (P) because I can prove that such action will not result in a Utopia (R), or We should not help England (P) because I can disprove the thesis that we should help England whenever England goes to war (R). But what the chancellor should have proved was that it was not in the interest of the United States to help England in 1940. His evidence should have shown (if such evidence were available) that we would have been better off by not helping England at that time. The wise man will always choose the better when he cannot get the best.

Another example: A group of law students were discussing the abilities of the various members of the freshman class. One of them insisted that Littleton, a student whose class recitations contained frequent references to Schopenhauer, Nietzsche, and other philosophers, was a true genius. His friends turned upon him with withering scorn and the challenge, "A genius! What possible basis is there for calling him a genius?" "Well," came the immediate response, "he's no damn fool!"

In debates this type of diversion is of frequent occurrence. One of the debaters may seek to divert the issue to one which his opponent will find more difficult to prove or to one which he can more easily prove. X asserts that "all corporation executives are opposed to labor unions," and then adduces evidence to prove that it would be absurd to believe that "all corporation executives are friendly to labor unions." But the proof of the falsity of the second proposition does not prove the truth of the first. Certainly it is not the case that *all* executives are friendly, for some are and some are not. But this is quite different from saying that none of them are friendly.

Similarly, if X asserts that "some executives are friendly," Y may then seek to prove that it is false to assert that "all are friendly." But Y is not disproving the falsity of X's statement; he is disproving a different one. This type of diversion is called an "extension," since it extends the opponent's statement beyond what was actually asserted.

7. Special Pleading

We ought to furnish adequate evidence for our beliefs, and this means that we ought to state the evidence as fairly and completely as it is possible to do so. To deliberately select evidence which is favorable to our thesis and to conceal unfavorable evidence is to violate this law. Few human beings are capable of perfection in this matter. Charles Darwin was an outstanding example of a thinker who conscientiously sought to find all the possible evidence which might upset his theory and who candidly admitted the gaps in his account of the evolution of life. At the opposite pole we find the fabled geologist who worked out a highly original theory concerning the rock formations in a certain valley. The examined evidence confirmed his theory, and he was in a state of exultation over the sensation which his paper would make in scientific circles. He walked up a hill to enjoy "his" valley, when his eye fell on a large boulder, a type of rock which should not have been there if his theory were true. He thereupon put his shoulder to the boulder and pushed it down the other side of the hill!

"Special pleading" is the evasion committed by speakers or writers who carelessly or deliberately overlook "negative" facts. The following is an example: "The New Deal of the early thirties was a disaster. It unbalanced the budget, increased the national debt, passed unconstitutional legislation, etc, etc." This argument tells us that the New Deal was a disaster "because of the following list of facts . . ." But this listing of evidence, whether true or not, is very one-sided. No mention is made of facts on the other side. Its structure: "P is true." Why? "Because of the following list of facts: Q, R, and S." But facts A, B, and C, which might tend to disprove P, are ignored, either carelessly or deliberately.

The term "special pleader," however, should not be used for those who merely fail to state the evidence completely, for complete evidence is often an unattainable ideal. Outstanding examples of this evasion are found in political debates where each side claims all the credit and finds nothing but ill in its opponent's records. Lawyers are also notorious special pleaders, since their chief purpose is to win the case rather than to find the truth. Witnesses in a law court who swear under oath are required to testify to the truth, the whole truth, and nothing but the truth. This is obviously a precaution against special pleading. Each part of the affirmation is necessary. Otherwise the witness might tell the truth part of the time and lie the rest of the time. He could then say that he had told "the truth," but not "nothing but." Or he might tell only the truth but leave out a substantial part of it. Thus the requirement that he tell the "whole truth."

Exercises

A. The following group contains examples of each of the evasions of
the law of rationality. The correct answers are found at the end
of this set, but the student should attempt to identify each example before looking up the answers. The seven evasions are the
following:

> (1) The appeal to authority (Argumentum ad Verecundiam).
> (2) The appeal to emotion.
>> (a) The appeal to one's own emotions.
>> (b) The appeal to the emotions of others (Argumentum
>>   ad Populum, ad Misericordiam, Appeal to Laughter).
> (3) The Argumentum ad Hominem (Poisoning the Wells).
> (4) Argumentum ad Ignorantiam.
> (5) Begging the Question (Reasoning in a Circle).
> (6) Diverting the Issue (Diversion, Extension).
> (7) Special Pleading.

In each case find the proposition (P) in issue. Show the structure of the evasion in the following way: "P is true (or false) because . . ." Then state the nature of the evasion.

> 1. Your argument that the Taft-Hartley Law has contributed
>   to labor unrest is without merit, since you are an Interna-
>   tional Representative of the CIO and would therefore be
>   against the act no matter how good it was.
> 2. A wholesaler sued a retailer for $200, claiming that he had
>   shipped that amount in goods to the defendant and had not
>   been paid. The retailer claimed that he had paid the bill.
>   The wholesaler–plaintiff stated that he had no record of the
>   payment. The retailer–defendant then said that the court
>   should dismiss the case, since the plaintiff could not disprove
>   his claim that he had paid the bill.
> 3. Every slip of the tongue is significant in that it reveals some
>   unconscious and suppressed desire. There can be no question
>   about the truth of this statement, since it was put forward by
>   Sigmund Freud, the founder of psychoanalysis.
> 4. Henry, a determinist, believes that human beings have no
>   free will. He argues that in all choices between two courses of
>   action, the strongest impulse will prevail, i.e., that the
>   strength of the impulse decides the issue, not the "will."

How do we know that the strongest impulse always prevails? By the very fact that it prevailed.

5. I feel that if we don't prevent the establishment of life tenure for the Chief Executive, the republic eventually will be undermined and destroyed. The New Deal is the height of totalitarian nationalism. Our Republican tradition is based upon uncompromising independence and the interests of the republic. (Alfred M. Landon, 1941.)

6. Jones says that he is in favor of an army draft at the present time. Smith: "But why? We are not at war." Jones: "This is a period of crisis." Smith: "Well, so far as I am concerned, I favor the time-honored constitutional way of doing things." Jones: "But in time of national crisis we must disregard the constitution."

7. Under the capitalistic system there are many poor people, there is waste of men and materials, cut-throat competition, the glorification of the acquisitive instinct, depressions on the one hand and inflation on the other. This proves that the system is thoroughly bad and should be discarded.

The above arguments may be analyzed as follows:

1. "The proposition: 'The Taft-Hartley Law has contributed to labor unrest (P)' is a false proposition because you are a certain kind of person." Ad hominem.

2. "I paid the $200.00 (P). This is true, since you cannot disprove it." Ad ignorantiam.

3. "Every slip of the tongue is significant because Freud says so." Freud was a great psychologist, but scientific psychologists still debate the truth of many of his theories. In any case, what is the evidence for this probandum? Ad Verecundiam or appeal to authority.

4. P: "The strongest impulse always prevails (hence no freewill)." How do we know that it does? "Because it does." This is begging the question.

5. These are highly "loaded" remarks. President Roosevelt had just been re-elected to his third term, but "life tenure" is a figment of the imagination. "The height of totalitarian nationalism" is an inflammatory rather than an informative description of the New Deal. Mr. Landon had a point, but he submerged it in emotive language. His probandum is not clear, but it seems to be "You ought to vote Republican." Appeal to emotion.

6. This is an example of a diversion. The question is whether it is right that "we should have an army draft at the present time (P)." Smith diverts the issue to "the constitutional way of doing things," and Jones falls into the trap. (The draft is constitutional.)

7. Highly selected and one-sided facts to prove that "capitalism is bad (P)." Special pleading.

B. Analyze this group as before. Each type is represented by one example.

1. The attorney for the defense handed his brief to the barrister with the written notation, "We have a very poor case. Abuse the plaintiff's lawyer." Which evasion was he recommending?

2. "Educated people do not believe in the devil."
"But I know some college graduates who do."
"I said *educated* people; the college graduates you refer to aren't really educated, because if they were, then they wouldn't believe in the devil."

3. How do we know that this man is guilty of having committed this well-planned crime? I have encountered many examples of crime in my experience, but never one so well-planned as this one. Consider the circumstances of this crime carefully, and I am sure that you will agree with me that it was unusually well-planned.

4. Since it is impossible to prove that immortality is false, there being absolutely no positive evidence against it, we may rest assured in the confident belief that our souls are immortal.

5. Religion brought intolerance into the world, denied freedom of thought, retarded scientific progress, and was a divisive influence in that it separated group from group, each creed believing that it alone was good and all others bad. Therefore religion has done more harm than good.

6. Why do I think the Demlican party is the best? Because that is the way my father voted.

7. I know that there will never be an atomic war because I just couldn't bear to think about what will happen to the human race if there is such a war.

C. Identify the evasions in the following and explain your answers. State the probandum in each case.

1. But, Doctor, surely your advice that I should cut down on my smoking for health reasons cannot be sound, since I see that you yourself are a chain smoker.

2. Vivisection is wrong because it is wrong to dissect living animals for experimental purposes.

3. Free enterprise is not as good a system as socialism. I need only point out to you that free enterprise does not work perfectly. There are losses as well as profits, depressions as well as booms. Letting everyone decide things for himself will not result in a perfect state.

4. *Open the door, Richard* must be the greatest song ever written. No other song ever became so popular in so short a time, and since music is written for the public, what the public approves of must be the best.

5. Modern art is greater than traditional art because all the best critics say so. Who are the best critics? You can identify them by the fact that they prefer modern art to traditional art.

6. Our senator is about the worst we ever had. I just can't stand his sanctimonious manner and his preaching to other countries in a holier-than-thou manner. And I feel like screaming whenever I hear that he is making another junket to Europe.

7. Russia has real freedom, and capitalism allows no freedom. What proof do I have? Because, by definition, capitalism enslaves the workers.

8. What does this child psychologist know about raising children! He doesn't even have any children of his own.

9. ELMER: I oppose all forms of imperialism, both the Russian type and the type represented by the Marshall Plan.
   PHIL: But the Marshall Plan is not imperialism in the usual sense of that term.
   ELMER: Oh, so you think that the Marshall Plan represents a policy of pure benevolence on the part of the United States?

10. Every human being believes in God whether he admits it or not, for this belief is universal in the human race.

11. The universe must have had a beginning. There have been many philosophers and scientists during the last 2,000 years who have tried to prove that the universe had no beginning. It is generally agreed that not one of these "proofs" will stand up.

12. PARENT: If you expect to graduate from college you will have to put more time in your studies.
    SON: In other words you want me to give up all my social

and athletic activities and do nothing but study from morning until night!

13. Dromedary cigarettes are without question easiest on the throat and most healthful. Our private statistical researches prove beyond doubt that more doctors smoke Dromedary than any other brand.

14. "Crime is a disease." "Well, but how about J. P., the head-waiter, who went to jail for income tax evasion? He seemed like a normal man to me." "Oh, he was sick, very sick." "But how do you know that?" "By the very fact that he committed a crime, for crime is a disease."

15. This witness is not telling the truth for he was convicted of perjury some years ago.

16. I would not hire X as a professor at this University. I have reason to believe that he is a communist.

17. Segregation must prevail, for it can be proved scientifically that human beings differ in all sorts of ways.

18. We'll give this here hoss thief a fair trial, but send to town for a good strong rope.

19. A Chicago newspaper commented as follows on ex-President Truman's statement that "we won that war for freedom": "Whose? The Poles? The Lithuanians? The Hungarians? The Yugoslavs? They were all freer before the war for freedom. They are all, and many others besides, enslaved now."

20. Will the farmer benefit by the increased wages which labor will receive if we raise our tariffs? There is no question that he will, since labor will buy more of the products of the farm.

21. Since I have tried every conceivable way I can think of to solve this puzzle, and have gotten absolutely nowhere, I can only conclude that there is no solution for it.

22. We should not prepare for war, for from so wicked a thing as war there can come only doom immeasurable.

23. You say that the United States has the highest living standards of any nation in the world? I can disprove that statement by pointing to the sharecroppers in the South. Is that what you mean by a high living standard?

24. The Constitution of the United States embodies a truly good form of government, for its founders were unquestioned experts in political theory.

25. Commerce students should not be required to take courses in liberal arts such as literature and philosophy. Why not? Because such courses are not worth taking.

26. I would not hire X as a professor at this university. I believe that he is prejudiced against Jews, Catholics, and Negroes.

27. I shall prove that the corrupt Demlican Party does not deserve your support and that the reliable Republocrat Party does.

28. If every person over sixty were given a pension of $200 per month, then they would buy more goods; this would increase the need for workers, whose wages would rise, and they in turn would raise their standard of living. Business would be kept at a high level, and everyone would benefit.

29. I pay no attention to writers who criticize communism for they are all prejudiced. The fact that they criticize communism is in itself proof that they are prejudiced.

30. Karl Marx and F. Engels, in the *Communist Manifesto:* "But don't wrangle with us so long as you apply, to our intended abolition of bourgeois property, the standard of your bourgeois notions of freedom, culture, law, etc. Your very ideas are but the outgrowth of your bourgeois production and bourgeois property, just as your jurisprudence is but the will of your class made into a law for all, a will whose essential character and direction are determined by the economic conditions of existence of your class."

31. Bishop Wilberforce scored a telling hit in his famous debate with Thomas Huxley on the subject of evolution. He simply inquired casually whether Huxley was descended from the monkeys on his mother's side or his father's side of the family. (Clarke).

32. Salesman to undecided customer: "Shall I wrap it up, or do you wish to have it delivered?"

33. A pacifist argued that all wars are morally evil. When a friend asked if he meant that we should not fight even if an enemy attacked us, he answered, "But no one will attack us."

34. A railroad spokesman said, "The Union's spokesman accuses us of speaking the language of the railroads. We wouldn't dream of suggesting that he speaks the language of the unions."

35. Aristotle stated that "the good" meant that which the good man approves. *(Nichomachean Ethics.)*

36. How long, oh America, will you tolerate the misrule of the party in power? They have squandered public funds and denied the people the services they are entitled to; they have raised taxes and unbalanced the budget; they have inflated

the currency and raised interest rates; they have allowed foreign goods to be sold in this country and they have antagonized our friends abroad; it's time for a change!

37. Nietzsche: "Those who disagree with me when I say that mankind is corrupt prove that they are already corrupted.

38. The ideas of "progress" and "individualism" are products of eighteenth century philosophers, and they reflect the special conditions of that age. So these ideas are out of date today and not valid for our society with its different social and economic conditions.

39. Psychological hedonism is the theory that every human action is always motivated by the individual's desire to benefit himself alone in what he does. If the opponent of this theory presents the case of a marine who threw himself on a grenade, giving up his own life in order to save his buddies from certain death, the psychological hedonist is not impressed. He argues that it must have been done for selfish reasons, as proved by the very fact that it was done.

40. A well-known editorial writer wrote isolationist editorials for the *New York Daily News* and interventionist articles for *Collier's* in 1940. Would this information have been relevant to the truth of what he said in either publication?

41. The House of David sect in Benton Harbor, Michigan, was reported to believe that every member of the sect was immortal. When it was pointed out that the members showed the same mortality rates as other groups, the answer was that those who died were not true believers, since if they were they would not have died.

42. In 1941, in a radio debate, Frederick J. Libby argued that it was against the best interests of the United States to help England or otherwise meddle in the "European" war. Thomas Y. Elliot remarked that Mr. Libby's objections were without merit, since he was head of a "Christian Pacifist" organization, which was opposed to all wars, whether they were aggressive or defensive and for whatever reason they might be fought. Mr. Libby accused Mr. Elliot of the argumentum ad hominem. Was his objection justified?

43. "In what grave and important discussion," a Van Buren editor asked, "are the Whig journals engaged? How are they enlightening the public mind and supplying material for that deep and solemn reflection which befits a great people about to choose a ruler? We speak of the divorce of the bank and the state; and the Whigs reply with a dissertation on

the merits of hard cider. We defend the policy of the administration; and the Whig answers, 'log cabin,' 'big canoes,' 'Go it, Tip, come it, Ty.' We urge the re-election of Van Buren because of his honesty, sagacity, statesmanship, and show the weakness and unfitness of his opponent; and the Whigs answer that Harrison is a poor man and lives in a log cabin. We show that he is not a poor man, that he does not drink hard cider except from choice, that his home is not a log cabin but a fine house; . . . the Whigs reply, 'No matter, the prairies are on fire.' " (*J. B. McMaster, A History of the People of the United States:* Vol. 6, p. 565, D. Appleton-Century Company, 1906.)

44. "Treason can never prosper. What's the reason?
That when it prospers none will call it treason."

Chapter 7

Syllogisms, Propositions, and Terms

Section I: Introduction to the Syllogism

In the previous chapter we noted the significance of the law of rationality, which requires that the evidence or reasons should be sufficient to prove our beliefs or conclusions. We also noted the distinction between arguments containing conclusive proof and arguments in which evidence is merely sufficient to establish probabilities. The remainder of Part Two will be devoted to the principles of conclusive proof, or *validity*.

The argument is the fundamental unit of reasoning. We shall study various types of arguments, but our chief emphasis will be devoted to the *syllogism,* one of the basic forms of deductive reasoning. The syllogism will be defined, in a very broad sense, as an argument in which two premises lead to a conclusion. The importance of this form of reasoning has been recognized by logicians since the time of Aristotle (384–322 B.C.), though Aristotle, it may be noted here, treated it in a limited manner, and analyzed only one of its types. Much misunderstanding, however, is still prevalent concerning the nature of the syllogism. It has been called "artificial" and "outmoded." We shall endeavor to show that such criticisms rest on misunderstandings, and to justify, at least in part, the following statement by the American philosopher, W. P. Montague.

> Far from being artificial or outmoded, the Aristotelian syllogisms are the blood and flesh, or at least the connective tissue, of all human discourse; and indifference to the logical laws which they exemplify is intellectual triviality, for it means indifference to the laws of any possible universe that the intellect can comprehend. (*The Ways of Things,* Prentice-Hall, 1940, p. 35.)

154

We shall begin our discussion of the syllogism with the simplest kinds of examples, and develop the complexity of the subject by gradual stages. In order to facilitate our understanding of the logical form of such arguments we shall state them in the schematic form show below. This form of presentation, which misleads many persons into thinking that syllogisms are "artificial," is adopted because it clearly indicates the structure of the argument. Thus:

> All men are mortal.
> Socrates is a man.
> Therefore,   Socrates is mortal.

The form of this syllogism is "artificial" in the sense that people do not argue in this schematic form. In ordinary discourse, as Montague has put it, the same argument might go like this: "Socrates, yes, even the divine Socrates, must be mortal, because we know that he is a man, and, alas we have to remember that whoever is man is also mortal." We shall deal with arguments in ordinary language in due course, but we will use the schematic form whenever we wish to clarify the logical structure of a syllogism.

Let us now consider the essential nature of syllogistic reasoning. Consider the following set of circles:

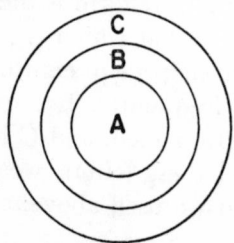

There are three circles, marked A, B, and C. B is inside C, and A is inside B. We shall now construct a syllogistic argument concerning these circles: If a circle B is inside a circle C, and A is inside circle B, then A must be inside C.

Stated schematically, we find:

> B is inside C.
> A is inside B.
> Therefore,   A is inside C.

If the premises of this syllogism are granted, then we must accept the conclusion. In this simple example we find the essential meaning of "validity": *An argument is valid when the premises necessitate the conclusion.* If it is impossible, granted the truth of the premises, that the conclusion should be false, then the argument is valid. If the reader grasps this simple example of valid reasoning, then he will be able to understand the more complicated examples, for all rest on principles of the same order.

In a valid argument, the truth of the premises guarantees the truth of the conclusion. Why is this so? We shall not attempt to answer this question, if indeed an answer is possible, but we will assume that we live in the kind of world in which such things are so and that the "light" of reason guides us correctly in such matters. If we know that a letter is inside an envelope and that the envelope is locked in a trunk, then it follows that the letter is inside the trunk. In any event, we shall assume that such reasoning is logically correct.

If we now return to the Socrates syllogism, we shall find that its validity rests upon the same principles. Its form or structure is exactly the same as the circles illustration. As logicians interested in validity, we are concerned with form or structure, rather than with content. The form is the framework or mold; the material or content is that which is poured into the mold. The use of symbols will help us to exhibit forms, and we shall therefore use symbols frequently. Let us then substitute the letters A for Socrates, B for men, and C for mortal. If we now draw circles for each of these letters, we will have exactly the same circles illustration we used above:

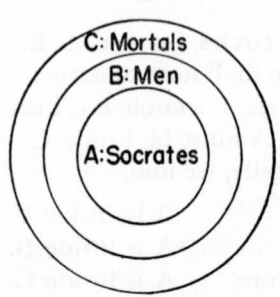

Note that the order of the *premises* of an argument is immaterial. We might have stated our argument as follows:

Socrates is a man.   A is inside B.
All men are mortal.   or   B is inside C.
Therefore, Socrates is mortal.   Therefore, A is inside C.

Diagrams enable us to "see" the structure of arguments with the eye of the senses as well as with the eye of the mind, and we shall resort frequently to diagrammatic illustrations. The use of these diagrams in logic is similar to their use in geometry. They are not indispensable, but they are very helpful aids in reasoning. We shall usually use circles, but other types of diagrams might also be used, such as maps. For example, examine the following syllogism:

The residents of the 15th ward are residents of the North Shore.

The residents of the Gold Coast are residents of the 15th ward.

Therefore, The residents of the Gold Coast are residents of the North Shore.

This syllogism might be illustrated by the following map:

This map shows that the syllogism is valid, just as the circles do. The circles, however, are easier to draw, and are generally preferred.

An introductory word concerning the relationship of "validity" to "truth" may be considered at this point.* A valid argument is one in which the premises "necessitate" the conclusion. This means that *if* the premises are true, then the conclusion must be true, or, stated in a different way, that it is impossible for the premises to be true and for the conclusion to be false.

* A more thorough discussion will be found in Chapter 14, Section II, page 329.

The actual truth or falsity of the premises is irrelevant. We ask: "If we *assume* that the premises are true, would the conclusion have to be true?" In Part Two we shall be concerned with structure, not with content; with the *form* of the argument rather than with the *truth* of what is stated. Thus (1) an invalid argument may be composed of true statements, and (2) a valid argument may be composed of false statements. Examples of each of these possibilities are as follows:

> (1) All Muscovites are human beings.
>   All Russians are human beings.
> Therefore, All Muscovites are Russians.

> (2) All Holy Rollers are chain-smokers.
>   All Moslems are Holy Rollers.
> Therefore, All Moslems are chain-smokers.

The first of these syllogisms is invalid, even though each statement is true. It is invalid because the premises do not logically justify the conclusion. (The reasons for its invalidity will be discussed later.) The second syllogism is valid, even though each of its constituent statements is false. Its form is exactly the same as our circles illustration, as you will find if you substitute *A* for Moslems, *B* for Holy Rollers, and *C* for chain-smokers. A valid argument is one in which the premises necessitate the conclusion. *If* these premises were true, then this conclusion would have to be true. A wholly satisfactory argument, of course, is one in which the premises are true, and the reasoning valid; but our only concern at present is with the meaning of validity.

Section II: The Categorical Proposition and Its Parts

In the last section we became acquainted with some simple examples of syllogistic reasoning. We saw how the validity of an argument could be exhibited through the use of circles or other types of diagrams. In the course of our study we shall find that not all syllogisms are so simple as those we have examined, and we shall also learn that syllogisms are not all of the same type. We have begun with examples of the "categorical syllogism," and shall deal with such syllogisms exclusively in the first few chapters of Part Two. We shall then go on to study hypothetical and alternative syllogisms. Syllogisms are classified on the basis of the types of propositions which enter into their construction. We shall, accordingly, study different types of propositions.* The same thought, moreover, may be expressed by different types of propositions. As examples of different types of propositions which may express the same thought, consider the following: (1) "Good readers are persons who find logic an easy subject," and (2) "If a person is a good reader then he finds logic an easy subject." The first of these is categorical, which means "unconditional"; the second is hypothetical, or "conditional." The first simply states a fact without conditions. The second, that something will be the case on the condition that something else will hold. But for the time being, we shall confine our attention to categorical propositions.

Our first task is to analyze categorical propositions which contain subjects and predicates. These terms are defined as follows:

Subject. The thing or entity of which we assert something.
Predicate. That which is asserted of the subject.

Examples: The desk is brown. "Desk" is the subject; that of which we make an assertion. "Brown" is that which we assert of the subject. Or: Dogs are animals. "Dogs" is the subject, and "animals" the predicate. When we speak of "subject" in logic, we always mean the *complete* subject. In "The desk which was bought five years ago and which was moved out of this room yesterday by two men wearing blue jeans is an antique" all the words preceding the verb "is" constitute the subject.

A categorical proposition (of the subject-predicate type) is made up of various elements: (1) The subject and predicate are called *terms.* Thus there are two terms; a *subject term,* and a *predicate term.* (2) There is the *copula* (a word meaning "that which joins"), which joins the subject term to the predicate term. The copula will always take a form of the verb "to be." ("Men *are* mortal." "This section *is* hard to understand." "I *am* a student of logic.") Note, however, that "is" and "are" are copulas only when they link the subject to the predicate. In

---

* A proposition, as we learned earlier, is a sentence which is either true or false. Not all sentences are either true or false; for example, directive sentences or interrogative sentences. A proposition, in other words, states that something *is* or *is not* the case. We need not know whether a sentence is true or false in order to call it a proposition, as in "There is oil beneath this building." We do not know whether this statement is true or false, but it is surely one or the other.

"Students who are conscientious are bound to succeed" only the second "are" is the copula. The first is simply part of the subject term. And finally, (3) there are the "quantifiers," words such as "all," "some," "no," or "none," which indicate the extent to which we refer to the members of the subject term, as in "All men are mortal" or "Some women are fickle." When no quantifier is stated, "All" is generally understood. Individual subjects like "This desk" and "Socrates" have no quantifiers.

In graphic form, the proposition consists of the following elements:

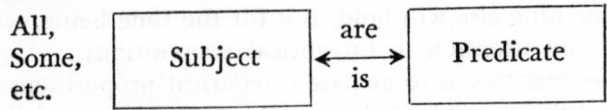

Exercises

Identify the subject term, predicate term, copula, and quantifiers (if any):

1. Some movie stars are happily married.
2. All birds are members of a class of vertebrata called "aves."
3. Socrates is mortal.
4. Dogs are friendly animals.
5. Birds which are in the hand are things equivalent to two in the bush.
6. The ships which sailed last night are sloops which are very fast.

Section III: The Class-Analysis of Subject-Predicate Propositions

We shall interpret all subject-predicate propositions as asserting that two classes have certain relations to each other. This means that we shall think of the subject term as referring to a class of individuals or things, and similarly with the predicate. Let us carefully define the meaning of "class." A class means a group of things, or a collection of things having some characteristic in common. This characteristic may be a "natural" one, as in the group of things called "mammals." The common characteristic may also result from an arbitrary act of selection, as in

"The people you saw on the street today." These people constitute a group having in common the fact that they were seen by you today. The class may consist of individuals who do not take more than two lumps of sugar in their coffee. Thus there are no limitations on grouping any entities into a class. We may even find a common characteristic between "a very heavy elephant" and "the thought of the square root of minus one in an angel's mind." They belong to the class of things which were used as illustrations in this paragraph.

Every entity may be said to belong to an infinite number of classes. Thus "tiger" belongs to the following classes and to an infinite number of others: existing things, physical things, living things, things found in jungles, in zoos, things which inspired the poems of William Blake, and so on.

A class, then, is any collection of things having some common characteristic. The members of a class need not be actually existing things. We may speak of "sprinters who can run one hundred yards in less than nine seconds" or "human beings who are without sin," though neither class has any members. A class having no members is called a "null" class.

The importance of thinking of subjects and predicates as classes of things will soon become evident when we begin to test the validity of syllogisms by the use of diagrams. When we think of "Orioles are birds" as representing two classes of things, the manner in which the circles should be drawn is immediately apparent. Similarly with "Birds are living organisms." These propositions may be diagrammed separately or they be combined, as in the following:

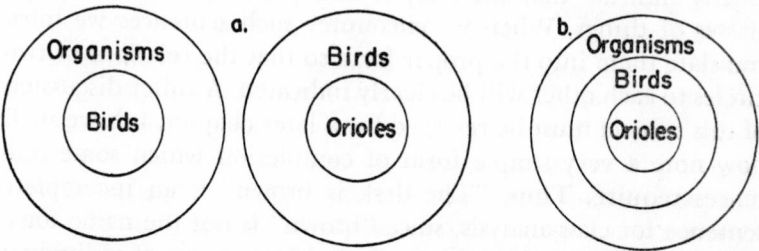

These relationships may also be exhibited by a "map" that emphasizes the fact that the classes are always collections of individuals. In the following "map" diagram each small circle stands for an individual member of the class to which it belongs:

LIVING ORGANISMS

```
┌─────────────────────────┬─────────────────────────┐
│  o o o o o o o o         │  o o o o o o o          │
│                         │                         │
│  o o o o o o o o         │  o o o o o o o          │
│     PLANTS              │   ANIMALS               │
│                         │         ┌───────────────┤
│  o o o o o o o o         │         │ Birds         │
│                         │  o o o   │ o o o o o o   │
│  o o o o o o o o         │         ├───────────────┤
│                         │         │ Orioles       │
│  o o o o o o o o o       │  o o o o │ o o o o       │
└─────────────────────────┴─────────┴───────────────┘
```

An important qualification of the above remarks must now be noted. Some sentences have single individuals as their subjects, as in "Ferdinand is a non-belligerent bull" or "This book is a logic text." In such cases the subject term is stated to be a *member* of the predicate class, and is not *included* within it. In other words, *class-inclusion* refers to the relationships of two classes to each other; *class-membership* to the relationship when the subject term is an individual. But though we shall have occasion to note situations in which this distinction is an important one, we shall nevertheless usually treat an individual subject in the same way as we treat a class. We shall use a circle to diagram the individual subject. We shall treat the individual, for most purposes, as a class having only one member and *include* it within another class.

The form in which many sentences are stated may not clearly indicate that the subject and predicate terms refer to classes of things. When we encounter such sentences we must translate them into the proper form so that the relations of two circles to each other will be clearly indicated. A fuller discussion of this subject must be reserved for a later chapter, but we shall now note a very simple form of completion which some sentences require. Thus, "The desk is brown" is an incomplete sentence for class-analysis, since "brown" is not the name for a collection of individual things. A class is made up of individual things, each of which could be pointed to, and it would be impossible to point to a "brown." When either subject or predicate is stated as an *adjective,* we must always add the "completing complement," or noun, in order to refer to a collection of individual things. Completed, the above sentence would read, "The desk is a brown thing." The sentence "All men are mortal" requires the addition of "beings," or we could simply add an "s" to "mortal," for "mortals" is a noun that refers to a class.

We shall now introduce the symbol <, using it to mean "class-inclusion" (or class membership). When this symbol stands between two classes, for example, A < B, we shall interpret it as meaning "A is (are) included in the class of B." The symbol is actually a substitute for the copula, and it emphasizes the relationship of the inclusion of one class in another. The grammatical copula *are* represents the more traditional type of usage; the symbol of inclusion "<," the more modern usage. We shall use both. Frequently, however, we shall find that the symbol expresses our meaning more accurately, especially when the subject is an individual. Thus, "Franco is a dictator" really means "Franco < dictators," i.e., "Franco is in the class of dictators." The symbol emphasizes the fact that the predicate class is a plural noun. Note carefully the exact words for which the symbol < stands: It means *"are included in the class of"* or *"is a member of the class of."*

Exercises

Restate the following sentences, substituting the symbol of class-inclusion (<) for the copula, and supply the missing quantifier and the completing complement where necessary. The predicate should be stated in the plural form in all cases. Read each proposition orally, using the words for which < stands.

For example: Suppose the sentence is, "Judges are trustworthy." We supply the missing quantifier "all" and add the completing complement "persons." The sentence now reads: "All judges are trustworthy persons." Using the symbol of class-inclusion we get: All judges < trustworthy persons. This is read as "All judges are included in the class of trustworthy persons."

1. Some movie stars are happily married.
2. Americans are peace-loving.
3. All philosophers are reflective.

4. Ferdinand is gentle.
5. Liberals are idealistic.
6. Liberals are idealists.
7. Her eyes are blue.
8. This book is a logic text.

Section IV: Affirmative and Negative Propositions

Propositions are classified according to their *quantity* and *quality*. The difference between "all" and "some" or between "none are" and "some are not" is a difference in quantity; the difference between affirmative and negative is one of "quality."

The propositions we have thus far examined have all been affirmative in quality. Each sentence asserted that a certain predicate may be affirmed of a subject. All have been of the form "S *is* P," using "S" for the subject of a categorical proposition and "P" for its predicate. But a categorical proposition may also assert that a certain predicate *cannot* be affirmed of a subject, i.e., that the predicate is *excluded* in whole or in part from the subject class. The presence of words like "no" or "not" usually indicate that a proposition is negative, as in "No S is P," or "Some S's are not P's," or "S is not P." Examples of such negative propositions in words are: "No men are angels," "Some men are not egoists," "Jayne Glamour is not an actress."

Note carefully the following sentences: "Nurses are non-combatants," "Nurses are not combatants." These sentences have the same meaning, but the first is stated affirmatively; the second, negatively. The difference between them centers in the copula. Does the copula indicate that the subject *is* something-or-other, or that it *is not?* There are many adjectives and nouns which are prefixed by "non," but the use of such terms does not make the propositions negative. The question is whether the negation belongs to the copula. "S is P" and "S is non-P" are both affirmative, but "S is not P" is negative. Note carefully that the form "No men are angels," (No S is P) asserts that angelic qualities cannot be affirmed of men. It means "Men *are not* angels," or "S *is not* P"; hence it is negative.

The symbol "$<$," we noted above, stands for class inclusion. It is an affirmative symbol. The corresponding negative symbol is "$\nless$" which stands for class-exclusion. When we say "S is not P" we mean that the class S is excluded from the class P (in whole or part, depending upon the quantifier). "$\prec$" stands for the words "are excluded from the class of." This symbol will be explained in greater detail in Section VI.

Exercises

Distinguish the copulas as affirmative or negative.

1. He is unwise.
2. He is not unwise.
3. No S is P.
4. No metals are non-conductors.
5. Some women are not intuitive.
6. Some nonfanatics are enthusiasts.
7. S is not non-P.
8. All non-S are non-P.
9. No non-fools are persons who do such things.
10. Teetotalers are persons who do not drink hard liquor.

Section V: Universal and Particular Propositions

In the last section we distinguished between affirmative and negative categorical propositions. We shall now classify propositions as "universal" or "particular." This distinction is based upon the extent to which we make reference to the members of the class of things named by the *subject* term. When we refer to *all* of the members of the subject class, as in "All nations are preparing for war," the proposition is universal. When reference is made only to *some* of the members of the subject class, as in "Some nations are preparing for war," the proposition is called particular. The distinction between universal and particular propositions is one of "quantity." When the quantifier is "all" the sentence is universal; when it is "some" the sentence is particular.

Similarly with negative propositions. The sentence "No men are angels" is universal, for it refers to all men, rather than merely to some. The quantifier "no" indicates a universal proposition. "Some students are not athletes" with the quantifier "some" is obviously particular. The term "particular," by the way, comes from an older usage in which it meant "referring to a *part* only," i.e., part of a class, not all of it.

Propositions which have an individual person or thing as subject are also classified as universal. Thus, "H. G. Wells was a second-rate novelist" or "This pen has a ballpoint" or "Carlyle was not a great man" are universals, though their subjects consist of single persons or things. The justification for this usage is that when the subject is an individual we refer to all of the subject, not to part of it.

There are thus two types of universal propositions, those which use the quantifier "all" and those which have an individual as subject. The former are called "general" and the latter "singular." But both are universals.

It is easy to distinguish any universal proposition from a particular proposition if we remember that a particular proposition always uses the quantifier "some" or other word (such as "many," "few") indicating that only part of the subject class is being referred to.

When the subject class has no quantifier, as in "Women are fickle," we may be uncertain as to whether the writer is referring to all women or only to some. As previously indicated, we shall adopt the convention of interpreting such indefinite statements as referring to all, unless the context makes it clear that "some" is intended. When the context does not indicate which quantifier is intended, assume that the proposition is universal.

To sum up, there are two types of universal propositions, general and singular. A universal-general proposition refers to *all* of the members of the subject class; a universal-singular has as its subject a *single* individual person or thing. A particular proposition is one which speaks of *some* of the members of the subject class. In tabular form:

Universal:
  General—*All* men are mortal. *No* men are angels.
    (Look for the quantifiers "all" or "no.")
  Singular—*This* table is brown. *John* is not a dancer.
    (A single thing or individual is the subject.)
Particular:
  The quantifier is *Some,* or any word which designates less than the whole of a class.

Exercises

Classify the following propositions as universal-general, universal-singular or particular:

1. All fish live in water.
2. Some dogs are homeless.
3. No textbooks are thrillers.
4. That theory is discredited.
5. You are wrong.
6. Lazy students are failures.
7. T. S. Eliot is a British subject.
8. Those apples look edible.
9. Some apples are not tangy.
10. That group of men should be watched.
11. Human beings are never satisfied.

Section VI: The Four Types of Categorical Propositions

We have classified propositions in terms of quantity and quality: as universal or particular, and as affirmative or negative. Combining the four elements in the two classifications, we derive four different combinations, which we shall label as A, E, I, and O in accordance with the custom of logicians:

Universal-Affirmative	A	form
Universal-Negative	E	form
Particular-Affirmative	I	form
Particular-Negative	O	form

Henceforth, we shall use the letters A, E, I, and O to signify the combinations for which they stand. These letters were originally used by mediaeval logicians, who derived them from the first two vowels in the two Latin words, *affirmo* (I affirm) and *nego* (I deny). Thus the affirmative forms are A and I; the negative forms are E and O. We shall now study these forms in detail and we shall diagram them in four different combinations of circles, a method of diagramming invented by the Swiss mathematician and physicist Euler (1707–1783).

1. The A-form

Examples: "All Arabs are Moslems" and "Ali-Baba is a Moslem."

The A-form (universal-affirmative) has the two types shown in the examples, the general and the singular. Using the symbols "S" for subject and "P" for predicate, "All S is P" represents the general form and "S is a P" represents the singular. We are already acquainted with the universal and affirmative nature of these types.

In class terminology, we write "All S < P" or "S (an individual) < P."

The same type of circle diagram will be used for both:

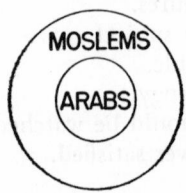

2. The E-form

Examples: "No Arabs are Hindus" and "Ali-Baba is not a Hindu."

The E-form (universal-negative) also has two types, general and singular. With respect to the *general* type, we recall that a universal proposition refers to *all* of the subject. The assertion that "No Arabs are Hindus" refers to *all* Arabs, for it states that each and every one of them is excluded from the class of Hindus. Similarly in "No logic texts are easy to read," we assert that all logic texts are outside the class of books which are easy to read. The E-form is thus universal, for it refers to *all* of the subject-class.

The E-form is negative for it denies that a certain predicate can be affirmed of the subject. It asserts that the subject does not belong to the predicate class; the relation of inclusion is denied *in toto*. This is the same as to say that the subject class is *completely excluded* from the predicate class.

The *singular* E-form, "Ali-Baba is not a Hindu," should be analyzed in the same manner. Here we say that the predicate cannot be affirmed of an individual, or that this individual is *excluded* from the predicate class. Individual subjects, as we saw earlier, are treated as universals.

In circles, we use the same form for the general and singular universal-negative. "No S is P," and "S (an individual) is not a P," are exhibited by two circles which have no point of contact, viz.:

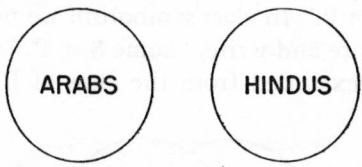

The symbol of class-exclusion, as we have noted, is "$\not<$," standing for the words "are excluded from the class of." The E-form in class terminology will take the following forms: "All Arabs $\not<$ Hindus," "Ali-Baba $\not<$ Hindus." These are read, "All Arabs are excluded from the class of Hindus," etc. Note carefully the sharp difference between the traditional statement of the E-form and its class statement: *"No S is P" and "All S $\not<$ P."* "No S is P" means that *all* of S is completely excluded from (outside of) the class of P.

3. The I-form

Example: "Some Arabs are Moslems."

The I-form (particular-affirmative) asserts that part of the subject class is included within the predicate class. "Some S is P." In diagrammatic form, we find that the S and P circles intersect:

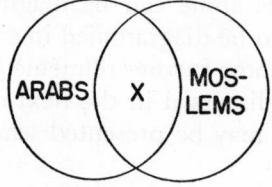

The area marked X indicates that there are individuals who are members of both classes.

In class symbolism: Some S < P.

4. The O-form

Example: "Some Arabs are not Moslems."

The O-form (particular-negative) asserts that some of the members of the subject class are excluded from, or are "outside of," the predicate class. This form is particular, since the quantifier is "some," and negative since it asserts that part of the subject *is not* in the predicate class. In the traditional manner we say, "Some S is not P." In class symbolism we use the symbol of exclusion once more and write, "Some S ⊄ P," which should be read, "Some S is excluded from the class of P."

In circles:

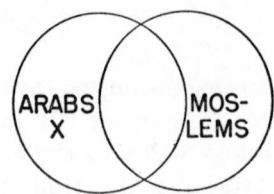

Note the position of the "X" in this diagram. It is in the subject circle outside of the predicate circle, and indicates that there are members of the subject class who are outside the predicate class. In the I-form, the position of the X indicated that there were some entities which were members of both classes.

The four types of categorical propositions reveal all of the possibilities in the relations of one class to another. There are four possibilities, covered by the forms we have designated under the letters, A, E, I, and O. One class is wholly or partially included within another, or it is wholly or partially excluded from another. These forms alone can be diagrammed in circles; a proposition which can be diagrammed in circles must be in one of these four forms. Some further refinements in the relations of these circles will be discussed in the next chapter.

The four forms may be presented schematically, as in the following table:

TYPES OF PROPOSITIONS		TRADITIONAL FORM	CLASS-TERMINOLOGY
A Universal-Affirmative	General	All S is P	All S < P
	Singular	X (an individual) is P	X < P
E Universal-Negative	General	No S is P	All S ⊄ P
	Singular	X (an individual) is not P	X ⊄ P
I Particular-Affirmative		Some S is P	Some S < P
O Particular-Negative		Some S is not P	Some S ⊄ P

The reader should carefully note the two forms of expression in which each type of proposition may be stated. The "traditional" form of expression states each type in ordinary language, and the "class-terminology" form expresses the same type in the symbols of class inclusion and exclusion. These different forms of expression are exactly equivalent to each other, and the reader should familiarize himself with these equivalences. Note in particular the two different ways in which the E-form is expressed.

Exercises

Classify the following propositions as, A, E, I, or O, and define each in terms of quantity and quality, (universal-affirmative, universal-negative, particular-affirmative and particular-negative).

1. No saints are sinners.
2. All politicians are interested in votes.
3. Some statesmen are politicians.
4. Some politicians are not statesmen.
5. Lewis is not a timid man.
6. Shakespeare is a great poet.
7. Some explanations are non-luminous.
8. Some types of non-compliance are worthy of chastisement.
9. All saints are excluded from the class of sinners.
10. Some citizens are excluded from the class of voters.
11. Those exercises are quite difficult.

Section VII: The Distribution of Terms

A new technical term, "distribution," must now be added to our logical vocabulary, and we will have completed our analysis of categorical propositions. This term is used in a precise and technical sense by logicians, and its customary meaning should be ignored. The understanding of this term is of great importance, since distribution is the fundamental idea in the analysis of the syllogism.

We shall speak of the "distribution" of terms. To say that a term is distributed means that we have referred to *all* of the members of the class designated by that term. Thus, when we say "All dogs are animals," the term "dogs" is distributed because we have referred to *all*. We have referred to each and every member of the class "dogs." In "Some books are texts" we have referred to only part of the class of "books," and the term "books" is undistributed.

We shall now examine the manner in which the A-E-I-O forms distribute their terms. Since it is quite easy to understand the notion of distribution when applied to the *subjects* of propositions, we shall dispose of this aspect of the problem very briefly, and then give a more extended discussion to the distribution of the predicate terms in each of the four forms.

The two universal propositions distribute their subject terms. The A-form (All dogs are mammals) distributes its subject "dogs" and the E-form (No crows are green birds) distributes its subject "crows." "No crows" refers to *all* crows, i.e., all crows are excluded from the predicate class.

The two particular propositions I (Some Americans are liberals) and O (Some Arabs are not Moslems) obviously refer to *some* Americans and *some* Moslems rather than to all, and so these subject terms are undistributed.

We turn now to the distribution of the *predicate terms* in each of the four forms.

1. The A-form: "All dogs are mammals."

This proposition does not say anything about *all* mammals. "Dogs" constitute only part of the class of mammals, so this sentence refers only to *some* mammals. "Mammals" is an undistributed term in this sentence. We may now generalize our analysis of this proposition: The predicate term is undistributed in every A-form proposition. Similarily we may generalize each of the analyses of the other forms.

In the typical A-form proposition, as in the one above, the predicate class is larger than the subject class. But the two classes may be co-extensive, as in "All triangles are 3-sided figures." In this case we know (from our knowledge of mathematics) that the subject class and the predicate class have the same members. But *as such,* an A-form proposition of the form "All S is P" tells us that its subject is distributed but it does *not* tell us that the predicate is. We shall therefore follow the rule that an A-form leaves its predicate undistributed. If we follow this rule we will never go beyond the information actually given to us.

We shall use the symbols "d" and "u" for distributed and undistributed. We may thus write our A-form as follows: All dogs (d) are mammals (u). Using S and P once more, and using the symbol of class inclusion, we have S(d) < P(u). Note that the quantifier "all" is unnecessary in this symbolic form, since "d" means "all." Note also that the singular A-forms are treated in the same manner as the general.

2. The E-form: "No crows are green birds."

The predicate term "green birds" is distributed here. The proposition states that "All crows are excluded from the class of green birds." This obviously means that *all green birds* are outside the class of crows, so an E-form distributes both its subject and predicate. We are given information concerning each and every member of both classes.

Using the symbols of distribution, our proposition may be written as "No crows (d) are green birds (d)." The student should become adept at translating all E-forms into class terminology, viz.: "All crows (d) are excluded from the class of green birds (d)," or "All crows (d) ⊄ green birds (d)." In completely symbolic form, this would read: S(d) ⊄ P(d). The singular E-form is treated in the same manner.

3. The I-form: "Some Americans are liberals."

The predicate term is undistributed. We are informed that the two classes, Americans and liberals, overlap, i.e., that some Americans are liberals and, conversely, that some liberals are Americans. We have received no information concerning *all* liberals. We have not been told that *all* liberals are Americans, but only that some are. Thus the predicate "liberals" is undistributed. In class-symbols: S(u) < P(u).

4. The O-form: "Some Arabs are not Moslems."

The predicate of an O-form is distributed. The proposition asserts that all Moslems are completely outside the group designated by the subject term. This will become clear if we remember that many of the Arabs of Lebanon are Christians. These Arabs are "some" Arabs, and none of them are Moslems, so all

Moslems are completely "outside of" these Arabs of Lebanon.

Another example may be helpful. If I say that "Some students are not Republicans," I refer to the entire class of Republicans. Look through the entire class of Republicans, I am saying, and you will not find any of these particular students. They are outside of the entire class. Any negative proposition, in other words, in saying "not" *excludes* its subject term from the entire class designated by the predicate term, and its predicate is distributed. The O-form in symbols: $S(u) \not< P(d)$.

Our discussion of the distribution of terms in the A-E-I-O forms may be summed up in the following table:

		Subject	Pred-icate	Traditional form	Class ter-minology
Universals	Aff. A	d	u	All Sd is Pu	Sd < Pu
	Neg. E	d	d	No Sd is Pd	Sd ≮ Pd
Particulars	Aff. I	u	u	Some Su is Pu	Su < Pu
	Neg. O	u	d	Some Su is not Pd	Su ≮ Pd

As an aid to memory, two simple summary principles will be helpful:

(1) Affirmative propositions (A and I) never distribute the predicate term.
(2) Negative propositions (E and O) always distribute the predicate term.

The distribution of the subject term is indicated by the quantifier and should be quite easy to figure out.

Exercises

Classify the following propositions (a) as affirmative-negative, (b) as universal-particular, (c) as general-singular (where relevant), (d) as A, E, I, or O, and (e) indicate the distribution of the subjects and predicates of each:

1. All composers are geniuses.
2. Johann Sebastian Bach is a genius.
3. No composers are geniuses.
4. Philip Emanuel Bach is not a genuis.
5. Some composers are geniuses.
6. Some composers are not geniuses.

Chapter 8

The Analysis of Categorical Syllogisms

Section I: The Definition of the Syllogism

A syllogism, in the broad sense of the word, is an argument made up of two premises and a conclusion. There are, as we noted in the previous chapter, different types of syllogisms, but we are at present concerned only with the categorical type, sometimes called the "Aristotelian" syllogism, since it was the only type recognized by Aristotle. A categorical syllogism is an argument made up of three categorical propositions, which contain between them three and only three terms.

Later on, we shall study non-categorical types of syllogisms. The fundamental distinction between the categorical and the non-categorical types lies in the types of the propositions of which the syllogism is composed. Categorical syllogisms are composed of categorical propositions, which are made up of terms. Such propositions are called "simple," as distinguished from propositions whose constituent elements are sub-propositions. The latter are called "compound." The following is an example of one type of compound proposition: "If all men are rational beings, then all men are entitled to justice." This proposition has two sub-propositions as its constituent elements: "All men are rational beings" and "All men are entitled to justice." Non-categorical syllogisms are based upon compound propositions. But we shall come to these later. For the time being we shall be concerned exclusively with categorical propositions and categorical syllogisms.

A categorical syllogism may be more precisely defined as an argument composed of two categorical premises and a categorical conclusion, containing three and only three terms, in which the three terms are combined in such a way that a term in one premise will be the same as the term in another premise, and the other two terms will be the same as the terms which appear in the conclusion. The reader need not bother to memorize this definition, since its meaning will become quite clear in a moment. The definition indicates that a relation between two classes of things is established by virtue of their relation to a third class. For example, let us suppose that we are concerned with the question as to whether hay fever is in the class of infectious diseases. The solution of this problem requires that we relate these two classes to a third class. We must seek for a third term which will connect the two terms with which we begin. We may connect them by the class of "allergy diseases." Since we know that "all allergy diseases are non-infectious" and that "hay fever is an allergy disease," we draw the conclusion that "hay fever is not infectious." This is an example of a categorical syllogism.

In this chapter we shall be concerned with the analysis of categorical syllogisms, with the primary aim of learning the rules of validity in such arguments. We shall also learn how to check the rules of validity by drawing diagrams. For clarity in presentation we shall begin by stating all syllogisms in a schematic or "artificial" form and deal with syllogisms as they appear in living discourse in a later chapter. The difficulties encountered in analyzing complicated syllogisms, as we shall see, are chiefly problems of language and not of form.

Section II: Basic Words in the Analysis of Categorical Syllogisms

The categorical syllogism is an argument containing two premises and a conclusion.

> All actors are egoists. ⎱
> All movie stars are actors. ⎰ *Premises*
> Therefore, All movie stars are egoists⎰ *Conclusion*

There are three propositions, each with a subject and predicate term. There are three different terms in the syllogism, each of which is used twice. The three terms (or classes of things) in our example are "actors," "egoists," and "movie stars." Each term is used twice, making three pairs of terms. Henceforth, when we speak of a "term" we must remember that it is used twice.

The terms are called "middle term," "major term," and "minor term." These words are defined as follows:

Middle term: The term which appears in *both premises.* Since each term is used twice, and twice only, the middle term does not appear in the conclusion. "Actors" is the middle term.

Major term: The *predicate* of the *conclusion* is called the "major" term. "Egoists," the predicate of the conclusion, is the major term. The major term also appears in the first premise, "All actors are egoists."

Minor term: The *subject* of the *conclusion* is called the "minor" term: "Movie stars." It also appears in the premise, "All movie stars are actors."

In analyzing syllogisms we shall use symbols for our three terms. The choice of symbols is an arbitrary matter. Traditionally, logicians have used M for the middle term, S for the minor term, and P for the major term, and we shall adopt this practice for the most part. Since S stands for the subject of the *conclusion* (minor term), and P for the predicate of the conclusion (major term), we must mark the minor and major terms in the conclusion before we can mark them in the premises.

Using these symbols, we use "S" for "movie stars," "P" for egoists, and "M" for "actors." Symbolized, our syllogism reads as follows:

All M are P.
All S are M.
Therefore, All S are P.

Another convenient way of symbolizing is to use the first letter of each term. This would give us A for actors, M for movie stars, and E for egoists, and we would have:

All A are E.
All M are A.
Therefore, All M are E.

The *major premise* is the premise which contains the *major term* (and the middle term), and the *minor premise* is the premise which contains the *minor term* (and the middle term). We must examine the conclusion of the syllogism to determine the minor and major terms: these are, by definition, the subject and predicate terms of the conclusion.

Exercises

Identify the middle term, major term, and minor term in the syllogisms below. Note that each type of term appears twice. Also identify the premises as major or minor.

1. All men are mortal.
   Socrates is a man.
   ∴ Socrates is mortal.
2. All politicians are opportunists.
   No statesmen are opportunists.
   ∴ No politicians are statesmen.
3. All A are B.
   No C are B.
   ∴ No C are A.
4. Some K are M.
   No N are M.
   ∴ Some K are not N.

Section III: Preliminary Analysis of Categorical Syllogisms

The analysis of a syllogism requires the application of certain techniques. We shall illustrate these techniques by applying them to the syllogism in Section I. (Since we have not yet examined the rules of validity, our analysis at this stage must be of a preliminary nature.)

Step 1. Write out the syllogism, symbolizing the terms with the letters S, P, and M, viz.:

All actors are egoists.
     M   P
All movie stars are actors.
     S   M
∴ All movie stars are egoists.
       S   P

Step 2. Identify each proposition as an A, E, I, or O form. We find that each of these propositions is in A-form. We then place the symbols for "distributed" (d) and "undistributed" (u) to the right of the symbols M, S, and P in each proposition. The chart on page 174 can be used as a guide for reference as to the distribution of subjects and predicates in the four forms. Our syllogism will now look like this:

A-form	All actors are egoists.
	$\overline{\text{M d}}$ $\overline{\text{P u}}$
A-form	All movie stars are actors.
	$\overline{\text{S d}}$ $\overline{\text{M u}}$
A-form	∴ All movie stars are egoists.
	$\overline{\text{S d}}$ $\overline{\text{P u}}$

Step 3. As a final step at this stage, "gather" the symbols, stating them in the class analysis form:

$$Md < Pu$$
$$Sd < Mu$$
$$\therefore Sd < Pu$$

Note that the quantifiers need not be stated when we use the symbols, since the signs of distribution indicate whether the propositions are A-E-I-O forms.

We are now ready to study the rules which determine whether a syllogism is valid or invalid.

Section IV: The Rules of the Categorical Syllogism

There are five rules which determine the validity of a categorical syllogism. A syllogism which complies with each of these rules, i.e., which violates none of them, is valid. A syllogism which violates any one of these rules is invalid.

The rules of the syllogism resemble the axioms of mathematics in that they are assumptions or principles which are not proved but accepted as true. But though we shall not attempt to prove the rules, diagrams and other forms of illustrations may help us to "see" that these rules must hold. As we noted earlier, if all of B is in C, and A is in B, then A must be in C. The principle involved in this reasoning may be generalized: If one class is wholly included within another, then any part of the first class is part of the second. Why is this so? Some thinkers hold that this is simply a characteristic of the language which we speak, others that logical relations are grounded in the nature of things, so that we simply "see" that these principles characterize the world in which we live. The latter view would appear to be nearer the truth. In any case, however, we must recognize that not all logical principles can be proved, since every proof requires the use of principles which are themselves not proved.

The five rules or axioms of the syllogism may be divided into two groups, as follows:

A. Rules concerning the proper distribution of terms (rules of quantity):

> Rule 1. The middle term must be distributed at least once.
>
> Rule 2. A term which is undistributed in a premise must also be undistributed in the conclusion.*

B. Rules concerning negative propositions (rules of quality):

> Rule 3. No conclusion is necessitated by two negative premises.
>
> Rule 4. If either premise is negative, then the conclusion must be negative.
>
> Rule 5. A negative conclusion cannot be drawn from two affirmative premises.

We shall now study these rules in detail. But before we analyze a syllogistic argument in terms of the rules, we should inspect it in order to determine whether it meets the definition of a categorical syllogism. It must have three and only three terms, each of which is used twice, with a middle term appearing in each of the premises.

Rule 1. The middle term must be distributed at least once.

Consider the following argument:

> All brain surgeons are highly trained men.
> All jet pilots are highly trained men.
> Therefore, All jet pilots are brain surgeons.

This foolish argument illustrates the following principle: the fact that two classes of things have one or more characteristics in common does not justify us in concluding that the two classes are identical, or even that one is included within the other. Brain surgeons and jet pilots share the characteristic of

---

* Note that this rule does not require that a term which is distributed in a premise must also be distributed in the conclusion. It means only that if a term is undistributed in a premise it must not be distributed in the conclusion. In other words, we must never go from "u" in a premise to "d" in the conclusion.

being highly trained men, but we can draw no conclusions about their relationships to each other from this information.

As logicians, however, we must exhibit the fallacy in terms of the technical rules of the syllogism. We begin by setting up the syllogism in accordance with our method of analysis:

A-form   All brain surgeons are highly trained men.
                  P d   M u

A-form   All jet pilots are highly trained men.
                 S d   M u

A-form ∴. All jet pilots are brain surgeons.
                 S d   P u

Rule 1 tells us that the middle term must be distributed at least once. We note that the middle term is "highly trained men" symbolized by "M." We note that "M" is undistributed ("u") in both premises. Rule 1 has been violated. This argument contains the fallacy of "the undistributed middle term."

Let us pause for a moment to examine the rationale of Rule 1. But first, let us be clear as to what "validity" means. A valid argument is one in which the conclusion necessarily follows from the premises. This means that if we grant the truth of the premises we *must* grant the truth of the conclusion. An invalid argument is one in which the conclusion is not thus necessitated.

The meaning of validity in this connection will become clearer if we illustrate by the circle diagrams. We ask the question: Is it possible to draw the circles in such a way that the premises will be shown to be true, without showing that the conclusion must be true? If we can do this then we have shown that the premises do not necessitate the conclusion.

The major premise tells us that "all brain surgeons are highly trained men." In circles:

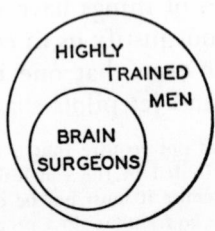

The minor premise tells us that "jet pilots are highly trained men." Now, this question: Can you put a circle for "jet pilots" inside the "highly trained men" circle without showing that jet pilots are brain surgeons? If you can, then you have shown that the conclusion drawn by the syllogism is not necessitated, and the argument is invalid. Thus:

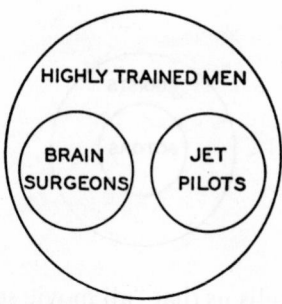

Note that it is of no importance that you are able to draw a diagram showing that the conclusion *might* be true. The only question is: Is it possible to draw a diagram in which the conclusion is *not* true? This is the only thing we need to show in order to demonstrate that the syllogism is invalid.*

* The premises require us to draw jet pilots *wholly within* the class of *highly trained men*. Thus there are five different ways in which the minor premise may be drawn in conjunction with the major premise:

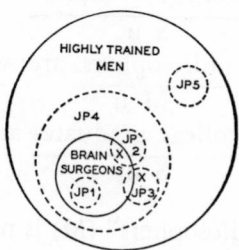

JP 1 shows jet pilots as wholly included within brain surgeons, JP 2 shows them as partially within, and JP 3 as partially outside; JP 4 shows *brain surgeons* as wholly within the class of jet pilots, and JP 5 shows jet pilots as wholly outside the class of brain surgeons. The conclusion asserted that JP 1 was necessitated by the premises; the diagram shows that this location of jet pilots is not necessitated. It is sufficient for our purposes to exhibit *one* possibility *other than* the conclusion asserted by the argument. In our illustration we drew "jet pilots" at JP 5 to show the invalidity of the argument.

"All actors are egoists":

In a valid argument, on the other hand, it is impossible to draw circles which show the premises to be true without at the same time showing the conclusion to be true. Let us illustrate with the "actors" argument, a valid syllogism. We begin our diagramming by drawing circles for the major premise,

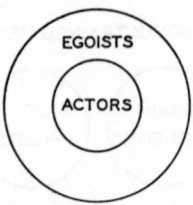

The minor premise tells us that "all movie stars are actors." Now the question: Can you draw the minor premise as required without showing that "All movie stars are egoists"? A glance will tell you that this is impossible, so the argument is valid.*

Here is another type of syllogism that involves the fallacy of the undistributed middle term: "Some college graduates are philosophers, and some philosophers are wealthy men; hence, some college graduates must be wealthy men." We set up this syllogism as follows:

I-form   Some college graduates are philosophers.
                          S u   M u
I-form   Some philosophers are wealthy men.
                          M u   P u
I-form   Some college graduates are wealthy men.
                          S u   P u

The middle term "philosophers" (M) is not distributed at least once. The diagram will exhibit the invalidity of this argument if we can draw circles which exhibit the truth of the premises without showing the truth of the conclusion. We proceed as follows: "Some college graduates are philosophers" gives us:

* Further refinements and special problems in diagramming syllogisms will be discussed in Sections VI and VII.

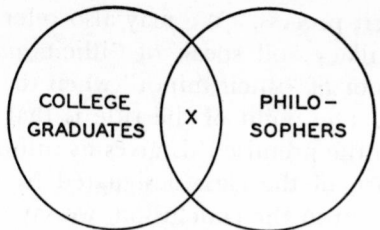

Now, can we draw a circle for "Some philosophers are wealthy men" without showing the conclusion drawn by the argument? We can:

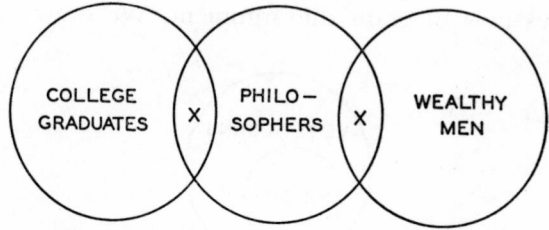

It is very important to note that the fact that the conclusion happens to be true is irrelevant with respect to the validity of a syllogism. The only question is: Do the premises *necessitate* the conclusion? From the premises given to us in this argument it does not necessarily follow that "some college graduates are wealthy men," so the argument is invalid.

Rule 2.   A term which is undistributed in a premise must also be undistributed in the conclusion.

The following syllogism contains a violation of this rule:

A-form   All Hindus are vegetarians.
          —————   —————————
            M d   P u
E-form   No Sikhs are Hindus.
          ————   ——————
           S d   M d
E-form   No Sikhs are vegetarians.
          ————   ——————————
           S d   P d

Note that "vegetarians" is undistributed (u) in the premise and distributed in the conclusion. The rule states that a term which is undistributed in a premise must not be distributed in the conclusion. The violation of this rule is called "illicit distribution" or "illicit process." We may also refer to the term in- volved in the fallacy and speak of "illicit major" (as in the syllogism above) or of "illicit minor" when the fallacy involves the minor term. The point of the rule is that when a term is undistributed in the premise this gives us information concern- ing *some,* or part, of the class designated by the term. If we distribute this term in the conclusion, we say something about *all* of this class, and this is to "out-talk" our information. It is not fallacious, on the other hand, to go from "d" in the premise to "u" in the conclusion, for if the premise gives us information about "all" we can then draw conclusions about "some."

Let us now diagram the argument. We draw the major premise:

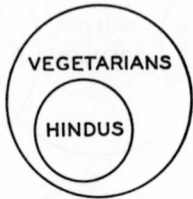

We now ask our key question: Can we draw a circle for the minor premise, i.e., showing the Sikhs class outside the Hindus class, without showing that "no Sikhs are vegetarians," the con- clusion drawn by the syllogism? We can, viz.:

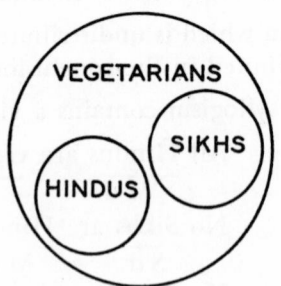

Rule 3. No conclusion is necessitated by two negative premises.

Here are two negative premises:

No marines are cowards.
No cowards are aviators.

The rule tells us that no possible conclusion can be necessitated by two negative premises. Why not? Well, consider the possible conclusions we might draw: (1) All marines are aviators, (2) No marines are aviators, (3) Some marines are aviators, and (4) Some marines are not aviators. (We could also reverse these subjects and predicates.)

We begin by diagramming "No marines are cowards":

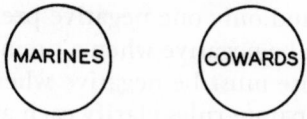

We must now draw "no cowards are aviators." The "aviators" circle must be outside the "cowards" circle, but no directions other than this are given. Aviators might be inside the marines circle wholly or partially, or outside wholly or partially. Whichever conclusion we draw (1–4) cannot be necessitated since there will be three other possibilities.

Rule 4. If either premise is negative, then the conclusion must be negative.

Rule 5. A negative conclusion cannot be drawn from two affirmative premises.

The last two rules are of lesser importance, since violations are rarely encountered, but they are necessary in order to complete the "system" of the rules of validity. An argument may violate none of the first three rules and yet violate one of these, so we must check by all five rules in order to guarantee validity.

>   *Violation of Rule 4:*
>   All communists are Marxists.
>   Some Brazilians are not Marxists.
> ∴ Some Brazilians are communists.
>   *Violation of Rule 5:*
>   All men are rational animals.
>   All rational animals are moral agents.
> ∴ Some moral agents are not men.

The student will have little difficulty in showing that the conclusion in Rule 4 is not necessitated. The fact that some Brazilians exist outside the Marxist circle does not prove that they exist within the communist circle. Drawing a proper diagram for Rule 5 presents difficulties which will be discussed in Section VI.

We may now note that the last three rules concerning negative propositions may be summed up in one formula: If *negative* propositions are used in a syllogism, then one and only one premise must be negative and the conclusion must be negative. Rule 3 emphasizes "one and only one negative premise"; Rule 4 that the conclusion must be negative when a premise is negative; and Rule 5 that a premise must be negative when the conclusion is negative. But the separate rules clarify each aspect and show the three ways in which the formula may be violated.

Exercises

Analyze the ten syllogisms on pages 189–190 in accordance with the methods used in this chapter. Check for violations of the rules: if none of the five rules are violated then the syllogism is valid. Draw the circle diagrams to "illustrate" your answers in the first five syllogisms. Remember that in order to illustrate invalidity the diagrams need exhibit only one situation in which the premises are true and the conclusions false.

To illustrate the way in which these syllogisms should be analyzed, the first one is worked out for you:

Step 1. Copy the syllogism on your note-paper, adding the following notations:

(a) Symbolize middle, minor, and major terms by M, S, and P, using each symbol twice.

(b) Identify each of the three propositions (two premises and conclusion) as A, E, I, or O forms.

(c) Place the signs for distributed (d) or undistributed (u) to the right of the symbols M, S, and P. (The distribution signs follow automatically after you have identified the A-E-I-O forms.)

Syllogism No. 1 will now look like this:

A-form   All Republicans are free-enterprisers.
———————————   ———————————
            M d   P u

E-form   No Democrats are Republicans.
                    ‾‾‾‾‾‾‾‾‾   ‾‾‾‾‾‾‾‾‾‾
                        S d   M d

E-form ∴. No Democrats are free-enterprisers.
                  ‾‾‾‾‾‾‾‾‾   ‾‾‾‾‾‾‾‾‾‾‾‾‾‾‾‾
                      S d   P d

For convenience in analysis we shall now "gather" the symbols of our syllogism, as follows:

$$M\ d \quad < \quad P\ u$$
$$S\ d \quad \not< \quad M\ d$$
$$S\ d \quad \not< \quad P\ d$$

Step 2. We check now for violations of the rules. Rule 1 tells us that the middle term must be distributed at least once. We note that M is distributed twice. No violation here. We then check for a possible violation of Rule 2, that a term undistributed in a premise must also be undistributed in the conclusion. We find that P was "u" in the major premise and "d" in the conclusion. Violation of Rule 2. The syllogism is invalid. It is unnecessary to check the remaining rules if you find that one rule has been violated.

Step. 3. Draw a diagram to show that the premises of this argument may be true and the conclusion false. We shall designate the terms by the symbols instead of words. Begin by drawing the major premise:

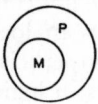

Now, can we draw "No S is M" without showing that "No S is P"? Yes, as follows:

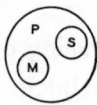

The drawing illustrates the invalidity of the syllogism.

Syllogisms for
   analysis.
      1. All Republicans are free-enterprisers.
         No Democrats are Republicans.
         ∴. No Democrats are free-enterprisers.
      2. All bankers are golfers.
         All middle-aged men are golfers.
         ∴. All bankers are middle-aged men.

3. Some Hindus are vegetarians.
   All Brahmins are Hindus.
∴. Some Brahmins are vegetarians.
4. All Republicans are free-enterprisers.
   No Socialists are free-enterprisers.
∴. No Socialists are Republicans.
5. All ministers of the gospel are shepherds of men.
   Some teachers of philosophy are not ministers of the gospel.
∴. Some teachers of philosophy are not shepherds of men.
6. Some believers in democracy are advocates of a planned society.
   Some advocates of civil rights are not advocates of a planned society.
∴. Some believers in democracy are advocates of civil rights.
7. No Democrats are Republicans.
   Some Republicans are not isolationists.
∴. Some Democrats are not isolationsts.
8. Some Russians are not communists.
   All communists are fanatics.
∴. Some fanatics are not Russians.
9. All Republicans are protectionists.
   All conservatives are Republicans.
∴. Some protectionists are not conservatives.
10. All beginning students in logic are students whose knowledge of the rules is superficial.
    No beginning students in logic are persons without rational capacity.
∴. Some students whose knowledge of the rules is superficial are not persons without rational capacity.

Section V: The Diagramming of Syllogisms

The diagramming of syllogisms in circles is an art which requires a thorough understanding of its principles, and, in some cases, a more refined analysis of the logical forms than we have as yet presented. This section will be devoted to this problem.

Let us restate our aims in diagramming arguments. We have learned the rules to which a valid syllogism must conform. We have learned the meaning of validity, viz.: a valid argument is one in which it is impossible for the conclusion to be false when the premises are true. We have also learned that if it is possible to draw the circles in such a way that the conclusion might be false though the premises are true, then the argument is invalid. And one further point before we proceed: Though the diagrams are not essential for proving validity, since the rules are sufficient for this purpose, the diagrams give us visible or "geographical" pictures of the relations of the members of classes to each other, so that we can see just why the argument is valid or invalid.

The chief difficulty in diagramming is that some ingenuity is often required to find a diagram which conforms to the premises and yet reveals that the conclusion need not follow. And worse, the Euler circles, while accurate as far as they go, do not adequately cover the full meaning of the A-E-I-O forms and do not furnish us with a sufficiently good instrument for diagramming all possible syllogisms. We shall therefore now present a supplementary interpretation of the diagrams for the A-E-I-O forms and we shall then have an adequate tool for all syllogisms which use these forms.*

1. The A-form

"All A is B" is diagrammed by Euler as:

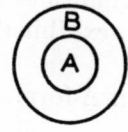

This diagram indicates that all of A is included within B, but it also shows some of B is outside of A. Now, this is normally the case in A-forms, as in "all dogs (A) are animals (B)." "Dogs" is the smaller class, and there are animals other than dogs. But this is not necessarily true in all A-forms. In "all triangles (A) are three sided figures (B)," A and B are *coextensive,* and there is no B outside of A.

In other words, the Euler diagram for A is correct insofar as it shows that A is *at least* as large as, or coextensive with B (never smaller), but it is misleading in that it indicates that B is always larger than A. Since the A-form does not necessarily imply the latter and since the Euler diagrams may indicate valid-

* An alternative method of diagramming will be found in the appendix.

ity if the second possibility is ignored, these circles are inadequate to handle all the possibilities in arguments containing A-forms.

To illustrate: The syllogism illustrating the violation of Rule 5 on page 187 (Men are rational animals and rational animals are moral agents, so some moral agents are not men) is invalid, but its invalidity cannot be shown by the ordinary Euler diagrams. It would be quite pointless to diagram this argument as shown below:

The point of diagramming an invalid argument is to show graphically that the premises may be true and the conclusion false, but this diagram indicates that the conclusion is true. It appears from these circles that some moral agents are outside the class of men. This indicates that we need an improved method of diagramming to exhibit the invalidity of this argument.

We shall now draw an A-form as follows:

The B-circle is shown by a broken line to indicate that B may or may not be larger than A. Thus an A-form has two possibilities: (1) in which B is a larger class than A, and (2) in which B is coextensive with A. These possibilities are shown below. (The dot between A and B stands for "both"):

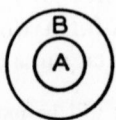   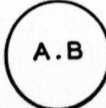

Let us now rediagram the last syllogism considering the possibility that the A-form may be represented by possibility 2. If the subjects and predicates are coextensive, the diagram will look like this:

The class of men, in other words, may be coextensive with the class of rational animals (it actually is!), and the class of rational animals may be coextensive with that of moral agents. Our drawing now shows that the premises of this syllogism may be true but that the conclusion that "some moral agents are not men" does not necessarily follow from the premises.

In a valid argument the conclusion will be necessitated whichever interpretation we give to the A-form diagrams.

2. The E-form

"No A is B" is diagrammed by Euler as:

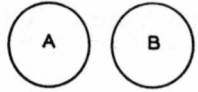

These circles are fully adequate for all possibilities arising under this form.

3. The I-form

"Some A is B," diagrammed by Euler as:

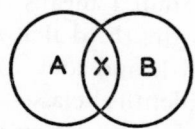

suggests that there may be some A that is outside of B (and some B outside of A). But these conclusions do not necessarily follow from "Some A are B" if we give it what logicians call a "strict interpretation." The nature of "strict interpretation" may be made clear by an example: A careful thinker who likes to travel visits the Melanesian Islands, and he observes natives eating betel. All the natives he has observed eat betel, but he cannot say that all Melanesians do (though they possibly may), nor can he say that some do not, and so he reports that "some Melanesians eat betel." A logician, reading this statement will interpret it as follows: He says some do; he has not said that some do not; so he means that *at least* some do and *possibly all* eat betel. This is the strict interpretation of an I-form: At least some A are B and possibly all A are B.

In ordinary speech "some A are B" usually means "not all are," but this is not the strict interpretation used in logic. In other words, from "some A are B" we cannot conclude "some A are not B." "Some A is B" should be represented by the following diagram:

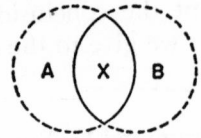

The solid lines indicate what we definitely know, or are sure of, namely, that at least some A are B. But the following possibilities may also hold in fact:

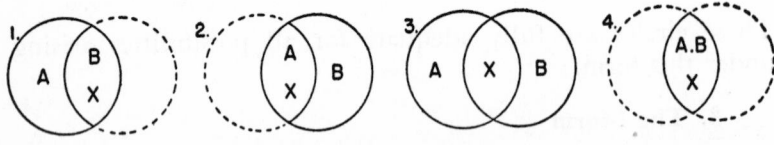

Note that the original solid lines and the "x" are present under each interpretation. Diagram 1 means that all B are A *; Diagram 2 that all A are B; the third that some A are B, but also that some A is outside of B and some B outside of A; and the fourth that A and B are identical classes. (The broken lines may be eliminated from each interpretation.)

---

* "Some A is B" is convertible with "Some B is A." The latter leaves open the possibility that all B is A.

4. The O-form

"Some A is not B" is diagrammed by Euler as:

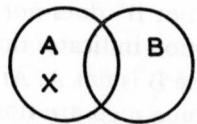

This suggests that some A may also be inside B. "Some A is not B" does not imply that some A *is* B to the careful thinker. Let us illustrate with our globetrotter once again. He is now among the Eskimos. He has heard tales about the blubber diet of Eskimos and he makes inquiries. Those interviewed tell him that they do not eat blubber. He now reports that "some Eskimos do not eat blubber." In ordinary language this would suggest that some of them do, but not to a logician. Strictly interpreted the statement means "At least some Eskimos do not eat blubber, and possibly none do." It is also possible that some do, but a valid argument must satisfy *all* of these interpretations of "Some do not," not merely one.

We shall represent the O-form by the following diagram:

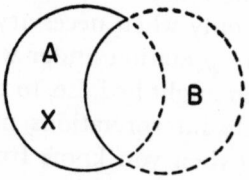

The solid lines indicate what we are sure of, marked by the "x." This new diagram may refer to the following factual situations:

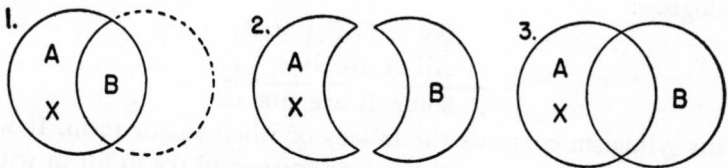

Here again the original solid portion marked "x" is present under each interpretation, i.e., each shows that "some A is not B."

But the first interpretation indicates that some A is not B and that all B is A. This would be the case in "Some animals (A) are not dogs (B)" for all dogs are animals. The second diagram is equivalent to the ordinary E diagram. It indicates that, strictly interpreted, "Some A is not B" does *not* mean that "Some A is B." The third interpretation indicates that some A is not B, that some A is B and that some B is not A. An illustration of the last situation is found in "Some men are not poets"; for some men *are* poets, and some poets are not men.

When the A-E-I-O forms are interpreted with the new diagrams, the broken lines may be discarded for each interpretation. Note also that where the diagram requires it, the two possibilities in the meaning of "All A is B" may be represented by either

TYPE 1   TYPE 2

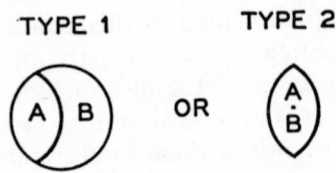

When we diagram arguments, we should use the simpler Euler circles where these are adequate. The special diagrams should be resorted to only when necessary. Remember that we need find only one interpretation under which the premises are true and the conclusion might be false, to prove an argument invalid. Try the possible interpretations until you can find an appropriate diagram (when you know from the rules that the argument is invalid).

We shall now present another illustration of the use and value of the new method. Assume that we have the following syllogism:

Some C is not A.
All A are B.
∴ Some B are not C.

This syllogism commits the fallacy of illicit major term. If we draw a diagram for one of these premises and try to fill in with the other in order to show that the premises may be true and the conclusion false, we will find that the ordinary Euler circles will not do the job. The following diagram, for example, is obviously not helpful:

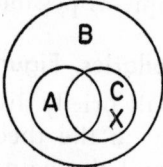

This diagram does *not* exhibit the invalidity of the syllogism, since it does not show that the premises might be true and the conclusion false. Rather, it appears to indicate that the conclusion is true, for some of the B circle is outside the C circle. We need a diagram which will show that these premises do not necessarily result in the conclusion presented.

The invalidity of this argument can be shown very clearly by the use of our new method of diagramming. We shall use Type 1 under the O-form above to diagram the major premise. This will show that Some C is not A and also that All A is C. If we now interpret the minor premise All A are B as involving the possibility that A and B are identical classes, we have the following:

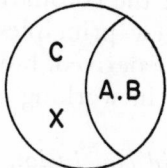

The new diagram reveals graphically that if some C is outside of A and all A is B, it does not necessarily follow that some B is outside of C. (Everything in the circle is part of C.) The same results would follow if the A class were smaller than the B class.

Exercises

Draw circle diagrams for syllogisms 6–10 on page 190. Use the ordinary Euler diagrams or the revised diagrams, whichever will suit your purposes. The problem in each case, to repeat, is to find a diagram that will indicate, by a geographical picture, that the premises of an argument may be true and the conclusion false. Make your diagram as simple as possible.

Section VI: The Corollaries, Figures, and Moods

In this section we shall briefly discuss two matters of theoretical interest pertaining to the theory of the syllogism: the corollaries of the rules, and the figures and moods of the syllogism. These matters are of interest in showing how the principles of the syllogism may be organized into a deductive system.

1. The corollaries.

The five rules of validity are sufficient for the testing of the validity of all syllogisms. No other rules are necessary. These rules play a role in the theory of the syllogism somewhat comparable to that of the axioms in Euclidean geometry. The axioms of geometry are undemonstrated, or "primitive" propositions which are used to prove theorems. In a similar manner we may use the five rules to demonstrate derived rules or corollaries (theorems) and we may then use such derived rules in the testing of syllogisms. But the corollaries are not indispensable, since they contain no new principles. Our discussion of the manner in which they are derived, however, will furnish an interesting logical exercise in working out the implications of a deductive system.

Corollary 1. No valid conclusion may be drawn from two simple particular premises.

This corollary states that no conclusion can be validly derived from the combinations of two I-forms, two O-forms, or an I and an O. We already know that two O-forms are an impossible combination, since no conclusion follows when both premises are negative (Rule 3). Let us consider the other two possibilities.

Suppose that both premises are in the I-form. Then no terms will be distributed. The middle term will then be undistributed, and Rule 1 will be violated. Let us now suppose that we have an I and an O in the premises. Only one term will now be distributed (the predicate of the O). The distributed term must be the middle term to satisfy Rule 1. But the conclusion of the syllogism must be negative (Rule 4). If the conclusion is negative, then its predicate must be distributed. But both the major and minor terms were undistributed, so the major term cannot be distributed without violating Rule 2. We have thus proved that the corollary must hold on the basis of the rules.

There is, however, an important exception to the corollary we have just proved. Note that we proved the rule for "simple" particular propositions. This qualification must be explained. A particular proposition refers to *some* of the subject, i.e., less than all. But there are many different ways in which we may refer to less than all of the members of a class. We may say "a few," "one-half," or "most" S's are P's. All of these are interpreted as meaning "some," i.e., less than all. But a particular proposition beginning with "most," which means "more than one-half," is a "special" as distinguished from a "simple" type of particular, for which Corollary 1 will not hold. For consider an argument such as the following:

Most of the students in this college are students of Latin.
Most of the students in this college are students of logic.
Therefore, Some of the students of Latin are students of logic.

If more than half of the students study Latin and more than half study logic, then some students must study both subjects, since "most" means "more than half." A map diagram will illustrate the situation:

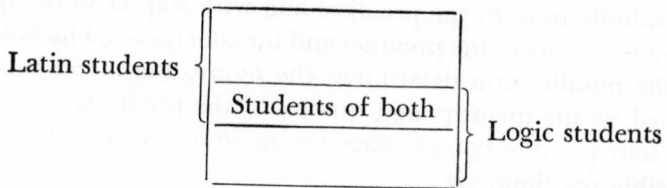

Latin students
Students of both
Logic students

This syllogism is valid despite the fact that it appears to violate Rule 1 and Corollary 1. It is a special type of case, whose validity is based upon mathematical relations. The corollary will therefore hold for all combinations of particular premises except when both have the quantifier "most."

Corollary 2. If one premise is particular, then the conclusion must be particular.

If one premise is particular, then the other must be universal (Corollary 1). Both premises cannot be negative (Rule 3). This leaves the following possible combinations of premises: AI, IA; AO, OA; EI, IE. We must prove that each of these six combinations cannot yield a valid conclusion which is universal.

Let us consider AI, or IA. Can the conclusion be a universal? It cannot be E, for a negative conclusion would violate Rule 5. Nor can it be an A. For AI or IA contains only one distributed term, which must be the middle term (Rule 1). If the conclusion were an A, the minor term would be distributed, violating Rule 2.

Combinations AO and OA. The conclusion cannot be an A (Rule 4). Nor can it be an E, for the premises contain two distributed terms, one of which must be the middle term (Rule 1). An E-form distributes both subject and predicate, and at least one of these terms must have been undistributed in the premises. The same reasoning applies to the combinations EI or IE.

So much for illustrations of the manner in which corollaries are demonstrated. The reader may try his hand at proving the following: Corollary 3: The premises must contain at least one more distributed term than the conclusion, and Corollary 4: No conclusion can be validly inferred from a particular major premise and a negative minor.

2. The figures and moods of the syllogism

Syllogisms may be classified with respect to the position of the middle term in the premises and with respect to the quantity and quality of the premises and the conclusion. The position of the middle term determines the *figure;* the *mood* is determined by the quantity and quality of the propositions. There are four possible figures, since the middle term may take four possible positions, viz.:

Figure 1	*Figure 2*	*Figure 3*	*Figure 4*
M . . . . P	P . . . . M	M . . . . P	P . . . . M
S . . . . M	S . . . . M	M . . . . S	M . . . . S
S . . . . P	S . . . . P	S . . . . P	S . . . . P

The moods are determined by the various combinations of A-E-I-O forms. When both of the premises and the conclusion are A-forms, the mood is called "AAA." The first letter stands for the major premise, the second for the minor, and the third for the conclusion. If the major premise is an A, the minor an E, and the conclusion an E, the mood is AEE.

Let us now compute the number of different syllogistic forms which are possible, taking account of the different combinations of moods and figures. Since there are four types of propositions and three propositions in a syllogism, there are four times four times four or sixty-four possible combinations of moods. These combinations may be arranged in four types of figures, so that we have four times sixty-four or 256 possible syllogistic forms. Most of these forms are invalid. We can easily eliminate the invalid forms by applying the rules and corollaries to each possible combination of premises. Thus, both premises cannot be negative (Rule 3). This eliminates all syllogisms whose premises are in the moods EE, EO, OE, and OO. Both cannot be particular (Corollary 1), and IE is ruled out by Corollary 4. This leaves us with only eight possible combinations of premises which can yield valid conclusions in some or all of the figures: AA, AE, AI, AO, EA, EI, IA, and OA.

The next problem is to determine which combinations of premises are valid in each of the figures. For example, premises AA or AI cannot be valid in Figure 2, for the middle term is the predicate in each premise in that figure, and if the premises are affirmative, the middle term will be undistributed. We shall now state some special corollaries which determine the rules of validity for each figure, but we shall not prove these corollaries. Their proof will follow the general procedure we used in proving the general corollaries concerning validity.

Figure 1:
   Corollary 1. The minor premise must be affirmative.
   Corollary 2. The major premise must be universal.
Figure 2:
   Corollary 1. The premises must differ in quality.
   Corollary 2. The major premise must be universal.

Figure 3:
    Corollary 1. The minor premise must be affirmative.
    Corollary 2. The conclusion must be particular.

Figure 4:
    Corollary 1. If the major premise is affirmative, the minor must be universal.
    Corollary 2. If either premise is negative, then the major must be universal.
    Corollary 3. If the minor is affirmative, the conclusion must be particular.

The mediaeval logicians worked out a set of mnemonic lines to aid the student in memorizing the valid moods of each figure, viz.:

Ba*r*ba*r*a, *C*e*l*a*r*e*nt*, *D*a*rii*, *F*e*r*ioque prioris;
*C*esa*r*e, *C*a*m*est*r*es, *F*est*in*o, *B*a*r*o*k*o secundae;
*D*a*r*apt*i*, *D*isa*m*is, *D*at*is*i, *F*e*l*apt*on*, *B*o*k*a*r*do, *F*e*r*ison habet;
Quarta insuper addit . . .
*B*ra*m*a*nt*ip, *C*a*m*e*n*es, *D*i*m*a*r*is, *F*esapo, *F*res*is*on.

The names in all these lines were invented, the instructions being in Latin. The first line gives us the valid moods in the first figure; the second, the valid moods in the second figure; and so on. The italicized letters in each name indicate the mood. Thus a syllogism in Barbara is one having A-forms in premises and conclusion. The interested reader may wish to determine which moods are valid in each figure, with these suggestions as his guide. These classifications are of course unnecessary if our sole interest lies in the testing of syllogisms for validity, the five rules being sufficient for that purpose. The systematic organization of the rules and corollaries, however, has great theoretical interest, as indicating the nature of a deductive system, the subject of the concluding section of this chapter.

Section VII: A Note on Deductive Systems

We are now familiar with the meaning of deduction. Granted certain premises we can deduce conclusions which necessarily follow from these premises. A *deductive system* refers to a collection or body of propositions which are so organized that some serve as the premises and the others as conclusions which necessarily follow from the premises. An example of such a deductive system is found in Euclidean geometry, a model for all such systems since 300 B.C. Euclid's premises, or "assumptions," include the following elements: (1) Undefined terms, such as "length" and "breadth," (2) definitions, such as the definition of a "line" as a "breadthless length," (3) axioms, or "common notions," [e.g., "Things equal to the same thing are equal to each other." "The whole is greater than any of its parts."] (4) postulates,* such as "All right angles are equal," and (5) rules of procedure, such as "It is possible to draw a straight line from any point to any other point."

From these assumptions Euclid deduces theorems, which follow from the assumptions as the conclusion follows from the premises of a valid argument. A famous example is the Pythagorean theorem: "The square formed on the hypotenuse of a right triangle is equal to the sum of the squares formed on the other two sides."

The relation of the rules of the syllogism to the corollaries resembles that of the assumptions to the theorems in the Euclidean system, the rules serving as assumptions (axioms or postulates) and the corollaries as theorems. This collection of propositions is thus a simple example of a deductive system.* *

Some further comments on the nature of a deductive system may be helpful. (1) The postulates of an ideal deductive system should possess three characteristics: independence, consistency, and sufficiency. "Independence" means that the postulates should not be reducible to each other, for, if they are, then the reducible postulates would be theorems. "Consistency" refers to the fact that the postulates should not result in inconsistent theorems, and "sufficiency" means that they must be adequate to yield all the known truths concerning the set of

* Euclid's postulates differ from his axioms in that the latter are "common notions" which are "generally accepted" outside of geometry, whereas the postulates are introduced by geometry itself. Strictly, the axioms are assumptions which are taken from outside the field of a given science, postulates those which are introduced by the given science; but we shall treat both as assumptions of the deductive system.

* * For a more thorough discussion of these matters the interested reader should see M. R. Cohen and E. Nagel, *An Introduction to Logic and Scientific Method*, Harcourt, Brace and Company, 1934, Chapters 4 and 7; and J. N. Keynes, *Formal Logic*, 4th ed., The Macmillan Company, 1906, pp. 287 ff.

propositions to which they are applied, i.e., all of the propositions in this set must be deducible from the postulates. (2) The postulates of a given system are not proved within that system. If they could be proved then they would be theorems rather than postulates. Whether they can be proved in some other fashion is simply irrelevant in the given system, the sole interest lying in the deducibility of the theorems from the assumptions. Thus, though Euclid's axioms and postulates seem "self-evident," this is not proof that they are true. It follows that *any* set of postulates may serve as the basis of a deductive system, but in practice the important systems are those in which the axioms are in "agreement" with the real world in some sense. A valuable system, moreover, is one which will yield significant theorems. (3) Finally, we should not think of the axioms as being first in the order of *discovery*. They are first, or fundamental, only in a logical sense and are discovered *after* there already exists a collection of propositions forming the body of a science. The formal scientist, such as Euclid or Aristotle, then seeks for a small number of assumptions from which the known truths concerning the subject matter may be deduced as theorems.

As we proceed in our introduction to logic we shall discuss other types of syllogisms. These, as we shall see, may be translated into the "Aristotelian" forms we studied in this chapter. But we shall also encounter other formal truths concerning deduction which cannot be reduced to the syllogistic form. This suggests that the entire field of logic cannot be organized into a completely systematic formal science, and indeed this was the prevailing view during the two thousand or more years following Aristotle's work. Beginning in the nineteenth century, however, with the work of George Boole and other logicians, in particular the great work of Whitehead and Russell in their *Principia Mathematica* (1910–1913), an important advance occurred in logical theory. Modern "symbolic" or "mathematical" logic has sought to demonstrate that *all* of the principles of logic may be proved on the basis of a small number of assumptions in an abstract deductive system. The exposition of this aspect of the new logic, however, belongs to a more advanced work than the present one.

Chapter 9

Semantics and the Syllogism

Section I: The Need for Semantical Analysis

We have studied the rules of the syllogism and have learned how to distinguish a valid from an invalid argument. But though we now know the rules, our ability to analyze syllogisms is still very limited. This is true for two reasons: (1) Our analyses have been limited to examples presented in the schematic or artificial form suitable for the clearest possible exhibition of the structure of the argument analyzed, and (2) our analyses have been confined to arguments in which the propositions clearly indicated the relationships of the three terms to each other. It is easy to apply the rules when syllogisms are presented in such ready-made form, but in living discourse syllogisms are not presented in schematic form, nor are the terms always easily identifiable. In order to remedy these limitations and to acquire the ability to analyze arguments as they occur in everyday discourse, we shall investigate a number of semantical problems. We shall learn how to translate everyday language into its correct logical form, and we shall also study the principles of "equivalences" in propositions. Propositions stated in different forms may express the same meanings, and transformations from one form into another may be required for syllogistic analysis.

The need for further analysis of meanings will become apparent when we examine the following syllogism:

All healthy people are non-alcoholics.
No unhealthy people are strong.
∴No strong people are alcoholics.

This syllogism appears to contain five terms ("unhealthy people," "strong people," "healthy people," "non-alcoholics," and "alcoholics"), and thus it appears to violate the requirement that a syllogism must have three and only three terms. But, as we shall presently learn, the first premise may be translated into "all alcoholics are unhealthy people," since this proposition has identically the same meaning as the first premise. We now have only three terms, and a valid syllogism.

Section II: Sentences in Irregular Forms

A categorical proposition must be stated in one of the A-E-I-O forms. Such forms indicate the manner in which two classes are related to each other in inclusion or exclusion. In everyday discourse, however, propositions may not clearly indicate the relations of two classes to each other, and in such cases we must translate the sentences into the correct form.

The necessity for this translation may be clarified by a somewhat farfetched analogy. The rules of the syllogism give us a kind of logical machine for testing arguments. This logical machine may be compared with a stamping machine that impresses stampings on pieces of metal. The pieces are inserted into the machine, a lever is pressed, and out comes the stamped piece. But the machine will not accept any piece of metal. The metal must be of the proper size and shape for insertion into the machine. Now, our logical "machine" is one into which we insert arguments. After the argument is "inserted," we press the lever (the rules), and out comes the argument stamped "valid" or "invalid." But the logical machine also requires that the pieces (the propositions) must be in the proper form for insertion, and "proper form" here means that the class relationships must be clearly indicated. Thus every proposition must be stated in strict A-E-I-O form, with all of the constituent elements, such as the quantifier, the copulas, the signs of inclusion or exclusion, and the names of the two classes, in their proper places. The chart below demonstrates for us the framework for each A-E-I-O form, with blank spaces which are to be filled in by the names of the subject and predicate classes.

		Traditional forms		*Class terminology*
A-form	General:	All ____ are	____	All ____ < —
	Singular:	X	is a ____	X < —
E-form	General:	No ____ are	____	All ____ ⊀ —
	Singular:	X	is not a __	X ⊀ —
I-form	:	Some __ are		Some __ < —
O-form	:	Some __ are not __		Some __ ⊀ —

Every proposition must be stated in one of the forms shown above, for no others can be used in the analysis of categorical syllogisms. We turn now to the analysis of sentences as they are stated in ordinary language. Such sentences may not be in the forms shown above, and we must learn how to make the proper revisions in order to shape the propositions for insertion into the logical machine.

1. Grammatical revisions

Before we analyse a sentence into its class relations, we must clearly identify the subject and predicate. In "Little has been accomplished by fanatics" the subject is "fanatics." "Fanatics," we are saying, "are persons who have accomplished very little." In "All take great risks who put their eggs in one basket" the "who" modifies "all," and the sentence should read, "All persons who put their eggs in one basket are persons who take great risks." The copula ("are") now separates the subject from the predicate.

2. The missing quantifier

We noted earlier that every logical proposition must have a quantifier and must therefore begin with "all," "no," "some," or, in the case of singular propositions, with the name of or reference to an individual thing or person. When no quantifier is stated, assume that the proposition is universal, unless it is quite clear from the context that "some" is intended. Where there is any doubt, assume that "all" is meant. Thus, in "College students are idealists" the speaker must be understood to mean "all." We are not certain that he meant "some." But in "Human beings live until the age of one hundred" it is obvious that "some" is intended.

3. The missing complement

We noted earlier that the *completing complement* must be added to adjectives and other phrases in order to indicate classes. Thus, in "All lions are mild" the predicate term does not clearly indicate a class. "Mild" is not the name of a class. If it were, we would be able to point to its members, but we cannot point to a "mild." However, when we add the completing complement "creatures" or "animals," our sentence will clearly refer to two classes of things. The proposition must clearly indicate that the circle representing the subject can be drawn inside another circle representing the predicate, and each circle must be named by a noun which designates a class of things.

In a sentence such as "Militarists are losing ground," "losing ground" is not a noun which names a collection of things. We must add the complement "persons who are," and we then have the class: "persons who are losing ground." But do not add complements when classes are clearly designated, since the simplest adequate statement is the most desirable. Note, too, that the subject term may also require its complement, as in "The foolhardy are losers." Add "persons" to "foolhardy" and add the quantifier "all," and we get "All foolhardy persons are losers."

Exercises

Restate the following sentences so that the subjects and predicates will clearly refer to classes of things, i.e., groups or collections of persons or things. Do not add complements to nouns. Where necessary, add expressions such as "things which are _____" or "persons who are _____," but where such simple words as "persons" or "things" are sufficient, you will simplify your statement by limiting yourself to a one-word complement. Also add the quantifier where it is missing.

1. Movies are entertaining.
2. She is a blonde.
3. The members of the orchestra are tuning their instruments.
4. The reflective are philosophers.
5. The narrow-minded are prudes.
6. Short skirts are on the way out.
7. Bobby-soxers are disappearing.
8. Those who are loyal to their country are patriots.
9. Blessed are the meek.
10. Happy are they who enjoy their work.

4. The missing copula

Many sentences omit the copula. We must supply it in such cases. Thus, in "Some fish fly" the copula is missing, and we must also add the complement to the predicate. The sentence will then read, "Some fish are flying creatures." Note that the operation of supplying the copula is always a two-fold one, since the completing complement will always be required for the predicate term and perhaps for the subject as well.

Another example: "Some ancient Oriental peoples worshipped the sun." We must supply the copula and add the complement so that the predicate will clearly indicate a class. Restated it reads, "Some ancient Oriental peoples are persons who worshipped the sun."

The following suggestion may be helpful to the student: Always identify the subject first, i.e., the complete subject. The copula should be stated immediately after the subject term. If you have difficulty in recognizing the subject in some cases, look for the main verb, and the subject will immediately precede it.

Exercises

Restate the following sentences by supplying the copula, complements, and quantifier when necessary. Express the copula in the forms of "are" and "included in the class of" ($<$). Be sure that the predicate is stated in the plural form.

1. Kangaroos jump.
2. Beginners make mistakes.
3. Children like to play games.
4. All atoms contain electrons.
5. Grass grows.
6. Evolution accounts for design.
7. He ridicules others who has never accomplished anything worthwhile.
8. All agree with me who are not ignorant of the facts.
9. They jest at scars who never felt a wound.
10. The people scurried to shelter when they heard the approach of the bombers.

5. Exclusive Propositions

a. The rule of transposition.

An exclusive proposition is one beginning with the words "only" or "none but." "Only men are priests." "None but adults are admitted." Such sentences do not clearly state the relationship of two classes to each other. "Only _____ are _____" is not a permissible form, and it will not be found in the chart on page 206. The subjects and predicates are not clear, and until they are it would be impossible to draw circles to represent these propositions or to fit them into our schedule of appropriate forms and yet retain the same meaning as the original statements.

Take the sentence "Only men are priests." How shall we draw the circles? Obviously we cannot draw a small circle representing men inside a large circle representing priests, for the sentence does not state that *all* men are priests. We therefore require a different type of translation. We require a restatement which can be diagrammed and which will have a meaning equivalent to that of the original sentence. The sentence can be translated into "All priests are men." This carries the meaning of the original sentence and is in proper class form. This simple example gives us our rule of translation: Whenever a sentence is in the form "Only (or none but) S is P" (where S stands for the subject and P for the predicate), we shall change the "only" to "all" and *reverse the order* of the subject and predicate. The exclusive sentence carries the meaning that all of the members of the class denoted by the (original) predicate are included in the class represented by the (original) subject.

A diagrammed statement of this type of translation may be helpful:

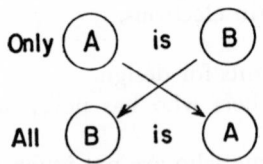

or

From the statement: "Only *fools* are *misers*."

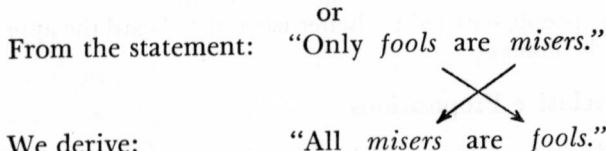

We derive: "All *misers* are *fools*."

Exercises

Translate the following exclusive propositions into propositions revealing class relationships, by eliminating expressions such as "only" and "none but." The expression "none but" has exactly the same meaning as "only."
1. None but S is P.
2. Only sissies are cry-babies.
3. None but Democrats are New Dealers.
4. Only declarative sentences are propositions.
5. Only persons who suffer from inferiority complexes are persons who wish to dominate others.

b. Procedure for complex cases.

More difficult types of translation are found in sentences in which the completing complement may be missing in one or both terms. The basic procedure to be followed in such translations is as follows:
1. Before we attempt to change the exclusive sentence into an A-form categorical proposition, we should check to determine (a) that each term has its completing complement and (b) that the exclusive sentence has a copula. Be sure that the complements and the copula are present before you proceed.
2. Transpose by reversing the order of the subject and predicate terms around the copula, and add the quantifier "all."
   Let us examine some examples, in an increasing order of difficulty:
   (i) "Only the narrow-minded are censors." "Narrow-minded" requires the complement "persons" and Step 1 is now satisfied. By Step 2 we have "All censors are narrow-minded persons."
   (ii) "Only citizens can vote" requires the copula as well as a complement for the predicate term to satisfy Step 1. It is advisable to add the copula first, immediately after the subject term, viz.: "Only citizens are. . . ." Are what? Obviously "persons who can vote." This completes Step 1. By Step 2: All persons who can vote are citizens.
   (iii) "Only the brave deserve the fair" is the most difficult type, for this requires complementing both subject and

predicate as well as adding a copula. Follow this procedure to complete Step 1: (1) Add a complement to the
subject, then (2) supply the copula, and finally (3) complement the predicate. A problem arises with respect to
the predicate noun. It is not "fair persons" for this
would fail to account for the words "deserve the." The
correct predicate is "persons who deserve the fair," and
Step 1 completed gives us: "Only brave persons are
persons who deserve the fair." By Step 2: "All persons
who deserve the fair are brave persons."

Exercises

Translate the following exclusive sentences into A-form propositions, following the procedures given to you under (b) above.
A. The following examples require complementing the subject, the
predicate, or both. Do not add complements to nouns.
  1. None but the unhappy are geniuses.
  2. None but the imaginative are poets.
  3. Only the curious are wise.
  4. None but good citizens are desirous of the general welfare.
  5. Only those who put others at ease are really polite.
  6. None but gentlemen are deserving of the fair.
  7. Only those who suffer from inferiority complexes are agres-
     sive.
B. The following require adding the copula **as** well as completing
   complements:
  8. Only religious persons pray.
  9. Only women bear children.
  10. Only vulgar persons talk like that.
  11. None but cowards die more than once.
  12. Only the curious get burned.
  13. Only the musical appreciate modern music.
  14. Only the brave deserve the fair.
  15. Only those who can, do.

6. Negative sentences

Like other sentences in ordinary language, negative sentences may lack complements and copula, and these must then
be supplied in order to fit such sentences into the "logical ma-

chine." Such sentences should be restated as standard E- or O-forms. Negative sentences also present special types of linguistic problems.

The quantifiers "none" or "nothing" indicate E-forms. "None of the greedy are happy" has a copula, so we need only change "none of" to "no," add complements to subject and predicate, and we get "No greedy persons are happy persons." "Nothing human frightens me" requires a copula as well as complements for subject and predicate, viz.: "No human things are things which frighten me."

The exact meaning of an E-form becomes clearer when we translate "No S are P" into "All S $\not\subset$ P." In class-analysis form our two E-forms will read: "All greedy persons $\not\subset$ happy persons" and "All human things $\not\subset$ things which frighten me."

We shall now examine a type of sentence which is ambiguous in its construction, i.e., amphibolous. Take, as example, "*All* Polynesians *are not* easygoing." Note carefully that this sentence is not in strict E- or O-form. Its structural skeleton is "All ___ are not ___." No such skeletal form will be found in the chart on page 206. This means that the sentence does not assert a precise relationship between two classes, since there are only four ways in which this can be done. Because only sentences in the four structural forms will fit into our "logical machine," we must therefore find, if possible, an E- or O-form equivalent.

We shall adopt the convention that sentences which present the "All ___ are not ___" formation will be rephrased as O-forms, unless an E-form is obviously intended. Simply change the "All" to "Some." Our example rephrased: "Some Polynesians are not easygoing persons." This rule is in accordance with customary usage. "All Russians are not communists" means "Some Russians are not communists" not "No Russians are communists." "All _____ are not _____" usually means "Not all _____ are _____," i.e., "Some _____ are not _____." But occasionally an E-form is intended, as in "All men are not sinless." This should be rephrased as "No men are sinless."

In the absence of a quantifier a negative sentence usually indicates an E-form as in "Misdemeanors are not crimes." This obviously means "No misdemeanors are crimes."

Exercises

Restate the following negative sentences in strict E- or O-forms. Add complements and the copula where necessary. Restate each E-form proposition in the two forms "No S is P" and "All S $\nless$ P."

1. No sparrows sing.
2. No Englishmen make good coffee.
3. Men are not sinless.
4. All labor leaders are not idealists.
5. All the students in this class will not get A's.
6. None of those who violate the rules will receive special consideration.
7. None of the faint-hearted were present at our great victory.
8. Nothing which makes sense is beyond my comprehension.
9. All who proclaim devotion to ideals are not sincere.
10. All that glitters is not gold.
11. The selfish individual is not a lover of his fellow-men.
12. Shostakovich's Fifth is not as great as Beethoven's Fifth.
13. No prejudiced person is included in the class of Christians.
14. What is not considered proper is not always wrong.
15. Plays cannot be judged by merely reading them.

7. Exceptive sentences

Translating an "exceptive" sentence into standard form requires more complex procedures than we required in our other translations.

A sentence of the form "All *except* A are B" (or "All *but* A are B") means that only A's are not B's.* "All but lazy students will graduate," means *"Only* lazy students will *not* graduate." If we translate this into an A-form we get "All students who will not graduate are lazy."

But this translation does not convey the entire meaning of "All but lazy students will graduate." If we combine this sentence with "John is a lazy student" as a minor premise we could not logically draw the conclusion that John will not graduate, for the two premises contain an undistributed middle term. Now, though the meaning of an exceptive sentence is somewhat

---

* This form of translation was suggested to me by Professor Donald Cliver of the University of Missouri.

ambiguous in this respect, the usual interpretation would be that our exceptive sentence contains "No lazy students will graduate" as part of its meaning. Since this meaning is not contained in "All students who will not graduate are lazy," we must add the second meaning to the first in the form of a conjunctive sentence (one which joins two propositions by the conjunct "and") as follows: "All students who will not graduate are lazy *and* no lazy students will graduate."

The following procedure is used in translating exceptive sentences:

(1) Translate "All but A is B" into an exclusive sentence, and negate the predicate term, viz.: "Only A's are not-B's." In categorical form we have "All not-B's are A's."

(2) Translate "All but A is B" into an E-form, with the original subject and predicate, viz.: "No A's are B's."

(3) Now combine the two translations into a single conjunctive proposition: "All not-B's are A's, and no A's are B's."

As we shall learn in the next section, "No A is B" is the equivalent of "All A is not-B" (or "non-B"), and so we can restate our conjunctive proposition as:

"All non-B's are A's, and All A's are non-B's."

Exercises

Translate the following exceptive sentences by following the procedure outlined above.

1. All but science majors take General Science.
2. All but military personnel were evacuated.
3. All except those who repent will be damned.
4. In 1947 the Ford Motor Company, for the first time in its history, permitted smoking by employees during working hours. The announcement read: "All employees except women office employees may smoke."

Section III: Equivalent Propositions

Different sentences may express exactly the same thoughts and meanings. They will then express equivalent propositions. Thus the sentence "Hitler is dead" has the same meaning as

"Hitler is not alive"; "No men are angels" has the same meaning as "No angels are men"; and "All just men are unprejudiced" means the same as "All prejudiced men are unjust." The three pairs of propositions we have just noted are examples of the logical processes called "obversion," "conversion," and "contraposition," the subject matter of this section. Though our immediate concern with these processes lies in the equivalences of language, we shall also note that these are also processes of reasoning, usually called "immediate inference." "Immediate" here means that we draw inferences from a single proposition, as distinguished from syllogistic, or "mediate" inference, in which we draw a conclusion concerning two classes because of their relation to a third class that "mediates" the inference.

The study of equivalent propositions has many values, not least of which is the realization that there is more than one way of stating the truth. In the search for truth it is not the language that is important but the ideas expressed. A difference in verbal formulation does not mean that there is a difference in meaning. We often find that apparent differences of opinion disappear when we learn that the difference is merely one of verbal formulation. This study will make us more keenly aware of equivalences in meanings, an awareness of which will be found indispensable in the analysis of many arguments.

1. Obversion

Obversion is a process whereby we change a proposition into its equivalent by *changing* its *quality* (but not its *quantity*), and by *negating* its *predicate*.

Example: A-form   All men are fallible.
             E-form   No men are infallible.

The A-form obverts into the E-form. The E is thus the obverse of the A.

These two propositions have exactly equivalent meanings. Note that the obverse contains two negations. We changed the proposition from affirmative A to negative E, and we negated the predicate from "fallible" to "infallible." The basic principle underlying this process is that two negations result in a positive statement, similar to the "double-negative" rule in grammar.

The child who says "I ain't got none" is, strictly speaking, saying that he does have some, though we will not usually mistake his meaning. "He did not fail to attend" means that he did attend. In algebra, too, we learned that the multiplication of negative numbers results in a positive number. The same principle also applies with respect to terms. The negation of "infallible" is "fallible"; the negation of non-combatant is "combatant."

We shall now introduce a new symbol "∼" called the "tilde," or sign of negation. Its verbal equivalent is "non," "in-," "un-," "im-," etc. If "B" stands for "fallible persons" then "∼B" stands for "non-fallible persons." We may thus express obversion symbolically as follows:

All A are B

obverts into: No A are ∼B.

Note the two steps: (1) Change the universal affirmative A-form into the universal-negative E-form (change quality, never quantity), and (2) negate the predicate term. (Do not tamper with the subject term!)

Note that "All C are ∼D" obverts into "No C are D." The negation of ∼D is ∼∼D, and the latter is the same as D.

The table on page 218 shows the manner in which all four types of propositions are obverted. Note (1) that there is no change in the quantity of the proposition. Universal propositions remain universal; particulars remain particular. (2) The quality of the proposition changes from affirmative to negative and vice-versa. (3) The predicate term is negated. (4) The subject term remains unchanged.

Two further points should be noted. (5) Examine carefully the obversion of I- and O-forms. The change in quality that takes place by changing "are" in the I-form to "are not" in the O-form, and vice-versa, is an operation entirely distinct from that of negating the predicate term. (6) Note the simplicity of the operations of obversion as stated in the "class-analysis" symbols. Only two operations are required. (1) We change < to ≮ (or vice-versa) and negate the predicate symbol. (Due allowance must of course be made for changes in the signs of distribution in the predicate term when we go from affirmative to negative and from negative to affirmative.)

Original A	Ad $<$ Bu	All A are B.	All men are mortal.
Obverse E	Ad $\not<$ ~Bd	No A are ~B.	No men are non-mortal.
Original E	Ad $\not<$ Bd	No A are B.	No liberals are appeasers.
Obverse A	Ad $\not<$ ~Bu	All A are ~B.	All liberals are non-appeasers.
Original I	Au $<$ Bu	Some A are B.	Some bankers *are* golfers.
Obverse O	Au $\not<$ ~Bd	Some A are not ~B.	Some bankers *are not* non-golfers.
Original O	Au $\not<$ Bd	Some A are not B.	Some Communists *are not* Russians.
Obverse I	Au $<$ ~Bu	Some A are ~B.	Some Communists *are* non-Russians.

When we obvert sentences in ordinary speech, difficulties may arise concerning the proper negation of the predicate term. It is, in general, preferable to negate by the prefix "non-," which expresses simple negation, rather than by prefixes such as "un-" and "in-" which often express antitheses, or words of contrary meaning. Consider "He is trustworthy" and "He is not untrustworthy." "Not untrustworthy," or the "not—un—" formation in general, appears to express a lack of certainty, though many people, especially the British, use this type of expression to express obversion. When the British send communiqués from war fronts announcing that they "were not unsuccessful," they mean that they were successful. To be safe, use the prefix "non," though other prefixes may sometimes correctly express simple negation. Note also that the simple negation of "large" is "non-large," (*not* "small"); the negation of "rich" is "non-rich," (*not* "poor"). People may be "non-rich," though far from poor.

Exercises

1. Obvert the following:

   a. Some X is Z.
   b. No L is M.
   c. Some R is not S.
   d. All ~A is ~B.
   e. Some R is not ~S.
   f. All puns are crimes.
   g. Some Chicagoans are gangsters.
   h. No planets are stars.
   i. Some books are not texts.
   j. Some chess players are non-athletes.
   k. All nonappeasers are wise men.
   l. No nonreaders are nonflunkers.
   m. Only A is B.
   n. Only the brave deserve the fair

2. Obvert: Germany invaded Russia on June 22, 1941. (Restate in logical form before you obvert. Remember too that a singular subject has no quantifier.)

3. Additional examples, if desired, will be found on page 171.

4. Are the following inferences justified? If not, which rule of obversion was violated?

a. All volunteers are patriots. Hence, all non-volunteers are unpatriotic.

b. All anonymous donors are wholly unselfish, so donors who sign their names are not wholly unselfish.

c. All letter writers who refuse to sign their names are cowards. Therefore, no writers who sign their names are cowards.

5. It is a useful exercise to draw circles in order to see why the obverse has the same meaning as the original proposition. Thus, if "All A is B," then the area outside the B circle is "~B," and since no A is outside the B circle, it follows that "No A is ~B." In the diagram:

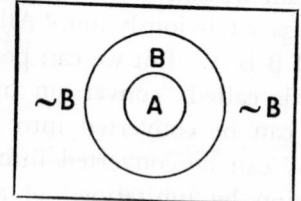

Draw and explain similar diagrams for the E-, I-, and O-forms.

2. Conversion

"No men are angels" has exactly the same meaning as "No angels are men." For obviously, if all men are excluded from the entire class of angels, then all angels must be excluded from the entire class of men. The two propositions are equivalent in meaning, though the order of their subjects and predicates is reversed. The subject of the first proposition has become the predicate of the second. The process whereby we pass from one proposition to another by reversing the order of the subject and predicate is called "conversion." This process is a legitimate one when the second proposition has the same quantity and quality as the first and when there is no "illicit distribution" of terms in the second proposition. When we apply this process to the A-E-I-O forms, however, we shall see that the E-forms and I-forms convert simply; A- and O-forms do not. A special kind of conversion may be applied to A-forms, however, as we shall note. Let us look at each form separately.

The E-form. An E-form may be converted, as in the example above, into a new proposition exactly equivalent in meaning to the original proposition. If all of A is excluded from B, then all of B must be excluded from A.

The I-form. "Some Americans are Communists" also means that "Some Communists are Americans." The original sentence states that there are some individuals who are both Americans and Communists. Obviously, then, there are some individuals who are both Communists and Americans. This gives us the rule that an I-form can be converted into a converse that is exactly equivalent to the original sentence. If some A are B, then some B must be A. If circle A overlaps B, then circle B overlaps A.

The A-form. Can we convert "All dogs are animals" into "All animals are dogs"? Obviously not. "All A is B" cannot be converted into "All B is A." But we can perform an operation on A-forms which is called "conversion by limitation." "All dogs are animals" can be converted into "Some animals are dogs." "All A is B" can be converted into "Some B is A." * Thus the "conversion by limitation" of an A-form yields a *partial* converse. It is important to note, however, that conversion by limitation gives us a new proposition that is *not equivalent in meaning* to the original one.

The process of distribution will explain why A-forms cannot be converted simply, like E- and I-forms. An E-form distributes both terms, and so does its converse. In the I-form, both terms are undistributed; similarly in the converse. But in the A-form, the predicate is undistributed, and if we convert it simply (i.e., without limitation), the original undistributed predicate would be distributed in the converse, as in going from "Ad < Bu" to "Bd < Au." The general rule of conversion with respect to distribution is that the converse must not distribute a term that was undistributed in the original proposition (cf. Rule 2 of the syllogism). The fact that we have informa-

---

* The conversion of an A-form requires certain assumptions concerning the existential import of propositions. This problem will be discussed in Chapter 11, Section IV.

tion concerning *some* members of a class does not warrant an assertion concerning *all* of its members.

One further point. In formal logic we are interested in valid inferences. We have stated the rule that "All A is B" cannot be converted into "All B is A." But suppose we have an A-form such as "All triangles are three-sided figures." We know that B is A in this case, i.e., that all three-sided figures are triangles. We may use this information as we please, but we did not derive this information by a formal logical process from "All triangles are three-sided figures." A formal logical process is concerned with form, not with content (or outside knowledge), and it is formally illegitimate to derive "All B is A," from "All A is B." To say this is illegitimate simply means that the latter might be true, and the former false. This is what is meant by "invalid argument."

The O-form. Can we convert "Some women are not mothers" into "Some mothers are not women"? Obviously not. The rule: An O-form cannot be validly converted. To do so would result in an illicit distribution of the original subject term, for we would go from "Au ≮ Bd" to "Bu ≮ Ad." The subject A would be undistributed in the original and distributed in the converse.

Once again we note that outside information may tell us that the converse of an O-form *happens* to be true. Take the example: "Some students are not women." We also know that "Some women are not students." But the point is that if we are given "Some A is not B," we cannot necessarily conclude that "Some B is not A."

The following table summarizes the possibilities in conversion. Remember that only E- and I-forms convert into equivalent propositions, that A-forms convert by limitation only, so that the converse is not equivalent to the original proposition, and that the O-forms do not convert at all. Note also that the *singular* A- and E-forms are not usually convertible.

	E-form	I-form	A-form
Original	No A is B (Ad ≮ Bd)	Some A is B (Au < Bu)	All A is B (Ad < Bu)
Converse	No B is A (Bd ≮ Ad)	Some B is A (Bu < Au)	Some B is A (Bu < Au)

Exercises

1. Convert the propositions in Exercise 1 in the preceding exercises.
2. Are the converses of the following propositions justified?
   a. All communists praise Russia, so those who praise Russia must be communists.
   b. Since some Germans were not Nazis, it follows that some Nazis were not Germans.
   c. Some Indians are non-Hindus, so some non-Hindus are Indians.
   d. No New Dealers are conservatives. Then no conservatives are New Dealers.
   e. All movies are masterpieces, so some masterpieces must be movies.
3. Are the following examples of conversion formally justified? Are the converses true in fact? Explain your answers.
   a. All men are rational beings. Therefore, all rational beings are men.
   b. Some baseball players are not golfers, so some golfers are not baseball players.
   c. Some coins are not pennies, so some pennies are not coins.
   d. Some human beings are not professors, so some professors are not human beings.
4. Convert: Americans enjoy a higher standard of living than Europeans.
5. Of which error in conversion is Alice guilty, according to her logical friends in Wonderland?

   The Hatter asked, "Why is a raven like a writing desk?"
   Alice replied, "I believe I can guess that."
   "Do you mean that you think you can find out the answer to it?" said the March Hare.
   "Exactly so," said Alice.
   "Then you should say what you mean," the March Hare went on.
   "I do," Alice hastily replied; "at least—at least I mean what I say—that's the same thing, you know."
   "Not the same thing a bit!" said the Hatter. "Why, you might just as well say that 'I see what I eat' is the same thing as 'I eat what I see'!"
   "You might just as well say," added the March Hare, "that 'I like what I get' is the same thing as 'I get what I like'!"

"You might just as well say," added the Dormouse, which seemed to be talking in its sleep, "that 'I breathe when I sleep' is the same thing as 'I sleep when I breathe'!"

(HINT: "I mean what I say" means "The things which I say are the things which I mean.")

3. Contraposition

The contrapositive of a proposition is the obverse of its converted obverse. To obtain the contrapositive we must perform three steps: obvert, then convert, then obvert once again. Let us illustrate this three-step procedure by an example of contraposition:

Original:	All metals	are conductors.	All M are C.
1. Obvert:	No metals	are non-conductors.	No M are $\sim$C.
2. Convert:	No non-conductors	are metals.	No $\sim$C are M.
3. Obvert:	All non-conductors	are non-metals.	All $\sim$C are $\sim$M.

This process may be applied to all A-form propositions, without exception. Note the symbols with which we begin and end: "All M are C" becomes "All $\sim$C are $\sim$M." The contrapositive of an A-form is thus another A-form, with the original subject and the original predicate reversed in order and both negated. The contrapositive of "All S is P" is "All $\sim$P is $\sim$S." The contrapositive of "All wizards are magicians" is "All non-magicians are non-wizards." The student should learn how to perform this process in both the one step and in the three step procedure.

The contrapositive of an A-form is always equivalent in meaning to the original proposition. This must be the case, since the obverse of an A-form (1), the converse of an E-form (2), and the obverse of an E-form (3) are equivalent to the propositions which are obverted and converted. The contrapositive of an O-form also results in an equivalent proposition. Thus, "Some A is not B" is equivalent to "Some $\sim$B is not $\sim$A." The E-form yields a partial contrapositive, and the I-form has no contrapositive. But we shall find little occasion to use contraposition except in the A-forms and will therefore not discuss this operation further.

Exercises

1. Exercises on contraposition: State the contrapositives of the following A-forms before you work out the three steps, and then prove your answer through the three steps:
   a. All Brahmins are Hindus.
   b. All communists are subverters.
   c. All men are mortal.
   d. All persons who fail in logic are non-studious.
   e. Only members are admitted.

2. On equivalence: Which of the following pairs are equivalent to each other? (The test of equivalence is whether or not you can translate back into the original proposition):
   a. All A are B and All ∼B are ∼A.
   b. All A are B and All ∼A are ∼B.
   c. All A are B and No ∼B are A.
   d. Some A are not B and Some B are not A.
   e. Some A are not B and Some ∼B are not ∼A.

3. On equivalence: Match the numbered proverbs with the lettered proverbs below. Do you regard the matched proverbs as having equivalent meanings?
   (1) It never rains but it pours.
   (2) Kind hearts are more than coronets.
   (3) Just as the twig is bent the tree's inclined.
   (4) Know thyself.
   (5) Carrying timber into a wood.
   (6) First come, first served.
   (7) Faint heart ne'er won fair lady.
   (8) A tempest in a teapot.
   (9) Don't put off until tomorrow what you can do today.
   (10) He who fights and runs away may live to fight another day.
   (11) Make hay while the sun shines.
   (12) Every man to his own taste.

   (a) Discretion is the better part of valor.
   (b) Troubles never come singly.
   (c) A mountain out of a molehill.
   (d) None but the brave deserve the fair.
   (e) There's nothing so kingly as kindness.
   (f) Strike while the iron is hot.
   (g) Like father like son.
   (h) One man's meat is another man's poison.

    (i) Carrying coals to Newcastle.
    (j) The proper study of mankind is man.
    (k) The early bird gets the worm.
    (l) No time like the present.

      (From George W. Crane's "Test Your Horse-Sense" Quiz in *The Chicago Daily Tribune*.)

Chapter 10

The Syllogism and Everyday Discourse

Section I: Syllogisms and Ordinary Discourse

We are now ready to analyze syllogisms as they are stated in ordinary discourse. We have learned how to make the linguistic transformations that are required when the essential relations of subject and predicate are obscured by "irregular" forms of expression. We should now be able to restate the syllogisms of ordinary discourse in the schematic form requisite for clear analysis.

We often reason syllogistically in ordinary discourse, but such syllogisms do not usually follow the pattern of the schematic form. They are more likely to occur in such forms as the following: "Certainly, we ought to have military training for our youth. These are critical times, aren't they? And shouldn't we have military training in critical times?"

We shall analyze syllogisms such as this one. We shall put the propositions into strict A-E-I-O forms, eliminating all unnecessary verbiage, rhetorical questions, etc., and then arrange the propositions in the schematic form we used earlier, with the premises first and the conclusion last. The syllogism above would then take the following form:

> All critical times are times when we ought to have military training for our youth.
> The present time is a critical time.
> ∴ The present time is a time when we ought to have military training for our youth.

The structure of this argument is now obvious, as is its validity.

In everyday discourse it is also customary to state an argument incompletely, because it seems unnecessary to state all the details. Someone tells us confidentially, "You know, all drunkards are short-lived. Well, poor John won't live very long." This argument is a syllogism in the form of an "enthymeme" (from two Greek roots meaning "in the mind"), i.e., part of the argument is unstated but understood. We supply the unstated but obvious premise that "John is a drunkard," and we have a complete syllogism.

In this chapter we shall analyze syllogisms as they might occur in ordinary discourse and will make frequent use of the devices for linguistic translations that we studied in the last chapter. As we noted earlier, the rules of the syllogism are easy to apply once we have properly analyzed the linguistic elements. But before we turn to the analysis of syllogisms, we must examine some special linguistic difficulties that arise in connection with the requirement that a syllogism must have three terms.

Section II: A Syllogism Has Three and Only Three Terms

The syllogism has been defined as an argument that has three and only three terms, but as yet we have not discussed the manner in which this requirement may be violated. Blatant violations do not usually occur in ordinary discourse. Thus, no one would be likely to argue in the following manner:

> All Englishmen eat roast beef with Yorkshire pudding.
> Zoroastrianism is a Persian religion.
> Therefore,———?

Since these two propositions contain four terms, they could not serve as the premises of a syllogism. There would be no middle term. An argument having the appearance of a syllogism, but containing four terms, is usually said to involve the "four-term fallacy." In the strict sense, such arguments are not syllogisms, but it will be convenient to refer to them as syllogisms involving "the four-term fallacy."

Though the four-term fallacy seldom occurs in the crude form of the illustration, it often occurs in a more subtle way. The ambiguity of terms may conceal the fact that a supposed middle term is really no middle term at all, but a word with two quite different meanings. The middle term, in other words, may be used equivocally. Let us look again at an example that we used earlier, on pages 56-7: "Science has discovered many 'laws of nature.' This is proof that there is a God, for a law implies the existence of a lawgiver, and God is the great Lawgiver of the Universe."

In more schematic form we have the following:
All laws₁ are rules which imply the existence of a lawgiver.
The 'laws of nature' are laws₂.
∴   The 'laws of nature are rules which imply the existence of a Lawgiver (God).

The middle term "laws" is used equivocally, so this syllogism has four terms. "Laws₁" is used in the sense of "legal laws," i.e., rules established by a governing body; "Laws₂" means descriptions of the uniformities among natural events. When we eliminate the equivocal uses of the middle term "laws" and substitute the proper definitions, we find the following argument:

All *rules established by a governing body* are rules which imply the existence of a lawgiver.

The 'laws of nature' are *descriptions of the uniformities of natural events.*

∴   The 'laws of nature' are rules which imply the existence of a Lawgiver (God).

Stated in this way, the four terms are glaringly obvious. But the four terms were not so obvious in the original argument, which had the appearance of a three-term syllogism because of the ambiguity of the word "law."

The student should examine every argument for possible violations of the three-term requirement. Note, however, that mere differences in terminology do not necessarily prove that four terms are used, as when synonymous expressions are used for the middle term, viz.:

> Those who believe that the state should be subordinate to the individual are opposed to the dictatorship of the proletariat.
> All anarchists are libertarians.
> ∴   All anarchists are opposed to the dictatorship of the proletariat.

In this argument the middle term is referred to by two different expressions: "libertarians" and "persons who believe that the state should be subordinate to the individual." Since both refer to the same referents, there are in reality only three terms. The term "libertarians" may be regarded as the subject of the major premise.

A merely apparent four-term fallacy may also occur when words of opposite meaning are used in an argument, as in

> All front-line fighters are combatants.
> All nurses are non-combatants.
> ∴ No nurses are front-line fighters.

In this syllogism we have apparent violations of both the three-term requirement and Rule 5, that a negative conclusion cannot be drawn from affirmative premises. But here we note a fundamental "rule of courtesy" which should be shown to all syllogisms: Do not assume that a four-term fallacy has occurred unless you have given the writer or speaker the benefit of every doubt. The reader should restate every syllogism as a three-term argument if this can be done without changing its meaning. When we give the last syllogism such courtesy, we find that the minor premise may be obverted into "No nurses are combatants," that there are thus only three terms, and that the syllogism is valid.

A different type of semantical violation of the three-term requirement is illustrated by the following example:

> All morally good men are concerned with human welfare.
> All virtuous men are morally good men.
> ∴ All virtuous men are concerned with human welfare.

Though this "syllogism" apparently has three terms, it really has only two since "morally good men" and "virtuous men" are synonymous terms. There is actually no reasoning from premises to a conclusion since the conclusion merely repeats the first premise in different language. Though such arguments are strictly speaking not syllogisms, we may refer to them as syllogisms involving the "two-term fallacy."

The four-term and two-term errors are semantical, rather than formal, in nature. The errors may be overlooked by carelessness in symbolization, as when we use the same symbol for different terms, or different symbols for the same term. We should therefore carefully check the language of every syllogism for possible violation of the requirement that a syllogism must have three and only three terms.

Section III: The Analysis of Syllogisms in Everyday Discourse

We shall now analyze syllogisms as they may occur in everyday discourse. The following procedure will be helpful to you in analyzing the syllogisms of the exercises:

Step 1. Your first task is to state the syllogism in schematic form, with the premises stated first and the conclusion last. To correctly identify premises and conclusion look for the "logical indicators," words like "because," "for," "since," which always precede a premise, and words like "hence," "so," "therefore," which introduce the conclusion. (Re-reading Section I of Chapter 6 may be helpful.)

Step 2. Be sure that each proposition in your syllogism is stated in strict logical form. (The possible structures of the standard forms are shown in the table on page 206.) Semantical revisions will be required when the argument uses rhetorical language or rhetorical questions. These irregularities should be eliminated. Make the proper grammatical revisions; add quantifiers, copula, and complements as necessary; translate exclusive and exceptive sentences; and revise negative sentences as required.

Step 3. The first two steps may adequately prepare the syllogism for the application of the rules. But other difficulties may need to be surmounted. You may have difficulty in correctly identifying the terms. When this occurs, carefully examine the conclusion, note its subject and predicate, and then try to find the common term in the premises. Further grammatical revisions may be required. Also recheck to see whether you have done everything required by Step 2.

It will sometimes be necessary to try out various hypotheses concerning the terms until we find the correct ones.

Step 4. Remember the "rule of courtesy" when the syllogism seems to have more than three terms. Use the rules of equivalence to obvert, convert, or contrapose in order to eliminate extra terms. Assume that the speaker had only three terms in mind until you have exhausted these precautions.

Step 5. Your syllogism is now stated in the proper schematic form. Symbolize the terms, show signs of distribution, gather the symbols together in class-analysis form for a symbolic statement of the structure of the syllogism, and analyze for validity.

Exercises

Restate the following syllogisms according to the instructions found in the five steps, and analyze for validity.

1. Since only citizens can vote, John must be able to vote, for he is a citizen.
2. Only the productive can be free, for only the productive are strong, and only strong people are free.
3. Since only the lucky make strikes, I must conclude that I am a very unlucky bowler, for I have not made a strike all winter.
4. Whatever is perceived by the senses is undoubtedly a fact. Then the existence of the soul cannot be a fact, since no one has ever perceived the soul by the senses.
5. Many great men have done very poorly in their studies while they were at college. I got low grades last semester. Can it be that I am a great man?
6. Decent newspapers cannot attain a wide circulation, for they decline to emphasize sensational material such as illicit love affairs and murders. We all know that papers which adopt such sensational methods invariably attain a wide circulation.
7. From Samuel Johnson's *Life of Cowley:* "Because the father of poetry was right in denominating poetry . . . an imitative art, these (metaphysical poets) will, without great wrong, lose their right to the name of poets . . . for they copied neither nature nor life."
8. The medical profession informs us that some stimulants are harmful to the human body. Everybody knows that all types of alcoholic liquor are stimulants; it follows, therefore, that some types of alcoholic liquor are harmful to the human body.

9. Nothing that makes sense ever puzzles me, and some of these exercises are quite puzzling. These exercises simply do not make sense.

10. The attorney for the defense argued; "It is a rule of the company by which my client was employed as a signal operator that express trains alone do not stop at his station. Now, the train in question stopped at his station, so he was undoubtedly correct in assuming that it was not an express train."

11. Every scientist will agree that true theories are theories which are confirmed by experiments. Now, we know that carefully formulated scientific experiments have confirmed Einstein's theory of relativity. Therefore it must be a true theory.

12. No unambitious people are successful, so no successful people are hedonists, for all ambitious people are non-hedonists.

13. No aggressive people are conscientious objectors, and all unaggressive people are friendly, so all unfriendly people are non-conscientious-objectors.

14. All Eskimos live in snow houses, and all people who like to live in snow houses would dislike our modern conveniences, so all Eskimos would dislike our modern conveniences.

15. All human beings are mortal, and all members of the genus homo sapiens are human beings, so all members of homo sapiens are mortal. (Does this example have three terms?)

16. The Dean says that all except the students with less than a "C" average will graduate. If you know that John has less than a "C" average, can you draw the conclusion that John won't graduate?

17. The *Digest* publishes what it considers the most interesting material that people want to read. Now, we know that an article doesn't have to be true in order to be interesting, and, since this magazine tries to publish interesting stories, we may conclude that its articles and stories are not entirely true.

18. If an argument is valid, and the conclusion is false, then a premise must be false. If we assume this principle then I can prove the falsity of A. E. Housman's theory that good poetry can be recognized by "the thrill down our spine." (*The Name and Nature of Poetry*). For though his own poetry is certainly good poetry, it does not send a thrill down my spine.

19. A Republican senator said that he disagreed with his party's chairman on key questions on domestic and foreign policy. If so, the chairman replied, then the senator is not a Republican, for the policies with which the senator disagrees are those for which the Republican party stands in the nation.

20. All who were present at the college senate meeting were members of the faculty, so I am justified in saying that no one present was not a member of the senate, since only faculty members belong to the senate.

21. If there is no reason to suppose that all his actions were praiseworthy and every reason to admit that no act is virtuous if it is not praiseworthy, then you can't argue that his actions were all virtuous.

22. The Eskimos are the only people who eat nothing but meat, and it is found that all Eskimos have good teeth. So we may conclude that no people who eat only meat have bad teeth.

23. A man is ennobled by the experience of finding himself faced by the choice between life and death. War provides the supreme situation in which men have to make this choice, so that if universal and perpetual peace could be attained, it would be at the price of robbing men of all ennobling experiences. (Thouless.)

24. Find a valid conclusion which would follow from the following premises: All of the incoming women freshmen at Indiana University disapprove of young men who neglect their studies in order to ride around in their flashy convertibles, and none of the incoming women freshmen at Indiana University seek to marry husbands who take the policies of either of the two major parties very seriously. Therefore?

25. It is a well-known fact that there are many pacifists in the U.S. today, and only people who are in favor of appeasing Russia are members of this peculiar sect. The pacifists feel that it is better to appease Russia than to go to war, even though appeasement may mean that communism will control the entire globe that we inhabit. Now, there is absolutely no question but that some persons who favor the appeasement of Russia are anything but loyal American citizens. The appeasers to whom I refer are in reality pro-communist, and they want Russia to take us over. Their talk about their desire for peace is nothing but a pretense. What these people really want is for us to disarm and thereby give Russia an easy path to conquest. It is thus apparent that at

least some, even if not all, pacifists can hardly be considered to be good American citizens.

Section IV: The Enthymeme

"Roosevelt made mistakes, for he was only human." This sentence states a syllogism in the form of an enthymeme, which we define as an incompletely stated syllogism. Only part of the complete argument is explicitly stated, the remainder being "within the mind." Completed, the argument would look like this:

> All human beings make mistakes.
> Roosevelt was a human being.
> ∴ Roosevelt made mistakes.

In everyday discourse we will find that syllogistic arguments are frequently stated in the form of enthymemes. In the example above it was unnecessary to state the major premise, "All human beings make mistakes," since it was obviously implied, and most speakers try to avoid "belaboring the obvious." Many arguments will be found to contain such unstated assumptions. Frequently, however, such assumptions are false or unjustified, and it is therefore important that we make our assumptions explicit, so that we may critically examine what is being assumed. This can be done only by completing the enthymeme.

Enthymemes may be classified into "Orders," to indicate the part or parts which are missing. There are four such Orders, as follows:

1. Major premise omitted

The illustration above omitted the major premise. Another example: "This cough syrup should help me, for it helped a man in St. Louis. I read his testimonial." The major premise, "Whatever helped a man in St. Louis will help me," is assumed.

2. Minor omitted

"Roosevelt will make mistakes, because all men make mistakes." The minor premise is missing here: Roosevelt is a man.

3. Conclusion omitted

"All men make mistakes, and the President is a man." The conclusion is obvious, but unstated. Another example, as told by Thackeray: "An old abbé, talking among a party of intimate friends, happened to say, 'A priest has strange experiences; why, ladies, my first penitent was a murderer.' Upon this, the principal nobleman of the neighborhood enters the room. 'Ah, Abbé,' here you are; do you know, ladies, I was the Abbé's first penitent, and I may promise you my confession astonished him.' "

4. The minor premise and the conclusion are omitted

This type is rarer than the others. It requires the *context* of a situation which indicates that an argument is intended. For example, assume that you are talking to a person whose boasting annoys you. You say, "Only an insecure person boasts about his achievements." Your hearer will supply the minor premise and the conclusion. The complete syllogism will read as follows:

> All persons who boast about their achievements are insecure persons.
> You are boasting about your achievements.
> ∴. You are an insecure person.

The problem of validity in the enthymeme must now be considered. In all of the examples considered, we completed the enthymeme into a valid syllogism. But consider the following: "Why do I say that X is a communist? He opposes loyalty oaths for teachers, doesn't he?" This is an enthymeme of the First Order, since the major premise is omitted. But what is the major? There are two possibilities: (1) All communists are opposed to loyalty oaths for teachers, or (2) All persons opposed to the loyalty oaths for teachers are communists. It is likely that the first interpretation was intended, in which case the argument would be invalid, since the middle term would be undistributed. If the second interpretation were intended, then the argument would be valid, but the falsity of this premise would be quite apparent. When one is in doubt as to which interpretation is intended, the argument should be analyzed in terms of both possibilities. Note also that questions concerning the truth of a premise are problems of material, not of formal logic.

Invalid enthymemes in other Orders will be quite obvious. The following is in the Second Order: "All Republicans believe in free enterprise, so you do not believe in free enterprise." This example contains an illicit major. A Third Order example: "All guilty individuals fail to pass the lie-detector test, and he failed to pass it." This argument contains an undistributed middle term.

Exercises

A. Complete the following enthymemes in strict categorical form. Each should be stated as a valid syllogism, unless it is obvious that an invalid argument was intended. State whether each is valid or invalid, and note the Order of the enthymeme. Linguistic irregularities should be handled as before. Note particularly, however, that the complete argument should have three terms, not four, five, or even six terms. It will be found helpful, in complying with the three-term requirement, to symbolize the subject and predicate of the conclusion by "S" and "P." Then find "M." Be sure that each term is stated in identically the same manner each time it is used.

1. This must be a good book—it was chosen by the Book-of-the-Month Club.
2. Liberals believe in freedom of speech, so he is not a liberal.
3. Remark made to an aggressive person: "When anyone acts aggressively it usually means that he is suffering from an inferiority complex."
4. All Republicans are against the "police state" so you must be a Republican.
5. Naturally, I consider him an intelligent man. He's a Democrat, isn't he?
6. Generals are notoriously poor chess players. I also play the game badly.
7. Don't take logic. You will have to work out a lot of exercises.
8. I don't see why I should be required to study Latin. Aren't all the worthwhile books translated into English?
9. We should have "socialized medicine" in the United States. Hasn't it worked well in England?
10. Robespierre's enemies accused him of having identified the "enemies of the state" with his personal enemies. "I deny the

accusation," he answered, "and the proof is that you still live."

B. State any set of two premises which will validly lead to the following conclusions (find a middle term):

1. No logical exercises are too easy.
2. Some payments for services rendered are not contemptible.
3. On rainy days, I dine alone.
4. Omar wished to remould this sorry scheme of things nearer to the heart's desire.

Section V: The Sorites

The sorites (rhymes with "nighties") is a series of syllogisms telescoped into one argument, as in the following:

All young men are idealists.	All Y are I.
All idealists are sensitive creatures.	All I are S.
All sensitive creatures are dissatisfied.	All S are D.
All dissatisfied creatures are unhappy.	All D are U.
∴ All young men are unhappy.	∴ All Y are U.

In this argument the first two premises lead to an unstated conclusion; namely, that "All young men are sensitive creatures." This unstated conclusion is then combined with the third premise, to yield the unstated conclusion that "All young men are dissatisfied," and so on. In other words, the conclusion of one syllogism is the premise of another, and all conclusions except the final one are unexpressed. The premises are so arranged that any two successive ones will contain a common term.

This form of the sorites is called the Aristotelian type. A second type, called the Goclenian sorites, proceeds in this way:

All living things are mortal.	All L are M.
All animals are living things.	All A are L.
All cats are animals.	All C are A.
∴ All cats are mortal.	∴ All C are M.

In the Aristotelian type, the first premise contains the subject of the conclusion, and the common terms of the premises appear first as a predicate and then as a subject. In the Goclenian type, the first premise contains the predicate of the conclusion, and the common term appears first as subject and then as predicate. Special rules for these sorites are as follows:

1. If negative premises are used, no more than one premise can be negative. In the Aristotelian sorites, it must be the last premise; in the Goclenian, the first.
2. No more than one premise may be particular or singular. If such premises are used, they must come first in the Aristotelian form, and last in the Goclenian.

Every sorites, however, may be stated in either form. The Goclenian sorites may be translated into the Aristotelian type by proceeding backwards from the last premise.

Exercises

1. Construct a valid Goclenian sorites having four propositions and containing a negative premise and a singular premise. Then restate in the Aristotelian form.
2. Classify the following sorites with respect to its form. Is it valid?

> The human soul is a thing whose activity is thinking. A thing whose activity is thinking is one whose activity is immediately apprehended and without any representation of parts therein. A thing whose activity is immediately apprehended without any representation of parts therein is a thing whose activity does not contain parts. A thing whose activity does not contain parts is one whose activity is not motion. A thing whose activity is not motion is not a body. What is not a body is not in space. What is not in space is insusceptible of motion. What is insusceptible of motion is indissoluble (for dissolution is a movement of parts). What is indissoluble is incorruptible. What is incorruptible is immortal. Therefore, the human soul is immortal. (Leibniz, *Confessio Naturae Contra Atheistas,* translated by H. W. B. Joseph, *An Introduction to Logic,* The Clarendon Press, pp. 355-6.)

3. The following examples of sorites are taken from Lewis Carroll's *Symbolic Logic.* Rearrange the premises in the Aristotelian order, making semantical changes as required:
   a. All babies are illogical.
      No one is despised who can manage a crocodile.
      Illogical persons are despised.
   ∴ No babies can manage crocodiles.
      (HINT: Symbolize each proposition by appropriate letters

("B" for babies, etc.) and then join premises having common terms.)

b. No terriers wander among the signs of the zodiac; Nothing that does not wander among the signs of the zodiac is a comet; Nothing but a terrier has a curly tail. ∴. All creatures with curly tails are non-comets.

c. Which conclusion may validly be derived from the following premises? All writers who understand human nature are clever; no one is a true poet unless he can stir the hearts of men; Shakespeare wrote Hamlet; no writer who does not understand human nature can stir the hearts of men; none but a true poet could have written Hamlet.

4. The following case may explain the reluctance of automobile dealers to sell cars to minors (legal infants):

On 21 April, 1928, the plaintiff, being a minor, entered into a contract with the defendant, by the terms of which he traded a Chevrolet truck, valued at $250, for a Dodge sport roadster, valued at $659.50. On 21 May, 1928, the plaintiff made a payment of $40.95 on his note. Thereafter the Dodge sport roadster was destroyed in a wreck; whereupon the plaintiff elected to disaffirm his contract, and now sues to recover $290.95, the sum of the value placed upon the Chevrolet truck at the time of the trade, to wit, $250 and the payment of $40.95 subsequently made on the note.

Stacy, Chief Justice: When an infant elects to disaffirm a contract, relative to the sale or purchase of personal property, other than one authorized by statute, or for necessaries, what are the rights of the parties?

(1) An infant may avoid such a contract, either during his minority or upon arrival at full age . . .

(2) Upon such avoidance, the infant may recover the consideration paid by him . . . with the limitation that he must restore whatever part of that which came to him under the contract he still has . . .

(3) Where the infant parts with personal property, he may, upon disaffirmance, recover the value of such property, as of the date of the contract.

In the instant case the plaintiff is entitled to recover the $40.95 which he paid on his note, together with the fair market value of the Chevrolet truck at the time of the trade. (Collins v. Norfleet-Baggs, Inc., Supreme Court of North Carolina, 1929.)

(HINT: Sum up the decision and the law in this case as stated by the Chief Justice in the form of an Aristotelian sorites. Begin with the singular premise: The plaintiff $<$ infants, etc.).

Section VI: The Relations between Terms Generalized

We have now completed our discussion of categorical syllogisms involving the relationship of class inclusion. These syllogisms used propositions containing subjects and predicates interpreted in terms of classes included within or excluded from each other. In later chapters we shall study the compound types of propositions composed of subpropositions rather than of terms. But before we leave the categorical type of syllogism we must note a special type which relates terms in relations other than that of class inclusion. Such syllogisms and the nature of "relations in general" will be our concern in this section.

Consider the valid syllogism:

A is older than B.
B is older than C.
∴ A is older than C.

This syllogism cannot be analyzed by the methods we have hitherto employed. If we put each proposition into "class" form, we shall find four terms: "A," "things older than B," "B," and "things older than C." But the argument is valid, and we must now inquire into the rationale of arguments such as these.

Subject-predicate categorical propositions relate terms to each other, but in a very special way, by class inclusion. Hitherto we have translated all possible relations between terms into the relation of class inclusion. But this procedure, though satisfactory in a great many cases, is not adequate for arguments such as the one above, and it thus becomes necessary to find a more flexible tool for handling other types of relations. In order to do this we must generalize the notion of "relations" and find a wider principle which will cover both the relation of class inclusion and other types of relations.

When we assert "$A < B$" we are saying that A is *related* to B in terms of class inclusion. We shall now use the symbol "(R)" for "related to," and we shall revise the previous symbolization to "A $(R_<)$ B." We may now assert new types of relations in the same manner. If we wish to say that A is older than B, we need not use the relation of class inclusion. We may use "o" for the relation of "older than" and symbolize the relationship as "A (R_o) B." This means that A is related to B in the relation of "older than." Similarly with other types of relations. The syllogism above may thus be symbolized as follows:

A (R_o) B.
B (R_o) C.
∴ A (R_o) C.

This type of argument may also be diagrammed, but not by circles. We may use a straight line to represent the different points on a line representing ages, from zero (0) to infinity (n), and we may then indicate the position of each term on the line, thus:

0   C   B   A   n

The diagram shows us that if A is older than B and if B is older than C, then A must be older than C. This is not startlingly new knowledge, but it serves as a simple illustration of the manner in which we may picture relations other than class inclusion, in order to test the validity of arguments in which they are used.

It should be obvious that some relations will permit valid argument and that others will not. Thus, if we know that A is the lover of B, and that B is the lover of C, we can conclude nothing with respect to the relations between A and C, nor indeed can we conclude that B is the lover of A. The relation of "lover of" does not permit such inferences. This makes it necessary to classify all relations, so that we may know which types of relations will yield valid inferences, and which will not. The relation of class inclusion, as we well know, is a type of relation which permits valid inferences. We shall now examine the special characteristics possessed by a relation which make such inferences permissible.

We shall classify relations under two general heads, *symmetry* and *transitivity,* each of which has three subdivisions.

1. Symmetry.

The three subdivisions are *symmetrical, asymmetrical* and *non-symmetrical.*

a. Symmetrical relations:
This type of relation is defined as a relation such that if A has it to B, then B *must* have it to A. Examples: equal to, unequal to, different from, cousin of, playing cards with, etc. In each case if A has the relation to B, then B has it to A.

b. Asymmetrical relations:
Here, if A has the relation to B, then B *cannot* have it to A. Examples: father of, older than, greater than, son of, at left of, etc. In each case if A has the relation to B, then B cannot have it to A.

c. Non-symmetrical relations:
Here, if A has the relation to B, then B *may* or may not have it to A. Examples: Lover of, helper of. If A is the lover of B, B may or may not be the lover of A.

2. Transitivity.

The subdivisions are similar: *transitive, atransitive, non-transitive.*

a. Transitive relations:
This relation is defined as a relation such that if A has it to B and B has it to C, then A *must* have it to C. The relation of "being older than" is such a relation, as are: equal to, ancestor of, class inclusion, etc.

b. Atransitive relations:
Here, if A has the relation to B and B has it to C, then A *cannot* have it to C. Examples are: father of, greater by half, etc.

c. Non-transitive relations:
Here, if A has it to B and B has it to C, then A *may* or may not have it to C. Examples are: lover of, unequal to.

These relations may also be combined as follows:
1. Transitive-symmetrical: equal to, contemporary of
2. Transitive-asymmetrical: greater than
3. Transitive-non-symmetrical: included in the class of
4. Atransitive-symmetrical: spouse of
5. Atransitive-asymmetrical: father of
6. Atransitive-non-symmetrical: nearest blood relative of
7. Non-transitive-symmetrical: cousin of
8. Non-transitive-asymmetrical: unrequited lover of
9. Non-transitive-non-symmetrical: lover of

We shall now consider the importance of these relations with respect to some inferences. "A < B, and B < C; therefore, A < C" is a valid inference because class-inclusion is a transitive relation.* "Older than" is also a transitive relation, and permits us to draw a similar type of inference. In other words, it is our knowledge that relations such as "class-inclusion" and "older than" are transitive relations which justifies us in drawing certain inferences.

We may now generalize the reasoning involved in the sorites. The Aristotelian sorites is a series of terms related by the transitive relation of class-inclusion. Thus if A < B, B < C, C < D, D < E, then A < E. For purposes of further simplification, this series of propositions may be stated as A < B < C < D < E. Such a series is called a "chain of relations," and indicates that any term at the left will be included within any term at its right, since "<" is a transitive relation. In interpreting such a chain, however, we should remember that it is a simplification of a sorites, with the connecting links omitted. In *reading* it, we must supply the missing links, viz.: "A is in B, and B is in C, and C is in D, and D is in E."

We may also generalize our previous analysis of the relation of conversion. We found that the E- and I-forms were convertible. In our new language, we may say that the relations of "being wholly excluded from" and "being partially included within" are symmetrical relations, so that if A has one of these relations to B, then B must have it to A. But the A-form relation of "being wholly included within" is a non-symmetrical relation, and from this it follows that the A-form is not convertible simply. The generalization of relations also permits conversions which would not be permissible under class relations. Thus "married to" is a symmetrical relation, and symmetrical relations are always convertible. If "A is married to B," we may thus convert into "B is married to A." If we interpreted the original statement in class terms, its meaning would be substantially altered and its conversion preposterous. We may also

---

* Note, however, that this inference will hold only for general universals and not for singular propositions, since class-*membership*, as distinguished from class-*inclusion*, is an atransitive relation. Where singular propositions are used in a syllogism, as in the familiar, "All men are mortal, Socrates is a man, etc.," the inference rests on the principles that if every member of class A is a member of class B, then any specified member of the first class must be a member of the second class.

now employ a new form of conversion, called "conversion by converse relation," when the relation is asymmetrical. Thus, "B is greater than A" converts by converse relations into "A is smaller than B." Similarly with "A is west of B" and "B is east of A."

We shall note further applications of these relations as we proceed. In particular, the importance of the transitive relation of "implication" will be emphasized. This relation, the most important relation in inference, will be discussed in the next chapter.

Exercises

A. Classify each of the following relations with respect to symmetry and transitivity:
   1. A is beating B.
   2. A is taller than B.
   3. A is a sister of B.
   4. A is the best friend of B.
   5. A is outside of B.
   6. A is "breathing down the neck of" B.
B. Which of the following inferences are valid? Explain why, in terms of the relations involved.
   1. A is the employer of B, and B is the employer of C. So A is the employer of C.
   2. A is heavier than B, so B is lighter than A.
   3. A is the twin of B, so B is the twin of A.
   4. A is a member of the Chicago Chamber of Commerce, and the Chicago Chamber of Commerce is a member of the United States Chamber of Commerce, so A is a member of the United States Chamber of Commerce.

Chapter 11

The Relations Among Propositions

Section I: Relations with Respect to Truth and Falsity

This chapter is a kind of interlude in our general analysis of syllogistic forms. We shall continue our discussion of relations, but our interest will now shift from the relations of *terms* to the relations of *propositions*. We shall examine the relations of propositions with respect to their truth values. Our fundamental problem will be this: given a pair of propositions, under what conditions does the truth or falsity of one proposition determine the truth or falsity of the other? As an example of this kind of problem, consider the following propositions, designated by the letters "P" and "Q":

P: All nummulites are foraminifers.

Q: No nummulites are foraminifers.

These propositions refer to actually existing things, but let us assume that the reader knows nothing concerning the truth or falsity of either P or Q. We may, nevertheless, discuss the relations of these propositions with respect to their truth values. Suppose we *assume* that one of these propositions is true. We can then draw inferences concerning the truth or falsity of the other. For example, if P were true, is it possible that Q might also be true? Obviously not. If P were true, Q would necessarily be false. P and Q cannot both be true. But both could be false, since they do not exhaust all the possibilities. *Some* nummulites might be foraminifers and some might not be. If the last situation prevails, then both P and Q would be false.

We see, then, that it is possible to discuss the truth relations of propositions even though we do not know which, if either, is true. Our problem is to determine how the truth or falsity of one proposition affects the truth or falsity of another. Consider another example. Our friends Bill and Jim are arguing once again:

BILL: No union has ever been justified in calling a strike.

JIM: No union has ever called an unjustified strike.

Bill and Jim, we note, are extremists. We know that both are wrong, since some strikes are justified and others are not. But in considering the logical relations of these propositions to each other, we must disregard our "outside" knowledge, in the sense that we may happen to *know* that a proposition is true (or false). We must consider only the truth values of the propositions to each other. We must ask, Does the truth of one of these propositions necessitate the truth of the other? Could both be true? Could both be false? The answers to these questions in the pair of propositions asserted by Bill and Jim will be exactly the same as in P and Q above, since the two pairs of propositions illustrate exactly the same relations.

Would the reader say that Jim *contradicted* Bill's statement in our example? If so, then the reader would be mistaken, for the logician defines "contradiction" as a relation such that, if one proposition of a pair is true, then the other must be false, and if one of the pair is false, then the other must be true. This is not the relation which holds in the two pairs of propositions we have examined. The relation holding between P and Q in these pairs of propositions is called "contrariety."

Let us now consider a pair of contradictory statements:

P: The first atomic bomb exploded on July 16, 1945.

Q: The first atomic bomb did not explode on July 16, 1945.

Once again we note that we must disregard the fact that we know that one of these statements happens to be true. Our logical questions are: Would the truth of P necessitate the falsity of Q? If P were false, would Q necessarily be true? When the answers to both of these questions is Yes, then the relation between the pair of propositions under consideration is called "contradiction."

One more illustration of a logical relation:

P: Nero was not the most cruel of all the Roman emperors.

Q: Commodus was not the most cruel of all the Roman emperors.

Here we have a new kind of relationship between P and Q. Both of these statements may be true. Neither Nero nor Commodus may have been the most cruel of all the emperors. If P is assumed to be true, then Q may or may not be true, and similarly, if Q is assumed to be true, then P may or may not be true. But now note what may not be so obvious, that P and Q could not both be false. If P is false, then Q would necessarily be true; if Q were false, P would necessarily be true. For consider: If P were false, then it would follow that Nero *was* the most cruel emperor. Since only one individual can be entitled to this distinction, Q, which says Commodus was not the most cruel, would then necessarily be true. When propositions are related in this manner, the relation is called "subcontrariety."

We shall consider seven relations in all: independence, equivalence, contradiction, contrariety, subcontrariety, superimplication, and subimplication. These seven relations are all the possible relations which two propositions may hold to each other in terms of truth and falsity. We shall now analyze each type of relation in detail.

Section II: The Seven Relations

Relation 1. Independence

The relation of "independence" means that two propositions have no bearing upon each other in terms of their truth or falsity. For example, P: "Shakespeare wrote Hamlet" is logically independent of Q: "Betelgeuse has a diameter approximately 300 times that of the sun." Though both of these propositions happen to be true, the truth or falsity of either determines nothing concerning the truth or falsity of the other. Their truth values are thus wholly irrelevant with respect to each other. Consider another pair: P: "Most children go to public schools" and Q: "Most children prefer to go to public schools." These are also independent, since from the truth or falsity of one of these propositions we could not necessarily conclude that the other is either true or false. As noted earlier we must disregard the actual truth or falsity of the propositions.

We shall define each type of relation by a table of "truth-values." The table for independence is as follows:

P true.....Q ?
P false.....Q ?

The question mark means "undetermined," i.e., we cannot know whether the proposition at the right side of the table is either true or false. Read as follows: If P is true, then the truth or falsity of Q is undetermined. Similarly for "P false." When propositions are independent, then both may be true, both may be false, or one may be true and one false. The truth or falsity of one has no bearing on the truth or falsity of the other.*

Relation 2. Equivalence

We have already learned the meaning of equivalences in propositions. We shall now define this relation: Two propositions are logically equivalent when the truth of one requires the truth of the other, and when the falsity of one requires the falsity of the other. In symbols:

P true.....Q true
P false.....Q false

Two equivalent propositions will alway be true together, and false together.

Relation 3. Contradiction

The logician defines contradiction in a precise manner. One proposition is the contradictory of another when the truth of one involves the falsity of the other and when its falsity involves the truth of the other. Both cannot be true and both cannot be false. The propositions P: "The Golden Plovers are noted for their gregarious habits," and Q: "Golden Plovers are not noted for their gregarious habits," fulfill the definition, and are thus contradictories. In symbols:

P true.....Q false
P false.....Q true

Both cannot be true; both cannot be false.

P: "All women are fickle," is the contradictory of Q: "Some women are not fickle." If P is true, then Q must be false. If P

* This means that independence is a symmetrical relation, as are equivalence, contradiction, contrariety, and subcontrariety. Q's relationship to P is the same as P's relationship to Q. Implication, however, is not a symmetrical relation.

is false, then it must be the case that at least some women are not fickle, i.e., Q will be true. Note also the symmetricality of the relation: If Q is true, then P must be false, and if Q is false, then P must be true.

Relation 4. Contrariety

This relation must be carefully distinguished from contradiction. P: "All women are fickle," and Q: "No women are fickle," are *not* contradictories, since both might be false. (Both *are* false, but we must ignore outside knowledge in considering the manner in which two propositions are related; it is sufficient to know that both *can* be false.) But note that if P were true, then Q would necessarily be false, and vice versa. P and Q are contraries. One proposition is the contrary of another when they are so related that both cannot be true, but both can be false. In symbols:

P true.....Q false
P false.....Q ?

Both can be false; both cannot be true.

The propositions P: "Washington was our greatest president" and Q: "Lincoln was our greatest president" are contraries. Both could not be true, but both might be false. Jefferson or some other president might have been our greatest president. If one of this pair of propositions is true, the other is false, but if one is false, the truth of the other remains undetermined.

Contraries, it may be noted, do not exhaust all possible alternatives, whereas contradictories do. The contradictory of P in the last paragraph would be, "Washington was *not* our greatest president."

Relation 5. Subcontrariety

Consider the following propositions: P: "Some people in the United States are eight feet tall" and Q: "Some people in the United States are not eight feet tall." Let us examine these propositions in the light of the relations we have studied thus far. The propositions are obviously not equivalent. Are they contradictories? No, because both might be true. It follows also that they cannot be contraries, since two contraries cannot both be true. What precisely is their relationship? *

Both can be true but both cannot be false. Consider: If P were *false,* we would then have to say that there were no people in the United States who were eight feet tall. If there are no such people, it follows that Q must be true. (On the other hand, if Q were false, it would follow that P was true.) When propositions have this type of relationship, they are called subcontraries. In symbols:

P true.....Q ?
P false.....Q true

Both may be true, but both cannot be false.

Note again that "some are" and "some are not" are interpreted strictly by logicians.* * "Some are" means "and possibly all." "Some are not" means "and possibly none." If P is true, i.e., if some people *are* eight feet tall, we cannot conclude that some *are not.* The truth of P allows the possibility that some are not, but does not guarantee it. Similarly, if Q is true, i.e., if some people *are not* eight feet tall, we cannot conclude that some *are.* The truth of either proposition leaves it an open question as to whether or not the other is true.

The relation of subcontrariety should be carefully compared with and distinguished from contrariety. In the former both propositions can be true; in the latter both can be false. In subcontraries the truth of one proposition leaves the other undetermined; in contrariety the falsity of one leaves the other undetermined. In subcontraries the falsity of one proposition involves the truth of the other. In contraries the truth of one involves the falsity of the other.

The following example of subcontrariety resembles the Nero and Commodus example above:

P: Carnera is not the worst heavyweight fighter of all time.
Q: King Levinsky is not the worst heavyweight fighter of all time.

* Propositions should be called independent only as a last resort, when careful study indicates that none of the seven logical relations are applicable.
* * Previously discussed under the I-form and O-form in Section V of Chapter 8.

The reader will find the definition applicable to this example. If it is false to say that Carnera *is not* the worst, then he *is* the worst. Q must then be true.

Relation 6. Superimplication

Consider the relations of the following:

> P: All contemporary French novelists are Existential-
> ists.
>
> Q: Some contemporary French novelists are Existen-
> tialists.

If P is true, then Q must be true. If P is false, Q is undetermined. For if it is the case that "all" of a group have a certain characteristic, then surely "some" must have that characteristic.* But if we merely know that it is false to say that "all" have it, then "some" *may* have it or "none" *may* have it. In other words, the falsity of the "all" leaves the truth of the "some" undetermined. In symbols:

> P true.....Q true
> P false.....Q ?

When two propositions are related in accordance with our table, the relation is that of superimplication. The reader should note that superimplication is not a symmetrical relation, as were the first five. If P is the superimplicant of Q, Q is *not* the superimplicant of P. In order to see the truth values from the "Q" point of view we must turn to the next relation, "subimplication," also an asymmetrical relation.

Relation 7. Subimplication

> P: Some contemporary French novelists are Existen-
> tialists.
>
> Q: All contemporary French novelists are Existen-
> tialists.

Note that this is a new relation, so that the "Q" sentence in the former relation is now called "P," and vice versa. In this new relation, if P is true, Q is undetermined, but if P is false, Q must be false. In symbols:

---

* But see section IV of this chapter for a different interpretation.

P true..... Q ?
P false..... Q false

If we know that "some" of a class have a certain characteristic, then "all" may or may not have it. But if even "some" do not have it, it is impossible that "all" should have it.

Superimplication and subimplication are correlative aspects of the basic relation called "implication."

When one proposition *implies* another, the first (the implicans, or "implying proposition") is *superimplicant* to the second (the implicate, or implied proposition), and the second proposition is *subimplicant* to the first. When one proposition implies another, the four statements in the following tetrad will hold:

(1) If the superimplicant is true, then the subimplicant must be true.
(2) If the superimplicant is false, then the subimplicant may be true or false.
(3) If the subimplicant is true, then the superimplicant may be true or false.
(4) If the subimplicant is false, then the superimplicant must be false.

The first two lines of the tetrad give us the truth values when we take the implicans as primary; the last two lines when the implicate is taken as primary.

An interesting example of the implicative relationship will be found in:

P: All Eskimos have blue eyes.
Q: No Eskimos have brown eyes.

Assuming that eyes can have only one color, then, if P is true, Q must be true, but if P is false, the truth or falsity of Q is undetermined. P is thus the superimplicant of Q since it fulfills the requirements of the definition. We may then look at the situation from the Q point of view, and we shall find that if Q is true, P is undetermined, but that if Q is false, then P must be false. Q is thus the subimplicant of P. This will become clear if you think about it for a while. If you don't see it, come back to it later.

In closing this discussion, we note that the relation of super-implication is the fundamental relation in the syllogism. Thus:

> P: All lemurs are mammals, and this animal is a lemur.
>
> Q: This animal is a mammal.

P is a compound proposition made up of two propositions, each of which might be the premise of a syllogism, and Q represents the conclusion of that syllogism. P implies Q, so that if P is true, Q must be true. The syllogism is valid. But if either or both of the premises were false, Q might or might not be true. Thus we have P true, Q true; P false, Q ?. This is the relation of super-implication.

Exercises

Write out the tables of truth values for the seven relations and keep the list before you. Identify the relations in the following pairs of propositions. Ask the following questions in each case: If P is true, is Q true, false or doubtful? If P is false . . . , etc.

1. P: Cleveland defeated Blaine in the presidential election of 1888.
   Q: Cleveland did not defeat Blaine in the presidential election of 1888.
2. P: Blaine was the Republican candidate in 1892.
   Q: Harrison was the Republican candidate in 1892.
3. P: No Polynesians eat cocoanuts.
   Q: All Polynesians eat cocoanuts.
4. P: No Eskimos eat blubber.
   Q: Some Eskimos eat blubber.
5. P: The Fifth is Beethoven's best symphony.
   Q: The Sixth is Beethoven's best symphony.
6. P: The Fifth is not Beethoven's best symphony.
   Q: The Sixth is not Beethoven's best symphony.
7. P: There is a book in this library which contains subversive ideas.
   Q: There is a book in this library which contains no subversive ideas.

8. P: All Eskimos live in snow houses.
    Q: Some Eskimos do not live in snow houses.
9. P: An atomic war will destroy mankind.
    Q: Human beings ought to abolish atomic warfare.
10. P: Swing music is first rate music.
    Q: Swing music is fourth rate music.
11. P: Some politicians are statesmen.
    Q: All politicians are statesmen.
12. P: Some of these exercises are easy.
    Q: Some of these exercises are not easy.
13. P: X is an artichoke.
    Q: X is a vegetable.
14. P: This book is not written in Chinese.
    Q: This book is not written in Japanese.
15. P: All Indians have blue eyes.
    Q: No Indians have green eyes.

Section III: The Square of Opposition

The term "opposition," as used in traditional logic, refers to the relations of propositions having the same subjects and predicates but differing in quality or quantity or both. The A-E-I-O forms may thus be "opposed" to each other when they embody the same subjects and predicates. We shall use the following group for illustrative purposes:

    A: All women are fickle.
    E: No women are fickle.
    I: Some women are fickle.
    O: Some women are not fickle.

No two of these propositions are independent of each other, since the truth or falsity of any one will involve truth values in the others. Nor are any two equivalent. But we shall find the other five relations exhibited among them. Thus, the A- and O- forms are contradictories, since their relation to each other fulfills the definition of contradiction which we stated earlier, namely, that if the truth of one of a pair of propositions involves the falsity of the other, and the falsity of one involves the truth of the other, then the relation is that of contradiction. E and I are also contradictories. A and E are contraries, since both cannot be true, though both can be false. I and O are subcontraries, since both could be true, but both could not be false. A is the superimplicant of I, and E of O. I and O are the subimplicants of A and E respectively.

The traditional logicians worked out an ingenious diagram called the "Square of Opposition," which embodies these oppositions, viz.:

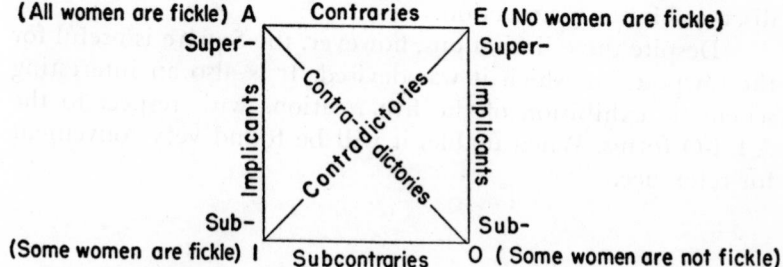

This diagram requires a word of explanation. The letters A-E-I-O at the corners stand for the propositions in the brackets, all of which have the same subjects and predicates. The diagonal lines connecting A and O, and E and I, marked "contradictories" mean that A-O and E-I are pairs of contradictories. The top line connecting A and E indicates that these are contraries, and the line between I and O that these are subcontraries. The vertical lines are marked "implicants," and the notations "super" and "sub" indicate that A is the superimplicant of I (E of O) and that I is the subimplicant of A (and O of E).

This diagram gives us an automatic device for detecting the relations of propositions *when they have the same subjects and predicates*. This limitation is very important for, as we already know, we may determine the relations between propositions which do *not* have the same subjects and predicates, as in relating "John is six feet tall" to "John is six feet, one inch tall." The relations of such pairs of propositions cannot be determined by the Square, for their predicates differ. But we know that they are contraries since they fulfill the definition of contrariety. The Square, then, does *not define,* but merely *illustrates* a limited application of the five relations.

The Square also has certain internal limitations. The universal propositions must be general, not singular, for singular propositions have no subimplicants. Furthermore, when we oppose singular A and E propositions to each other we find that the distinction between contradiction and contrariety disappears, as in "John is a great golfer" and "John is not a great golfer." Other limitations, based upon the re-interpretation of the meaning of universal and particular propositions, will be discussed in the next section.

Despite these limitations, however, the Square is useful for the purpose for which it was devised. It is also an interesting schematic exhibition of the five relations with respect to the A-E-I-O forms. When usable, it will be found very convenient for reference.

Exercises

The Square of Opposition should be used in working out these exercises.

A. Identify the relations among the following pairs:
1. P: Some women are not aviators.
   Q: Some women are aviators.
2. P: Some novelists are amoralists.
   Q: All novelists are amoralists.
3. P: Some politicians are crooks.
   Q: No politicians are crooks.
4. P: Some exercises in logic are not easy.
   Q: All exercises in logic are easy.
5. P: No Southern senators are Republicans.
   Q: Some Southern senators are not Republicans.
6. P: No Germans are pacifists.
   Q: All Germans are pacifists.
B. Complete the following chart, using T, F, and ? to symbolize True, False, and Doubtful. For example, if A is true, then its contradictory, O, must be false; its subimplicant, I, must be true; and its contrary, E, must be false.

If A is true, then I is ——, E is ——, O is——.
A is false, then I is ——, E is ——, O is——.
If I is true, then A is ——, E is ——, O is ——.
I is false, then A is ——, E is ——, O is ——.
If E is true, then A is ——, I is ——, O is ——.
E is false, then A is ——, I is ——, O is ——.

If O is true, then A is ———, E is ———, I is ———.

O is false, then A is ———, E is ———, I is ———.

C. The propositions in the following group are stated in irregular language. In order to place them on the Square, translations into the A-E-I-O forms are necessary. In some cases it may be necessary to obvert or convert them in order to obtain two propositions with the same subjects and predicates. Identify the relations after you have disposed of the linguistic problems.

1. P: Only the brave deserve the fair.
   Q: Some persons who deserve the fair are not brave.
2. P: None but geniuses write like that.
   Q: All persons who write like that are not geniuses.
3. P: Nothing difficult displeases me.
   Q: Some things which displease me are not difficult.
4. P: All men like jokes.
   Q: No persons who like jokes are men.
5. P: Some novelists are moralists.
   Q: Some novelists are amoralists.
6. P: Only the brave deserve the fair.
   Q: None of the brave deserve the fair.

D. Which problems on pages 253–4 could have been answered by reference to the Square?

E. Prove by using the relations of contradiction and contrariety that I and O cannot both be false, and that the falsity of I requires the falsity of A.

F. Criticize the following:

1. Granted that it is true that All wise men are mortal,
2. then No wise men are immortal
3. and No immortal beings are wise men.
4. Hence it is false that Some immortal beings are wise men,
5. and that Some immortal beings are not unwise men.
   But if this is false, it must be true that
6. All immortal beings are unwise men.
7. And that Some unwise men are immortal beings.
   (Creighton and Smart, *An Introductory Logic.* Copyright 1898, 1900, 1909, 1922, 1932 by the Macmillan Company and used with their permission.)
   (HINT: Are the terms properly negated, in the strict sense of contradiction?)

Section IV: The Existential Import of Categorical Propositions

Throughout our discussions of categorical propositions we have been making an unstated assumption concerning the existential import of propositions. We have assumed the existence of members of the classes referred to by such propositions. This assumption must now be made explicit for two reasons: (1) The careful thinker should be aware of the assumptions on which the validity of his reasoning depends, and (2) modern symbolic logic has shown us that the rules of inference of traditional logic sometimes depend upon certain unstated assumptions and that the possibilities of valid inference are different if we use a different set of assumptions. This matter deserves some attention.

In the classical logic the problem of "existential import" was never raised. In modern symbolic logic, however, the universal propositions (A and E) are interpreted as not asserting the existence of members of the class denoted by the subject term. Only particular propositions (I and O) assert existence. Following this re-interpretation of the existential import of the categorical propositions, we get new definitions of the A-E-I-O forms, viz.:

A: For any x, if x is an S then x is a P.
E: For any x, if x is an S then x is not a P.
I: There is an x such that x is an S and x is a P.
O: There is an x such that x is an S and x is not a P.

Note that the universals, in this interpretation, make no assertions that any S's exist. Take an A-form: "All margays are wild." In symbolic logic this is interpreted to mean that if anything is a margay then it is wild. Similarly, "No margays are wild" is interpreted to mean "If anything is a margay then it is not wild." The I-form, however, (Some margays are wild) does assert that there are margays: "There is an x such that x is a margay and x is wild" and similarly in the O-form.

Before we attempt to justify this new interpretation of the meaning of the A-E-I-O forms let us examine one of the consequences which follows from these definitions. It will now be illegitimate (without additional assumptions, to be examined presently) to deduce the truth of an I-form from the truth of an A-form (the relation of superimplication). Why is this? Examine the definitions of the A and I above. The A says that *if* anything is an S, then it is a P. The I: there *is* an x such that . . . In other words, we cannot derive an assertion concerning existence from a non-existential statement.

This point needs further clarification. We have heretofore assumed that "Some women are fickle" follows from "All women are fickle," but we are now told that this is an illegitimate inference. Nevertheless, the difficulty can be easily remedied if we recognize that the usual assertion that "All women are fickle" carries with it the tacit *assumption* that women exist. What we really mean, then, in making such an assertion, is something like the following: "If x is a woman, then x is fickle, and we assume that women exist" (or "If x is S then x is P, and assume that there are S's.") We can now infer that there *is* an x which is an S and a P, since there are S's and all S's are P's. Once we make the assumption of existence explicit, as an additional premise, the I follows from the A, as in the classical treatment of this matter. The importance of the new convention, then, is that we should be aware of the fact that we *have* made this assumption.

Let us now examine the justification for the new convention that universals should not be interpreted in an existential manner. Modern logic adopts this convention because of the undoubted fact that universals frequently refer to non-existential classes. As an example, examine the following A-form: "All world governments will bring more evil than good." We definitely do not mean that world governments exist, so that the interpretation "If there were a world government, then it would bring more evil than good" renders our meaning more accurately. Similarly many significant universals in the physical sciences must be interpreted in a non-existential manner, as Newton's first law of motion ("All bodies free of impressed forces will persevere in their states of rest or motion in a straight line forever"), for there are no bodies free of impressed forces.

It is thus apparent that some universals do not assert existence. Since it is desirable to have a uniform rule which will apply in all cases and since it is preferable to follow a strict interpretation which assumes as little as possible, modern logic interprets all universals as non-existential and supplements with the assumption of existence, when this is appropriate. In practice, of course, many universals are meant in an existential sense, and it is unnecessary to make this assumption explicit in everyday argument, but the point is that we should know what we are doing and not draw inferences concerning existing things when this is impermissible.

It may interest the reader to note some further consequences of the new conventions with respect to some previous inferences. The conversion by limitation of an A-form will be incorrect without the explicit assumption of existence. Similarly, it will be illegitimate to deduce a particular from two universal premises, as in the following example:

> No world governments are perfect organizations.
> All world governments are organizations which
>   abolish national sovereignty.
> ∴ Some organizations which abolish national sover-
>   eignty are not perfect organizations.

This syllogism is invalid if we adopt the convention that particulars affirm existence, whereas universals do not. We have hitherto assumed that this would be a valid argument.

Another very important consequence of the new convention is the radically different interpretation of the Square of Opposition which is now required. I and O can no longer be derived from A and E, for reasons already noted. A and E are not necessarily contraries, nor are I and O necessarily subcontraries, since both of the former pair might be true, and both of the latter false. This somewhat startling consequence follows from the new assumptions. Take the I and O propositions: "Some ghosts are in this room" and "Some ghosts are not in this room." Each of these is regarded as false, on the ground that these particulars assert that ghosts actually exist, and this is a false assertion. The I-form asserts "There is a ghost in this room," and the O: "There is a ghost which is not in this room." Since both are false, their contradictories, A and E, must both be true. It thus follows that "All ghosts are in this room" and "No ghosts are in this room" are both *true*. For if we grant that there are no such things as ghosts, we will also grant that all of them are in this room, i.e., "all of them that there are" are in this room, namely, none. And we will also grant that none of them are in this room. Thus, under the new existential interpretation, both an I and an O with the same subjects and predicates may be false, and the corresponding A and E true.

But these difficulties do not arise when we assume the existence of the subjects of universal premises, as is the rule in the traditional logic. And this brings us to the very important problem of understanding what is meant by "existence." Both the classical and modern logic use the concept of "universes of discourse." This means that by "existence," in some cases, we may mean existence in the actual world of space and time. In other cases a special kind of "existence" is referred to, i.e., membership in a "universe of discourse" other than the real one. Thus a novelist or dramatist may create a world of his own in which his characters enjoy a special kind of being, and the same holds for the creatures of myths. We argue about the character of Hamlet, we say that it is correct to define a mermaid as "half woman, half fish," and when we say "Some fairies are wicked creatures," we definitely do not mean to affirm existence in the real world (though the proposition is particular), but we do affirm existence of a special sort for the denizens of the Grimm fairyland.

In other words, though particulars assert existence and universals do not, we must also be careful to specify the kind of existence referred to. Both "Some Greek gods were lustful" and "Some Greek gods were not lustful," when interpreted in terms of the universe of discourse of the Greek mythology, cannot both be false, just as in the universe of discourse of a ghost story our earlier I- and O-forms could not both be false. In such universes, the corresponding A- and E-forms could not both be true. (Nor can they both be true when we deal with actual existents.) On the other hand, "All angels are immortal beings" makes no assertion concerning existence, even in the universe of discourse of angelology, for it is a universal proposition. From such a universal we could not infer that "Some angels are immortal beings" unless we explicitly assume that angels do exist in that universe. If we make this assumption, then the inference would be justified.

Section V: The Traditional "Laws of Thought"

Traditionally, the so-called "Aristotelian Laws of Thought" have been regarded as basic in all reasoning. These laws have been formulated in two different ways, for things (or classes), or for propositions, as follows:

1. The Law of Identity: For things, the law asserts that "A is A," or "anything is itself." For propositions: "If a proposition is true, then it is true."
2. The Law of Excluded Middle: For things: "Anything is either A or not-A." For propositions: "A proposition, such as P, is either true or false."
3. The Law of Contradiction: For things: "Nothing can be both A and not-A." For propositions: "A proposition, P, cannot be both true and false."

These laws, though not the only principles used in reasoning, are certainly basic in the sense that all reasoning presupposes them. These laws, of course, are really axioms, not psychological laws which purport to tell us how we actually think. They are not scientific laws of nature, for they are not descriptions of observed uniformities of behavior. These laws can also be violated as when people contradict themselves, or are inconsistent. When we think rationally, however, we always assume these axioms. We shall discuss their meaning and significance in connection with certain popular criticisms and misunderstandings.

1. The Law of Identity

For things. The law "for things" is used in widely different ways. As a logical relation identity is illustrated by equations such as $x = x$, or $x + 2x = 3x$, or statements such as "Mark Twain is Sam Clemens." The "is" here means that each name denotes the same individual.

When we say "Tables are tables" and "Cows are cows," we use the law as a principle of semantics. Unless terms retain identical meanings throughout a given unit of discourse and have fixed referents in their various occurrences, communication would be impossible.

In metaphysics the principle of identity is often interpreted to mean that permanence as well as change is a pervasive feature of reality. We shall expand on these usages in answering some criticisms of the law.

Some writers, in particular the late Count Alfred Korzybski and the General Semanticists, have attacked the law as false. Korzybski criticized the use of the "is" of identity, claiming that it results in such expressions as "Grass *is* green" or "Smith *is* a man" which are taken to mean that grass is identical with green or that the *name* Smith is identical with a man! The word, he tells us, is not the thing. This is all very true and instructive. It is an error, for example, to take the word "freedom" as a guarantee of a free society, but this is not a criticism of the law of identity but of foolish misapplication of the law. In any case it may be doubted whether the error he notes is actually responsible, as he claims, for his catalogue of the ills to which the spirit and flesh of modern man are heir, ills such as:

> . . . unrest, unhappiness, nervous strain, irritability, lack of wisdom, and absence of balance, the instability of our institutions, the wars and revolutions, the increase of "mental" ills, prostitution, criminality, commercialism as a creed, the inadequate standards of education, the low professional standards of lawyers, priests, politicians, physicians, teachers, parents, and even scientists . . .

Because of his belief that the Law of Identity is responsible for these evils, Korzybski believed that the crucial need of the twentieth century is the formulation of a new non-Aristotelian logic which will reject the Law of Identity.

Korzybski's basic criticism of the Law of Identity is that it is not true for a world that is in constant change. Things are in constant flux, he argues, so that nothing is ever the same from moment to moment. When we say that "a table is a table," we ignore the fact that the table *now* is different from what it was a moment ago. Hayakawa, in his *Language in Action,* as we noted in our earlier discussion of extension and intension, follows Korzybski's lead here. He asserts that "no word can ever have the same meaning twice" on the ground that the thing referred to has changed in the meanwhile and that our attitude toward it has also changed. Two answers may be given to this criticism:

(1) "The table *now* is different from what it was a moment ago." True, but unless words consistently referred to the same referent throughout a given unit of discourse, communication would break down. When one speaks of a table, he means a table, and is understood to mean a table, for anything is itself and not some other thing.

(2) The critics also confuse logical and physical identity. The problem here becomes a metaphysical one, involving the basic concepts of permanence and change. In the ancient world, the Greek philosophers first formulated this problem. Heraclitus, the philosopher of change, asserted that it was impossible for anyone to step into the same river twice, since the river was constantly changing. But Plato and Aristotle effectively criticized this doctrine of universal "flux" by noting that the statement "X has changed" requires that X retain its identity throughout the series of changes, for otherwise it would be impossible to say that X had changed. There is constant physical change in our universe, but also permanence or identity. The reader is undoubtedly a somewhat different person now from what he was before he began to read this discussion, but he must also be the same reader who began to read, for otherwise how could we say that *he* had changed? There can be no change except in relation to something that is constant.

For propositions. In the propositional formulation of the law of identity, we say that if a proposition is true, then it is true. This again is not so obvious as it appears, as we shall see when we consider some of the implications of this formulation. Does the reader believe that a proposition can be "true for one man and false for another," or that "what is true in one age of history is false in another age"? If so, he rejects the law of identity, for the law means that if a proposition is true, it is true for *all persons,* in *all times,* and in *all places.* But, the reader may urge, was not the statement "The earth is flat" true in the middle ages and is it not false today? The answer to the first part of this question is No. The earth was not flat in the middle ages, and to have called it such was to utter a false statement. People *believed* that the earth was flat, but believing a thing is so does not make it so. Their belief was false.

Another typical criticism of the law proceeds as follows: May not the time element, or the space element, make a proposition true for one time and place and false for another? For example, "It is cool today" may be true where we are, but false in the tropics, or false for us in July. But "It is cool today" is an unprecise statement of the speaker's meaning. To make it precise we must not only date it and locate it, but we must say something like the following: "The temperature is 41° F. at 1:15 P.M. in the shade at the meteorological station in Chicago, Illinois on March 31, 1960." *If* this statement is true, then it must be true for all time and places.

It is undoubtedly the case that men's beliefs differ, so that what *seems* true to one man will *seem* false to another. Confidence in one's beliefs is not always justified, nor is certainty always a guarantee of truth. We should remember that we may be mistaken in what we believe to be true. Truth is an ideal difficult to achieve, and in practice we may find it safer to say that a given belief appears to be probable in the light of the available evidence, rather than to say, "It is true." But if we know the truth, then we know the truth.

2. The Law of Excluded Middle

For things. Anything is either A or not-A, or anything is either A or its contradictory. We may assert that anything in the universe is either a piece of chalk or not a piece of chalk. A color is either red or not-red. Contradictories always exhaust the universe of discourse to which we refer.

Some critics urge that this is vicious "either-or" thinking, representing a "two-valued orientation" toward the world, whereas the world requires a "multi-valued orientation." There are, it is urged, infinite differences in things, so that it is false to say "Either A or not-A." For example, we should not divide men into two classes, the good and the evil, for there is some evil in the best of us, and some good in the most evil. The cartoonist Mauldin once illustrated the vice to which the critics refer. He pictured one man carrying a sign with the words, "Russia is never wrong." Another carried the sign, "Russia is always wrong." The critics of the law ask: Does not another alternative exist? Must Russia be either always right or always wrong?

These critics call our attention to a prevalent fault in thinking. A great deal of confused thinking falls into an "either-or" pattern. We often assume that there are only two possibilities in a situation or only two choices when there are more than two. We say "Either you are for us or against us" (you may be neutral); we say "Either we must establish a world government or an atomic war is inevitable" (the "cold war" may continue indefinitely). We shall call this "the error of insufficient options." But this type of thinking should not be confused with the law of the excluded middle. The criticism of the law noted above is based upon a confusion between contrariety and contradiction. The law of the excluded middle says that anything is A or its contradictory. Thus, a man is necessarily either rich or not rich, for "rich" and "not rich" are contradictories. But we cannot say that a man must be either rich or poor for these terms are contraries. The law does not require us to say that Russia is always right or always wrong, but only that Russia is either always right or not always right. In any pair of contradictory propositions one must be true and the other false.

Another type of criticism is based upon the alleged inadequacy of the law of the excluded middle in dealing with matters of *degree*. When a physician measures temperature, for example, he does not make his report in terms of hot or cold or even of fever or no-fever, but he states the degree of temperature. Granted, but the law is not a technique of scientific procedure. It is merely an axiom of reason. "Either the body temperature is 98.6° F. or it is not" is an instance of the law. (It is also significant to state whether or not the patient has a fever.)

Another example of the "degree" criticism is found in B. B. Bogoslovsky's *Technique of Controversy* in which he cites the example of a beard in order to expose this alleged weakness of the law. The point is this: suppose we say "Either Smith has a beard or he does not," and Smith is neither beardless nor does he have a full beard. Consider the difficulties. If we agree that 1,000 hairs make a beard and that 100 do not, we will also agree that 999 make a beard and that 101 do not. But is there some point, say 549 hairs, where we can say: This is not a beard but the addition of one hair will make it one? This seems absurd and the critics say that this proves the law inapplicable to things involving degrees. But the absurdity is based on the fact that it has never been important to define a beard precisely. The law of the excluded middle presupposes that our terms have been precisely defined.

Mastery of a college course is also a matter of degree, and so it also seems unrealistic to say "Either John has mastered the course or he has not." But in this case the administration of a grading system requires a precise definition of mastery, given in the minimum passing grade of 60. Fair or unfair, the student whose grade is 60 has "mastered" the course, one with a grade of 59 has not.

For propositions. A proposition is either true or false. "The street has been sprinkled" is either true or false. There is no middle ground between truth and falsity. Now, suppose that only part of the street has been sprinkled. Would it then be *both* true and false to say that the street has been sprinkled since it has been in part and has not been in part? Here again we find the necessity for precision in our statements. When we say "The street has been sprinkled" we usually mean that certain parts of it have been sprinkled. With respect to *these parts* our statement is either true or false. If the statement were interpreted to mean *"All* parts have been sprinkled" then this proposition too is either true or false.

Vagueness in the meaning of our terms is also responsible for the belief that some propositions are neither true nor false. "I am happy" and "We are enjoying prosperity" are examples of propositions which may be regarded as neither completely true nor completely false. But when the words are defined precisely, then, in some determinate respects the propositions will be either true or false. If we cannot define "happiness" or "prosperity," then we are not stating completely meaningful propositions, and truth or falsity apply only to meaningful propositions.

3. The Law of Contradiction

For *things,* nothing can both have and not have a given characteristic in precisely the same respect. This law asserts that nothing can be both A and the contradictory of A. A man cannot be both rich and not-rich at the same time and in the same respect. For *propositions,* we say that no proposition can be both true and false, in the same respects. The law of relativity tells us that an object may be moving for one frame of reference and at rest in another, but for any given frame of reference the object is not both moving and not-moving. It is perhaps needless to note that we are not always able to determine which of two contradictory propositions is true. But one must be true, and one false.

Exercises

A. Analyze and discuss the following items in terms of the preceding discussion:
1. Every seven years the cells in a human body change completely. How then can a man's debts be held against him for more than seven years, since he is no longer the same man?
2. Do the following items illustrate the law of identity?
   a. Those were the days when men were men.
   b. Let us call a spade a spade.
3. What happens when an irresistible force meets an immovable object?
4. According to the principle of contradiction, "animal" cannot be both vertebrate and invertebrate. But are not some animals vertebrate and others not?
5. Are the following statements both true and false?
   a. Heavy objects fall at the same speed as light objects.
   b. Water boils at 212° F.
   c. Hamlet was a man.
6. Does Aristotle use the principle of the excluded middle in the following quotation from his *Physics*?: "As every occurrence must be ascribed either to coincidence or to purpose, if the frequency of heat in the summer cannot be ascribed to coincidence or chance, it must then be ascribed to purpose."
7. Is the law of the excluded middle applicable to statements such as "John loves Mary"?
8. Is it necessarily the case that a nation will either win a war or lose it?

B. Study the following quotations and consider their points of agreement or disagreement with the text. Also answer the questions following each.
1. There is a venerable law of logic called the "law of excluded middle" which states that A is either B or not B. Thus a piece of paper is either white or not white. This is obviously true, and I shall not deny its soundness as a law of pure

logic. At the same time, we must notice that the kind of thinking embodied in this law may be dangerous and misleading when applied to a certain very common range of facts . . . All over human life we find properties which show continuous variation, and (just as in the case of white and black) we find this property obscured by the use of words implying sharp distinctions. "Sane" and "insane"; "good" and bad"; "intelligent" and "unintelligent"; "proletarian" and "capitalist," are pairs of opposites which show this property of continuous variation . . . Any argument, therefore, which begins in some such way as follows: "A man must be either sane or insane, and an insane person is absolutely incapable of reasonable thought . . ." is a dangerous piece of crooked thinking, since it ignores this fact of continuity. (R. H. Thouless, *How to Think Straight,* Simon and Schuster, 1939, pp. 119, 123.)

Question for discussion: Would a law court be guilty of "crooked thinking" if it sought to determine whether a person guilty of homicide was sane or insane?

2. All people tend to think of things in terms of good and bad, black and white, hot and cold, God and Satan, rich and poor, etc. . . . Since this two-valued orientation underlies most of our thinking except in technological matters, the outcome of almost all disagreements is that both sides are pushed to irreconcilable extremes . . . Illiterates and "uneducated" people are by no means alone in their two-valued orientation; controversialists in intelligent magazines and in learned journals are similarly conditioned. The reader will recall, for example, the situation in which André Gide found himself after the publication of his *Return from the USSR,* in which he had recorded, with an artist's rigid self-honesty, his impressions of the Soviet Union. Thousands of anti-communists clutched him to their bosoms as a brother, while thousands of his ideological allies gnashed their teeth at his "apostasy." For savages, for heresy-hunters like Mrs. Dilling, as well as for ideologically kosher intellectuals whether of the Left or the Right, there is no middle ground between black and white; it is *all* or *none*. This is what is meant, of course, by the "excluded middle" of Aristotelian logic. How far could modern engineering have got if we had thermometers which could give only two readings, "hot" and "cold" . . . ? (S. I. Hayakawa, "The Meaning of Semantics," *New Republic,* Aug. 2, 1939.)

    a. Which common error does Hayakawa criticize?

    b. Criticize his formulation of the law of excluded middle.

3. *A is A.*

The characters of Aphrodite (a sow) *now* are different from those one second earlier or one second later. Not by much, but by enough to destroy the perfection of identity. A rocket is always the same rocket. True for words, but not for that nonverbal event in space-time which blazes in glory and falls a charred stick as we watch it; not for a mushroom full-blown today and underground yesterday; not for a rose, withered now and lovely a week ago; not for an ice cream cone five minutes in the sun; . . . We have no knowledge of anything in the real world which is not a process, and so continually changing its character, slowly or rapidly as men measure intervals.

Everything is either A or not-A.

The law of the excluded middle might read: "Every living thing is either an animal or a plant." It was so employed by biologists for centuries. We still play the game of twenty questions on the animal, vegetable, mineral basis. In recent years a number of organisms have been studied which defy the distinction. A class of living things has been observed whose metabolism under certain conditions follows the classification of "plant," under other conditions that of "animal." Thus Euglena, a little unicellular water organism, becomes green in abundant sunlight and behaves like a "plant." Remove the light, the green color disappears, and Euglena proceeds to digest carbohydrates like an "animal," rather than synthesizing them like a plant. . . . The law of the excluded middle is an unreliable guide to knowledge. The law of contradiction—Nothing is both A and not-A—is equally unreliable. Euglena is both "plant" and "animal." (Stuart Chase, *The Tyranny of Words,* Harcourt, Brace and Co., pp. 228–30.)

Defend the laws of identity, excluded middle, and contradiction against Chase's criticisms.

4. The Law of Contradiction is afflicted with a similar falsity. It says "nothing can both be and not be." But anything that can change or have a plurality of relations defies it. It can both be and not be with the utmost ease. It is at one time and not at another. Or in one respect, and not in another. Or in one place, and not in another. Or for one purpose, and not for another. Or in one context, and not in another.

(F. C. S. Schiller, *Logic in Use,* Harcourt, Brace and Co., p. 38.)

Which qualifications are omitted from Schiller's formulations?

5. Life consists before all just in this, that a living creature is at each moment itself and yet something else. Life is therefore also a contradiction present in things and processes, continually occurring and solving itself; and as soon as the contradiction ceases, life also ceases and death steps in. (Friedrich Engels, *Anti-Duhring,* p. 120.)

This passage is characteristic of the Marxist thesis that contradiction is "objectively present in things and processes." Does Engels use "contradiction" in the logical sense? If not, what does he mean by the term?

6. In analyzing the Aristotelian codification, I had to deal with the two-valued, "either—or" type of orientation. I admit it baffled me for many years, that practically all humans, the lowest primitives not excluded, who never heard of Greek philosophers, have some sort of "either—or" type of evaluation. Then I made the obvious "discovery" that our relations to the world outside and inside our skins often happen to be, on the gross level, two-valued. For instance, we deal with day and night, land or water, etc. On the living level we have life or death, our hearts beat or not, we breathe or suffocate, are hot or cold, etc. Similar relations occur on higher levels. Thus, we have induction or deduction, materialism or idealism, capitalism or communism, democrat or republican, etc. And so on endlessly on all levels.

In living, many issues are not so sharp, and therefore a system which posits the general sharpness of "either—or," and so objectifies "kind," is unduly limited; it must be revised and made more flexible in terms of "degree." This requires a physico-mathematical "way of thinking," which a non-Aristotelian system supplies. (Alfred Korzybski, *op. cit.,* p. vii.)

Do Korzybski's illustrations include both contraries and contradictories? What relevance does this have with respect to his criticism of the law of the excluded middle?

Chapter 12

Compound Propositions and Syllogisms

Section I: Compound Propositions

Up to this point we have been concerned with categorical propositions. Such propositions have terms, i.e., classes, as their constituent elements. We now turn our attention to compound propositions which have propositions as their constituent elements.

Thus, "All men are rational beings" has the terms "men" and "rational beings" as its constituent elements. The compound proposition "If men are rational, then a world community is a possibility" has two propositions as its elements, namely, "Men are rational" and "A world community is a possibility." By analogy with chemical analysis we may think of categorical propositions as being composed of atoms (terms), and compound propositions of molecules (propositions).

There are three major types of compound propositions, each having a distinctive set of connective words, and each being made up of subpropositions, which we shall customarily symbolize by the letters p, q, r, etc., which stand for propositions. Following is a list of the different types, with examples of each:

Hypothetical: *If* prices continue to rise, *then* the unions will ask for wage increases.

Alternative: *   *Either* the nations will co-operate, *or* all will perish.

Conjunctive: Americans believe in freedom of speech **and** Americans speak English.

Each type will now be considered in detail.

---

* Many writers use the term "disjunctive" for what we call "alternative" propositions.

Section II: Hypothetical Propositions and Syllogisms

A hypothetical proposition is made up of two subpropositions connected by the words "if" and "then." The hypothetical proposition *"If* prices continue to rise *then* the unions will ask for wage increases" has two subpropositions. The first of these is called the "antecedent," the second the "consequent." We shall symbolize these by p and q. The structural form of the hypothetical proposition may thus be exhibited as follows:

If _____ p (antecedent) _____ then _____ q (consequent) _____
(Prices continue to rise)   (The unions will ask for wage increases)

"If p then q" means "If p is true then q is true" or "If what p asserts is the case, then what q asserts will be the case."

Let us now examine the precise meaning of the proposition: "If prices rise, then the unions will ask for wage increases." No assertion is made that either of the subpropositions taken alone is true. We have not said that prices will rise nor have we said that the unions will ask for wage increases. The only assertion we have made is that the consequent will follow if the antecedent occurs. *If* prices rise, we have said, then the unions will surely ask for wage increases.

Another meaning of this proposition is that if we find that the unions do *not* ask for wage increases, then we may conclude that prices have *not risen,* for if they had risen then the unions would have asked for increases.

This proposition, however, tells us nothing about what may happen if prices do not rise. There may be other reasons why unions ask for wage increases. Similarly, if we learn that the unions have asked for wage increases we cannot conclude that prices have risen, because of the aforesaid other reasons.

To sum up this expansion of the meaning of "If p then q," we have found that it involves four aspects:

1. If p is true, then q must be true.
2. If p is false, i.e., if p does not occur, then we can draw no conclusion concerning the truth or falsity of q.
3. If q is true (q occurred) then we can draw no conclusions concerning the truth or falsity of p.

4. If q is false (q did not occur) then we know p is false (did not occur).

It may be noted that the relation of p to q is that of implication. The relation of superimplication holds between p and q and that of subimplication holds between q and p. "If p then q" may thus be expressed in the form "p implies q."

2. Hypothetical syllogisms.

The rules of validity of the hypothetical syllogism are based upon the meaning of the hypothetical proposition.* The following hypothetical syllogism is an example of the so-called "mixed" type, i.e., it is made up of a hypothetical major premise, a categorical minor premise, and a conclusion:

If a battleship is gray, then it has been painted. (If p then q.)

p q

The battleship Missouri is gray.   (p)

p

∴ The battleship Missouri has been painted.   (∴ q)

q

We shall refer to the hypothetical premise as the "major premise," and to the second premise as the "minor." Note the latter carefully. It introduces a "special case," the battleship "Missouri." The minor premise asserts that our special case has the characteristic stated in the antecedent of the major premise; hence, we say that the minor premise "affirms" the antecedent, and we symbolize the minor premise by "p," i.e., p is true. But the minor premise might have informed us that the antecedent did not apply to the Missouri, i.e., that the Missouri was *not* gray. This is to deny the antecedent, i.e., to say p is false, or "not-p," symbolized by "$\sim p$." There are two other possibilities. The minor might have informed us that our special case has the characteristics of the *consequent* of the major premise (symbolized by "q") or that it does not have it (symbolized by "$\sim q$," i.e., q is false). These four possibilities give us four "figures" of the hypothetical syllogisms, which take their names from what the minor premise asserts. They are as follows:

---

* The concepts of distribution and class analysis are now irrelevant since we are no longer dealing with terms.

Figure 1. Affirming the antecedent:
If a battleship is gray, then it has been painted. If p then q.
The Missouri is gray (affirms antecedent). p
∴ It has been painted (affirms consequent).   ∴ q

The hypothetical major premise asserts that the consequent will be true if the antecedent is the case. The minor premise asserts that the antecedent is the case (affirmed) so we may properly affirm the consequent. This valid argument form is often referred to as *modus ponens.*

Figure 2. Denying the antecedent:
If a battleship is gray, then it has been painted. If p then q.
The Missouri is not gray (denies antecedent).   ~ p
∴ It has not been painted (denies
    consequent).   ∴ ~ q

Here the minor premise tells us that the Missouri is not gray. We cannot properly conclude that it has not been painted. It may be painted in a different color, such as white. The major premise asserts that a ship has been painted *if* it is gray, but it does *not* assert that it has been painted *only* if it is gray. "Denying the antecedent" is an invalid argument form.

Figure 3. Affirming the consequent:
If a battleship is gray, then it has been painted. If p then q.
The Missouri has been painted (affirms
    consequent). q
∴ The Missouri is gray (affirms antecedent).   ∴ p

The minor asserts that the Missouri has been painted. For the same reasons as above, this does not permit us to conclude that it is gray. This form is also invalid.

Figure 4. Denying the consequent:
If a battleship is gray, then it has been painted. If p then q.
The Missouri has not been painted (denies
    consequent).   ~ q
∴ The Missouri is not gray (denies
    antecedent).   ∴ ~ p

This form is valid. If the Missouri is not painted, then it certainly cannot be gray, since only painted battleships are gray.

When we deny the consequent of the major premise, then the antecedent must be false. Consider: If the antecedent is the case, then the consequent must be true. But if the consequent is not the case, then the antecedent cannot have occurred for if it had, then the consequent would have occurred. This valid form is called the *modus tollens*.

Exercises

A. State the figures of the following syllogisms, and note whether they are valid or invalid:

1. If p then q	2. If p then q	3. If p then q	4. If p then q
and $\sim q$	and q	and $\sim p$	and p
$\therefore \sim p$	$\therefore p$	$\therefore \sim q$	$\therefore q$

B. Analyze the following syllogisms for validity. Write out each with the hypothetical major premise stated first, the minor premise second, and the conclusion last. Underline the subpropositions of the major premise as p and q.

Two hints may be helpful in working out the last four exercises. Exercises 5 and 6 contain negative expressions. These may be symbolized by $\sim p$ or $\sim q$ as the case may be. Now, if the minor premise asserts $\sim p$ this would affirm, and p in the minor would deny $\sim p$, and similarly with $\sim q$ and q.

In exercises 7 and 8 note that a mixed hypothetical syllogism is always invalid when the minor premise denies the antecedent or affirms the consequent. But when the antecedent is affirmed or the consequent denied (Figures 1 and 4) then we must check the conclusion to determine whether it properly affirms the consequent, as in Figure 1, or denies the antecedent, as in Figure 4.

1. If a man can vote, then he is a citizen. John is not allowed to vote, so we may conclude that he is not a citizen.
2. If a man can vote, then he is a citizen. John can vote, for he is a citizen.
3. If a sailor desires submarine duty, then he must be a brave man. But Bill cannot be a brave man, for he did not desire submarine duty.
4. If this world is the work of a wise and beneficent Intelligence, it will exhibit evidence of wisdom and foresight. The most hardened skeptic is not able to deny that the world does, as a matter of fact, exhibit evidence of wisdom and

foresight. He should therefore admit that it is the work of such an Intelligence.

5. If he had good taste, then he would not make wisecracks at inopportune moments. But since he does make them, he lacks good taste.

6. If men are not wise, then they will not show reverence for those matters which are beyond their understanding. In my classes in the social sciences and philosophy, I have noted that the instructors often confess to an inability to explain some things and yet they do not show reverence for those matters. Is this not sufficient to establish the fact that they are not wise?

7. If all men were capable of perfection, then some would have attained it. But since no men have ever attained perfection, we may conclude that none are capable of it. (SPECIAL HINT: Does the conclusion *contradict* the antecedent?)

8. If some men were capable of perfection, then some would have attained it. But no men have attained perfection, so some men are not capable of it.

Section III: Special Aspects of Hypothetical Propositions and Syllogisms

We conclude our discussion of hypothetical propositions and syllogisms by considering such matters as ordinary language, equivalence, opposition, and "pure" hypothetical syllogisms and sorites.

1. Hypothetical syllogisms in ordinary discourse

a. Linguistic irregularities

In our study of categorical syllogisms we noted the necessity for the restatement of many propositions in order to make them fit into our "logical machine." Similar types of problems will be encountered when we analyze hypothetical syllogisms.

The hypothetical major premise must always be stated in the skeletal form: If —, then —. Some special types of irregularity will be frequently encountered: (1) Exceptive sentences, which use words such as "unless." Example: "Unless the fog lifts, the planes will be grounded." "Unless" is the equivalent of "if not," and we rephrase this sentence as "If the fog does not lift, then the planes will be grounded." (2) Words such as "when," "where," and "provided that" may be simply trans-latable into "ifs." Examples: "When we eliminate prejudice, this will be a better world." "Where science throws its searching light, ignorance disappears." "Provided that the weather is fa-vorable, crops will be excellent." Each of these sentences should be rephrased by beginning them with "if" and adding "then" after the commas. (3) The consequent may be stated before the antecedent, as in "He will co-operate if we give him what he asks for." This should be restated as "If we give him what he asks for, then he will co-operate." Another, stated in exceptive form: "No wills are legal unless witnessed by two persons." This is restated as "If wills are not witnessed by two persons, then they are illegal."

b. Hypothetical enthymemes

Hypothetical enthymemes should be completed as syllo-gisms, and they will be valid or invalid. The following argument is in the First Order: "The unions asked for wage increases, so prices must have risen." The major premise is presumably "If prices rise, then the unions will ask for wage increases." If so, the argument is invalid. A Second Order example: "If the future is like the past, then men will be dissatisfied. They will be." The missing minor here is "The future will be like the past." This argument is valid.

In the example "If Russia were a satisfied nation, then there would be no war, but Russia is not a satisfied nation" the conclusion is missing. The hearer is expected to conclude that there will therefore be a war. The completed argument will obviously be invalid, since the minor premise denies the ante-cedent. Difficulties may be encountered in Fourth Order enthy-memes in which only the major premise is stated. The following is stated sarcastically: "Sure, the Republicans will save the coun-try. All they have to do is to reduce the national debt by cutting taxes." This entire statement is the major premise of a syllogism: "If the Republicans will save the country, then they must reduce the national debt by cutting taxes." The hearer is expected to note that it is impossible to reduce the national debt by cutting taxes, so that it follows that the Republicans will not save the country.

Exercises

State the following arguments in the schematic form of the hypothetical syllogism and analyze for validity. Disregard all material other than the essential syllogistic structure.

1. They said that they would surely come if they could get a sitter, and I know that no sitters are available, so they will not come.

2. He said, "I shall come unless you hear from me by Saturday." We have not heard from him and Saturday has passed. We can conclude that he is coming.

3. If that isn't sound doctrine, then I don't know sound doctrine.

4. The prisoner was very nervous and we know that if he were guilty he would have acted in that manner, so we know that he must be guilty.

5. We should have "socialized medicine" in this country. Hasn't it worked well in England?

6. Robert Filmer argued as follows, in his *Observations Concerning the Originall of Government* (1652): "The king is not proved a tyrant by evidence that he disregards the law, for, if disregard of law be tyranny, courts of equity and all exercise of the pardoning power are tyranny; and such is not the case."

7. The following selection is taken from a discussion in which the author is examining various theories concerning the problem: "What makes conduct right or wrong?" The author now takes up the theory that "morally right conduct" means "conduct approved by one's community."

We usually approve such conduct as is approved by the community to which we belong, and condemn whatever our group condemns. May we not simply say, then, that morals are *mores*, the customs of a given people? Obviously these moral customs vary indefinitely.

The wildest dreams of Kew are the facts of Khatmandu,
And the crimes of Clapham, chaste in Martaban.

According to this conception, there is no one universal right and wrong; there are merely local and temporary standards, like the local spaces and times of relativity theory. Indeed, this view of morality is frankly relativistic. What is right for us, as a member of our community, may be a sin for a member of an alien group. It is a mortal sin for a Catholic to commit suicide, but it is a glorious deed (under certain circumstances) for a patriotic Japanese. . . . To be moral is simply to be true to the code of the group to which you belong.

This view of morality . . . makes . . . morality consist in *conformity.* . . . It gives us no reason to think that the particular code of our group is a *better* code than that of some other group. It gives us no leverage by which to *criticize* and *improve* the morals of our group. It allows no meaning at all to the concept of moral *progress.* However superstitious and stupid, or even cruel, the customs of our community are, they are, by definition, what is right—for us. The unthinking conformist is the moral man, the moral reformer is the immoral man—unless he converts his fellows to his view.

But we do not really believe this. We are all constantly criticizing the morals of our own group—not to say the morals of other peoples. And while a prophet is apt to be without honor in his own country during his lifetime, he is often rated by a later generation as the most moral man of his day, precisely because he rejected the inadequate moral code of his people. We all feel that moral judgments are more important than this definition of morality makes them out to be. (Durant Drake, *Invitation to Philosophy,* Houghton Mifflin Company.)

(HINT: Sum up Drake's argument in the fourth figure. Use p for the theory he discusses, and q for its logical consequences.)

2. Equivalence and Opposition of Hypothetical Propositions

a. *The equivalence of categorical and hypothetical propositions*

A given proposition may be stated either as categorical or as hypothetical, and convey exactly the same meaning in either form. Thus, "If a battleship is gray, then it is painted" may be stated in the categorical form as "All gray battleships are painted." Similarly, "All students of literature are well-read persons" may be stated in the hypothetical form as "If a person is a student of literature, then he is a well-read person." Every hypothetical proposition is translatable into an equivalent A-form categorical, and vice versa. An E-form is equivalent to an A-form by obversion and is hence also translatable, but particular categoricals do not have corresponding hypotheticals. Only universal general categoricals are equivalent to hypotheticals, singular propositions not being thus translatable.

The schematic form of the translations described above may be shown as follows:

All P's   are Q's.   If p, then q.
If it is a p then it is a q.   All P's are Q's.

The student may require some practice before he makes these translations with ease. The categorical equivalent of ordinary hypotheticals may require adding the words "All situations in which . . ." Suppose, for example, that we wish to translate the hypothetical, "If prices continue to rise, then the unions will ask for wage increases" into its corresponding categorical. The categorical propositions must be stated in terms of class inclusion: "All situations in which prices continue to rise are situations in which the unions will ask for wage increases." The hypothetical form of expression states the thought of this proposition more elegantly than does the categorical.

b. The opposition of hypothetical propositions

In this subsection we shall consider the possibilities of converting, contraposing, and contradicting hypothetical propositions.

Conversion. Since a hypothetical proposition is equivalent to an A-form, it cannot be converted. "If x is a man, then x is mortal" cannot be converted into "If x is mortal, then x is a man." We noted on an earlier occasion that we may happen to know, from outside information, that the converse of an A-form happens to be true. Similarly in the hypothetical: "If x is a triangle, then x is a three-sided figure." This proposition is not formally convertible, even though we may know that its converse is a true proposition.

Contraposition. The contrapositive of a categorical A-form is equivalent to the original proposition. Ad $<$ Bu is equivalent to $\sim$ Bd $<$ $\sim$ Au. (The original terms are reversed.) Similarly with hypotheticals. The component subpropositions are negated (contradicted) and reversed in order. Thus:

"If a man is wise, then he knows he is ignorant" contraposes into, "If a man does not know that he is ignorant then he is not wise."

Contradiction. One proposition is the contradictory of another when the truth of one implies the falsity of the other, and vice versa. How would you state the contradictory of "If prices rises, then the unions will ask for wage increases"? When we carefully examine the meaning of "If p then q," we find that it asserts the impossibility of p being true and q false, for it means "If p is true then q *must be* true." To contradict the impossibility of "p is true and q is false" we assert the actuality of this conjunction. The contradictory of our proposition, then, is "Prices rose, and the unions did not ask for wage increases." If we can point to a single instance where prices rose and the unions did not ask for wage increases then we have shown that the hypothetical proposition is false.

Note that "If p, then $\sim q$" is the contrary, not the contradictory of "If p then q," for both of these propositions may be false. The contradictory of "If p then q" is p and $\sim q$."

Exercises

A. *The equivalence of categorical and hypothetical propositions*

1. Translate the following propositions from the categorical into the hypothetical form, and vice versa:
   a. All cats are lovers of solitude.
   b. No exercises in logic are easy.
   c. Express trains alone do not stop here.
   d. If a person is a radical, then he is dissatisfied.
   e. If a person does not read, then he is not well-informed.
   f. If statesmen will show self-restraint, then war will be averted.

2. Translate the four figures of the hypothetical syllogisms concerning the battleship Missouri into their corresponding categorical forms, and note the validity of each. To which fallacies of the categorical syllogisms do Figures 2 and 3 correspond?

3. Analyze the following syllogism in hypothetical form:
It is a rule of the company by which my client is employed that express trains alone do not stop at his station. Since the train in question did not stop, how was he to know that it was not an express train?

B. *The opposition of hypothetical propositions*

1. Are any of the following propositions formally convertible?
   a. If statesmen will show self-restraint, then war will be averted.
   b. If men are not free to express their opinions, then opposition smolders beneath the surface.
   c. If a person is not infected with the typhus bacillus, then he does not have typhoid fever.
2. Contrapose exercises a, b, and c.
3. State the contradictories of a, b, and c.

c. *Pure hypothetical syllogisms and sorites*

Thus far we have analyzed mixed hypothetical syllogisms, in which the minor premise and conclusion were categorical propositions. But syllogistic arguments may contain hypothetical propositions exclusively. Such syllogisms are called *pure* hypothetical syllogisms. This form is illustrated by the following argument:

> If a man is young, then he is an idealist.   (If p, then q.)
> If a man is an idealist, then he is sensitive. (If q, then r.)
> ∴ If a man is young, then he is sensitive.   (∴ If p, then r.)

The validity of this argument may be explained in two ways. (1) The three propositions may be translated into categoricals, in which case the validity will be obvious. (2) Implication is a transitive relation, so that if p implies q and q implies r, then p implies r.

A pure hypothetical sorites may be constructed in a similar manner, there being no limit to the number of propositions which may be used. Assume that we are given If p, then q; if q, then r; if r, then s; and if s, then t. Since implication is a transitive relation, p implies t. It is also obvious that any proposition in the series will imply any proposition at its right.

The contrapositive of the series above is, If $\sim t$, then $\sim s$;

if $\sim s$, then $\sim r$, if $\sim r$, then $\sim q$; and if $\sim q$, then $\sim p$. In other words, the contradictory of any proposition at the right, in the *original* argument, will imply the contradictory of any proposition at its left.

We may also note here that a pure hypothetical syllogism may be *followed* by a categorical proposition, as if we had added "John is a young man" to the syllogism with which we began this discussion. We could then draw the conclusion that "John is sensitive." The complete argument would then be a mixed hypothetical sorites.

Exercises

1. The following propositions are given as true: If A, then X; if S, then M; if Z, then T; if M, then Z, if X, then S. Put them together as a series of implications. Then state the contrapositive of the series. Does $\sim$ Z imply $\sim$ X?

   (HINT: The two propositions which appear only once are obviously the two ends of the chain.)

2. Analyze the following argument as a hypothetical sorites followed by a categorical proposition. Draw the author's conclusion.

   If our diagnosis is correct and if capitalism is doomed to die from the self-contradiction which grows and gnaws like a cancer within its body, then we would seem to be faced with the necessity of choosing either the dictatorship that is fascism or the dictatorship that is communism. For choosing dictatorship means that we will have bureaucratic ownership or bureaucratic regulation by the state, in other words, the end of economic democracy and this means abolishing the rights and liberties of private property. When the rights of private property disappear, there will follow the abolishing of those other rights and liberties which constitute the essence of human personality and without which the human individual will be degraded to the status of a bee in a hive or a cog in a machine. Thus we are faced with the necessity of abandoning the democracy that we love. (Adapted from *The Ways of Things*, by W. P. Montague, Prentice-Hall, 1940, p. 628.)

(HINT: Symbolize the constituent propositions as follows: C: Capitalism is doomed, F: We must choose between fascism and communism, B: We will have bureaucratic ownership or bureaucratic regulation, P: The rights of private property will be abolished, D: The rights and liberties which constitute the essence of human personality will disappear.)

3. The author of the following believes that a science of values (of good and evil) is possible. He is seeking to refute an objection to the possibility of such a science:

> The first argument we shall consider is based on the freedom of the will. It is maintained that men are endowed with a faculty of arbitrary choice which renders human life and its values too unpredictable for scientific treatment. The argument, if valid, would eliminate not only the value-sciences, but also psychology and sociology. The latter must also depend upon a certain constancy in human nature. If freedom is conceived as pure indeterminism, in the sense of absolute chance, no science of human life is possible insofar as freedom obtains. Hence, if psychology and sociology can be scientific, this objection must be invalid. (M. Rader, *No Compromise*. Copyright 1939 by The Macmillan Company and used with their permission.)

(HINT: State the argument of the "free-willists" in the form: If p, then q; and if q, then r; p is true, $\therefore$ r is true. Rader's argument: If $\sim r$, then $\sim q$; and if $\sim q$, then $\sim p$; $\sim r$ (r is false), $\therefore$ $\sim p$ (p is false). Note that $\sim r$ is suggested, not explicitly stated.)

Section IV: Alternative Propositions and Syllogisms

1. The alternative proposition

Alternative propositions are compound, being made up of two constituent propositions joined by the connectives "either" —"or." "Either the nations will co-operate or all will perish." The subpropositions are called the first and second alternants. Using p and q to symbolize these alternants, we find the following structure:

Either $\dfrac{p \text{ (first alternant)}}{\text{(The nations will co-operate)}}$ or $\dfrac{q \text{ (second alternant)}}{\text{(All will perish)}}$

We shall read as "Either p or q" as "Either p is true or q is true," or "Either p is the case or q is the case," depending upon the sense of the proposition.

Let us now examine the meaning of an alternative proposition. The expression "Either p is true or q is true" is somewhat ambiguous. In ordinary language it may mean (1) that one alternant *at most* is true, or it may mean (2) that one at least, and *possibly both,* are true. In logic we take the latter interpretation.

For example, we learn that a politician has been involved in shady dealings. We say of him, "Either he is a fool or he is a scoundrel." One alternant at least, we say, must be true, and possibly both. He may be *both* a fool and a scoundrel. Similarly, in the structural illustration above, we say that at least one alternant must hold, but we do not exclude the possibility that both will occur, i.e., that the nations will co-operate and also perish.

2. The alternative syllogism

Alternative syllogisms are composed of an alternative major premise, a minor premise which affirms or denies one of the alternants, and a conclusion. There are thus four possible figures. The rules of validity of alternative syllogisms follow from the meaning of the alternative proposition. Since the alternative proposition asserts that one alternant at least is true, and possibly both, a valid argument results only when we deny one of the alternants and affirm the other. For if we are told that at least one of two propositions is true, and we learn that one of them is false, the other must be true. But if we learn only that one of them is true, no definite conclusion can follow concerning the other. It *may* be true, but it may not be. The alternative syllogism is thus valid when the minor premise denies; invalid when it affirms. Thus:

The Valid Figures:

Denying the first alternant:
Either X is a fool or he is a knave.
X is not a fool.
∴ X is a knave.

Denying the second alternant:
Either X is a fool or he is a knave.
X is not a knave.
∴ X is a fool.

The Invalid Figures:

Affirming the first alternant:
Either X is a fool or he is a knave.
X is a fool.
∴ X is not a knave.

Affirming the second:
Either X is a fool or he is a knave.
X is a knave.
∴ X is not a fool.

Exercises

1. Complete the following alternative major premises in such a way as to get two valid syllogisms in each case:
   a. Either you are lazy or you are inefficient.
   b. Either you dislike me or I have offended you.
   c. Either Roosevelt or Ruin.
   d. Either the government will control the amount of money in circulation or we shall never succeed in avoiding boom and bust in the business cycle.
2. Analyze for validity: Either it is raining or it is not raining. It is not raining. Therefore, it is raining.

3. Special aspects of alternative propositions and syllogisms

a. Inclusive and exclusive alternation

In inclusive alternation (the kind we have just discussed), one at least of the alternants is true, and possibly both are true. The rules of the alternative syllogism are applicable to such propositions. But consider the following alternative propositions:

Contradictories: Either the workers will get wage increases or they will not.

Contraries: Either he was in Chicago or he was in New York yesterday at noon.

These are examples of "exclusive alternation." We cannot say "and possibly both are true" for these sets of alternants. In the case of contradictories we know that at least one alternant *must* be true; in contraries that no more than one *may* be true. But if we know that one of the contrary alternants is true then we may say of this pair of propositions: "At least one alternant is true, but both are not true," i.e., "*p* is true or *q* is true, but it is not the case that both *p* and *q* are true." *

An exclusive alternative proposition is defined as one in which at least one of the alternants is true, but not both. Such alternation is sometimes called "strong" to distinguish it from "inclusive" alternation, which is also referred to as "normal" or "weak." Hereafter, we shall use "alternation" in the weak or inclusive sense.

b. The equivalence of alternative and categorical propositions

We learned earlier that every hypothetical proposition is equivalent to an A-form categorical. Similarly, every alternative proposition is equivalent to an A-form.

"All men are mortal" has as its corresponding equivalent alternative: "Either any being is *not* a man, or that being is mortal." Note that we contradict the first term of the categorical. The schematic representation in symbols:

Categorical: All x's that are *p* are   *q*
Alternative: Either x is   ∼*p* or x is *q*

Alternative: Either   *r* or *s*
Categorical: All   ∼*r* are *s*

To test the correctness of the equivalence of *"Either* a being is not a man *or* that being is mortal" to "All men are mortal," consider the truth of our alternative proposition for everything in the universe. The proposition states that at least one of the alternants, and possibly both, will be true for anything. Let us apply it to a piece of chalk, a dog, and a man. The first alternant is true for the chalk, since it is "not a man." Both alternants are true for the dog, and the second is true for man.

---

* Symbolically, this is stated as "(*p* or *q*) and ∼ (*p* and *q*)." The first set of parentheses tells us that at least one alternant must be true, and the second set of parentheses, preceded by the tilde, tells us that it is false to say that both *p* and *q* are true. This will be explained further in the next section.

c. Contradicting an alternative proposition

The alternative proposition "Either p or q" asserts that *at least one* of the alternants is *true*. To contradict such a proposition we must assert that *both* p and q are false. In symbols, we say that "$\sim p$ and $\sim q$" is the contradictory of "p or q." In words, "Either that child is ill or it has been spoiled" is contradicted by "That child is not ill, and that child has not been spoiled."

Exercises

A. The equivalence of alternative and categorical propositions

1. Restate the following propositions from the categorical to the alternative form and vice versa.
   a. All soldiers are brave.
   b. All high-ranking students are eligible for honors.
   c. Either you are over 21 or you cannot vote.
   d. Either a man must tell the truth or he must multiply his lies.

2. Restate the following syllogisms in alternative form. Only the major premise will require restatement; the minor premise either affirms or denies.
   a. All Hoosiers are Americans and all Texans are Americans, so all Texans must be Hoosiers.
   b. All Hoosiers are Americans and no Texans are Hoosiers, so no Texans are Americans.
   c. Decent newspapers cannot attain a wide circulation, for they decline to adopt sensational methods, and we know that papers which adopt sensational methods attain a wide circulation.

B. Contradict the following alternative proposition:

1. Either A or B, Either $\sim p$ or q, Either r or $\sim s$.
2. Either you are over 21 or you will not be admitted.
3. Either the nations of the world will establish a world organization which completely eliminates all national sovereignties or the destruction of the world in a third war is absolutely inevitable.

Section V: The Conjunctive Proposition and the Negated Conjunct

The conjunctive proposition is compound, since it is composed of two or more subpropositions joined by the conjunctive "and." Thus, "*p* and *q*" asserts that both *p* and *q* are true propositions. Note that the conjunctive proposition is true or false *as a whole*. It asserts that both *p* and *q* are true, so that if either one of them is false then the proposition as a whole is false.

We shall also find that a "negated conjunct" is an extremely useful form in inference. "*p* and *q*" means that both are true. The negation (or contradiction) of *p* and *q* is ~(*p* and *q*). This means that it is *not the case* that both *p* and *q* are true, and this in turn means that at least one of these conjuncts is false.

The contradictory of ~(*p* and *q*) *is* ~ ~ (*p* and *q*), and this is equivalent to *p* and *q*, since the two negations cancel each other out. To negate a "negated conjunct" then, we simply remove the negation sign and the brackets.

"It is not the case that both *p* and *q* are true" may be stated as "Not both *p* and *q*." A structural illustration of this form in words is:

Not both	*p* (first conjunct)	and	*q* (second conjunct)
	(We will reduce taxes)		(We will reduce the national debt)

In symbols, we have ~(*p* and *q*), which may be read as "It is false that both *p* and *q* are true, or as "*p* and *q* are not both true," or as "Not both are *p* and *q* true." Our illustrative proposition tells us that we cannot reduce both taxes and the debt or "Not both can we reduce taxes and reduce the national debt."

The meaning of a "negated conjunct" should be understood in an inclusive sense. It means that at least one of the conjuncts is false, but that possibly both are false. When we say that we cannot reduce both taxes and the debt, we mean that we may reduce taxes and not reduce the debt, or reduce the debt and not reduce taxes, or that we may reduce neither. The proposition simply rules out the possibility that we can do both, i.e., that both conjuncts can be true.

The reader should recall our discussion of inclusive alternation, in which "*p* or *q*" means that at least one alternant is true, and possibly both are true. "$\sim(p$ and $q)$" means at least one conjunct is false, and possibly both are false. If, however, we wish to express the impossibility of both conjuncts being false, as in "Not both is Hitler alive and dead," we shall need a conjunctive proposition of the form: "Not both is Hitler alive and dead, and Hitler is alive or he is dead." In symbols, using "A" for "Hitler is alive" and "D" for "Hitler is dead" we have "$\sim(A$ and D) and (A or D)." It will be noted that this is exactly the same form we used for exclusive alternation (page 288).

Negated conjuncts may also be used as the premises of syllogisms. Such syllogisms will be valid only when one of the conjuncts is *affirmed*. Since a negated conjunct asserts that one at least of the conjuncts is false (possibly both) we could draw no inference concerning the second conjunct if we were told that one was false. But if we know that one is true, then the other must be false.

One final point before we leave conjunctive propositions and the negated conjunct. The latter type can be shown to be equivalent to an A-form categorical proposition.

"All men are mortal" may be stated as "Not both can a being be a man and a non-mortal." The symbolic transformations are as follows:

Categorical:	All x's that are p's are q.
Negated conjunct:	Not both is x a p and a $\sim q$.
Negated conjunct:	Not both p and q.
Categorical:	All p are $\sim q$.

Note that the first "term" remains unchanged, the second is negated. A test of this equivalence may be shown by applying "Not both is a being a man and a non-mortal" to the piece of chalk, a dog, and a man. One at least of the constituent propositions must be false for everything, and possibly both are false. The first conjunct is false for the chalk, which is "not a man." Both conjuncts are false for the dog, and the second is false for a man.

The categorical equivalent of our illustrative proposition above will be "All situations (such as the present one) in which we reduce taxes are situations in which we will not reduce the national debt."

Exercises

1. State the contradictories of the following:
   a. A and B, $\sim(\sim$A and B), $\sim(\sim$A and $\sim$B).
   b. There will be no world government and there will be no third world war.
   c. It is impossible that a statesman should both protect his country's interest and sacrifice his country's interest.
2. Express the meaning of the following in symbols, assuming that the relations are to be understood in the exclusive sense.
   a. p or q; $\sim(r$ and $s)$; A or $\sim$A
   b. There cannot both be an irrestible force and an immovable object. (Use the symbols F and O).
3. Analyze for validity:
   a. You cannot have socialism and retain economic freedom. But we shall not get socialism, so we shall retain economic freedom.
   b. Not both can anyone indulge in racial and religious discrimination and believe in the fatherhood of God. You believe in the fatherhood of God, so you don't discriminate.
4. State the equivalent categoricals and negated conjuncts for the following:
   a. All students of literature are well-read persons.
   b. All situations in which prices go up are situations in which the unions will ask for wage increases.
   c. Not both can we work hard and not succeed.

Section VI: The Dilemma

1. The meaning of dilemma

A young man was considering the pros and cons of marriage. Being of a somewhat sombre and pessimistic turn of mind, his reflections took the following form: "If I get married, then I shall undertake grave responsibilities and worries. That's not so good. On the other hand, if I remain single, then I shall often be lonely without the companionship of some lovely woman. And that's not so good. What to do?"

This young man found himself confronted with a dilemma. A dictionary defines a dilemma as "a situation in which we are forced to make a choice between equally undesirable alternatives; in other words, a perplexing predicament." This is the way the term is popularly understood. This usage may even cover some "perplexing predicaments" in which the choices are between equally desirable alternatives as in the case of the child in Proust's *Remembrance of Things Past* who could not make up his mind when given the choice of two tempting kinds of dessert. For his alternatives were also undesirable: whichever one he chose, he would lose the other.

In debating, or argument generally, the dilemma is an effective rhetorical device for putting one's opponent "in a hole." Most dilemmas involve perplexing predicaments. But in logic, "dilemma" means a certain kind of logical structure, and its conclusions may be either pleasant or unpleasant. As a logical form the dilemma, as we shall see, combines some of the forms we have studied in this chapter and involves no new principles of proof.

2. The analysis of dilemmas

We shall now analyze a dilemma. The President, Senators, and Congressmen are confronted with dilemmas whenever they act on controversial legislation. Whichever way they act they will lose votes. The dilemma arises when the alternatives are of equal (or nearly equal) importance. Thus, when controversial labor legislation comes to the president's desk, the president may say to himself: "If I sign this bill, I will lose many labor votes. If I veto it, I will lose many conservative votes. But I must either sign or veto. Thus in either case I shall lose votes." This dilemma has the following structure:

If I sign this bill, then I will lose many labor votes, and
    p q
If I veto this bill, then I will lose many conservative votes.
    r s
But either I sign this bill, or I veto this bill.
          p r
Therefore, either I lose labor votes or I lose conservative votes.
                   q s

Note the structure of the argument. It is made up of two syllogisms in hypothetical form:

If p then q and   If r then s
p or r
$\therefore q$ or s

These elements are combined in the following manner. The major premise is a complex conjunctive proposition, made up of two hypothetical propositions. The minor premise is an alternative proposition in which the two antecedents of the hypotheticals in the major premise are affirmed. The conclusion, another alternative proposition, then goes on to affirm the consequents. This type of dilemma is called "constructive."

The dilemma should of course be stated in valid form. This requires that the antecedents of the major premise be affirmed, or its consequents denied. A dilemma in which the consequents are denied (the "destructive dilemma") is illustrated by:

If you were a loyal member of the party, then you would wish to support our leader when he is right; and if you were intelligent you would see that he is right. But either you don't wish to support him when he is right or you don't understand that he is in the right. Therefore, either you are not loyal, or you are not intelligent.

Stated symbolically, we have:

If p then q and if r then s
But either $\sim q$ or $\sim s$
$\therefore$ either $\sim p$ or $\sim r$

The types of dilemma we have analyzed above are called "complex," since the consequents and antecedents are different propositions. In "simple" dilemmas, either the antecedents are the same or the consequents are the same. Thus:

If p then q and if p then r If p then q and if r then q
But either $\sim q$ or $\sim r$ But either p or r
Therefore $\sim p$ or $\sim p$ (i.e., $\sim p$)   Therefore q or q (i.e., q)

3. The criticism of a dilemma

A dilemma may of course be formally invalid, but typically the criticism of a dilemma is based upon material rather than formal considerations. Let us suppose that you are in a debate. Your opponent charges that you are enmeshed in a dilemma from which you cannot escape and that this dilemma places you in an embarrassing predicament. Assuming that your opponent's argument is formally valid, there are nevertheless three possible modes of escape from the "embarrassing predicament" in which he claims that he has placed you. You may be able to "escape through the horns," or "take the dilemma by the horns," or "rebut." These defenses are based upon factual rather than formal considerations. If the facts are not with you, then you may find the dilemma "impregnable."

a. Escaping through the horns

The horns of the dilemma are the two alternants stated in the minor premise: "Either p or r." This implies that there are only two possibilities. But are these actually the only alternatives? If they are not, then we may "escape" through these horns by showing that there are other alternatives, such as t, etc. We then assert that p and r are not exhaustive of the possibilities, that we may escape the devil and the frying pan and not find ourselves in either the deep blue sea or the fire.

This form of attack cannot always be used. The young man contemplating marriage could not use this attack, since he must either remain single or get married. The alternatives exhaust the possibilities. But consider the following dilemma concerning the Caliph Omar, who ordered the destruction of the famous library at Alexandria, Egypt. He is reported to have reasoned as follows: "If these books contain the same doctrines as those of the Koran, then they are unnecessary. If they contradict the doctrines of the Koran, then they are pernicious. Destroy them!"

But there are other possibilities. Mathematical treatises, for example, do not contain the doctrines of the Koran nor do they contradict these doctrines.

Our analysis may be generalized. It is impossible to slip through the horns of a dilemma when the alternatives are genuine contradictories, since one or the other must hold, but it is possible to slip through the horns when the alternatives are contraries. In the last example the alternatives were contraries.

One final comment: Alternatives may not be contradictories, but circumstances may rule out a third possibility. Thus "sign the bill" and "veto the bill" are not formal contradictories, since one might do nothing. But our Constitution makes "doing nothing" equivalent to a veto under certain circumstances and equivalent to signing under others, so that there was no third alternative open to the President. No escape between the horns was possible.

b. Taking the dilemma by the horns

To "take the dilemma by the horns" means to deny the consequences alleged to flow from p or to deny the consequences alleged to flow from r. To do either one of these things (or both) is to deny the major premise of the dilemma. We deny that q follows from p or that s follows from r. A dilemma based on a false premise is a specious one.

The "not loyal or not intelligent" conclusion might be avoided by attacking the horn of the dilemma which says "If you were intelligent then you would understand that he is in the right." Possibly an intelligent person might find that the leader was wrong. Whether this is so or not, however, depends on the facts, or material truth, and not on formal considerations.

c. Rebuttal, or the "counter-dilemma"

This form of escape is sometimes effective where the others fail. Let us assume that the premises of the dilemma are true and the alternatives exhaustive. Escape from the embarrassing predicament may yet be possible. "A cloud may have a silver lining" just as "every rose has a thorn." Choices involve sacrifices, but sacrifices often bring compensating gains. The counter-dilemma emphasizes the silver lining. But, as we well know, it is not true without exception that every cloud has a silver lining, so this form of escape is not always possible. The facts of the situation must be considered in each specific case.

Thus our pessimistic young man might be told to look at the situation from a different point of view. "If you get married," we tell him, "you will not be lonely, and if you remain single then you will avoid the cares and responsibilities of marriage." Both alternatives now appear favorable, and his embarrassing predicament has been eliminated. What we have done here is to emphasize different aspects of the same factual situation. The same facts may appear desirable or undesirable, depending upon the point of view, as in the case of the child and his dessert.

Let us set the formal structures of the dilemma and counter-dilemma side by side:

Dilemma	*Counter-dilemma*
If p then q, and if r then s	If p then $\sim s$ and if r then $\sim q$
But either p or r	But either p or r
∴ Either q or s	∴ Either $\sim s$ or $\sim q$

The major premise of the counter-dilemma contradicts the original consequents and reverses their order. Note, however, that
the conclusion of the counter-dilemma is *not* the contradictory
of the conclusion of the original dilemma. "Either I will have
responsibilities or I will be lonely" is quite consistent with
"Either I won't be lonely or I won't have responsibilities." The
contradictory of the original conclusion would be: I won't be
lonely and I won't have responsibilities. The counter-dilemma
does not deny the facts stated in the original dilemma; it merely
looks at them in a different way.

But not all counter-dilemmas are effective, nor indeed do
all of them "make sense." Whether any one of the three attacks
we have noted is effective will always depend upon the facts of
the particular situation. An attack against a dilemma may be
strong, or it may be weak. There are no rules which determine
the persuasiveness of an attack; your own common sense must
be the judge.

Exercises

Restate the following dilemmas in proper form. Note whether
the dilemma is in valid form. Then determine whether the dilemma
can be effectively attacked by one or more of the three methods of
criticism.

1. If you don't believe in the capitalistic system, then why don't
   you go to Russia to live? If you do believe in it, then you
   should not criticize the manner in which it is operated. But
   either . . . , etc.
2. Either the conclusion of a syllogism is contained in something already stated in the premises, or it is not. If the conclusion merely states something already given in the premises, then it adds nothing to our knowledge, and is useless.

If the conclusion states something not given in the premises, then it is invalid. So every syllogism is useless or invalid.

3. If human actions are determined by heredity and environment, then we are not responsible for what we do. On the other hand, if human actions result from *uncaused* acts of the will ("free-will"), then we are also not responsible for what we do. So we should never blame anyone for anything, not even for failing to see the sense of this argument!

4. Either I am fated to pass my final exams or I am fated not to pass my final exams. If I am fated to pass, then I shall pass whether or not I prepare for them. If I am fated not to pass, I shall fail whether I prepare or not. So, in either case, study will be useless.

5. Either I am fated to pass this course or I am not fated to pass it. If I am fated to pass I shall do so whether I do the work correctly or not. If I am not fated to pass, the same. So why study?

6. A chess player's meditations: If my opponent made that move intentionally, then he was not wise; if unintentionally, then he was not lucky. But as I have known him long enough to know that he is neither wise nor lucky, I must conclude that he made the move neither intentionally, nor unintentionally. Which seems to put *me* in a dilemma, since it must have been one or the other. (Castell.)

7. The "Philosophy of an Airman" (quoted in *The Principles of Reasoning*, D. S. Robinson):

If you fly well, there is nothing to worry about.

If you should spin, then one of two things may happen: Either you crash or you don't crash.

If you don't crash, there is nothing to worry about.

If you do crash, then one of two things may happen: Either you are hurt or you are not hurt.

If you are not hurt, there is nothing to worry about.

If you are hurt, one of two things may happen: Either you are badly hurt or you are not badly hurt.

If you are not badly hurt, there is nothing to worry about.

If you are badly hurt, then one of two things may happen: Either you recover or you don't recover.

If you do recover, then there is nothing to worry about.

If you don't recover you can't worry.

INSTRUCTIONS: In analyzing this item, symbolize: "there is nothing to worry about" by N; "you fly well" by W; "you spin," i.e., "you do not fly well," by $\sim$W; "you crash" by C;

"you are hurt" by H; "you are badly hurt" by B; "you recover" by R. Then show how the argument uses the dilemmatic form to prove that N is implied by all possibilities. Can you pass through the horns of one of its premises?

8. A classical example of a counter-dilemma is illustrated by the following tale concerning Protagoras, the famous Greek sophist:

Protagoras, teacher of law and rhetoric, had agreed to give Eulathus instruction in law, rhetoric, and argumentation on the following terms: Eulathus was to pay half of the fee in advance, and the remainder after he won his first case in a court of law. Protagoras instructed Eulathus after receiving the down payment, but after the course was concluded Eulathus showed no interest in the practice of law. After waiting a reasonable time, Protagoras sued Eulathus for the balance of his fee; Eulathus conducted his own defence in the court. Protagoras presented the following dilemma to the judge:

"If the judge holds in my favor, then Eulathus must pay by judgment of the court, and if the judge holds in favor of Eulathus, then he must pay by virtue of our agreement, which requires that he pay when he wins his first case in court of law. But either the judge will hold in my favor or against me. Therefore in either case Eulathus must pay me."

Protagoras, however, had been an excellent teacher, and Eulathus was a shining example of the master's own method. Eulathus presented a counter-dilemma to the judge:

"If I win this case, then, by the judgment of the court, I do not have to pay Protagoras, and if I lose this case, then, by the terms of our agreement, I don't have to pay since I will not yet have won my first case. But either I win the case or lose it. Therefore, no matter how the decision goes, I need not pay."

(Questions: Was the agreement intended to cover this kind of case? Do the parties appeal to a single standard for the determination of the case? If you were the judge, how would you decide?)

Chapter 13

Symbolic Logic

Section I. What is Symbolic Logic?

Modern symbolic logic is a generalized treatment of formal logic which makes use of special symbols. The use of symbols in logical analysis is of course not new: Aristotle found it convenient to make a limited use of symbolic abbreviations. But modern logic symbolizes logical operations in a very thoroughgoing way.

The value of symbols is manifold. First, they can be precisely defined, thus eliminating the richness of ambiguity that attaches itself to the words of ordinary language. Symbols abbreviate lengthy expressions, thus simplifying exposition. The value of such abbreviations is well stated by A. N. Whitehead: ". . . by the aid of symbols we can make transitions in reasoning almost mechanically by the eye, which otherwise would call into play the higher faculties of the brain." * The use of symbols may also enable us to analyze arguments which might be too complex to unravel when stated in ordinary English.

One of the most important virtues of the new symbolic language lies in its power to simplify and systematize large numbers of complex statements. In recent years, many practical applications have been made of this power. Thus, engineers have been enabled to simplify very complicated switching systems, insurance companies have been able to provide for large numbers of contingencies by fewer provisions, and even legislation has benefited through the application of the new techniques by legal scholars. Symbolic logic has also contributed to the building of the large computers known as "thinking machines" or "electronic brains."

* Introduction to Mathematics.

In this chapter, we shall introduce the student to only a few of the concepts of the new logic. We shall limit our attention to some phases of the "propositional calculus" and to "truth-tables," and we shall not deal at all with the systematic treatment of logistic systems. Our chief concern will be to show how the new symbolic methods may be employed in the analysis of arguments.

Section II. Truth-Functions and Truth-Tables

We are already familiar with some of the basic concepts of symbolic logic, such as the notions of "negation" or "contradiction," "conjunction," and "alternation." We shall now introduce symbols for these notions and stipulate precise definitions for each.

The symbol for "negation" is already familiar: "$\sim$." If p stands for any proposition, then $\sim p$ means "not-p," or "p is false."

"Conjunction" is symbolized by a dot "$\cdot$" which stands for "and." Thus, "$p \cdot q$" means "p and q," or "p is true and q is true."

"Alternation" is symbolized by "v," from the Latin "vel," meaning "or." This symbol is usually called a "wedge." Thus, "p v q" is read as "Either p or q" or "Either p is true or q is true."

The symbols "p" and "q" which stand for any propositions, are called "logical variables," which are given "values" by substituting propositions for the letters. The concepts "not," "and," and "either—or" are called "logical constants" or "truth-functional connectives." "Truth-function" means that the truth-value of the proposition resulting from substitutions on the variables of "p v q," for example, will depend solely on the truth values of the propositions substituted.* Another useful expression is "substitution instance." Thus, "Either x is a fool or x is a crook" is a substitution instance of the truth function "p v q."

A "truth-table" is a device for defining truth functions. It shows us under what conditions the truth or falsity of its constituent propositions will make the function true and under what conditions false. Let us illustrate:

* There need be no relevant connection between p and q.

1. The contradictory function, "$\sim p$"

One proposition is the contradictory of another when they have opposite truth values: if one is true, the other is false and vice versa. If p is true, then $\sim p$ must be false; if p is false, $\sim p$ must be true. This is shown by the table:

p	$\sim p$
T	F
F	T

2. The conjunctive function, "$p \cdot q$"

The conjunctive "and" is defined as a connective which asserts the joint truth of any two propositions. Thus "$p \cdot q$" asserts that p is true and that q is true, or "both p and q are true." In ordinary language, propositions are usually connected in this way only when they have some relevance to each other, but "$\cdot$" merely asserts the idea of two (or more) propositions being jointly true. To illustrate with an odd pairing, "Nero lived in Rome $\cdot$ Norwegians catch sardines" is a true conjunctive proposition, since its constituent propositions are both true. This attention to truth-values without consideration of relevance is an important point in what follows.

The truth table for "$p \cdot q$" is shown as follows:

	p	q	$p \cdot q$
1.	T	T	T
2.	F	T	F
3.	T	F	F
4.	F	F	F

The first two columns, one headed by "p" and one by "q," are called the "guide" columns. On lines 1 to 4 we find the four possible combinations of the truth or falsity of p and q. (A convenient automatic way of writing these combinations is to alternate T's and F's under the p column and to run a pair of T's and then a pair of F's under q.)

The column to the right of the vertical line shows us the conditions under which "$p \cdot q$" is true or false. Since "$p \cdot q$" is true only when both are true, we find this shown only on line 1. The function is false when one or both of its constituent propositions are false.

3. The alternative function, "*p* v *q*"

The truth functional connective "v" stands for alternation in its *inclusive* sense. Thus, "*p* v *q*" will be true when *p* is true and *q* false; when *p* is false and *q* true, or when both *p* and *q* are true. This function is false only when both *p* and *q* are false. This is shown by the table:

p	*q*	*p* v *q*
T	T	T
F	T	T
T	F	T
F	F	F

We recall that there need be no relevance between the two subpropositions in a conjunctive function, whose truth is determined solely by the truth or falsity of the subpropositions. Similarly with respect to the two (or more) alternants: The alternative proposition "Either (it is true that) 2 + 2 = 5 or (it is true that) Hawaii is a state" is true, for the second alternant is true.

If we wish to express the notion of *exclusive* alternation, i.e., that *p* or *q* is true, but not both, we do so as follows: (*p* v *q*). ~(*p* · *q*). This is read as (*p* or *q* is true) and (it is false that both *p* and *q* are true).

4. The truth-functional "If—then"

We shall now discuss one additional concept of symbolic logic, the truth-functional "If—then" relation, symbolized by a horseshoe lying on its side: "⊃." The function "*p* ⊃ *q*" should be read as "If *p*, then, truth-functionally, *q*." This relationship, as we shall see, has some important resemblances to the ordinary hypothetical "If—then" relationship, but it also differs in important ways. We shall now define the relationship symbolized by "⊃," and this will be the sense in which we shall employ it throughout this chapter.

The conjunctive function has been defined as a relationship such that it is false except when both of its constituent propositions are true; an alternative function, on the other hand, is true except when both constituents are false. The truth-functional "If—then" ($p \supset q$) is defined as true except when the *antecedent* proposition is *true* and the *consequent* *false*. Its table is shown as follows:

p	q	$p \supset q$
T	T	T
F	T	T
T	F	F
F	F	T

Note that $p \supset q$ is false only on line 3 which shows p as T and q as F.

We shall attempt to explain the "rationale" of the truth function $p \supset q$ in the next section.

Section III. The Meaning of "$\supset$"

The most important thing to remember about the truth of a truth function is the absence of the requirement of relevance between the sub-propositions of the function. This absence of relevance is not a serious stumbling block in the conjunctive and alternative functions, but it is in the "If—then" function. The truth or falsity of this function is defined by the truth table, however, and the only check we need make in connection with the truth table is with respect to the material truth or falsity of the constituent propositions. Let us now try to "make sense" of this situation.

We recall our earlier treatment of "If—then" propositions. We learned that the contradictory of a hypothetical proposition (If p then q) asserts that the antecedent p is true and the consequent q is false. To prove the falsity of "If prices rise (p) then the unions will ask for wage increases (q)" we must show that prices rose (p is true) but that the unions did not ask for wage increases (q is false). In symbols, "$p \cdot \sim q$" is the contradictory of "If p then q." Further, we said nothing about how we prove that "If p then q" is true. We do not prove its truth by showing that p is true, nor that q is true (or p false or q false), but only by showing that there is an actual connection between p and q.

The truth-functional If—then relation agrees with our

earlier analysis in holding that "$p \cdot \sim q$" is the contradictory of "$p \supset q$." This is shown on line 3 of the table for "$p \supset q$." But "$\supset$" also means that "$p \supset q$" is true "functionally" when p is true and q true (line 1), when p is false and q true (line 2) and when p is false and q false (line 4). No "connection" between p and q is required in the "true" functional use of the If—then relation.

The contradictory of p is $\sim p$, and the contradictory of $\sim p$ is $\sim \sim p$, i.e., p. Similarly, if the contradictory of "$p \supset q$" is "$p \cdot \sim q$," then the contradictory of $p \cdot \sim q$, i.e., $\sim (p \cdot \sim q)$ is $p \supset q$. We may thus define "$p \supset q$" as "$\sim (p \cdot \sim q)$." This definition may be proved by truth tables:

| | | | | (A) | (B) |
p	q	$\sim q$	$p \cdot \sim q$	$\sim (p \cdot \sim q)$	$p \supset q$
T	T	F	F	T	T
F	T	F	F	T	T
T	F	T	T	F	F
F	F	T	F	T	T

We interpret this table as follows: At the left we find the guide columns for p and q. Since we use $\sim q$ in the function "$p \cdot \sim q$" we work up a table for $\sim q$. Its truth values, obviously, are opposite to those for q. Then we determine the truth values for $p \cdot \sim q$. A conjunctive function is true only when both its constituents are true. We find T's under both p and $\sim q$ only on line 3. The table for $\sim (p \cdot \sim q)$ is opposite to that for $p \cdot \sim q$. Then, at the end, we state the table for $p \supset q$. We find the last two columns, headed by (A) and (B), identical, showing that the two functions are equivalent.

This point may be summed up as follows: A truth-functional "If—then" statement is one in which it is *not the case* that its antecedent is true and its consequent false. In words, "If we have intelligent leadership, then war will be averted" ($p \supset q$) is equivalent to "It is false to say that we will have intelligent leadership and that war will not be averted" [$\sim (p \cdot \sim q)$].

Exercises

1. In the following, T and R stand for true propositions; F and L for false propositions. Which of these functions are true, and which are false? (Example: R · L is false, for a conjunctive function is true only when both of its constituents are true).

   a. T · R; F · T; R · L

   b. T v L; R v F; F v T, L v F

   c. F ⊃ L; R ⊃ T; L ⊃ R; T ⊃ F; R ⊃ L

   The following are called "complex" functions since they contain compound functions as elements. Start by checking the truth values of the elements (inside the parentheses), and then work outward, thus: (R ⊃ F) ⊃ (L ⊃ T)

$$\text{F} \quad \supset \quad \text{T}$$
$$\text{T}$$

   Note the manner in which we "short-circuited" the truth tables in this illustrative example. Use the same method on the following:

   (F ⊃ T) ⊃ (T ⊃ L); (R ⊃ F) ⊃ (T ⊃ L); (R ⊃ T) ⊃ (L ⊃ F)

Section IV. Ordinary Implication and Material Implication

In its ordinary usage "If p then q" states an implicative relationship between p and q. We have already learned that when one proposition (p) logically implies another proposition (q), the following relationship holds between them:

> If p is true, then q is true.
> If p is false, then q is undetermined.
> If q is true, then p is undetermined.
> If q is false, then p is false.

This relationship holds in "If x is a tall man, then x is a man." This illustration is an example of the "strict" use of the "If—then" implicative relationship.

There are also other kinds of "ordinary" implications in which this pattern may hold. In our illustration there was a logical necessity in the relation of the antecedent and consequent, but we may also set up similar relationships by definition, as in "If x is an artichoke then x is a vegetable." A causal relationship, in the sense of a sufficient condition, may yield a similar pattern, as in "If prices rise then the unions will ask for wage increases." Finally we may voluntarily set up an implicative pattern by our decision or fiat, as in "If you do that again then I'll spank you." There are thus four types of ordinary implication, i.e., of the ordinary use of the "If—then" relationship: the strict or logical, the definitional, the causal, and the decisional uses.

In all of these uses there is some kind of "connection" between the antecedent and the consequent. But the truth-functional If—then, symbolized by "⊃," which may be regarded as a fifth type, requires no connection between antecedent and consequent. This type is usually called *"material* implication," meaning that it is true or false depending exclusively on the material truth or falsity of antecedent or consequent, independently considered.

The reader may now raise the question: Why is the truth functional "If—then" relation called "material *implication*"? The reason is that though this function differs radically in meaning from ordinary implication, there are some fundamental similarities. We have already noted that *all* types of implication, including material, are proven false by showing the antecedent true and the consequent false. This indicates that "⊃" is at least a *minimal* meaning for "If—then," even though the latter expression usually means much more. Further, though a material implication is proven "true" merely by showing its antecedent to be false or its consequent true, the sequel will show that we get the same results in determining the validity of arguments whichever type of implication we employ.

A useful analogue of the relationship between ordinary and material implication may be helpful. Let us compare "strict" equivalence with "material" equivalence. "All whales are mammals" has the same meaning as "No whales are non-mammals." These are strictly equivalent, i.e., they are (must be) true or false together. But two propositions are materially equivalent when it is merely the case that both are true or both are false. Thus, "2 + 2 = 4" and "The Senate has 100 mem-

308   SYMBOLIC LOGIC

bers" are materially equivalent to each other since both are true. But there is no connection between these propositions. (We shall symbolize the notion of material equivalence by "≡.")

The meaning of material implication may be stated as follows: Except in the case where, as a matter of fact, the antecedent of an If—then statement is true and its consequent false, the antecedent (whatever it may be) materially implies the consequent (whatever it may be). Thus, any If—then statement with a false antecedent "counts" as true, as does any such statement with a true consequent. A false proposition thus implies anything and everything (true and false statements), and a true proposition is implied by any proposition whatsoever (true and false statements).

We shall close this long discussion by considering the so-called "paradoxes" of material implication. The innocent reader is apt to be puzzled by some examples of "true" material implications such as the following:

1. If Socrates did not drink the hemlock, then a triangle has four sides.
2. If white is black, then some roses are red.
3. If "July" contains four letters, then Nero fiddled while Rome burned.

The first counts as true because it has a false antecedent; the second because it has a false antecedent (or because it has a true consequent); the third because its consequent is true. Now, these are "paradoxes" only if we assume that any "implication" must have some logical connection between antecedent and consequent, but truth-functional "If—thens" disregard such connections.

It is possible, however, to bring the "sense" of these peculiar joinings of statements closer to ordinary language by showing the equivalences of truth-functional "If—then" statements to truth functional alternations. This will be done by showing that $p \supset q$ is equivalent to $\sim p \vee q$, and $p \vee q$ equivalent to $\sim p \supset q$. Let us show these equivalences by truth tables:

Table 1   Table 2

p	q	$\sim p$	$p \vee q$	$\sim p \supset q$		p	q	$\sim p$	$\sim p \vee q$	$p \supset q$
T	T	F	T	T		T	T	F	T	T
F	T	T	T	T		F	T	T	T	T
T	F	F	T	T		T	F	F	F	F
F	F	T	F	F		F	F	T	T	T

Table 1 shows $(p \vee q) \equiv (\sim p \supset q)$ and Table 2 shows $(\sim p \vee q) \equiv (p \supset q)$. Note that $\sim p \supset q$ is false only when $\sim p$ is true and q false, and that $\sim p \vee q$ is false only when both $\sim p$ and q are false.

These tables tell us that the following are materially equivalent propositions: "Either x is a fool, or he is a crook" is equivalent to "If x is not a fool, then he is a crook" $[(p \vee q) \equiv (\sim p \supset q)]$. Similarly, "Either x is not a man, or x is mortal" is equivalent to "If x is a man, then x is mortal" $[(\sim p \vee q) \equiv (p \supset q)]$.

These equivalences, of course, hold even though there is no connection between the constituent propositions of the respective truth functions. But possibly our "If—then" paradoxes will seem slightly less paradoxical if we translate them into equivalent alternative propositions. We will then derive the following:

1. Either Socrates drank the hemlock, or a triangle has four sides.
2. Either white is not black, or some roses are red.
3. Either "July" does not contain four letters, or Nero fiddled while Rome burned.

We know that an alternative function is true if either one of the alternants is true. In number 1 the first is true; in number 2 both are true; in number 3 the second is true. Since these alternative functions are true, their equivalent material implications must be true!

When we have a false material implication, we shall find an equivalent false alternative function: "If a triangle has three sides, then salt is sweet" is a false implication, and its equivalent, "Either a triangle does not have three sides, or salt is sweet" is a false alternative function.

Exercises

1. Which of the following are strictly equivalent; which materially equivalent?
   a. No women are pilots; no pilots are women.
   b. Desdemona was loved by Othello; Othello loved Desdemona.
   c. Shakespeare wrote Hamlet; Shakespeare wrote Othello.
   d. Van Buren defeated Harrison; white is black.
2. Which type of implication is illustrated in the following:
   a. If everybody is happy, then Hawaii is the fiftieth state.
   b. If he is a piccolo player, then I'm the Admiral of the Swiss Navy.
   c. If one wishes to lose weight, then he should eat less.
3. State the equivalent alternative or implicative functions for the following and exhibit the equivalences by constructing truth tables:
   a. "If Stevenson defeated Eisenhower, then 3 is greater than 2."
   b. "Either $2 + 2 = 4$ or a square has 4 sides."

Section V. The Interdefinability of Truth Functions

The conjunctive, alternative, and materially implicative truth functions are definable in terms of each other, supplemented by the use of the negation function. What we mean in saying that these functions are "interdefinable" is that we can find truth-functional equivalences among these functions in terms of the truth tables. The interdefinitions are as follows:

1. Material implication defined by the use of "$\sim$" and "v": $(p \supset q) \equiv (\sim p \lor q)$
2. Alternation defined by the use of "$\sim$" and "$\supset$": $(p \lor q) \equiv (\sim p \supset q)$

These two equivalences were explained on pages 308–9.

3. Material implication defined by the use of "$\sim$" and "·": $(p \supset q) \equiv \sim(p \cdot \sim q)$

This equivalence was shown on page 305.

4. Conjunction defined by "$\sim$" and "$\supset$": $(p \cdot q) \equiv \sim(p \supset \sim q)$

The contradictory of $(p \supset q)$ is $(p \cdot \sim q)$. Now, in order to state the contradictory of "$p \supset \sim q$" we need a conjunctive function in which the antecedent is affirmed and the consequent denied, viz.: "$p \cdot q$." We thus have the equivalence $\sim(p \supset \sim q)$ $\equiv (p \cdot q)$. [The negation of $(p \supset \sim q)$ is $(p \cdot q)$.] If we now reverse the order of the equivalent expressions we have $(p \cdot q) \equiv$ $\sim(p \supset \sim q)$ which gives us our definition of conjunction in terms of "$\sim$" and "$\supset$."

In words: "Prices will rise and wages will rise" $(p \cdot q)$ is equivalent to "It is false to say that 'If prices rise, then wages will not rise'" $[\sim(p \supset \sim q)]$.

5. Alternation defined by "$\sim$" and "$\cdot$": $(p \vee q) = \sim(\sim p \cdot \sim q)$

We recall the meaning of the alternative function "$p \vee q$." It asserts that at least one and possibly both of the alternants are true. It is false only when both p and q are false. Thus the contradictory of $p \vee q$ is $(\sim p \cdot \sim q)$ which asserts that both are false. In symbols, $\sim(p \vee q) \equiv (\sim p \cdot \sim q)$. Our next step requires the negation of both sides of this equivalence. This step will yield a new equivalence: $(p \vee q) \equiv \sim(\sim p \cdot \sim q)$. This is the equivalence we undertook to demonstrate.

In words: "Either you are very bright, or you knew the answer" $\equiv$ "It is false to say that you are both not very bright and that you did not know the answer."

6. Conjunction defined by "$\sim$" and "$\vee$": $(p \cdot q) \equiv \sim(\sim p \vee \sim q)$.

The following steps will make this equivalence clear. The contradictory of $(p \cdot q)$ is $\sim(p \cdot q)$. The last expression, a negated conjunct, means that at least one of the conjuncts is false, i.e., p is false or q is false, or both are false, (i.e., $\sim p \vee \sim q$), and so we have $\sim(p \cdot q) \equiv (\sim p \vee \sim q)$. Negating both sides we get $(p \cdot q) \equiv \sim(\sim p \vee \sim q)$.

In words: "Lincoln and Washington were both great men" is equivalent to "It is false to say either that Lincoln was not a great man or that Washington was not a great man."

We shall now sum up these interdefinitions in tables, for convenience in reference. Note that implication and alternation have equivalents in negated conjuncts, and that the conjunctive proposition has equivalents in the contradictories of implications and alternations. We also include a table for the "negated conjunct" function.

Implicative	$p \supset q$	Alternative	$p \vee q$
Alternative	$\sim p \vee q$	Implicative	$\sim p \supset q$
Negated conjunct	$\sim(p \cdot \sim q)$	Negated conjunct	$\sim(\sim p \cdot \sim q)$
Conjunctive	$p \cdot q$	Negated conjunct	$\sim(p \cdot q)$
Implicative	$\sim(p \supset \sim q)$	Implicative	$p \supset \sim q$
Alternative	$\sim(\sim p \vee \sim q)$	Alternative	$\sim p \vee \sim q$

Exercises

A. *On Interdefinitions of Truth Functions*

1. Translate the following implicative functions into alternative and "negated conjunct" functions; the alternatives into implications and negated conjuncts; the conjunctives into the contradictories of implicative and alternative functions; and the negated conjuncts into implications and alternations:

   a. $r \supset s$ d. $\sim r \supset \sim s$ g. $\sim r \vee \sim s$
   b. $r \vee s$ e. $\sim r \cdot s$ h. $\sim(\sim r \cdot \sim s)$
   c. $r \cdot s$ f. $\sim(r \cdot s)$

   i. Either the treasurer neglected his duties, or he connived in the embezzlement of the funds.
   j. Not both can a person put forth his best efforts and not succeed.
   k. If he is a piccolo player, then I'm a monkey's uncle.

2. Show the equivalences of your translations in exercises a. through h. by the truth tables. Place the letter A above the original function and B above its translation, as in the truth table on page 305.

B. *"Chains of Implication"*

Instructions: Implication is a transitive relation, so that if p implies q, and q implies r, and r implies s, then p must imply s. Stated symbolically, if we are given $p \supset q$, $q \supset r$ and $r \supset s$, then $p \supset s$. This series of implication may be simplified in the form of a "chain of implications" shown as $p \supset q \supset r \supset s$. Any proposition in this series will obviously imply any proposition at its right. This chain, however, is only a simplified way of stating the series of implications shown above, and should be *read* as "p implies q, and q implies r, etc."

The contrapositive of the chain may be shown as $\sim s \supset \sim r$

$\supset \sim q \supset \sim p$. Thus, the contradictory of any proposition at the right, in the *original* argument, will imply the contradictory of any proposition at its left.

1. The following propositions are given: $a \supset x, s \supset m, z \supset t,$ $m \supset z, x \supset s$. Put these together as a chain of implications. Then state the contrapositive. Query: Does $\sim z \supset \sim x$?

2. The following are given: $b \supset c, \sim c \vee d, \sim(d \cdot \sim e),$ $\sim f \supset \sim e.$

    Translate the non-implications into implications. Then arrange in the form of a "chain of implications." (Note that one of the functions must be contraposed in order to get it into the chain.) Then contrapose the entire chain.

3. The following are given: $a \supset x, x \supset s, b \supset g, \sim(g \cdot z),$ $t \vee o, \sim o \vee m, t \supset z.$

    a. Translate the non-implications into implications.

    b. Arrange as a chain of implications. To do this, find your "end" propositions, (which appear only once) by first eliminating the pairs, counting a variable and its contradictory as a pair. Then make your pairs perfect by contraposing. Some "trial and error" may be necessary before you make the proper changes.

    c. Now contrapose the entire chain of implications found in b.

    d. Are the following functions true if the chain is true?

    1. $\sim s \supset \sim m.$ 3. $\sim x \vee g.$

    2. $\sim s \supset \sim z.$ 4. $\sim(\sim b \cdot \sim x).$

4. Examine the following for validity, symbolizing as shown below:

    The United States will support either a ban on atomic testing or general disarmament. But if the U.S. supports the abolition of atomic weapons, then the U.S. will not support general disarmament. Further, if the U.S. supports a ban on atomic tests, then the U.S. will become a second-rate military power. It follows, then, that either the U.S. will not support the abolition of atomic weapons, or the U.S. will become a second rate military power.

    Symbolize the propositions as follows:

    B: The United States will support a ban on atomic testing.

    D: The United States will support general disarmament.

    A: The United States will support the abolition of atomic weapons.

    S: The United States will become a second-rate military power.

Section VI. Complex Propositions and Bracketing

Complex propositions contain one or more compound constituent elements. An example: If price control is to work (p), then either the people must be willing not to buy in black markets (q) or black markets must be ruthlessly stamped out (r). The consequent of this implication is an alternative, i.e., a compound proposition. In order to symbolize this proposition we must use parentheses in order to show that the major relation is implication, thus: $p \supset (q \vee r)$.

In our study of ambiguity we considered the question, "How much is $3 \times 2 + 4$?" The question is emphibolous, but there is a rule of arithmetic which tells us to perform the multiplication before the addition. Now, a similar ambiguity would arise if we symbolized our proposition above by $p \supset q \vee r$. This is ambiguous as it stands, for it may mean $p \supset (q \vee r)$ or it may mean $(p \supset q) \vee r$. The former statement means "*If p is true, then* either q or r is true"; the latter, "*Either p implies q is true, or r is true.*" To avoid such ambiguities we shall employ parentheses and brackets as needed.

Complex propositions may also have other *complex* propositions as their constituent elements. These will need brackets as well as parentheses. To illustrate: We recall the "First Figure" of the hypothetical syllogism, or "Modus Ponens": "If p is true then q is true; p is true; therefore q is true." This argument form can be stated symbolically as a complex implication,* as follows: $[(p \supset q) \cdot p] \supset q$. The antecedent gives us the two premises, and the brackets show us that the major relation is implication.

The following: $[(p \supset q) \cdot (r \supset s) \cdot (p \vee r)] \supset (q \vee s)$ is the symbolic form of the Constructive Dilemma. It takes some practice to learn how to express the major relationships of a complex proposition in words. The proposition above tells us that if the whole of the bracketed conjunctive antecedent is true then the consequent will be true, or "IF it is true that p implies q and that r implies s and that either p or r is true, THEN it follows that q or s must be true."

Statements of much greater complexity are of course possible, and we soon reach a point where restatement of a com-

---

* "Therefore" may be interpreted as "implies."

plex function in the words of ordinary language becomes extremely difficult. The advantage of working with symbols is thus quite apparent.

Exercises

Use parentheses and brackets to show several different possible interpretations of the major relationships in the following:
(a) $p \cdot q \vee r$, (b) $p \supset q \cdot r$, (c) $p \vee q \supset r$, (d) $p \supset q \supset r$,
(e) $p \vee q \cdot r \supset s$, (f) $p \supset q \supset r \vee s \cdot q$

Section VII. Truth Tables and Argumentation

We shall now show how the truth tables may be used to test the validity of arguments. We shall distinguish between arguments, "argument forms," and laws of logic.

We are already familiar with the nature of an argument as a unit of discourse which contains premises and a conclusion, viz.:

If you wish to understand this material, then you will read it carefully.

You do not read it carefully.

Therefore, you do not wish to understand it.

We are also familiar with "argument forms," which contain "statement variables" instead of statements. The argument-form for the above argument reads:

$$\text{If } p \text{ then } q.$$
$$\sim q$$
$$\therefore \sim p$$

This is the Modus Tollens argument form, shown as an implication under (G) below. Its validity may be shown by the truth tables, as follows:

(A)	(B)	(C)	(D)	(E)	(F)	(G)
p	q	$\sim p$	$\sim q$	$p \supset q$	$(p \supset q) \cdot \sim q$	$[(p \supset q) \cdot \sim q] \supset \sim p$
T	T	F	F	T	F	T
F	T	T	F	T	F	T
T	F	F	T	F	F	T
F	F	T	T	T	T	T

We have headed the columns with letters for convenience in reference. We interpret this table as follows. Column
E shows the truth values for $(p \supset q)$ and F shows the values for
$(p \supset q) \cdot \sim q$. The truth values for F (a conjunctive proposition)
are determined by seeking for lines on which T's are shown for
both $p \supset q$ (E) and $\sim q$ (D). This occurs only on line 4. To fill
in values under (G) we must use T's for all cases except when
the antecedent, $[(p \supset q) \cdot \sim q]$ (F) is true, and the consequent,
$\sim p$ (C) is false. We check under columns F and C and find that
we must use T's exclusively.

The truth tables, in other words, tell us whether or not
the two premises (D and E) materially imply the conclusion
(C). In a valid argument form the implication which states
the full argument will have nothing but T's under it, meaning
that this form is valid for all values of p and q.

To test any argument, then, we may test the implicative
function of which the given argument is an instance. If the
tables show that the implicative function is true for all possible
values of its variables, then it is a "law of logic" and the argument which is a substitution instance of this function is valid.
The implication under (G) in our example is thus a law of logic.

A law of logic is a "tautology," i.e., a function whose substitution instances are necessarily true whatever may be the truth
values of its variables. It has nothing but true substitution instances. A function is said to be "contingent," on the other
hand, when it has both true and false substitution instances.
Thus, "$p \vee \sim p$" is a tautology, for it has nothing but true substitution instances. The function "$p \vee q$," however, is contingent, for its substitution instances are both true and false. Its
instances will be true for some values of p and q and false for
others. (The falsity of both p and q will make the instance false.)
Similarly the function "$p \supset q$" is contingent, for its substitution
instances will be true or false depending upon the truth values
of p and q.

We shall now show how the *invalidity* of an argument
form may be exhibited by the truth tables. We shall examine
a "second figure" syllogism, the fallacy of "denying the antecedent": $[(p \supset q) \cdot \sim p] \supset \sim q$.

(A)	(B)	(C)	(D)	(E)	(F)	(G)
p	q	$\sim p$	$\sim q$	$(p \supset q)$	$(p \supset q) \cdot \sim p$	$[(p \supset q) \cdot \sim p] \supset \sim q$
T	T	F	F	T	F	T
F	T	T	F	T	T	F
T	F	F	T	F	F	T
F	F	T	T	T	T	T

We see under (G) that our implication is true on lines 1, 3, and 4 and false on line 2. This means that it is sometimes the case that $\sim q$ will be true when the antecedent of this implication is true but also sometimes not.

Since the premises of this argument form may be true and the conclusion false, it is an invalid argument-form, and thus the implicative function which states the full argument is not tautologous. It is contingent, true or false depending upon the truth values of p and q. (Materially implicative functions are true except when the antecedent is true and the consequent is false.)

Thus far we have shown how the truth tables reveal necessary or (tautologous) functions and contingent functions. Some expressions, on the other hand, are self-inconsistent or self-contradictory, e.g., $(p \cdot \sim p)$. The truth tables will show nothing but F's under this function:

p	$\sim p$	$p \cdot \sim q$
T	F	F
F	T	F

If we *negate* a necessary or tautologous function the truth tables will show F's for any combination of the variables. Similarly the negation of an inconsistent expression will show only T's.

We may also formulate a truth table to test argument forms involving more than two variables, as in

$$\{[(p \text{ v } q) \supset r] \cdot \sim r\} \supset (\sim p \cdot \sim q).$$

To set up a table for three variables, write the tables for p and q, then repeat these tables below (alternating T's and F's under p, doing the T's and F's twice alternately under q), and then write four T's and then four F's under r.* After we do the three guide columns for p, q, and r, we then do tables for the truth functions, viz.:

p	q	r	$p \vee q$	$(p \vee q) \supset r$	(A) $[(p \vee q) \supset r] \cdot \sim r$	(B) $\sim p \cdot \sim q$	(A) $\supset$ (B)
T	T	T	T	T	F	F	T
F	T	T	T	T	F	F	T
T	F	T	T	T	F	F	T
F	F	T	F	T	F	T	T
T	T	F	T	F	F	F	T
F	T	F	T	F	F	F	T
T	F	F	T	F	F	F	T
F	F	F	F	T	T	T	T

This table has been abbreviated because of space limitations. Interpret as follows: After the three guide columns we find the tables for $(p \vee q)$, then for $(p \vee q) \supset r$. The latter function is false only when $(p \vee q)$ is true and r is false (lines 5, 6, and 7). The conjunctive function under (A) is the antecedent of our original argument form. It is true when both the implication function of the second column is true and when $\sim r$ is true (i.e., when r is F in the guide column). We find this combination of conjuncts only on line 8. Next, under (B) we show a table for $(\sim p \cdot \sim q)$, the consequent of the original argument form. This is shown as T when both p is false and q is false (lines 4 and 8).

Our problem is to determine whether the argument form is valid. The argument asserts that the function under (A) implies the function under (B). This is shown in the last column. We find that there is no case where the antecedent is true and the consequent is false. Thus there are nothing but T's in the last column. In other words, there are no circumstances in which this implication is materially false, and so the expression is a law of logic.

* For four variables, repeat the tables for three (below) and then add eight T's and eight F's at the right of these tables, and so on, for five or more variables.

Exercises

1. Use the truth tables to prove that the following argument forms
   are laws of logic:
   a. $(p \supset q) \supset (\sim q \supset \sim p)$
   b. $[(p \supset q) \cdot (q \supset r)] \supset (p \supset r)$
   c. $[(p \vee q) \cdot \sim q] \supset p$
   d. A Principle of Summation: $(q \supset r) \supset [(p \vee q) \supset (p \vee r)]$
   e. A Principle of Association: $[p \vee (q \vee r)] \supset [q \vee (p \vee r)]$
   f. A Principle of Distribution: $[p \cdot (q \vee r)] \supset [(p \cdot q) \vee (p \cdot r)]$
   g. $[(p \vee q) \vee r] \equiv [p \vee (q \vee r)]$
   h. $[(p \supset q) \cdot (r \supset s)] \supset [(p \vee r) \supset (q \vee s)]$

2. Transform the following argument into an equivalent argument which will be a "substitution instance" of the law stated in
   "h" above by translating the constituent propositions into the
   appropriate functions:
   Either he is not a thief, or he is a scoundrel; and it is false that
   he is both vicious and not unhappy. Therefore, if it is false to
   say that he is neither a thief nor a vicious person, then if he is
   not a scoundrel he is unhappy.
   Symbolize as follows: T: he is a thief; S: he is a scoundrel; V:
   he is vicious; U: he is unhappy.

Section VIII. Complex Arguments

1. Complex Syllogisms

The truth tables furnish us with a convenient method for
testing the validity of arguments. But this method is an incon-
venient one when the propositional variables are numerous. An
argument *form* containing four variables requires sixteen lines;
one of five requires thirty-two lines, etc. The ordinary methods
of deduction are much simpler for the analysis of such arguments, and it is to these methods that we now return.

Take the argument form: $\{[(p \cdot q) \supset (r \vee s)] \cdot (\sim r \cdot \sim s)\} \supset$
$\sim p \vee \sim q$. This complex function can be dealt with as a hypothetical or implicative syllogism in the Fourth Figure, viz.:

$$(p \cdot q) \supset (r \vee s)$$
$$\sim r \cdot \sim s$$
$$\therefore \sim (p \cdot q) \equiv \sim p \vee \sim q$$

The minor premise, we note, is the contradictory of the consequent of the major premise, and we conclude by contradicting the antecedent. The contradictory of $(p \cdot q)$ is $\sim(p \cdot q)$, which is equivalent to $\sim p \vee \sim q$.

Here are four typical implicative major premises involving four variables:

(1) $(p \cdot q) \supset (r \vee s)$
(2) $(p \vee q) \supset \sim(r \cdot s)$
(3) $(p \supset q) \supset (r \cdot s)$
(4) $\sim(p \cdot q) \supset (r \supset s)$

Valid syllogisms may be constructed by affirming antecedents or by denying consequents. Let us see how antecedents may be affirmed. Note that (1) has a conjunctive antecedent. This must be affirmed in its entirety, i.e., both p and q must be true. But not so with the other three. In (2) it is obviously enough to affirm either alternant to make the antecedent true. In (3) it is sufficient to assert that p is false or q true to make the antecedent implication true. The function $p \supset q$ is equivalent to $\sim p \vee q$. In (4) it is sufficient to assert that either disjunct is false to make $\sim(p \cdot q)$ true.

Fourth Figure syllogisms have minor premises which contradict the consequent. For convenience in reference, here are the contradictories of the four consequents in our "typical" premises.

(1) $(r \vee s)$ has as its contradictory: $\sim r \cdot \sim s$
(2) $\sim(\sim r \cdot s)$ has as its contradictory: $\sim r \cdot s$
(3) $(r \cdot s)$ has as its contradictory: $\sim(r \cdot s)$ or $\sim r \vee \sim s$
(4) $(r \supset s)$ has as its contradictory: $r \cdot \sim s$

2. Some special aspects of complex propositions and arguments

a. Contraposition

The contrapositive of $p \supset q$, we recall, is $\sim q \supset \sim p$. We contradict and reverse the antecedent and consequent. Thus the contrapositive of $[(p \vee q) \supset (r \supset s)]$ is $[(r \cdot \sim s) \supset (\sim p \cdot \sim q)]$. The contraposition of a "chain" argument or sorites proceeds in a similar manner.

b. Equivalences among complex propositions

The complex function $(p \text{ v } q) \supset (r \supset s)$ has an implicative major relation. To translate this into one with an alternative major relation, we use $(p \supset q) \equiv (\sim p \text{ v } q)$ as our model. We contradict the antecedent $(p \text{ v } q)$ of our complex function into $(\sim p \cdot \sim q)$ and will then have $(\sim p \cdot \sim q) \text{ v } (r \supset s)$.

c. Contradicting a complex proposition

Suppose we wish to contradict the complex function $(p \text{ v } q) \supset (r \supset s)$. We recall that the contradictory of $p \supset q$ is $p \cdot \sim q$. The contradictory of the consequent $(r \supset s)$ is $r \cdot \sim s$, and so the contradictory of the complex function is $(p \text{ v } q) \cdot (r \cdot \sim s)$.

3. A sample analysis of a complex sorites

Assume that we are given as true premises the following: "$(p \text{ v } q) \text{ v } r$," "$q \supset s$," "$r \supset t$." Prove that $\sim p \supset (s \text{ v } t)$ must be true.

We must first combine the premises into a meaningful series of implications. We proceed as follows. We recall law "g" on page 319. This tells us that $(p \text{ v } q) \text{ v } r$ may be restated as $p \text{ v } (q \text{ v } r)$, and this is equivalent to (1) $\sim p \supset (q \text{ v } r)$.

We shall also need to use law "h" on page 319. This tells us that $[(p \supset q) \cdot (r \supset s)] \supset [(p \text{ v } r) \supset (q \text{ v } s)]$. We use the law in this way: We combine the premises $q \supset s$ and $r \supset t$ of our problem into the conjunctive function $(q \supset s) \cdot (r \supset t)$. We now use law "h," which tells us that the conjunctive function just stated implies (2) $(q \text{ v } r) \supset (s \text{ v } t)$. We may now substitute that which is implied for the premises which imply it, and we can now put our new functions (1) and (2) into a series of implications: $\sim p \supset (q \text{ v } r)$ and $(q \text{ v } r) \supset (s \text{ v } t)$, from which it follows that $\sim p \supset (s \text{ v } t)$.

Exercises

1. Write the symbolic structures of the following syllogisms and check for validity:
   a. If our lives are to be wholly unblemished with unhappiness,

then we must have our cake and we must eat our cake. But since we cannot do both, we shall not be completely happy in this world.

b. If price regulation were both economically sound and politically feasible, then it should not be the case that economists would disapprove of it or that politicians would shy away from it. But since it is false to say either that economists approve of it or that politicians do not shy away from it, we must conclude that price regulation lacks economic soundness and political feasibility.

c. Zeno argued: In order to move, a body must either move in the place where it is or it must move in a place where it is not. But a body cannot move in the place where it is, for so long as it remains in the place where it is, then it is at rest in that place. And it is obviously impossible for a body to move in a place where it is not. Therefore it is impossible for a body to move at all.

Symbolize as follows: M (a body moves), I (a body moves in the place where it is), N (a body moves in a place where it is not).

2. State the contrapositives of the following, eliminating negation signs outside of brackets where possible.
   a. $(p \supset q) \supset (\sim r \text{ v } s)$
   b. $(p \cdot q) \text{ v } (r \supset \sim s)$
   c. If you were either fairly conscientious or not lazy then you would get to class on time.

3. a. State 2a and 2c in alternative form.
   b. State 2b in implicative form.
   c. Contradict all the items in exercise 2.

4. The following premises are given: $\sim A \text{ v } B$, $B \supset \sim(E \cdot F)$, $H \supset (E \cdot F)$, $N \supset K$, $O \supset L$, $\sim(\sim K \cdot \sim L) \supset H$.

   These functions should be put into a chain. In order to do this you will find it necessary to make use of the laws of logic "g" and "h" on page 319. Substitute the propositional variables of the exercise for those in the law, as in the sample analysis on page 321. Be sure that you make your substitutions consistently.

5. Given the following premises:
   a. Either democracy will triumph, or communism will triumph, or neither will triumph. (Symbolize by D v C v N.)
   b. The triumph of democracy implies that the U.S. will oppose Russian ambitions, or that the U.S. and Russia will settle their differences. [$D \supset (O \text{ v } S)$]
   c. If the U.S. opposes Russian ambitions, then the Republicans will return to power. ($O \supset R$)

1111111

d. If the U.S. and Russia settle their differences, then a new party will come to power. (S ⊃ P)

e. If it is not the case that both the Republicans will not come to power and that a new party will not come to power, then the Democratic party will be turned out of office. [∼(∼R · ∼P) ⊃ T]

f. If either communism triumphs or neither democracy nor communism triumphs, then the U.S. will adopt a one-party system. [(C v N) ⊃ I]

Arrange these premises in an ordered sequence of implications. If these premises are accepted as true, and some years hence it is the case that the Democratic party is not turned out of office, would it follow that the Democratic party is the only party in the United States?

The Logic of Truth:
Scientific Methodology

Part Three

The Logic of Truth:
Scientific Methodology

Chapter 14

Truth and Probability

Section I: Deduction and Induction

In Part Two we studied the nature of formal reasoning, or deduction. A valid argument, we learned, is one in which the premises necessitate or imply the conclusion. Given certain premises, we deduce or exfoliate their implications. A valid argument is simply one having a certain form or structure, the truth of the premises being assumed or taken for granted. In Part Three we shall seek to determine the meaning of the assertion that a given proposition is in fact true. We shall examine the logical methods employed in determining truth, and we shall give particular attention to the methods of science, since scientific method is the logical discipline which is most successful in the discovery of truth.

We shall now be concerned with the logic of "induction." Inductive reasoning seeks to establish true propositions concerning the facts of experience, based upon observations of such facts. Its ultimate goal is to find true generalizations concerning nature's laws. It develops methods, usually called scientific methods, for deriving such generalizations from experience. This is a quite different goal from that set up by formal logic which merely seeks to deduce the consequences or implications of propositions and to determine whether an argument is valid or invalid. But it would be a mistake to think that inductive logic and deductive logic are mutually exclusive. For inductive logic (or scientific method) is concerned with the adequacy of the evidence to establish its conclusions. These are problems of "proof," and wherever there is a question of proof the canons of formal logic are relevant.

During the Middle Ages, before the rise of modern science,

a widespread method of philosophers and scientists was to begin discussions by citing "the authorities" (i.e., principles drawn from the Scriptures, the writings of the Church Fathers, the works of the ancient Greek philosophers, particularly Aristotle), and then to apply these principles by deductive reasoning. These thinkers did not, in general, question the truth of their basic assumptions; they used their logical acumen to find contradictions and inconsistencies in the authorities, and to draw out new implications. But modern science is distinguished by two special characteristics. The first is its critical or questioning spirit, which refuses to accept any statement as true merely because the authorities say that it is true (or because someone claims that he has a "self-evident intuition" of its truth). In the second place, science regards the appeal to the facts of actual experience as the ultimate test of the truth of any proposition.

Some mediaeval thinkers did not regard the test of experience as the ultimate guide even with respect to matters of fact. Thus, a professor of astronomy at the University of Pisa looked through Galileo's telescope, which revealed facts inconsistent with Aristotle's cosmology. But he thought it more likely that his senses deceived him than that Aristotle was wrong. Thus there is an important contrast between deductive procedures, which begin with assumed principles, and scientific methods, which appeal to the facts for truths; but, as we shall see over and over again, science also uses deductive reasoning. The ultimate goal of the scientist, moreover, is the organization of all knowledge into a deductive system in which the special principles of all fields of investigation will be deducible from a few simple laws.

Though induction may furnish the ultimate grounds on which we base our premises, deduction is an indispensable aspect of science and all rational thought. The sciences of arithmetic, geometry, and other branches of mathematics are imposing structures which are purely deductive in nature. "Without deduction," as Chapman and Henle have said (*The Fundamentals of Logic,* Scribner, 1933), "we could prove nothing, science at its present stage of development would be impossible, and rational discourse would be a misnomer. We cannot acquire genuinely new truths by deduction; but we can, by its means, determine exactly what we mean, predict the future, and infer what the past must have been."

We shall therefore not dispense with the principles of deductive reasoning in our investigation of scientific methods. Nevertheless, we do have a new kind of problem: How do we establish the truth of a factual proposition? In the beginning of our study of logic we noted that we were to consider three problems: (1) the nature of meaning, (2) the nature of validity in argument, and (3) the nature of truth. We shall be concerned primarily with the third problem throughout Part Three.

Section II: Validity and Truth

"Valid" is an adjective which characterizes *arguments*. An argument is valid when the premises necessitate the conclusion. "True," on the other hand, is an adjective which characterizes *propositions*. A true proposition is one which "corresponds to the facts" or correctly describes the facts. We shall accept this definition of truth throughout our discussions in Part Three. Before we proceed further, however, let us summarize some of the things we have learned concerning the relationship of validity and truth.

When we analyze an argument for validity, we do not concern ourselves with the truth or falsity of the premises or conclusion. Validity is determined by one and only one test: Do the premises imply or necessitate the conclusion? The problem of validity, then, concerns itself solely with the form or structure of the argument.

The truth or falsity of the statements in an argument are irrelevant with respect to its validity; the argument may be valid though its premises are false and the conclusion false, as in:

> All Americans are heavy drinkers.
> All heavy drinkers are Prohibitionists.
> ∴All Americans are Prohibitionists.

or though its premises are false and its conclusion true, as in:

> All capitalists favor the abolition of private ownership of industry.
> All Socialists are capitalists.
> ∴All Socialists favor the abolition of private ownership of industry.

If the premises of a valid argument are true, however, then the conclusion must be true. A valid argument cannot have true premises and a false conclusion.

Similarly, the truth or falsity of the premises is irrelevant with respect to *invalidity*. The following argument is invalid though each statement in it is true:

> All Manitobans live in the northern part of North America.
> All Canadians live in the northern part of North America.
> ∴ All Manitobans are Canadians.

Now, when we claim that we have proven the truth of a conclusion by deductive logic, we must be understood as presupposing the truth of our premises. If the familiar Socrates syllogism is taken to prove his mortality, this is because we presuppose an "If it is true that" before each premise, thus:

> (If it is true that)   All men are mortal.
> and (if it is true that)   Socrates is a man.
> Then (it is true that)   Socrates is mortal.

By contrast, consider the valid "Socialists" argument. Though that argument *formally* proves its conclusion, the *truth* of the conclusion has not been *demonstrated*, since the premises are false.

We turn, now, to a new problem, the problem that is to concern us throughout Part III. It is one thing to *assume* the truth of the propositions used as premises. But our new problem is to determine whether these propositions are *actually* true or false. Take, for example, the Socrates syllogism. In that argument we assume in the major premise that all men are mortal. Most persons would agree that that statement is in fact true. But is it? Suppose we are asked for proof that this premise is in fact true. How should we proceed? Two methods are possible. We might deduce the truth of "all men are mortal" from other premises, thus:

> All animals are mortal.
> All men are animals.
> ∴ All men are mortal.

If asked to prove that "All animals are mortal," we might deduce this from the premises that "all living things are mortal," and "all animals are living things," and so on. But obviously, such proof lives on borrowed premises, and we never rid ourselves of the qualification "provided the above premises are true," and these premises themselves need proof. But we demand that this deductive chain be broken, and that our deductions be based on a premise of which we can say, "This proposition is true—period." In the end our deductions must have a stop if we are not, in despair, to give up the search for truth. We require a non-deductive basis for our chains of reasoning. How shall we find it? We find it in our experiences. We believe that living things will die because they have died in the past. Is this conclusive proof that all living things will die in the future? No. We may be warranted in our certainty that some living things have died, but it can be only probable that what happened in the past will also happen in the future. Nevertheless, whether we say that our premise is true or probable, we seem to have found a means whereby we may break the deductive chain in the proof of a premise. Deduction is never absent in proof, but something new has been added, namely, the appeal to experience.

Section III: The Meaning of Truth

We have seen that the truth of the conclusion of a valid argument can have no greater certainty than the truth of its premises and that the validity of an argument is wholly independent of the truth or falsity of its premises. We also defined truth as "correspondence with the facts." We shall now examine some of the implications of this definition.

If a true proposition is one which corresponds to the facts, then a true proposition must be true for all men at all times and all places. This, indeed, was the conclusion we reached in our discussion of the "Laws of Thought." If a proposition correctly describes the facts, then it cannot be said to be a correct description for one man and not for another. Correctness is determined by objective considerations, upon the facts and the evidence. Truth is thus an objective, or public affair, and does not depend upon anyone's feelings.

The position stated above is opposed by "relativists," who

hold that the truth of a proposition is relative to time, and place, and circumstance. Differences of opinion exist on all matters, says the relativist, and this is because each individual's ideas are based upon his own past experiences in a given environment. Since no two individuals have exactly the same experiences, truth will be different for each. We have already examined this position in some detail. Little need be said here, except to note a retort which may be made to the relativist: "If all ideas are the result of past experience, or 'conditioning,'" we may say to him, "then your relativistic theory is itself the product of *your* past experiences, and therefore not 'true' for any but those who have had your experiences." Thus this view appears to end in self-stultification.

Nevertheless, though the relativistic view must be rejected if our definition of truth is accepted, it does call attention to an important consideration, namely, that differences of opinion are often quite legitimate. The candid observer will be deeply impressed by the actual variety of opinions which men hold on all matters of real importance. Consider the differences of opinion on matters political, both at home and in the international sphere. Consider the differences with respect to religious truth, and consider the different interpretations of the events which lead to the breaking up of a friendship! But these differences of opinion do not mean that truth is relative. They mean only that no one may really *know* which of two interpretations is the correct one. We should say "This proposition is *true*" only when we *know*. In practice, however, our emotions, biases, and prejudices affect our judgments; and wishful thinking leads us into error. Self-righteous people will always think that they are right about everything, but truth depends upon the correspondence of a proposition with the actual facts.

We must therefore distinguish between the *truth* of a proposition and the *belief* we may have in its truth. The statement, "The earth is shaped like a flat disk and floats on water," is a false proposition because it incorrectly describes the facts, but it was once believed true. People were once ignorant of things we know today, and we are also beset by ignorance in many matters. But if we really know that a given proposition is true, then its truth will never change, provided that we state it with the proper precision and limit it to a specific area of investigation.

Here the reader may interpose an objection. Granted, he may say, that the relativistic view must be rejected and that the truth does not change. Granted that it was false to say that the earth is flat. But how can we be certain that the earth is a spheroid? Perhaps *our* view is only an opinion, and later investigation may prove that *we* are wrong. In other words, how can we ever be sure that a given proposition does correspond with the facts? We made mistakes in the past and we may be in error today. The absolutes of today may be the untruths of tomorrow. Is not truth then an unattainable ideal, so that we can never be sure that we have attained it?

Questions such as these lead to a view which we shall call "probabilism," which holds that we can never be certain that we have attained the truth and that we must be content with varying degrees of probability. Certainty in factual propositions, it is held, is an unattainable ideal. Before we discuss this view further let us seek to clarify what we mean by "degrees of probability," in relation to truth. Let us then think of truth and falsity as the two poles of a line, running from 0(zero), which stands for "absolutely false" to 1(unity) which stands for "absolutely true," viz:

0(.001)	.10	.30	.50	.70	.90	(.999)1

This diagram indicates that when we are certain that a proposition is true, we say that it has a probability of 1; when we are certain that it is false, that it has a probability of 0. A probability of .50 means that we are wholly uncertain, leaning neither to truth nor falsity. Translating the specific degrees into their equivalents in ordinary expressions, we may say that .10 means "highly improbable"; .30 "improbable"; .70 "probable"; and .90 "highly probable." The percentages .001 and .999 stand for cases where we are "practically certain," allowing only for a very remote possibility that we are in error. These figures are of course only approximations.

The reader may have noted that the word "probability" has been used in two different senses, as meaning (1) some definite degree of probability, whether it be .10 or .90, and (2) "more than 50 per cent." The latter is the popular sense of the term and means that something is more likely to happen than not. When we say "possible but not probable," we use the term in this sense. We shall use the word in both senses, but we will usually specify the degree when we use it in its broader sense. The context will also make clear which sense is meant.

Another clarifying remark before we proceed. An important distinction should be drawn between a probability judgment and the judgment that a proposition is true or false. A proposition is true or false regardless of whether we have the evidence available to us or not. Either the facts correspond, or they do not. But a probability judgment is always relative to the available evidence. For example, the statement, "Russia and Germany have signed a pact of friendship," was highly improbable to most observers in the light of the available evidence on August 23, 1939, immediately before the pact was announced to the world. The statement was true, but improbable in the light of the evidence which was known to outsiders. A well-informed foreign correspondent would have been justified in saying that the statement was improbable, even though a sufficiently astute observer might have predicted it on the basis of "inside information" concerning the motives of the principal actors in that political drama. Probability judgments will thus vary with every change in the evidence. We have indicated a case where a true proposition appeared to be improbable. Similarly, a false proposition may appear to be highly probable. Thus every probability judgment must be qualified by the words "in the light of the evidence which is available."

Let us now apply our diagram in estimating the strength of some of our beliefs. "Moses led the Jews out of Egypt." Would you say that this statement is absolutely true and that error is inconceivable? Another: "The leader of Germany between 1933 and 1945 was a man named Hitler." Most of us would say "absolutely certain." But is it possible that the prevailing belief is based upon a gigantic hoax which was played upon the whole world? Such an interpretation is highly improbable, but is it *possible?* Let us press the point further. Is it possible for you to doubt whether you are reading these lines now? Is it possible that you are dreaming and that your alarm clock may ring in a few minutes, waking you from your dream? Descartes, the seventeenth century French philosopher, believed that there was *only one* statement which he could not possibly doubt, namely, that he himself existed. For doubt, he said, implies the existence of a doubter. But he thought it possible to doubt everything else.

We return now to the point of view called "probabilism." The probabilist argues that no factual proposition can ever be absolutely certain. Take the proposition "People are living in Alaska at this moment." If we can conceivably be mistaken, he says, then we have not reached certainty, or "unity." The probability may be as high as .99 or even .999999 but it must be less than unity. Similarly in, "There are lovers of boogie-woogie on the planet Mars." This has a probability of almost zero, but not quite; shall we say .00000001? If the probabilist is correct, then we can never be sure that any proposition concerning the world is true or false in a conclusive sense. We must always allow for the possibility that any belief, no matter how certain it may appear, may turn out to be in error.

The probabilist view is based upon two chief arguments: (1) Human beings have made mistakes in the past even when they were most confident that they had discovered the truth. They may be mistaken today. (2) All perception involves interpretation and inference.

The second argument refers to the fact that when we perceive, let us say, a table, we *see* a brown-colored patch of a certain shape, and then we *interpret* this patch as a table. Interpretation is thus involved in perception, and the interpretation may be mistaken. Thus, the traveler on the desert who "sees" an oasis in the distance may be seeing only a mirage. The radio listener may "hear" the burning of wood in a campfire, and the sound of a man walking through the snow. But it is only the crumpling of cellophane and the crunching of soapflakes in a projection booth. Human beings may also suffer from delusions and hallucinations. Under the influence of alcohol a man may falsely believe that he sees bats flying around in his room. These are some striking examples of "observations" which are mistaken.

We shall not explore, much less attempt to dispose of, the metaphysical or epistomological issues raised by the probabilist point of view except to note some of the arguments which a critic of this view might advance. With respect to the first argument, that our past mistakes are a reason for present doubt, does not the probabilist regard it as absolutely certain that we have made such mistakes in the past? If we are not certain that we have made mistakes, we admit the possibility that we have never been mistaken in any matter whatsoever and that our judgments were always absolutely true. But surely it is certain that we have made mistakes. Similarly, if someone tells us that "no knowledge is certain," then we may say that the speaker contradicts himself, for he asserts that at least one proposition is certain, namely, the proposition just quoted.

With respect to the argument concerning perception, the critic might urge that some perceptions must be absolutely veridical, for otherwise we could not know that hallucinations were errors. Thus, when we are in a normal state of health and sobriety, we are simply not mistaken in our everyday judgments concerning the existence of the chairs and tables around us. Such observations, on the "common sense" level of experience, furnish the basis of all human knowledge and also enable us to distinguish between correct and incorrect perceptions.

Doubt would thus appear not to be warranted in some cases, the critic might continue, but in others it may be not only proper but obligatory. The important distinction is between the easy cases and the difficult ones, i.e., between cases where interpretation and inference involve the possibility of error and those in which they do not. The theories of a physicist concerning the structure of the atom are probable rather than certain, for error is possible here, but when the physicist takes a pointer reading which indicates +.745 the physicist is certain *that he is taking a pointer reading* and that the number he is looking at is somewhere between .6 and .9. When there is the slightest possibility that we may be mistaken, let us modestly admit it. But we *know* of at least one person in the world who had parents, and we know that it is false to assert that "all grandfathers can run around the circumference of the earth in less than ten seconds." And would it not be rather odd for one to say, "The available evidence makes it highly probable that I was not drowned ten years ago, but I must admit the possibility that I may be mistaken"?

Finally, the critic might urge, the statement that one proposition is more probable than another is itself not merely probable, for otherwise we should find ourselves saying that "it is probable that it is probable that it is probable" ad infinitum. It is more probable that there is life on the planet Mars than that there are beings there who enjoy boogie-woogie and "Dixieland." When we say "more probable" we mean just that, and not that it is probably more probable.

We shall close this long discussion with a few general remarks. For practical purposes we assume that some propositions are true, rather than merely probable. In any case, in a given investigation we must assume the truth of a host of propositions whose truth is not in question in that particular investigation. But at least some of these assumptions may themselves be questioned in later investigations. This is the point of view of the scientist, who is, in general, concerned with matters involving probability rather than certainty. The scientist is satisfied with verification which gives high probabilities. But even though certainty is not attainable in scientific problems, this does not mean that "one opinion is as good as another." Beliefs based on good evidence are more likely to be true than not, and our concern in all cases will be to determine on what evidence our beliefs are based. The fundamental question, one which will be raised over and over again in our discussion of scientific method, will be: WHAT IS THE EVIDENCE?

Section IV: The Meaning of Empirical Probability

Thus far we have indicated some of the ways in which we apply judgments of truth and probability. We shall now examine the *meaning* of probability judgments. But first we must distinguish two types of probability, the *empirical* and the *a priori* (pronounced ā' prī·ō'rī). "Empirical probability" means the probability which is based upon past experience, as that alcohol will probably cause intoxication. Thus far all of our illustrations have been of this type. A priori means "in advance of experience," or "prior to experience." Mathematics is an a priori science. We know in advance of seeing the beasts that two kangaroos plus two kangaroos will add up to four kangaroos. A priori probability is essentially a branch of mathematics, and its applications can be calculated mathematically with complete precision and exactness. It is most conveniently illustrated by games of chance. Thus, since there are 38 slots on a roulette wheel, a player's chances of getting a given number are 1/38. The probabilities may be calculated in advance of experience if we assume that the wheel is so constructed that there is an equal chance that the ball will fall on any number. The basic formula for all probabilities is $p = f/n$, in which p stands for probability, n for the total number of possibilities, and f for the "favorable" event, or the event which we seek to measure. Probability may also be defined by $f/f + u$ in which u stands for the "unfavorable" events.

Mathematical or a priori probability is a deductive science whose rules are clear and results precise, granted certain assumptions. This type will be considered in more detail later. The remainder of this section will be devoted to the meaning of empirical probability (also called "experiential"). In this type we find a general absence of mathematical exactitude, though here, too, as in a priori probability, we shall use the fraction f/n. We shall now be satisfied with rough approximations to the fraction. As examples, consider the probabilities that there will be another war within the next ten years, or a reversal in business during the next two years. Exactly how probable are these predictions? Exactness is unattainable, but surely some predictions are more sensible than others. We might say that we did not know the exact probability of a turn in the business cycle, but that its probability was less than .9 and more than .1. In any case, as it has been well said, empirical probabilities are "the very guide of life." A successful adjustment to the world around us requires that one should know how to "bet" on the future: to know which events are more likely to occur than others. The wise man can predict better than the uninstructed man. Justice Oliver Wendell Holmes had this view of probability in mind when he described himself as a "betabilitarian." Our confidence in our predictions or beliefs, he said, is indicated by the manner in which we would be willing to bet.

When we speak of an event as probable in the empirical sense we mean that it is more likely to be the case than not. "More likely than not" must be clarified. When we say that it is probable that any redhead will be hot-tempered, that Shakespeare wrote the plays attributed to him, that the theory of evolution is more probable than the "special creation" theory, or that it is probable that Caesar crossed the Rubicon, in what senses do we mean "more likely to be the case than not"? When an agent of the FBI finds a man in the possession of the ransom bills paid to a kidnapper who is still at large, what justifies the agent in believing that it is probable that the holder of the ransom notes is guilty of the crime?

All of these examples, as we shall see, use the basic concept "in most cases," though it is also possible to reach a rough approximation to specific percentages of the probabilities. Let us illustrate, first, by considering the association of redheads and hot tempers. (The figures used in this illustration are purely imaginary.) If we say it is probable that any redhead is likely to be hot-tempered, we mean that *most* are, so that there is a greater-than-even chance that any one taken at random will be hot-tempered. Or we might state the percentage, by stating that 60 out of 100 are hot-tempered. This would mean a probability of .6. We might use the f/n fraction, thus: $\dfrac{RH^{ht}}{RH}$ which puts all redheads into the denominator and redheads possessing the special characteristic into the numerator.

In the same manner, we reach conclusions concerning the probability that the holder of the ransom money is the kidnapper. (The police, of course, will generally follow any clue, no matter how small the probability may be.) But the problem of "in most cases" is somewhat more complex when we consider the probability of a historical proposition.

When we say that it is highly probable that Caesar crossed the Rubicon, it may appear that the concept "in most cases" is inapplicable, for surely we do not mean that he did so "in most cases." Nevertheless, our concept is applicable here also. What we mean when we say that such judgments are probable is something like the following: "Whenever we have had evidence in quantity and quality like the evidence which supports the proposition 'Caesar crossed the Rubicon,' then, in the great majority of cases, the occurrence of the event attested to has been confirmed in all subsequent investigations." Our fraction f/n in this case may be represented by $\dfrac{E^t}{E}$ in which the denominator "E" stands for all cases in which we have had this kind of evidence (in quantity and quality) and "E^t" for all cases in which such evidence has turned out to be reliable, and the proposition attested to, true. A similar analysis applies to a prediction that another economic depression will occur within a given limited period of time, say five years. We ask, "How often have situations like the present one developed into depressions during such a period of time?" Comparisons of present situations with past ones will of course be complicated by the presence of new factors, and new experiences and attitudes; but there are also similar factors present. Though our judgment will be anything but mathematically precise, nevertheless, the wise man is more likely to reach a correct estimate of the probability than the uninstructed man. We must also take into account our present, and perhaps future, inability to predict human behavior with precision, since the variables involved in human decisions are exceedingly various, and this, too, will affect our judgment. But our estimate of the probability of an economic depression will depend on our evaluation of the f/n fraction.

One further complication. In some cases we may find a wholly uniform experience, as when we find that all zebras have stripes, and know of no exceptions. Our f/n fraction will now equal 1, since the numerator and denominator will have the same size. But we must qualify our prediction concerning future observations of zebras by also considering the following question: What is the probability, on the basis of past experiences with observations of this type, that a generalization without known exceptions will prove to be true in all of the as yet unexamined cases?

We know that at one time all observed swans were white and then black swans turned up in Australia. Thus, though the probability that *all* zebras (both the observed and the unobserved) are striped, may be high, it is far short of certainty. In any case, it cannot be determined with the exactness of mathematical probability.

Empirical probabilities, then, are based on past experience. The procedures just described, we may note, are also used by insurance actuaries, who must estimate the probabilities with respect to life-expectancy. If, in a given area, we find that of 10,000 individuals aged thirty, 9,500 live to their fortieth years, then the probability that any individual at random in this area of the age of thirty will reach forty is .95. As conditions change, insurance rates change, but this is the basis of the predictions. The famous Lloyds institution in London will generally furnish insurance on *any* future event, using these theories of empirical probability as its guide. Though the race does not always go to the fastest horse and the best jockey, it usually does.

Section V: Probability and the Syllogism

We shall now examine the manner in which probability judgments are related to the problems of validity in syllogistic reasoning. The rules of validity are very much like the rules of mathematics. The product of 26×26 is 676. If a student answered this problem with 675, his answer would be completely wrong, though very close to the truth. We shall find a similar situation with respect to validity. An invalid argument may also be "quite close" to validity. Though validity is either attained completely or not, nevertheless some invalid arguments may be better than others, just as 675 would be a better answer in the arithmetic above than would be 179.

We shall now discuss some arguments whose conclusions contain the term "probably." The following argument, a valid one, presents no difficulties:

> If a person has red hair, then he is probably hot-tempered.
> Smith has red hair.
> ∴ Smith is probably hot-tempered.

Now examine the following invalid argument:

> If a theory is true then it will be confirmed by experiment.
> The theory of relativity has been confirmed by experiment.
> ∴ The theory of relativity is (probably) a true theory.

In this syllogism the minor premise affirms the consequent. Is the argument "saved" by inserting the word "probably" into the conclusion? Now, there is no question that the argument is an invalid one without the word "probably," but most persons would agree that the argument, valid or invalid, is a satisfactory one for the scientist. Why is this? And why is it that the following argument cannot be "saved" by the use of "probably"?

>   All Chinese drink tea.
>   X drinks tea.
> ∴ X is (probably) Chinese.

The term "probably" does not make good sense here. Let us explore this problem.

In our discussion of formal logic we learned that validity was determined by form and structure and that we were to ignore our outside knowledge. But we are now interested in material (or actual) truth as distinguished from formal truth, and our actual knowledge becomes relevant. We noted earlier that an A-form proposition could not be converted simply, without limitation. But we may happen to know that the simple converse of a given A-form is true as a matter of fact. If we know this then we may assert our knowledge. For example, the following syllogism is invalid:

>   If a figure is a triangle, then it is three-sided.
>   This figure is three-sided.
> ∴ It is a triangle.

But we also know that "All three-sided figures are triangles." If we add or substitute this as a premise, then our new argument will be valid. The point is that if all we know is that "A is a B," we cannot conclude that "All B's are A's," but if we know more, then we can use our knowledge.

Every A-form proposition such as "All A are B" can be converted into "Some B are A." But "some" is a very vague quantifier. It covers all quantities from "more than none" to "just short of all." Take the following proposition: "All true theories are confirmed by experiment." Normally, it converts into, "Some theories confirmed by experiment are true." But if we *know* that the great majority of theories confirmed are true theories, then we may say, "Most confirmed theories are true." And this is equivalent to, "If a theory is confirmed by experiment, then it is probably true."

We may now restate our syllogism above, using our actual knowledge, and say:

If a theory is confirmed, then it is probably true.
The theory of relativity is confirmed.
∴ The theory of relativity is probably true.

In other words, when we know that the major premise of an invalid argument of this type has a true converse containing the terms "probably" or "most," we may substitute this converted proposition as the new major and construct a new argument in which a probable conclusion may be validly derived. The next three examples will help to clarify this point:

(1)

All communists eat food.
Joe Doakes eats food.
∴ Joe is a communist.

(2)

All communists favor the abolition of private property.
Joe favors the abolition of private property.
∴ Joe is a communist.

(3)

All communists follow the Russian foreign policies with complete consistency.
Joe follows the Russian foreign policies with complete consistency.
∴ Joe is a communist.

All of these arguments contain undistributed middle terms. But they have varying degrees of merit. The problem here is the manner in which we may materially convert their major premises. In Number 1 we may say, "Some (a small minority) persons who eat food are communists." In Number 2 we may say, "Some (a larger minority) persons who favor the abolition of private property are communists." (Socialists are not communists.) In Number 3 we may say, "The overwhelming majority of persons who follow the Russian line are communists." Thus the conclusion in Number 1 has a probability close to zero, in Number 2 it is too uncertain to warrant the conclusion, but in Number 3 the conclusion is very highly probable, even though it is not conclusive.

In other words, many invalid arguments may be transformed into valid arguments containing conclusions which are probable when we know that the major premise may be converted into a proposition which states a probability.

Section VI: A Priori Probability

We return now to the discussion of a priori, or mathematical, probability. Probabilities in this field are worked out on a purely formal basis by deduction from certain axioms and assumptions. Strictly speaking, this field of thought is a branch of mathematics, rather than of logic, but we consider it here in order to add to our understanding of probability and because it furnishes a splendid example of a deductive system which exfoliates the implications of basic axioms.

When a coin is tossed in the air, we say that the probability that the coin will fall heads uppermost is $\frac{1}{2}$. This probability is known before we toss a coin, and it is unnecessary to toss coins to determine it. In fact, tossing coins is wholly irrelevant to the a priori probabilities. This is because we make certain assumptions and deduce their consequences in a purely formal manner. We assume that the coin will fall when tossed, that it will not fall on its edge, that it is so balanced that it will not have a tendency to fall on one side rather than the other, and that it is not controlled in any way. If these assumptions are made, then there are two possibilities, each of which is equally probable. Using the fraction f/n, we find that one of two possibilities is favorable, and the probability is $\frac{1}{2}$. In the same manner, and with similar assumptions, we find that the numbers on a die give us six "equiprobable" possibilities. The probability of getting a given number, such as a "4," is thus $\frac{1}{6}$. The probability of getting a spade from a deck of 52 cards is $\frac{13}{52}$.

The deductions we make in this field simply exfoliate the meaning of our assumptions. Experiments are unnecessary in determining our meanings. "If there are two equiprobable possibilities and one is favorable, then our chances are one in two." But a new question now arises: Are *actual* coins perfectly balanced? To say that they are is an empirical judgment of which we cannot be absolutely certain. Nor can we be certain, in general, of lack of manipulation. Crooked gamblers, as is well known, load the dice in their favor. But we do find, when large numbers of coins are tossed, that they fall as we should expect them to in accordance with the a priori probabilities. The variations from the norm are negligible in large numbers, and we may assume that coins are perfectly balanced in fact. Thus, when we throw a coin 1,000 times, we should expect to get somewhere in the neighborhood of 500 heads and 500 tails.

Let us be perfectly clear as to the meaning of a priori probability. It gives us a calculus of chances. It does not tell us that heads and tails will fall in equal amounts, but merely that that is the most likely possibility. The coins might all fall heads, since this is a conceivable possibility, but the odds against such an occurrence are fantastically high. But it might occur. The chances against four bridge players all getting "perfect" hands, each with single suits, has been estimated as 1 in 2,235,197,406,-895,366,368,301,560,000. Such a combination of hands may not occur in thousands of years of playing, or it may occur twice tomorrow, but the probability is that it will occur once in the number given above. In the long run, the a priori probabilities do tend to be approximated, but in any case, these are the expectations. But note that there is no "law of averages" which controls probabilities. It is not certain that there will ever be four perfect hands, though it is probable that there will be if sufficient hands are played.

The failure to understand the nature of a priori probability is responsible for an error which is usually called "the gambler's fallacy." Let us assume that we intend to toss a coin 1,000 times. The first 20 tosses turn up tails. How would you bet on the next toss, provided you were sure that the coin was a fair coin? The gambler's fallacy is the assumption that there is a better than even chance that the next toss will fall heads, on the ground that heads are "overdue." The assumption is that the "law of averages" must fulfill itself, that there must be 500 heads and 500 tails in 1,000 tosses, so that the heads must now make up for lost time. But coins have no memories of past tosses, nor do they have consciences. The odds on the twenty-first toss are exactly the same as on any other. The a priori probability is always ½ on any toss.

If the objection is raised, "But isn't it probable that 1,000 coins will fall in the proportion of 500 each?," the answer is Yes. "Then won't the heads have to make up their due proportions?" To this the answer is No. A priori probabilities refer only to the future in the sense that past events do not affect the f/n fraction with respect to future tosses. If the first 20 tosses show tails, we must then revise our expectations as to the total results when the 1,000 tosses will have been completed. Since there are 980 tosses to go, with a probability of 490 heads and 490 tails, the probability for the total (including the 20 tosses) will be 490 heads and 510 tails.

Coins never "make up" for past performances. Nor do dice or roulette wheels. The only sensible inference when 20 tails fall in a row is the possibility that the coin is not perfectly balanced, so that the greater probability would then lie in favor of tails. Or the coin may have been manipulated. But even a fair coin may fall tails 20 times in a row.*

In the next section we shall examine some theorems which follow from the fundamental principles of a priori probability. This section (and the exercises in group F) may be skipped by those not particularly interested in the more technical aspects of probability theory.

Section VII: The Calculus of Mathematical Probabilities

We shall now work out some of the applications of a priori probability as applied to complex events. This subject is dealt with in mathematics under the title "Theory of Combinations and Permutations." Our basic formula is f/n but we shall deal with matters in which it is difficult to determine the total possibilities. Once we do that, the rest is easy.

Let us start with a simple problem. What are the chances of getting two heads in a row (or two heads with two coins)? We must first consider the total number of possibilities. Two coins may combine with each other in four different ways. Using "H" for heads and "T" for tails, the four possibilities are: H-H, H-T, T-H, and T-T, in which the first letter stands for one coin, the second for the other. We shall call this list our "table" for two coins. Since there are four possibilities and H-H appears once, the chances of getting two heads is one in four, or ¼. Now another problem. What is the probability of getting

---

* An amusing commentary on the "gambler's fallacy" is the fact that many gamblers also believe in an opposite fallacy. This is the belief that if a dice player wins several times in a row then "luck must be with him" (the dice are "hot"). The fallacious inference is now drawn that his chances of winning on the next throw are greater than his mathematical chances.

at least one head? There are four possibilities, in three of which we will find at least one head. The probabilities are ¾. The probability of getting *only one* head is 2/4, since only H-T and T-H satisfy the last requirement.

Let us now examine the manner in which we work out similar problems in connection with two dice, where the possibilities are much more complex, since two dice may combine with each other in thirty-six different ways. The six numbers on one die may each combine with each of the six numbers on the other. The following is our table for two dice, in which the first number stands for the number which appears on the first die and the second for the number which appears on the second:

TABLE FOR TWO DICE

6–6	5–6	4–6	3–6	2–6	1–6
6–5	5–5	4–5	3–5	2–5	1–5
6–4	5–4	4–4	3–4	2–4	1–4
6–3	5–3	4–3	3–3	2–3	1–3
6–2	5–2	4–2	3–2	2–2	1–2
6–1	5–1	4–1	3–1	2–1	1–1

The probability of getting two 6's is thus $\frac{1}{36}$, since there are 36 possibilities, only one of which is favorable. The probability of getting a combination which totals 7 is $\frac{6}{36}$, since the following combinations total 7: 6–1, 5–2, 4–3, 3–4, 2–5, and 1–6. The probability of getting a 4 is $\frac{3}{36}$, since there are only three combinations which total 4: 3–1, 2–2, and 1–3. Since there are 6 ways in which to make a 7 and only 3 in which to make a 4, it is exactly twice as easy to make a 7 as it is to make a 4. In 36 throws, 7 will probably appear 6 times and 4 only three times. The "odds" in favor of 7, as compared with 4, are thus 2 to 1.

We shall now examine the theory which underlies the calculation of the probabilities of complex events from the knowledge of their components. There are three different types of combinations of events, which we shall call "Exclusive," "Independent," and "Dependent" (or "Combined").

1. Exclusive Events

Exclusive events are events which are strictly alternative, or "exclusively alternative." If one such event occurs, then the others cannot occur. When a coin is tossed, "heads" and "tails" are strictly alternative events; since both cannot occur, one excludes the other. Similarly the numbers on a die are strictly alternative, since only one can appear.

To determine the probability of getting one of two or more strictly alternative events we add their separate probabilities. Thus the probability of getting either 5 or 6 on a die is $\frac{2}{6}$ ($\frac{1}{6}$ plus $\frac{1}{6}$). The probability of getting either 2 or 3 or 4 is $\frac{3}{6}$ ($\frac{1}{6}$ plus $\frac{1}{6}$ plus $\frac{1}{6}$). The probability of getting either the combination 5-6 or the combination 6-5 with two dice is $\frac{2}{36}$, since each combination has a probability of $\frac{1}{36}$. The probability of getting T-H or H-T with two coins is $\frac{1}{4}$ plus $\frac{1}{4}$, and so on.

Note that when we have strictly alternative or mutually exclusive events, "either x or y . . . or n," and add all of the probabilities together, the total will be 1, or unity. The probability of getting either 1, or 2, or 3, or 4, or 5, or 6 on a die is thus "1," i.e., "unity." The probability that *some* number will appear is "unity." Similarly the probability of getting at least one of the 36 combinations with two dice, or at least one of the four combinations with two coins is also 1.

2. Independent Events

Two events are independent when the occurrence of one has no effect on the occurrence or non-occurrence of the other. Thus the probability of getting a head on one coin has no effect on the getting of a head on the other coin. What is the probability of getting two heads? Since these events are independent, we multiply the separate probabilities: $\frac{1}{2} \times \frac{1}{2}$ is $\frac{1}{4}$. The probability of getting three heads in a row is $\frac{1}{2} \times \frac{1}{2} \times \frac{1}{2}$ or $\frac{1}{8}$. The probability of getting two 6's is $\frac{1}{6} \times \frac{1}{6}$ or $\frac{1}{36}$. These are the probabilities of favorable events. We may also compute the probability of the unfavorable event. The chance of getting an unfavorable event is $1 - f/n$. If we know the probability of the favorable event, we may subtract it from 1, since $1 - f/n = u/n$, in which "u" means "unfavorable." The fraction f/n plus u/n will always equal unity. The probability of not getting a 6 with one die is thus $1 - \frac{1}{6}$ or $\frac{5}{6}$. The probability of not getting a 6 with two dice? The chances of not getting a 6 on each is $\frac{5}{6}$. Since the events are independent, we multiply the separate probabilities and we have $\frac{5}{6} \times \frac{5}{6}$ or $\frac{25}{36}$.

3. Dependent or combined events

The typical problem here is one such as this: What is the probability of getting *at least one* head with two coins? This probability cannot be obtained by multiplying $\frac{1}{2} \times \frac{1}{2}$ since we do not require heads on both coins. Thus we are not dealing with strictly independent events. A head on either coin will settle the issue. Nor can we add $\frac{1}{2} + \frac{1}{2}$ since we are not dealing with exclusive events. The probability of getting *at least one* head involves "dependent" events, since what we need on the second coin depends upon what we get on the first.

Let us shift the problem to a different one. What is the probability of getting *only one* head? Two combinations satisfy this requirement: T-H plus H-T. These combinations are strictly alternative events. For the probability of *either* one, add the separate probabilities: $\frac{1}{4}$ plus $\frac{1}{4}$ is $\frac{1}{2}$. This is the probability of only one head. Now, the problem of getting *at least one* head means that we can also use H-H. This is also strictly exclusive of the others, and we add its probability ($\frac{1}{4}$) to the previous probability, so that the probability of getting at least one head is $\frac{3}{4}$.

This problem may also be solved in a simpler manner by subtracting the probability of the *un*favorable event from 1. The remainder will give us the favorable event. We recall that $f + u = 1$, so that $1 - u = f$. Thus, if we want at least one head, the unfavorable event would be "no heads." The probability of no heads is obtained by multiplying the probability of no heads on the first coin (tails) by no heads on the second coin (tails). The probability of "no heads" is thus $\frac{1}{4}$ ($\frac{1}{2} \times \frac{1}{2}$). Then subtract $\frac{1}{4}$ from 1 and we have $\frac{3}{4}$, the same as before. The favorable plus the unfavorable event always add up to unity.

The same methods apply to two dice. In order to find the probability of getting *at least one* 6, start with the simpler problem of getting *only one* 6. Two possibilities satisfy this problem. We must get "no 6" on the first die and a 6 on the second, or vice versa. Let us use the symbol X for "no 6." The two favorable possibilities are thus X-6 and 6-X. These are strictly exclusive so we must add their separate probabilities. The probability of X is $\frac{5}{6}$, that of 6 is $\frac{1}{6}$. We then have X-6 ($\frac{5}{6} \times \frac{1}{6}$) plus 6-X ($\frac{1}{6} \times \frac{5}{6}$). This gives us $\frac{5}{36}$ plus $\frac{5}{36}$ or

$\frac{10}{36}$. For *at least one* 6 we may also use the combination 6-6. Its probability is $\frac{1}{36}$. The probability of getting *at least one* 6 is thus $\frac{11}{36}$. To confirm this result consult the table of dice.

By the indirect method, we must subtract the possibility of getting no 6's from 1 and we will then have the probability of getting at least one 6, since "no 6" is the contradictory of "at least one 6." (By the law of the "excluded middle" either we will get "at least one" or "none at all," for the probabilities of these events exhaust the possible cases). To get *no* 6's we must get "X" on both dice. These probabilities are multiplied: $\frac{5}{6} \times \frac{5}{6}$ or $\frac{25}{36}$. The probability of getting at least one 6 is thus $1 - \frac{25}{36}$, or $\frac{11}{36}$.

There are of course many more difficult problems in the calculus of probabilities, but we have indicated the general theory and some of the important theorems.

Exercises

A. *The Distinction between Validity and Truth*

Judge Jerome Frank attacked what he called "the slavish adherence of lawyers to that instrument of reasoning which was worshipped by all men of the Middle Ages—formal logic." The following discussion purports to show how logic misleads us:

The school board of Seattle is reported to have insisted that all teachers, as a condition of procuring employment in the Seattle schools, should sign a contract by which they would agree not to join a teacher's union. Suppose that a suit were brought to compel the school board to hire teachers without imposing this condition. If a court were to decide such a suit in favor of the school board, an analysis of its opinion would show that its reasoning was apparently based upon a "fundamental principle." The court would argue that one who is under no duty to enter into a contract with another may stipulate any condition he pleases as a condition to entering into a contract. This principle the court would take as its major premise. It would then state, as a minor premise, that the school board is under no duty to enter into a contract with any particular teachers . . .

This method of syllogistic reasoning, which is that of formal logic, is the method used by the courts today. Because of its use, the court's conclusions appear inescapable and inevitable. This seeming machine-like certainty, however, is artificial and conceals a fatal weakness. For a decision against the school board might have been rendered, and, if so, could have been justified, with reasoning which would have seemed similarly inevitable. The court could have argued thus: Officials administering the trust of public office may not unreasonably discriminate between applicants for employment . . . (There is your major premise.) To deny employment to a teacher because he refuses to agree not to join an organization of teachers is an unreasonable discrimination. (And there is your minor premise.) . . .

The weakness of formal logic is now exposed. The court can decide one way or the other and in either case can make its reasoning appear equally flawless. Formal logic is what its name indicates; it deals with form and not with substance. The syllogism will not supply either the major premise or the minor premise. The "joker" is to be found in the selection of these premises. (Jerome Frank, *Law and the Modern Mind*, Coward-McCann, 1949, pp. 65–6.)

Defend formal logic against Frank's criticism.

B. The Meaning of Truth

1. The author of the following selection argues that all truth is relative to the state of the body and mind at the time of perception. Is he somewhat inconsistent in referring to "a fascinating novel of genuine quality"?

The old illustration that 2 + 2 equals 4, whether one be sick or well, should be finally exploded. A number has more concreteness, because of the definite character of its associations, than a visual image or auditory sensation, but the process of perception is similar and the agreement or disagreement as to the nature of the impression is dependent equally upon the state of the body and mind at the time of perception. To a man suffering with paresis, 2 and 2 may make 11 or 7 or 5, just as to a man afflicted with toothache, a fascinating novel of genuine quality may be dull and of little value. (V. F. Calverton, *The Newer Spirit*, Liveright, 1925.)

2. A relativist argued: "A person's conception of what is true depends upon the manner in which he was conditioned by his environment and group customs. Western peoples thus have one set of conceptions, such as a reliance upon the methods of science, but Eastern peoples have a different kind of standard. They rely on mysticism as the source of truth. Thus there can be no 'absolute' truth, for every 'truth' is such only for those who have been conditioned to accept it. We criticize them, but they have an equal right to criticize us." Discuss.

3. A relativist says, "All American school teachers, without a single exception, are members of the Communist Party." This statement, he argues, is true *for him*. If you disagree, he says, you mean only that the statement is false *for you*. Discuss.

4. Pyrrho, the ancient Greek sceptic, dogmatically denied the possibility of human knowledge, either with respect to the senses, morals, or logic. Pyrrho's disciples, it may be recalled, refused to mourn him after he died, on the ground that they could not be sure that he was dead. Distinguish "probabilism" from Pyrrhonic scepticism.

C. *On Empirical Probability*

1. How would you answer the sorcerer in the following?

Dr. Livingstone was trying to dissuade an African sorcerer from his fetishistic ways of invoking rain. "You see," he said, "that after all your doings, it sometimes rains, and sometimes does not, exactly as when you do nothing at all."
"But," replied the sorcerer, "it is just the same with you doctors. You give the patient remedies, and sometimes the patient gets well, and sometimes he dies, exactly as when you do nothing at all." (A. Wolf, *Exercises in Logic and Scientific Method.* Copyright 1939 by The Macmillan Company and used with their permission.)

D. *Probability and Syllogisms*

Explain Holmes' "deductions" in the second paragraph of the following by constructing appropriate syllogisms. Indicate the general rules which Holmes assumes as his major premises; note that his observations constitute his minor premises, and complete the syllogisms with the conclusions stated in the second paragraph. Are his syllogisms valid? Can they be interpreted as "probability-syllogisms"?

Our visitor bore every mark of being an average common-place British tradesman, obese, pompous, and slow. He wore rather baggy gray shepherd's check trousers, a not overclean black frock-coat, unbuttoned in the front, and a drab waistcoat with a heavy brassy Albert chain, and a square pierced bit of metal dangling down as an ornament. A frayed top hat and a faded brown overcoat with a wrinkled velvet collar lay upon a chair beside him. Altogether, look as I would, there was nothing remarkable about the man save his blazing red head and the expression of extreme chagrin and discontent upon his features.

Sherlock Holmes' quick eye took in my occupation, and he shook his head with a smile as he noticed my questioning glances. "Beyond the obvious facts that he has at some time done manual labor, that he takes snuff, that he is a Freemason, that he had been in China, and that he has done a considerable amount of writing lately, I can deduce nothing else."

Mr. Jabez Wilson started up in his chair, with his forefinger upon the paper, but his eyes upon my companion.

"How in the name of good fortune, did you know all that, Mr. Holmes?" he asked. "How did you know, for example, that I did manual labor? It's as true as gospel, for I began as a ship's carpenter."

"Your hands, my dear Sir. Your right hand is quite a size larger than your left. You have worked with it and the muscles are more developed."

"Well, the snuff, then, and the Freemasonry?"

"I won't insult your intelligence by telling you how I read that, especially as, rather against the strict rules of your order, you use an arc and compass breastpin."

"Ah, of course, I forgot that. But the writing?"

"What else can be indicated by that right cuff so very shiny for five inches, and the left one with the smooth patch near the elbow where you rest it upon the desk."

"Well, but China?"

"The fish which you have tattooed immediately above your wrist could only have been done in China. I have made a small study of tattoo marks, and have even contributed to the literature of the subject. That trick of staining the fishes' scales of a delicate pink is quite peculiar to China. When, in addition, I see a Chinese coin hanging from your watch-chain, the matter becomes even more simple."

Mr. Jabez Wilson laughed heartily. "Well, I never!" said he. "I thought at first that you had done something clever, but I see that there was nothing in it after all." (A. C. Doyle, *The Red-Headed League*.)

E. On A Priori Probability

1. "I haven't seen John's new convertible, but the probability that it is red is $\frac{1}{2}$, since there are only two possibilities: it is red or not-red." Criticize.

2. What is the probability that the next birth in your neighborhood will be a boy? What assumptions did you make? Are they true?

3. Which hand is it more difficult to acquire in a bridge game, a hand containing 13 spades, or a hand containing Q, 10, 4 of spades, J, 9, 7 of hearts, 10, 8, 4 of diamonds, and Q, 6, 5, 2 of clubs?

4. A baseball player has made only one error in 200 chances. What is the probability that he will field the next chance without an error? What would the probability be if he had fielded 200 chances flawlessly? Would it make any difference if we assumed that the next chance would be a normal one and the player was alert? Does this problem involve empirical or a priori probabilities, or a combination of both?

5. A checker keeps tab on the numbers which fall on a roulette wheel. There are 38 numbers, so that the probability is that each number will fall 50 times in every 1,900 revolutions of the wheel. The checker finds the results for the first few numbers after 1,900 revolutions: number 1(48), number 2(55), number 3(47), number 4(79), number 5(43), number 6(14), number 7(51), number 8(49). Would this information be relevant to the making of a bet on any of these numbers?

6. Five cards are dealt to you from a pack of 52. Four of your cards are hearts. What is the probability that the top card in the deck is a heart?

7. Five cards are dealt to you once again. You have no ace or 9. What is the probability that the top card is either an ace or a 9?

8. Captain Marryat, in the novel *Peter Simple*, tells us of the midshipman who, during a battle, stuck his head through the first hole made in the side of his ship by an enemy cannon ball, because, he said, "by a calculation made by Professor Inman, the odds were 32,647 and some decimals to boot, that another ball would not come in at the same hole." (H. A. Larabee, *Reliable Knowledge*.) Comment on the midshipman's reasoning.

9. It is sometimes argued that if six chimpanzees were set to work pounding six typewriters at random for millions of years, they would in time write the works of Shakespeare, since all possibilities would be realized if they were given enough time. They would write much nonsense of course, but by mere chance they would be likely to hit the keys necessary to write anything whatsoever. Do you agree?

10. In his books, *New Frontiers of the Mind* and *The Reach of the Mind*, J. B. Rhine, Director of the Parapsychology Laboratory of Duke University, claims to have established the reality of clairvoyance, or the awareness of objects without the use of the senses. A series of "extrasensory perception," or "ESP" tests, was conducted in which subjects were asked to identify concealed cards. A simplified 25-card deck was devised, containing only five variations in design—star, rectangle, cross, circle, and wavy lines. Subjects were then asked to identify the cards as they were placed face down on a table. On the basis of chance, the probability is that a subject will score an average of five hits per 25 cards. According to Professor Rhine, one subject scored an average of 6.85 hits per run of 25 cards for more than 3,500 runs; another scored an average of more than 18 hits per 25 through a series of 74 runs through the deck, one of these runs giving a perfect score of 25 and several above 20. These facts, says Professor Rhine, have strongly established the case for clairvoyant extrasensory perception, since a perfect run should occur only once, according to one calculation, in over 298,023,223,876,-953,125 times! The odds are 100 to one that no one will average 8 or better for even three runs in succession, and 10,000 to one that no one will average 5.77 cards in 100 runs. Nevertheless, according to a reported poll taken among 352 psychologists in 1939, only 5 accepted ESP as established, with only 26 considering it "likely."

Do you believe that the case for ESP has been established, granted that the *facts* cited above are true?

F. The Calculus of Mathematical Probabilities

1. Compute the probabilities of the following: (a) 4 heads in a row, (b) three 6's in a row, (c) a 4, 5, or 6 with one die, (d) at least one head in three throws.

2. A man argued that since the probability of throwing a 6 with one die was $\frac{1}{6}$, the probability of throwing a 6 with

two dice was $\frac{2}{6}$, with 3 dice, $\frac{3}{6}$; with 4 dice, $\frac{4}{6}$; with 5 dice, $\frac{5}{6}$; with 6 dice, $\frac{6}{6}$; with 7 dice, $\frac{7}{6}$, etc. Point out his error.

3. When we toss 3 coins, there are 8 possible arrangements of the 3 coins: 1 of 3 heads, 1 of 3 tails, 3 of 2 heads and 1 tail, and 3 of 2 tails and 1 head. What is the probability that you can toss at least 2 heads with the 3 coins?

4. The possibilities with 4 coins are 16 in number: 1(4 heads), 4(3 heads, 1 tail), 6(2 heads, 2 tails), 4(3 tails, 1 head) and 1(4 tails). What are the probabilities that you can toss at least 2 heads with 4 coins?

5. A slot machine has three wheels with 20 characters on each wheel. One wheel has two jackpot symbols; the other two have one each. What are your chances of hitting the jackpot if the machine is not "rigged"?

6. Compute the probabilities in the dice game known as "craps." Instructions and rules follow:

   a. The "shooter" wins if he throws a combination totalling 7 or 11 on the first throw, and loses if he throws 2, 3, or 12 on the first throw.

   b. If some other number is thrown, such as 4, the shooter must then throw another 4 before he throws a 7 to win. If he throws 7 before 4, he loses.

   c. The possibilities for the various numbers are as follows:

Number	Ways of making	Combinations
2	1	(1–1)
3	2	(1–2, 2–1)
4	3	(3–1, 1–3, 2–2)
5	4	(4–1, 3–2, 2–3, 3–2)
6	5	(5–1, 4–2, 3–3, 2–4, 1–5)
7	6	(6–1, 5–2, 4–3, 3–4, 2–5, 1–6)
8	5	(6–2, 5–3, 4–4, 3–5, 2–6)
9	4	(6–3, 5–4, 4–5, 3–6)
10	3	(6–4, 5–5, 4–6)
11	2	(6–5, 5–6)
12	1	(6–6)

$\overline{36}$ possibilities

   d. Compute the chances of the shooter's losing. The shooter may lose on the first throw by throwing a 2, 3, or 12, and he may lose after throwing a 4, 5, 6, 8, 9, or 10 on the first throw. Since the probabilities of throwing (and losing) in these different combinations are strictly alternative, the separate probabilities should be added.

e. Special attention should be given to the probabilities of loss when a number from 4 to 10 is thrown. Suppose that 4 is thrown. This number will probably be thrown 3 times in 36 throws. (See the middle column above: Ways of making). We must now compute the probability of *losing* when 4 is thrown on the first throw. There are twice as many possibilities of making a 7 as there are of making a 4, since 4 occurs $\frac{3}{36}$ (3 times in 36) and 7 occurs $\frac{6}{36}$ (6 times in 36). In 9 attempts to make a 4 before a 7 the shooter will probably succeed three times and fail six times. He will lose six times out of nine, or $\frac{2}{3}$ of the time. Thus the probability that any shooter will lose via the number 4 is $\frac{3}{36} \times \frac{2}{3}$. (He will throw "4" $\frac{3}{36}$ of the time, and if he does, lose $\frac{2}{3}$ of the time).

f. Compute the probabilities for losing via the other numbers in the same manner, add the probabilities together, and you will have the shooter's chances of losing. Subtract this fraction from 1 and you will have the shooter's chances of winning.

g. It will be found convenient to translate all your fractions into fractions having a denominator of 990.

Chapter 15

Hypotheses and
Scientific Method

Section I: Concerning the Proof of a Proposition

If a proposition corresponds with the facts, then it is a true proposition. This definition of truth is pleasingly simple, but difficulties arise when we seek to apply it to actual cases. The proposition "I have a $1,000 bill in my wallet" is false, for it obviously does not correspond to the facts, but such correspondence or lack of correspondence is not so easily determined in propositions such as Einstein's famous statement that "the universe is finite but unbounded." Our basic question in this chapter will be: How do we determine whether a proposition does or does not correspond to the facts? We shall emphasize the manner in which the scientist answers this question, for scientific method is the most trustworthy method for testing the truth of propositions. Our discussion, however, will aim only at delineating the logical essentials of the method and we shall avoid entering into the details of the highly developed techniques which are used in elaborate research. We shall also seek to emphasize aspects of the scientific method which have some relevance to everyday thinking. The difference between the careful thinker in ordinary affairs and the scientist who develops reliable methods of inquiry is, as we shall see, one of degree rather than kind. It has been said that every man has something of the poet and lover in him. We may add that he is also something of a scientist.

Our present concern is with the methods of proof which may be used in testing the truth of a proposition. The basic problem here arises when we ask, Is proposition "P" true? Now, there are two ways in which the investigation into the truth of a proposition may be initiated. "P" may be a familiar "truth" which we suddenly decide to question. Most of us, of course, never raise such questions, especially where matters of "common knowledge" are concerned. Such ideas are regarded as immune from criticism, and false ideas enjoy long lives. Prejudices abound with respect to the activities of groups about which we know very little, such as Wall Street bankers, liberal political organizations, and racial and religious minorities. But the great thinkers in each generation question the basic presuppositions or assumptions of their times. Such men see problems in "accepted truths" that others take for granted. Questions may also result in scientific revolutions, as when Einstein questioned the accepted definition of "simultaneity." But more typically, propositions become candidates for testing by scientific methods when they are advanced as suggestions for the solutions of problems. A typical scientific problem is the search for the cause of a disease, as in cancer research. The cause of this disease is as yet unknown. Many hypotheses are suggested, i.e., propositions in the form "X is the cause." These propositions are then subjected to careful testing to determine truth or falsity.

We have just noted the two ways in which our basic question arises. It is also important to note that there are two general methods of proof which may be used in determining the truth or falsity of a proposition. These are the direct and the indirect methods. By direct proof we shall mean proof by simple observation; by indirect proof, cases in which logical reasoning, as well as observation, is required. To illustrate: The proposition "There are four yachts in the harbor" may be verified by direct observation. We see the yachts, and seeing is believing. (At least usually.) But there are many propositions which cannot be verified in this manner—statements concerning past events, for example. We cannot see Caesar crossing the Rubicon today, nor can we "see" a gas expanding when heated, since the gas is invisible to the eye. In such cases indirect methods of proof are required. The proposition "A gas expands when heated" is tested by heating gas in a cylinder. We see the piston moving up. Such indirect proof requires logical reasoning in addition to observation. We must deduce the consequences which will follow if our proposition is true, and we then experiment to determine whether these consequences actually occur. Our reasoning takes the following form:

> If gas expands when heated, then the piston will move up when the gas is heated.
> The piston did move up when the gas was heated.
> Therefore, it is true (or probable) that gas expands when heated.

We note that our reasoning has taken a syllogistic form. Though the syllogism is invalid, it justifies a highly probable conclusion.

The indirect method of proof is a very useful one in science. The secrets of nature are not always open to inspection by the naked eye, nor does the microscope always reveal them. Many of the significant propositions in science cannot be verified directly. We therefore ask what observable consequences will follow if the proposition is true. This is deduction. We then go to observation to find out if these consequences do in fact occur. Science thus involves both empirical and rational elements: observation and logical reasoning. Observation, of course, is the indispensable prerequisite of all truth concerning matters of fact and experience, and it is the ultimate ground of all truths concerning nature. But we could not go very far without the aid of logic.

Section II: Problems, Facts, and Hypotheses

All investigation begins with questions or problems. Philosophy, Aristotle said, begins in wonder. So does science. The testing of the truth of a proposition begins with the question, Is it true? All reflective thinking, as John Dewey has insisted over and over again, is a problem-solving activity. Reflective thinking differs from daydreaming, reverie, and other nonlogical forms of thinking in that it explores and analyzes the conditions which will resolve a difficulty. When the smooth tenor of untroubled existence pursues its placid course, we do not think reflectively. We must have something to think about, a problem which requires solution.

Let us imagine a motorist driving along a narrow country lane. He pays a minimum of attention to the mechanics of his car or to the condition of the road, though he is of course on the lookout for wandering livestock and other possible occupants of the road. But if he has "nothing on his mind" he indulges in reverie. This reverie is suddenly broken when he sees a cow standing astride the road, and he stops his car. The cow is eating loose alfalfa which had fallen on the road from a farmer's wagon. If our motorist cannot drive off the road to go around the cow because of "soft shoulders" then he must get the cow off the road. He has a problem, and he must think reflectively to find a solution. He removes the alfalfa from the road and the cow follows the alfalfa. This was a practical problem. But other types of problems may have occurred to our motorist while he was driving. He might have wondered why gasoline trucks drag iron chains on the ground after them. For him this would have been a theoretical problem, since it did not involve a practical difficulty. This distinction between practical and theoretical problems also characterizes two types of scientific problems, those concerned with the practical conditions of human welfare, and those which are concerned primarily with the enlightenment of the human mind. Problems concerning the chemical constitution of the stars, or Copernicus' problem concerning the relationship of the earth to the sun were primarily theoretical problems. But reflective thinking, in any case, always starts with a problem.

Our emphasis on the role of the problem in reflective thinking will help us to understand the nature of scientific method. In particular it will help us to see the inadequacy of a conception of science fostered by nineteenth century positivism, which thought of science as a fact-collecting agency. This view regards the scientist as a man who goes out into the field of nature with a notebook, jots down the description of what he observes, classifies his material, and then draws generalizations. But this view is inadequate, for at least two reasons. First, the world is full of a bewildering variety of things. What shall we note, and what shall we ignore? Effective observation of nature must have a purpose; one must know what to look for. We must go to nature with questions or problems, and the scientist must note the facts relevant to his problems. In the second place, "the facts" are not items which can always be directly observed, so that when we say, "Look at the facts," there may be nothing to see. These two criticisms deserve further discussion.

1. Observation requires hypotheses

Significant observations do not usually occur unless we are looking for something. In looking at a painting, or listening to music, or reading a book, the trained observer, i.e., the man who is familiar with the field, will observe infinitely more than the untrained person. The artist, said Leonardo da Vinci, sees what others catch only a glimpse of. He knows what to look for. In the same manner, no scientist makes observations without a plan of observation. He starts with a problem, e.g., the nature of the rock formations in an area. He examines the rocks with some definite goal in mind. He develops a suggested solution of some specific problem. Such suggested solutions are called "hypotheses," the working tools for the solution of problems. He has a "theory" as to how the rocks are formed, and then he looks for proof, for verification of his hypothesis.

Looking must have a purpose, to determine whether certain specific things are or are not present in nature. A detective needs a clue, and the scientist needs a working hypothesis which will be confirmed or rejected by the facts. If a hypothesis is refuted, the scientist must then revise or even abandon that hypothesis, and try out a new one. "How odd it is," said Charles Darwin, the father of modern evolutionary theory, "that anyone should not see that all observation must be for or against some view, if it is to be of any service." On another occasion he said, "No one can be a good observer unless he is a good theorizer."

Significant observation requires that we look for something specific, that we have a "point of view." But this method of "purposeful observation" also involves a pitfall. There is the danger that preconceived notions may lead to a biased point of view. The observer may then see only what he wishes to see, in line with his wishful thinking. He may not note the negative instances or exceptions to the rule he seeks to verify. Observation, in other words, should be selective, but it should not be "subjective."

There is also a certain sacrifice the observer must make for the advantages of purposeful observation. He will usually ignore facts which may have great significance for problems in which he is not interested. This point is well illustrated by an anecdote concerning Darwin and a fellow scientist who were searching for certain fossils in the North of England. They were interested in the theory of evolution and were not then aware of the glacial theory. Years later, Darwin revisited this region, and he was now astonished to discover how clearly marked were the glacial ridges on the rocks. He had not noticed them earlier because he was not looking for them. Modern archaeologists have recognized this aspect of selective observation, i.e., that we do not see what has no significance for us, and have accordingly established a methodological rule for the opening of new excavations. The archaeologists who discover ancient monuments or buildings will not excavate the site completely, but will leave part of the "find" untouched; for they may otherwise ignore important clues which a later generation will be aware of, in the same manner as Darwin became aware of the glacial markings.

2. What are "the facts"?

We have noted the importance of selective observation, centering around a problem, in our first criticism of the "fact-collecting" conception of science. The second inadequacy in this view is that the facts cannot be directly observed. When we are told to "base our ideas on the facts," the question arises, "What *are* the facts?" We may not know what the facts are! The distinction between a hypothesis and a fact, moreover, is often a tenuous one. It would seem appropriate, at this point, to inquire into what is meant by "fact."

The word "fact" has several senses. We shall note two important ones. When we say that a true proposition corresponds with the facts, we use the word "fact" for those existences in space and time which are what they are, independent of our theories, our knowledge, and our beliefs about them. These "facts" are simply there, awaiting our discoveries of them. In a second sense, however, "fact" means an established truth. We use "fact" in this sense when we say that "it is a fact that the earth is round." But at one time this view was regarded as a fantastic hypothesis by many persons who believed that the roundness of the earth involved the absurd consequence that the people in the antipodes (the other side of the earth) would have to walk upside down, like flies on a ceiling. What was once regarded as a "wild theory" is now accepted as a fact because the evidence overwhelmingly supports the hypothesis that the earth is round. The difference between what is called "hypothesis" and what is called "fact" (in the second sense) is thus one of degree only. Hypotheses become facts when the evidence becomes sufficiently convincing. The popular distinction between "fact" and "opinion" points to a similar distinction. An opinon is a theory, the evidence for which is inconclusive. When we prove our opinion, it becomes a fact.

To say that we should "go to the facts," then, may beg the question, for we may not know what they are. "The facts" cannot always be observed by simple inspection. Highly indirect modes of observation, mediated by hypotheses, may be necessary to find out what the facts are. Thus, very complicated deductions and mathematical calculations are required to test hypotheses concerning the internal structure of the atom. An observer in a physicist's laboratory watching an experiment might see the physicist watching the needle in a galvanometer. The reading is $+ .745$, and this reading may confirm a hypothesis concerning the atoms. But there was no direct observation of the facts. When Copernicus formulated his heliocentric theory concerning the revolution of the planets around the sun, he rejected the geocentric notion that the earth is motionless, with the sun, moon, and stars revolving around it every twenty-four hours. Did he merely observe the facts? No. Direct observation tells us that it is the sun which is in motion. But we now say that it is a fact that the earth moves.

Note also that there may be an element of hypothesis even in what we think of as direct observation. We see stars in the heavens. What we actually see are gleaming specks of light. We interpret these specks of white light as stars because of our hypotheses. I see a friend on the street, walk up and slap him on the back, but alas! I have annoyed a stranger. I acted on a hypothesis, which erroneously interpreted the facts. Interpretation is always somewhat hazardous, involving a leap into the unknown. Similarly, the desert traveler who "sees an oasis," sees an image, but his image does not correspond to anything in the real world.

The central element in scientific thinking is thus problem-solving, and the hypothesis is the central tool in such thinking. We have been using the terms "theory" and "hypothesis" synonymously in this discussion, but it should be noted that "theory" is often used in a more specialized way, as in the physical sciences, where it refers to the fundamental principles underlying a science. The "atomic theory" is used in this latter sense, since the atomic theory underlies various branches of the physical sciences.

We shall now turn to the analysis of scientific method to examine the manner in which the scientist proceeds in his search for the solution of problems.

Section III: The Logical Analysis of an Example of Scientific Thinking

The following example of scientific thinking is an abridged version of an incident in A. J. Cronin's novel, *The Citadel* (Grosset and Dunlap, pp. 57–60):

Andrew tore open the envelope. It was a message from Dr. Bramwell:

Come round at once. I want you to help certify a dangerous lunatic.

. . . . . .

Andrew threw on his things in three minutes. Accompanying him down the road, Annie told him as best she could about Emrys. He had been ill and unlike himself for three weeks, but during the night he had turned violent and gone clean out of his mind. He had set upon his wife with a breadknife. . . .

. . . . . .

"Acute mania." Bramwell rolled the words over his tongue with tragic grandeur. "Acute homicidal mania. Clear evidence, I think!"

"It sounds pretty bad," Andrew answered slowly. "Well! I'll take a look at him. . . ."

He went over to Emrys, and at first he hardly recognized him. His face seemed swollen, the nostrils thickened, the skin waxy. . . . Andrew spoke to him. He muttered an unintelligible reply. Then, clinching his hands, he came out with a tirade of aggressive nonsense. . . . [1] . . . . A silence followed. Andrew felt that he ought to be convinced. Yet, inexplicably, he was not satisfied. Why, why, he kept asking himself, *why* should Emrys talk like this? Supposing the man had gone out of his mind, what was the cause of it all? He had always been a happy, contented man—no worries, easygoing, amiable. Why, without apparent reason, had he changed to *this?* [2]

There must be a reason, Andrew thought doggedly; symptoms don't just happen of themselves. Staring at the swollen features before him, puzzling, puzzling for some solution of the conundrum, he instinctively reached out and touched the swollen face, noting subconsciously, as he did so, that the pressure of his finger left no dent in the edematous cheek. [3] *

All at once, electrically, a terminal vibrated in his brain. [4] *Why* didn't the swelling pit on pressure? Because—now it was his heart which jumped!—because it was not true edema, but myxedema.** [5] He had it, by God, he *had* it! No, no, he must not rush. Firmly, he caught hold of himself. He must not be a plunger, wildly leaping to conclusions. He must go cautiously, slowly, be sure!

Curbing himself, he lifted Emrys' hand. [6] Yes, the skin was dry and rough, the fingers slightly thickened at the ends. Temperature—it was subnormal. Methodically he finished the examination, fighting back each successive wave of elation. Every sign and every symptom—they fitted as superbly as a complex jigsaw puzzle. The clumsy speech, dry skin, spatulate fingers, the swollen inelastic face, the defective memory, slow mentation, the attacks of irritability culminating in an outburst of homicidal violence. Oh! the triumph of the completed picture was sublime. [7]

Rising, he went down to the parlor. . . . "Look here, Bramwell— . . . I don't think we ought to certify Emrys . . .

"In my opinion Emrys is only sick in mind because he's sick in body. I feel that he's suffering from thyroid deficiency—an absolutely straight case of myxedema." [8]

The *Citadel* incident will now be analyzed in order to show how scientific thinking typically follows eight steps, or phases, in the solution of a problem. We shall begin with an outline of the eight steps, and then show how each is a phase of the problem in *The Citadel*. Frequent reference back to the example

* Edema is the medical term for "a morbid accumulation of a waterlike fluid in organs or tissues of the body." Strictly, Cronin should have said "apparently edematous cheek," for, as he notes in a moment, the swelling in Emrys' cheek is not really due to edema.
** A disease associated with the thyroid gland and characterized by swelling of the face, dryness of the skin, and progressive mental deterioration.

will help the reader in following the discussion. (The numbers in the example refer to the steps.)

The Eight Steps

(1) The situation which generates the problem.
(2) The formulation of the problem.
(3) Observation of facts relevant to the problem.
(4) The use of previous knowledge.
(5) The formulation of the hypothesis.
(6) Deduction of the implications of the hypothesis.
(7) Testing of the hypothesis.
(8) Conclusion: The hypothesis is confirmed or disconfirmed.

1. The situation which generates the problem

Every scientific problem has a "background." There is some disturbing situation which must be set right, whether the disturbance be of a practical or theoretical nature. In our example Andrew notes certain peculiarities in Emrys' behavior. Emrys, hitherto a well-adjusted individual, is acting very strangely.

2. The formulation of the problem

Why, Andrew asks himself, does Emrys act in this manner? What is the cause of the observed peculiarities in his behavior? This is the problem generated by the disturbing situation. The formulation of a problem initiates the scientific inquiry. Note that the problem should be formulated in a precise manner. It should be "localized" and admit of a definite answer. "What's wrong with the world?" is not a scientific question, as Will Rogers well knew when he quipped that both he and Bernard Shaw knew that the world was all wrong, but that neither of them knew what was the matter with it.

We shall fumble aimlessly if we seek to solve a vaguely defined problem. The precise "definition" of the problem may require further analysis by breaking a large problem into smaller parts, or additional observations. Only those with knowledge of the field of investigation, moreover, are able to formulate problems precisely.

3. Observation of facts relevant to the problem

Andrew now seeks for the facts which may be connected with his problem. He touches Emrys' swollen cheek and notes that the pressure of his finger leaves no dent in the flesh. Only a trained observer, of course, is capable of making the fine discriminations which are required in situations such as this one.

Now, why did Andrew touch Emrys' face? There are many facts concerning Emrys (the color of his eyes and hair, his height and reach, and so on) which Andrew ignored. Andrew was concerned only with the *relevant* facts, i.e., those which might suggest a clue or hypothesis for the solution of his problem. How did he know which facts are relevant? This brings us to Step 4:

4. The use of previous knowledge

The scientist, in seeking to solve a problem, brings a fund of previous knowledge to his task. His recognition of relevance depends on this knowledge, which tells him to look for answers in certain directions and not in others. The scientist begins an investigation with many provisionally accepted assumptions as to what *may* be the solution of his problem. These assumptions may not be consciously present in his mind, but they are there.

Previous knowledge is also indispensable in the formulation of the hypothesis, or Step 5.

5. The formulation of the hypothesis

A hypothesis is a suggested solution of a problem. Andrew's hypothesis is that "Emrys has myxedema." Obviously, only a trained investigator could have thought of this hypothesis, based on his previous knowledge (Step 4). An untrained individual cannot diagnose a disease, because he doesn't know what symptoms to look for or how to interpret what he sees.

From his study of medicine Andrew knows that myxedema *might* account for Emrys' behavior, and that myxedema is characterized by various symptoms, among which is swollen flesh that does not pit on pressure. This "law" of medical science may be stated hypothetically: "If a patient has myxedema, then he will have swollen flesh, etc." Andrew's hypothesis is based on this knowledge, even though the hypothesis comes to his mind "like a flash." His mind went through a rapid process of reasoning, the steps in which were not at the foreground of his consciousness. His reasoning is syllogistic, in the form of an enthymeme, with the major premise omitted: "He has swollen flesh, etc. . . . Therefore, he has myxedema." The major premise is the law of medical science just referred to, and when we complete the syllogism it reads as follows:

> Emrys (is acting strangely and) has swollen flesh (Step 3).
> If one has myxedema then he will act strangely and have swollen flesh (Step 4).
> ∴ Emrys has myxedema (Step 5).

His reasoning proceeds from the observed fact (the minor premise), through the rule (major premise), to the hypothesis (conclusion). The syllogism is invalid, since it affirms the consequent, but the conclusion has a measure of probability, since the major premise can be "converted" into "If one acts strangely and has swollen flesh, then he probably has myxedema."

It should be noted that Andrew regards this hypothesis as merely a tentative solution until he has further evidence or proof. He now desires to test his hypothesis and we proceed to Step 6.

6. Deduction of the implications of the hypothesis

This step is also not formulated consciously in Andrew's mind. But we may discern the following pattern: "I must test my hypothesis. But how? This thing must be reasoned out, so I need an indirect proof. I must deduce the consequences of my hypothesis. If my hypothesis is true, what further facts should I observe in the patient? He should have spatulate fingers, etc., etc." Once more we find a hypothetical proposition, in which the hypothesis is the antecedent, and the deduced implications the consequent. Thus:

If Emrys has myxedema   then he will have spatulate fingers, etc.
    (the hypothesis)   (the deduced implications)

The purpose of deducing (or exfoliating) the implications of the hypothesis is that we will then have a definite prediction that certain observable facts will be found, if the hypothesis is true. We can then perform a test to determine whether these predicted facts are actually present. Step 6 is obviously dependent upon our previous knowledge, as were Steps 3 and 5. We are now ready for the test.

7. Testing the hypothesis

Andrew finds the predicted facts by further observation. The purpose of the test is to find whether the consequences do or do not in fact occur. In some cases an experiment may be required in Step 7, but an experiment, as Susan Stebbing has observed, is simply "a deliberate observation in the light of a definite expectation as to what will be observed." An experiment often involves special kinds of apparatus, but these are not indispensable. In any case, both experimental and non-experimental observation are forms of observation.

8. Conclusion: The hypothesis is confirmed or rejected

Andrew draws the conclusion that Emrys is suffering from myxedema. His hypothesis was confirmed by his further observations. If the observations in Step 7 had been negative, however, then either further analysis or a new hypothesis would have been required.

Note that Steps 6–7–8 also form a unit of syllogistic reasoning, like Steps 3–4–5. Step 6: "If he has myxedema, then he will have spatulate fingers." Step 7: "He has spatulate fingers." Step 8: "Therefore, he has myxedema." Once again, we can only say "probably." But the probability of the hypothesis has now been increased greatly for it rests on stronger evidence. The probability of a patient's having a particular disease increases, other things being equal, with the number of the observed symptoms.

If the hypothesis had been *disconfirmed* by negative evidence, our syllogism would then have been in the fourth figure. If Step 7 had shown that Emrys did *not* have spatulate fingers, etc., then Andrew would have concluded that he did not have myxedema. Does this mean that a negative experiment gives us certainty rather than probability? No, for we can never be certain that our premises are absolutely true. A negative experiment, however, gives us a more conclusive proof than a positive one. It is often possible that some other hypothesis might also account for the known and observed facts, but if the deduced facts are *not* present, then that particular hypothesis cannot be true, with the qualifications above noted. When a hypothesis is proved false, we must return to Step 3 and make a fresh start in the search for a new one.

Before we go on to discuss some further general features of scientific thinking and methods, it may be helpful to sum up our discussion of the *Citadel* case. We shall list the eight steps in tabular form, showing the application of each to the *Citadel* illustration:

The Eight Steps of Scientific Method	*Application to the* CITADEL *case*
1. The situation which generates the inquiry.	1. There is a disturbing situation which must be set right: Emrys, a hitherto well-adjusted individual, is acting strangely.
2. The precise formulation of the problem.	2. What is the cause of Emrys' symptoms and behavior?
3. Observation of the relevant facts.	3. Andrew notes that Emrys' swelled flesh does not pit on pressure.
4. The use of previous knowledge.	4. Andrew knows that myxedema is characterized by mental deterioration and swelled, nonedematous flesh. He uses this knowledge in Step 5. (Step 3 is also based on his knowledge that the condition of a patient's flesh is apt to be a significant symptom.)
5. The formulation of the hypothesis.	5. Andrew puts Steps 3 and 4 together: myxedema fits the observed facts. His hypothesis: Emrys has myxedema.
6. Deduction from the hypothesis: If the hypothesis is true, certain consequences can be predicted.	6. If Emrys has myxedema, then he should have *all* of the symptoms that characterize the disease, including

The implications of the hypothesis tell us what facts will verify or confirm the hypothesis.

7. Testing the hypothesis, by further observation or experiment.

8. Conclusion: the hypothesis is confirmed or not confirmed.

symptoms that have not as yet been observed: dry, rough skin, spatulate fingers, etc.

7. Andrew observes that Emrys has all the characteristics of myxedema: dry, rough skin, spatulate fingers, etc.

8. Andrew draws the conclusion that Emrys has myxedema.

Section IV: Some General Considerations Concerning Hypotheses And Negative Experiments

In this section we shall discuss the criteria of a good hypothesis and some special problems arising in connection with negative experiments. We shall also discuss the form of proof known as the "Reductio ad Absurdum."

1. The Criteria of a Good Hypothesis

In the *Citadel* case, Andrew found his hypothesis in his previous knowledge. He applied a previously known rule to the case before him. But his problem was a relatively simple one when compared with those theoretical problems which result in the discovery of new laws of nature. Sir Isaac Newton and Albert Einstein were men of great imaginative power, who saw relations in nature that had never been previously suspected. Great scientists, like great artists, are men of imagination.

Whatever the scientific problem may be, however, the good hypothesis is one which successfully solves a problem. In thus functioning successfully the hypothesis must do certain things. First, it must account for the facts which are already *known*. This means that, before we put it to the test of proof, it should account for the facts which have been observed in the specific investigation at hand, i.e., it should be consistent with our previous knowledge. In the *Citadel* case, Andrew's hypothesis met this first requirement, for the hypothesis of myxedema accounted for the observed fact that Emrys' flesh was swelled.

Our first requirement, however, calls for judicious interpretation. Great scientists sometimes appear to show a bland disregard of "the facts." Let us examine the instructive illustration afforded by Mendeleyev, the great Russian chemist who discovered the law of the periodicity of the chemical elements. Mendeleyev formulated a hypothesis which did *not* account for all of the facts. In 1869, the year in which he formulated his hypothesis, 63 chemical elements had been isolated, but these elements had no apparent logical relationships to each other. Mendeleyev believed that if the elements were arranged in groups according to their atomic weights, then their other properties could be explained as periodic functions of their atomic weights. But two of the elements, tellurium and gold, could not be fitted into the suggested pattern, for their atomic weights were not in accordance with his hypothesis. His attitude may be summed up as "So much the worse for the facts." He argued that the atomic weights of these recalcitrant elements had been miscalculated, and it later turned out that he was correct. Mendeleyev did not, of course, think that a hypothesis could be true if it were not in accordance with the facts; he simply had the boldness to predict that "the facts" were not really facts. The student of the history of science will find that many scientists are reluctant to give up plausible hypotheses despite negative experiments. When a scientist hits upon a novel explanation that appears to give a new insight into the laws of nature, he may hold tenaciously to his hypothesis despite the consideration that his hypothesis does not account for all of the known facts. His faith in his idea may be so great as to justify him in disregarding hostile facts on the ground that it is in the facts, and not in his idea, that error resides. In the end, the facts reign supreme, but there may be legitimate controversies as to just what they are.

A second requirement of a good hypothesis is that it should be *verifiable* in terms of the facts. It should be capable of being tested, that is, we should be able to prove it or disprove it. In the typical case, a prediction is made that certain facts will be observed, and we either observe these facts or we do not. Andrew made such a prediction. His verified prediction corroborated his hypothesis and strengthened its probability. Predictions are particularly impressive when they predict facts the existence of which would otherwise have been unknown. Einstein, for example, predicted that if his hypothesis of relativity were true, the sun would deflect the path of a ray of starlight. He predicted a deflection of 1.75 seconds. The verifying experiment showed a deflection of 1.65 seconds. No deflection had previously been suspected.

Though a good hypothesis should be verifiable by observation, this does not mean that a hypothesis which cannot be so verified is worthless. A speculative hypothesis concerning the origin of the solar system has a measure of probability when it accounts for the known facts, and when it is stated in such a way that its implications *might* be observed under the appropriate conditions. It is important to note that a legitimate working hypothesis always involves the possibility of its being proved *or disproved* by the occurrence or non-occurrence of observable events. If this condition is not present, then the suggestion is only a pseudo-hypothesis. As an illustration of such a pseudo-hypothesis consider the thesis that all human choices are motivated by the desire to achieve the greatest amount of pleasure and the least amount of pain for oneself. An interesting popular exposition of this thesis, called "psychological hedonism," will be found in Mark Twain's *What is Man?* This thesis is not a hypothesis, since it is not possible to disprove it by any conceivable experiment. For no matter what evidence we present against it, the proponent of the thesis will say that the evidence proves his point, even when we cite the martyr who goes to the stake for his religious beliefs. No distinction is made between the type of evidence which would support the thesis and the type which would disprove it. This is another example of "begging the question" or "arguing by definition."

Typically, a hypothesis is verified after its consequences are deduced. In some cases the available facts may be so numerous (or convincing) that a given hypothesis which accounts for all of them may be highly probable *without further deduction of its implications*. For example, the reader may arrive at his home one evening and find his rooms in a state of disarray, the dresser drawers pulled out, clothing strewn on the floor, and his prized oil paintings gone. These immediate observations make the hypothesis, "My home has been burglarized" highly probable, without the necessity for deducing its implications and making a prediction. The observed facts present a relatively "complete picture," and every observed fact points in the direction of the hypothesis.

Whether we deduce the implications of our hypothesis or not, however, the hypothesis should account for all of the available evidence. The items which make up this evidence may be said to "converge" on the hypothesis which accounts for them. Thus, if the hypothesis "H" accounts for the evidence, made up of facts a, b, c, d, e, f, etc., we may say that these facts "converge" on "H." This situation may be represented by a diagram:

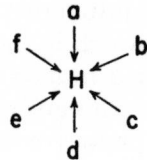

A third requirement for a good hypothesis is that it should be *simple*. This means that, other things being equal, where two hypotheses explain a given set of facts, and where each is verified by prediction, the simpler of the two should be preferred. Copernicus used this principle in advancing his hypothesis—that the earth moves around the sun—when he pointed out that the science of astronomy would be greatly simplified if the sun, rather than the earth were taken as the center in determining the movements of the planets. "Ockham's razor," a maxim attributed to William of Ockham, the mediaeval philosopher, tells us that "entities should not be multiplied beyond necessity." There are also cases, of course, where no choice between two rival hypotheses, on the ground of simplicity, is possible. The two theories of light now used by physicists afford a good illustration of this point. Newton's corpuscular theory and Huyghen's wave theory explain the known facts equally well. Both are equally "simple." In such cases, as Sir William Bragg once remarked, "We have to work with both theories. On Mondays, Wednesdays, and Fridays we use the wave theory; on Tuesdays, Thursdays, and Saturdays we think in streams of flying energy quanta or corpuscles."

It should be noted, however, that "simple" is a vague term. The hypothesis that "God is the cause of all things," including every movement of your body, is a "simple" explanation in one sense, but not at all simple in another, since it requires special explanations as to why He caused each particular motion of your body. The more complex physiological explanation of these movements in terms of muscular contractions is thus the "simpler" of the two hypotheses.

2. Negative Experiments and the "Reductio ad Absurdum"

Step 6 states the consequences which follow from the hypothesis. When the test (Step 7) confirms these consequences and when we draw the conclusion that the hypothesis is true, we have an invalid syllogism which is "saved" by adding the word "probably." But when Step 7 negates the consequent of Step 6, the syllogism is a valid one. This gives us the rule that a negative experiment has a higher probative value than a positive one, but even a negative experiment can give us no more than probability. As noted earlier, we have no guarantee that our major premise was absolutely true, nor that our testing procedure was flawless, at least in complicated problems. Errors may have crept into our calculations, and relevant factors may not have been analyzed properly. An interesting example of a negative experiment which contained such errors is found in the experiments of Bishop Needham during the eighteenth century. At that time biologists were concerned with the question as to whether life can be generated spontaneously from non-living matter. Spallanzani, an Italian priest, performed experiments to prove the theory of biogenesis, i.e., that all living things have parents, including germs. He sterilized a liquid, put it into a sealed flask protected from the dusts of the surrounding air, and found that his liquid remained sterile. Unless it was exposed to the air it remained free of germs. Needham, an English priest, sought to disprove the theory of biogenesis. He boiled a liquid, thus sterilizing it, put it into a flask, and plugged the top tight with a cork. After a period of time he found germs in his flask. This appeared to him to be a convincing refutation of the theory of biogenesis, since if living things are reproduced only by other living things, there should have been no germs in his flask. But germs *were* present, so the theory appeared to be disproved. Spallanzani, however, showed that Needham's experiment was worthless since his flask had not been properly sealed. The germs were able to push their way through the porous cork into the flask.

The use of negative cases gives us a syllogism in which the consequent is denied. This type of reasoning is also used in the form of argument called the "Reductio ad Absurdum," in which we "reduce to the absurd," i.e., we prove a proposition by showing that its contradictory is absurd, or false. We take the contradictory of the theory we wish to prove, deduce its implications, show that these implications are absurd, and we have then disproved the contradictory of our original theory. If its contradictory is false, it must be true. As an example, suppose that we wish to prove that the moon is uninhabited. We proceed as follows:

1. Assume that the contradictory of H is true: The moon is inhabited. Let us call this H'.
2. Deduce the consequences of H': If the moon is inhabited, then its creatures live without air. (These implications are based upon our knowledge.)
3. It is impossible for living creatures to live without air. (Denies the consequent.)
4. Therefore, H' must be false.
5. Therefore, H must be true (for H is the contradictory of H').

Note that Steps 1–4 in this proof correspond to Steps 5–8 in our previous notation. The Reductio, of course, gives us no greater certainty than the certainty of the premises in Steps 2 and 3.

One final point. In some problems, several different hypotheses may be available as possible solutions. Step 5 will then be formulated as an alternative proposition, e.g., "The cause of X is either A, or B, or C, or D." We then deduce the implications of each, and test each. If all but one are eliminated, the remaining hypothesis is probably the cause. This is not conclusive proof unless we can be certain that the four hypotheses exhaust all the possibilities, i.e., that no other hypothesis can explain the facts, in addition to the other reservations which are required.

Section V: Supplementary Comments on the Eight Steps

The aim of our eight-step analysis is not psychological analysis but logical analysis. We have sought to clarify the roles of observation, hypothesis, deduction, and testing in the solution of scientific problems. Our analysis may not be exemplified in every detail in any given case of scientific thinking. It is obvious that Step 4, for example, does not appear in that order even when the steps follow each other chronologically. There may be a telescoping of the steps, as in the *Citadel* case, and new variations may be added, but in general these eight steps will appear. In poetry, similarly, we find that few poets adhere with rigidity to a given rhythmical pattern, such as an iambic pentameter. This may be the basic rhythm, but the meaning of the words in a line of verse often requires accents which depart from the strict scanning of the meter. But underlying the departures, there is a definite pattern. So it is with scientific method.

Our pattern requires certain modifications when we deal with purely rational problems, as in mathematics, chess, or puzzles. The important thing in such problems is the suggestion of hypotheses and the mental elaboration of their implications. Observation is incidental to deduction. We deduce consequences in the mind and accept or reject these implications.

Some examples: In a chess game, I explore the possibilities. I wish to capture my opponent's Queen. It occurs to me that I can attack successfully if I move my knight to KB5. Now, if I move my knight, then he will move here, and I will then move there, and he will do this, and I will do that, etc. Then I note that my position will be weakened, without compensating gains, and try another possibility. Puzzles and "brain-twisters" give us similar types of problems. Suppose we had the following problem presented to us:

(A) .   .   . (B)
.   .   .
(C) .   .   . (D)

Copy these dots on a sheet of paper, ignoring the letters. Then draw four straight lines, without removing your pencil from the paper, and without retracing any lines, so that the lines will go through all of the nine dots. The reader will now try out various hypotheses, by the trial-and-error method, and may shortly con-

clude that all of the obvious suggestions are impossible. A sense
of defeat is typical at this point. The reader may now be given
a helpful hint: The instructions permit a line to extend out
beyond a series of dots. This hint suggests new hypotheses. But
there are no rules which will guarantee success in working out
such problems. Imagination in selecting fertile hypotheses is of
the essence. But we must also persist in trying out new hypotheses and deducing the consequences of each possibility. (The
solution of our problem will now be given: Start at the dot near
A, and run the line out beyond B. Then come back through the
middle dot between B-D and the middle dot between C-D to a
point below C. Then up to A and back to D through the center
dot.)

Our general pattern may be varied in yet another way. In
working out a problem we may find that new problems are generated by our investigations. We will then have a primary problem and subsidiary problems. When a patient visits a physician,
the physician's primary problem is that of curing the patient.
But before the physician can formulate a hypothesis for the
cure, he must diagnose the patient's illness. This becomes the
subsidiary problem, and the physician must work through
the eight steps toward a solution of this problem. The solution
of the problem of diagnosis then becomes the third step in the
primary problem of cure. In this case the subsidiary problem appears in connection with the *observation* of the relevant facts.

The subsidiary problem may also occur at other stages, as in
the *proper formulation* of the *hypothesis*. Let us use a famous
murder mystery as our example. A dead child was found in a
field outside of a large city. A preliminary problem concerned
the cause of death. The hypothesis of murder was easily verified
by the condition of the body. The next problem is the primary
one: Who committed the murder? We shall now set forth the
steps in the solution of this problem, omitting Steps 1 and 4
for simplification:

2. Primary problem: Who committed the murder?
3. Observation: A clue is found in a pair of glasses.
5. Hypothesis: The owner of the glasses is the murderer. But a
   hypothesis must be specific, and so we take up a subsidiary
   problem:
   2. Who is the owner of the glasses?

    3. Observation: Careful examination of the type and make gives us the name of the manufacturer. The manufacturer informs us as to the dealers who handle these glasses in the vicinity of the murder. A list of customers is then obtained: A, B, C, D, etc.

    5. Hypothesis: Either A, B, C, D is the owner of these glasses.

    6. If D was the owner, then he was in the woods on the day of the murder. (We assume that we have eliminated A, B, and C)

    7. D was in the woods.

    8. D is probably the owner of these glasses.

5. The hypothesis is restated: D is the murderer.

6. Deducing the implications: If D is the murderer, then further incriminating evidence will be found connecting D with the murder.

7. Testing the hypothesis: We find such incriminating evidence.

8. Conclusion: D is (probably) the murderer.

    Similarly, the problem of *verification* may raise a subsidiary problem. A classical example of an ingenious experiment which verified an important hypothesis in physics will be found in Galileo's *Two New Sciences* (Northwestern University Press). Galileo (1564–1642), the great Italian physicist, was interested in the fall of bodies through space. His famous experiment, in which he dropped weights from the top of the Leaning Tower of Pisa, showed that the speed with which bodies fall to the earth does not depend upon their weight, provided that we neglect the resistance of the air. He also knew that the speed of falling bodies increases as they approach the earth. He assumed that the increase in speed occurred in accordance with a general law of nature. He now became interested in the manner in which the change of speed occurs, i.e., just what is the law of motion of a falling body? Two suggestions came to his mind. The first was that the speed increased with the *space* traveled, i.e., that the speed was proportional to the distance a body falls through space. (The greater the distance, the greater the speed.) He rejected this hypothesis. He then tried a second suggestion, that the speed varied with the *time* of the fall, so that the change in velocity would be proportional to the time interval. He deduced the consequences of this hypothesis and found that they were not self-contradictory. He formulated his new hypothesis as follows: The speed of a falling body increases in direct proportion to the time of the fall. He wished now to test his hypothesis. This presented a difficult problem, since he had no accurate clocks with which to measure the speed of the fall. He then deduced the implication that the *distance* fallen would be proportional to the square of the time taken. In other words, the distance traversed after two seconds should be four times as great as after one second; after three seconds, nine times as great, and so on. But how was he to test this consequence? He then set up two kinds of apparatus with which he could measure distance and time. He set up an inclined plane, with a smooth groove, and rolled a ball down the groove. For the measurement of time, he used a vessel containing water which trickled through a pipe into a small glass. He then permitted the ball to roll one quarter of the length of the incline and measured the time elapsed by the quantity of water which flowed into the glass. The ball was then rolled the full length of the incline, and now there was twice the former amount of water in the glass. In other words, in double the time there was four times as much distance. In this way he discovered that "the spaces traversed were to each other as the squares of the times." When the time factor was multiplied by three, the space factor was multiplied by nine, and similarly for all other quantities.

Section VI: The Problem of Verification in History and the Law Courts

In this section we shall consider some problems in assessing the value of evidence in historical investigations. We shall also consider the problem of proving the guilt of an accused person in a court of law, since this, too, is a historical investigation involving the truth of propositions concerning past events.

In general, the historian is concerned with three types of logical problems. He must verify specific propositions concerning specific events: Did Caesar cross the Rubicon? He seeks for explanations of important events: Why did Franklin D. Roosevelt seek a third term? What were the fundamental causes of the Revolutionary, Civil, and World Wars? A third problem is the search for a general law of history. The Marxian thesis that economic or materialistic causes are responsible for the fundamental happenings of history is an example of one hypothesis in the last field. We shall be concerned, in what follows, with the first problem, concerning the verification of specific propositions. We shall simply note that the method of "proof" in the two latter fields usually involves search for a pattern of explanation which will place the relevant facts in an intelligible order. Though conclusive proof for such explanations is an unattainable ideal, each hypothesis will usually be of value in pointing to some significant factor which might otherwise have been overlooked. Limited as the theory of economic determinism may be in explaining history, it has nevertheless revealed a causative factor which is of great importance in many situations.

Let us now turn to propositions concerning specific events in the past. The first obvious point is that the past cannot be inspected directly. Each past event is a unique event which cannot be repeated again in exactly the same form. The problem is: Did such and such an event occur? The only basis on which we can answer this question is in terms of the evidence. Every such proposition concerning the occurrence of a specific event must be regarded as a hypothesis, as a candidate for proof, and will have a varying degree of probability depending upon the quality and quantity of the evidence which supports it. Authority, "what everybody knows," and rumor are not evidence. How does the historian assess his evidence in proving such hypotheses?

The historian uses observation of the remains of the past—monuments, inscriptions, and other tangible objects. He examines the writings of men and women who were witnesses of events or who reported hearing about them. These reports constitute the memory of the human race. The Greeks rightly made Memory the muse of history. Two important types of problems arise when we consider the writings of the past. The first question is: Is the document genuine, i.e., was it written by the person purporting to have written it? The original document may have disappeared, and we must use a copy. Is the copy a correct one? The second question concerns the competence of the witness: Who is the witness? Was he a reliable person who could be trusted to tell the truth? Even if we grant that he was not a liar, did he have special biases which might distort his judgment and lead him to give distorted testimony? Was he a competent observer who would be likely to give an accurate account of what he witnessed? To what extent do independent witnesses give substantially similar accounts of the same events? Was the witness suggestible, so that he would be likely to be easily led by a questioner? And so on.

Was Jonah a historical character? Can we be absolutely certain of his existence because he is mentioned in the Bible? Can the Bible be mistaken in this particular instance? What is the evidence on which you base your judgment? According to the Moslems, the Koran was revealed to Mohammed by God, "sent down" through the Angel Gabriel, thus making him the true and final prophet of God's will. Pious Moslems are absolutely certain that this event occurred, but the historian asks, What is the evidence, and how reliable is it? The Moslems also report many miracles, i.e., violations of the natural order of cause and effect in the world. Such reports are based upon the testimony of witnesses, but the belief that this testimony is true is a hypothesis, which must be supported by adequate evidence. One must also consider other hypotheses, e.g., that the witness was mistaken. The scientific thinker judges the evidential value of such hypotheses by the principle of probabilities. Which is the more likely, that the witness was mistaken or that the miracle occurred? The scientist does not dogmatically deny the occurrence of unusual events merely because they do not fit into his preconceived theories, but he asks for the evidence in each case.

Similar problems of verification occur in a law court when facts are in dispute. The law distinguishes between two kinds of evidence: the testimony of witnesses and circumstantial evidence. Circumstantial evidence means evidence of facts or circumstances from which the fact in issue may be inferred. In a criminal case such evidence means facts associating an individual with the crime: fingerprints, personal possessions or clothing, possession of stolen property, and so on. Neither type of evidence can give probability of more than varying degrees. Let us look at an example of circumstantial evidence in a criminal case.

A streetcar conductor was robbed and murdered. A mask and food were found at the scene of the crime. The police suspected that N was the murderer, for the following reasons: N was identified by a witness as having been seen running away from the locality of the crime shortly after it occurred. When the police searched his room they found thread of the same kind as that in the mask. They also found hair-tonic having the same odor as that of the hood. Four days after the murder, N attempted to leave town without bothering to collect his unpaid wages from his employer. Witnesses testified that N had told them that it would be easy to hold up a streetcar conductor. The watchman in the plant where he worked reported that his .32 caliber revolver, the type with which the conductor was killed, was missing for several days before the murder was committed. N's shift at the plant started at 6 P.M., but on the night of the murder he did not report until 1:15 A.M. N's defence was that he had decided to take a walk on the night in question; that when he was near the scene of the crime a man ran by saying that there had been a murder, and so he ran too. Now, the evidence in this case is very powerful and convincing, and establishes a high probability of N's guilt, but it does not give certainty. It is *possible* that N was innocent, despite this evidence, i.e., even if all the facts cited are true. We should remember, too, that circumstantial evidence is based upon the reports of investigators, and these reports may be mistaken. Evidence may even be "planted." But when we now turn to the evidential value of testimonial evidence we also find only probabilities, not absolute certainty. Witnesses may be honestly mistaken, and they may also commit perjury. Even the confessions of individuals are subject to some doubt. Innocent persons have "confessed" in order to shield others; confessions may be extorted by illegal means, such as torture or drugs; and there are always the neurotics who rush in to confess to sensational crimes.

In a trial-at-law a witness presents his testimony on "direct" examination. His testimony is then subject to cross-examination. Hearsay evidence, i.e., evidence not within the personal knowledge of the witness, but the mere repetition of what he has heard others say, is usually excluded. Such evidence is excluded, not because it is irrelevant, but because it does not permit of the safeguard of cross-examination. Witnesses may also be called to establish the credibility or to throw doubt on the credibility of a witness' testimony.

Probability, in other words, is all that can be hoped for, whichever type of evidence is used. The question is: How good is the evidence (whether it be circumstantial or testimonial)? Though laymen hold circumstantial evidence in suspicion, lawyers and logicians are more acutely aware of the possibilities of error in testimony. But neither type should be esteemed or disparaged in a wholesale manner. Further, if certainty of proof were required, few, if any, accused persons could be convicted. We should also note that the courts establish different standards of proof for civil and criminal cases. In a civil case, all that is required is that one party prove his case by a preponderance of the evidence. But in a criminal charge, the state must prove a person guilty "beyond a reasonable doubt." This means that no "reasonable man" would doubt that the accused has been proved guilty. The hypothesis, in other words, must have a very high probability before conviction is justified. Certainty is not required.

Exercises

A. On the Criteria of a Good Hypothesis

1. Is it possible to test the hypothesis that there are mountains on the side of the moon that no human being has ever seen?
2. Galileo's telescope revealed mountains on the moon. A contemporary astronomer argued that there could be no mountains on the moon, for Aristotle said that the heavenly bodies are perfect spheres. The astronomer argued that there appear to be mountains, but that the valleys are filled with an invisible substance, so that the moon is in reality a perfect sphere. Galileo retorted that if we may postulate invisible substances, he would postulate that there are invisible mountains on the moon extending far beyond the apparent peaks.
   Discuss in terms of the testability of hypotheses.
3. In a criminal trial the prosecution has a dossier of facts built up by painstaking investigation. In amassing their evidence the police work with clues that serve as tentative or working hypotheses. The jury is asked to decide whether these facts justify the hypothesis that "X is guilty." Explain the

difference between the use of the eight steps by the police and the jury. Use the case on pp. 383–4 as a basis for your discussion.

B. *The Analysis of Scientific Thinking: The Eight Steps*

The following account of the discovery of the cause of pellagra by Dr. Joseph Goldberger is based upon the story as told in Chapter 11 of Paul de Kruif's *Hunger Fighters* (Harcourt, Brace and Co.). De Kruif's material is freely adapted in what follows.

In the second decade of the twentieth century an old disease called "pellagra" had become epidemic in the southern states. The disease was also endemic, i.e., its occurrence was confined to some localities and not others. One village might be affected; a neighboring one not. Pellagra is characterized by gastric disturbances, skin eruptions, and nervous derangement. Medical opinion at the time inclined to the belief that the disease was caused by an unknown microbe. Dr. Goldberger was sent to Mississippi by the U. S. Health Service to find a way of eliminating the disease. His work in discovering the cause of pellagra was quite remarkable, especially in view of the fact that he worked without the aid of specialized laboratory equipment.

Goldberger's problem: What is the cause of pellagra? He observed the fact that the sufferers were always in contact with other victims. Since this is the consequence which would be expected if the disease were caused by microbes, i.e., it would be "catching," he adopted the tentative hypothesis that the disease was caused in this manner. He then reasoned that if microbes were the cause, persons in close contact with the victims should catch the disease. But in the first hospital he visited, he found that the orderlies, nurses, and doctors who were in close contact with the victims never caught the disease. This led him to discard the hypothesis that the disease was caused by germs. It was now necessary to find and try out another hypothesis. He continued his observations. He found that only the poor suffered from the disease. He noted that the victims' diet consisted of corn-meal mush, hominy grits, and like foods, but practically no milk or fresh meat. On one occasion, while visiting an orphanage, he noted that only the children in the 6–12 age group had the disease. In investigating this clue he found that the children under six were given milk and the children over twelve were fed meat. The orphanage's funds were limited, so they skimped on the food of the 6–12 group, who were too young to work (and so did not "deserve" meat) and who were beyond the "baby" stage, the stage when milk was regarded as essential. This fact suggested the hypothesis that a diet lacking in milk and fresh meat was the cause of the disease. He then reasoned out the consequences of this hypothesis, namely, that remedying these deficiencies in diet would cure the disease. He procured a sufficient amount of milk and fresh meat for the children at the orphanage. All cases of pellagra disappeared.

INSTRUCTIONS:
Analyze this account in terms of the eight-step analysis. Two complete analyses will be required: first, of the discarded hypothesis, and then of the confirmed one.

C. Hypotheses in Criminal Cases: Circumstantial Evidence

In 1932 the Lindbergh baby was kidnapped and murdered. Bruno Richard Hauptmann was arrested after paying for gasoline at a filling station with a banknote which had been part of the $50,000 ransom. During his trial and after the verdict of "guilty," Hauptmann protested his absolute innocence and insisted, even at the very last moment before he was executed, that he had had nothing to do with the crime. He also asserted that he had no knowledge of any person or persons who may have been involved in the crime. The evidence against him was purely circumstantial. No witnesses testified to having seen him at or near the scene of the crime when it occurred. Following are some of the items of circumstantial evidence presented by the prosecution to prove his guilt:

1. When arrested, Hauptmann had $20 of the ransom money in his pockets, and concealed under a board in his garage was an additional $14,600. (His defence was that this money, identified as the ransom money, had been left in his possession for safe keeping by a friend named Isador Fisch, just before Fisch left for Europe, where he died.)

2. Hauptmann had been in the habit of keeping a personal financial record up to the time of the kidnapping. The record showed that just prior to April 2, 1932 (the date on which the ransom money was paid) he had $203.90 in a savings bank, and owned about $100 in stocks. He opened brokerage accounts in the same month, depositing about $17,000 for the purchase of stocks. He was shown to have acquired new money in the amount of $44,486 between the

time of the kidnapping and the time he was arrested. His stock transactions showed a net loss of over $5,000. He quit his job during March, when the kidnapping occurred, and his wife quit her job in a bakery shortly thereafter. He bought a new car, made a hunting trip to Maine, and a motor trip to Florida. His wife made a trip to Europe.

3. The kidnapper's ransom notes indicated that the author was a German, as was he. An expert identified the ransom notes as being in Hauptmann's handwriting.

4. The handwriting on a note left in the nursery after the kidnapping was the same as that of the ransom notes. These notes were sent to Dr. J. F. Condon, a retired school-principal, who acted as the intermediary. Dr. Condon arranged to meet the writer of the notes in a cemetery, where he paid him the ransom money after receiving the baby's sleeping garment as proof that the recipient of the money was the kidnapper.

5. Condon testified that Hauptmann was the man with whom he sat on a bench at the Woodlawn cemetery and to whom he later paid the ransom at St. Raymond's cemetery. Lindbergh identified Hauptmann's voice as that of the man in the latter cemetery.

6. The lumber used to make the kidnap ladder was traced to the National Mill Work and Lumber Co., in the Bronx. Hauptmann had worked there, and bought lumber there. He was an expert carpenter. One rail on a ladder section was made of wood identical with the wood in Hauptmann's attic, from which part of a floorboard had been ripped out. Four nail-holes in the rail matched exactly four nail-holes in the attic joist from which the wood had presumably been ripped. Chisel marks on the ladder were made with a three-quarter-inch Stanley. Hauptmann had a set of Stanley chisels from which the three-quarter-inch size was missing.

7. The nails used in the ladder were found to have the same microscopic defects as nails found in Hauptmann's home.

8. Paper like that of the ransom notes was found in his home.

9. The print of a wrapped foot outside the Lindbergh home was similar to Hauptmann's footprint. So was the footprint of the man who received the ransom.

10. The kidnap ladder broke as the kidnapper was descending. Ground marks beneath the baby's bedroom indicated that the kidnapper may have injured his leg. Hauptmann

walked with a cane for a few weeks after the crime, and was treated by a doctor later.

11. He worked near the Lindbergh home shortly before the kidnapping.

12. An automobile seen near the Lindbergh home shortly before the kidnapping was of the same make, color, and model as Hauptmann's.

13. A taxi driver identified Hauptmann as the man who gave him one dollar to deliver a note to Dr. Condon.

14. He revealed a reluctance to answer questions, and gave surly responses, such as "Leave me alone."

15. He had a criminal record in Germany before coming to the United States.

16. In his testimony he stated that he lent $2,000 to Fisch. Previously he had said that Fisch gave him the ransom money for safe keeping.

17. Pencilled on a shelf in his closet was Dr. Condon's address and telephone number. This was a 1932 number; it had since been changed. When asked where he had obtained the number Hauptmann answered, "I must have read it in the newspaper about the story." The telephone number had never been published.

Questions:

1. If you were a member of the jury, would you regard the evidence as proving Hauptmann guilty beyond a reasonable doubt?

2. Which items of the evidence did you consider most cogent?

3. Show how this case illustrates the principle of "the convergence of evidence."

D. *Hypotheses in Criminal Cases: Testimonial Evidence (The Sacco-Vanzetti Case)*

This case was a *cause célèbre* during the 1920's. Two anarchists named Sacco and Vanzetti were convicted of murdering Parmenter and Berardelli in a payroll robbery. They pleaded their complete innocence. The trial and conviction occurred during the period of the so-called "Red Scares," of the early 1920's. Following are some excerpts from Justice Felix Frankfurter's book *The Case of Sacco and Vanzetti* (Little, Brown and Company, 1927):

So far as the crime is concerned we are dealing with a conventional case of payroll robbery resulting in murder. At the trial the killing of Parmenter and Berardelli was undisputed. The only issue was the identity of the murderers. Were Sacco and Vanzetti two of the assailants of Parmenter and Berardelli, or were they not? This was the beginning and the end of the inquiry at the trial; this is the beginning and the end of any judgment now on the guilt or innocence of these men. . . .

The character of the testimony of the five witnesses who definitely identified Sacco as in the car or on the spot of the murder demands critical attention.

Splaine and Devlin were working together on the second floor of the Slater and Morrill factory, with windows giving on the railroad crossing. Both heard the shot, ran to the window, and saw an automobile crossing the tracks. Splaine's identification of Sacco, as one of the occupants of this escaping car, was one of the chief reliances of the prosecution. Splaine, viewing the scene from a distance of from 60 to 80 ft. saw a man previously unknown to her, in a car traveling at the rate of from 15 to 18 miles per hour; she saw him only for a distance of about 30 feet, that is to say, for from one and a half to three seconds; and yet she testified:

"The man that appeared between the back of the front seat and the back seat was a man slightly taller than the witness. He weighed possibly from 140 to 145 pounds. He was muscular, an active looking man. His left hand was a good sized hand, a hand that denoted strength."

Q.—"So that hand you said you saw where?" A.—"The left hand, that was placed on the back of the front seat, on the back of the front seat. He had a gray, what I thought was a shirt,—had a grayish, like navy color, and the face was, what we would call a clear-cut, clean-cut face. Though here (indicating) was a little narrow, just a little narrow. The forehead was high. The hair was brushed back and it was between, I should think, two inches and two and one-half inches in length and had dark eyebrows, but the complexion was a white, peculiar white that looked greenish." (R. 114–5.)

Q.—Is that the same man you saw at Brockton? A.—It is.

Q.—Are you sure? A.—Positive.

The startling acuity of Splaine's vision was in fact the product of a year's reflection. Immediately after Sacco's arrest the police, in violation of approved police methods for the identification of suspects, brought Sacco alone into Splaine's presence. (R. 121, 130.) Then followed in about three weeks the preliminary hearing at which Sacco and Vanzetti were bound over for the grand jury. At this hearing Splaine was unable to identify Sacco:

> Q.—"You don't feel certain enough in your position to say he is the man?" A.—"I don't think my opportunity afforded me the right to say he is the man." (R. 132.)

When confronted with this contradiction between her uncertainty forty days after her observation and her certainty more than a year after her observation, she first took refuge in a claim of inaccuracy in the transcript of the stenographer's minutes. This charge she later withdrew and finally maintained:

"From the observation I had of him in the Quincy Court and the comparison of the man I saw in the machine, on reflection I was sure he was the same man." (R. 133.)

Questions:

1. (The evidence cited here is only a fraction of the total.) How convincing do you regard the testimony of Mary Splaine?
2. What conclusions, if any, do you draw with respect to the comparative value of circumstantial evidence and testimony?
3. Do you have an opinion on the probable guilt or innocence of these men? On what evidence is your opinion based?

E. The Problem of Organic Evolution

What is the origin of all the myriad forms of life found on the earth? The theory of evolution holds that during countless ages of development, all forms of life originated by descent through gradual or abrupt modifications from earlier forms which trace back to the most rudimentary organisms. The theory of "special creation" holds that all of the living beings were created by God in their present forms, the present species being lineal descendants of the originally created species.

The evolutionist presents evidence from various fields of investigation, briefly summarized as follows:

1. Paleontology: Rocks contain fossils. The "record of the rocks" reveals that the oldest rocks show only the more elementary forms of life. The older fossil-bearing rocks contain only fishes and plants. As we proceed through the later rock strata we find a greater complexity and variety of living forms. The evolutionist also notes the fact that no fossil has ever been found in a "wrong" rock stratum.

2. *Geographical distribution:* Isolated regions show striking differences in their forms of life, e.g., the Australian kangaroo.

3. *Comparative anatomy:* There are anatomical similarities in various large groups of living creatures. The arms of man, the forelegs of the dog and frog, the wings of birds are all based on the same structures. The blood of related species, as man and the ape, shows chemical resemblances.

4. *Embryology:* "Ontogeny recapitulates phylogeny." This means that the stages in the development of an individual organism "summarize" the historical stages in the development of the species. Thus some warm-blooded animals pass through the "fish stage" in their embryonic development.

5. *Vestigial organs:* Human beings and other living things have organs which are vestigial, i.e., of no use today, but presumably inherited from evolutionary ancestors who had them and found them useful. The vermiform appendix is the most striking example.

6. *Breeding:* By cross and selective breeding, animals and plants are produced which differ greatly from previously known varieties.

The arguments of the "special creationists" are based on positive (religious) and negative (scientific) grounds. They argue that special creation is in accordance with the Word of God as revealed in the Book of Genesis and that the sacred quality of the human soul presupposes special creation. On scientific grounds, they argue that the proof for evolution is not conclusive, since there are many gaps (missing links) in the evolutionary record, and that breeding has never succeeded in producing a new species.

Questions:

1. Which of the two rival theories do you regard as the more probable? Why?
2. Do you regard evolution as a theory or a fact? Why?
3. How does the special creationist account for the various types of evidence presented by the evolutionist? In this respect, which of the two hypotheses is the simpler?
4. "Special creationists use a double standard of criticism; a

severe one for the theory of evolution, and an uncritical one for their own theory." Comment on this statement.

F. Did Shakespeare Write "Shakespeare's Plays"?

Very little is known concerning the life of William Shakespeare. The available facts, however, indicate that he was a man of lowly origin and scant schooling. It has therefore been regarded as incredible that such a man could have written those plays which reveal as remarkable a genius as the world has ever known. Controversies over the authorship of the plays have raged for many years. From time to time the names of other writers have been suggested for the honor of authorship, such as Sir Francis Bacon, Marlowe, Raleigh, and others. A fairly recent candidate for the honor is one Edward de Vere, the 17th Earl of Oxford. The case for de Vere has been presented by Louis P. Bénézet, in his *Shakspere, Shakespeare, and de Vere* (Granite State Press, 1937).* Bénézet holds that the author of these plays must have been a man with certain characteristics. The writer of the plays, he says, must have been (1) a student of the classics, (2) an aristocrat of feudal ancestry, (3) a warrior, (4) one versed in the law, (5) one with skill in music, (6) one familiar with Italy and France, (7) a member of the Red Rose family, (8) one careless of money, (9) one who was known to be a poet aside from the "Works of Shakespeare," (10) one closely associated with plays and players, (11) one the facts of whose life fit with the self-revelations of the sonnets, (12) one who was known to be a playwright apart from the "Works," (13) one who "bore the canopy," and (14) one whose associations with the Earl of Southampton were so close that he would feel free to dedicate works to him.

The problem: Who wrote these plays? There are several hypotheses. The hypothesis that a given individual is the author, says Bénézet, implies that he had the fourteen characteristics. Bénézet holds that few of these requirements fit Bacon. In Shakespeare's case, if the author of the plays is regarded as the William Shakespeare who died in Stratford-on-Avon in 1616, only No. 10 may hold, he contends. But he says that all fourteen requirements are fulfilled by de Vere, and he therefore regards that hypothesis as established. A strong point in de Vere's favor is the fact that he was a poet and that his extant poetry is written in a style bearing many similarities to the style of the Shakespearean sonnets. To the question, why

* Discussed in greater detail by Frye and Levi, *op. cit.*, Chapter XVII.

did he not sign his name to the plays?, Bénézet cites the aristocratic conventions of the time that practically prohibited individuals of Oxford's rank from acknowledging that they published verse and plays.

Other reasons given for rejecting Shakespeare's authorship are the facts that his death appeared to have attracted no notice in Stratford or in London, and that the Shakespeare who died in Stratford requested that the following lines be engraved on his tomb:

> Good friend for Iesus sake forbeare
> To digg the dust encloased heare
> Blest be ye man yt spares thes stones
> And curst be he yt moves my bones.

These lines do not bear the mark of genius.

On the other side of the case we may cite Ben Jonson's remark, in the dedicatory poem to the First Folio of 1623, that "he loved Shakespeare this side of idolatry." Ben Jonson was the most powerful literary figure among Shakespeare's contemporaries.

Questions:

1. Do you regard Bénézet's hypothesis as verified in terms of the evidence? Why, or why not?
2. If your answer to the last question is negative, who in your opinion is the author of Shakespeare's plays? Why?

G. A Historical Problem

A historian, studying the policies of the Communist party of the United States, finds the following facts: After the first world war until 1935 the party vigorously attacked American "capitalists" and all other political groups, including liberals, progressives, and non-communist radicals. The moderate Socialists were denounced as "social fascists" and referred to as "Enemy No. 1" as late as 1933–4. In 1933 Hitler came to power in Germany and destroyed the German Communist party. In 1935 the American Communists decided to collaborate with Socialists and other democratic parties in a "Popular Front" against Nazism and Fascism. The Catholic Church was also invited to join the united front. This policy was coincident with the same policy adopted by the Communist International at its 1935 Congress. On August 23, 1939 the Soviet Union and Nazi Germany signed a non-aggression pact, and the Soviet Union thenceforth gave Germany diplomatic support in its war against the Western powers. The American Communists ceased their campaign against fascism and sought to prevent American aid to Britain and France in their war against Hitler. They denounced as "war-mongers" those who wished to aid England and France in what the Communists referred to as the "imperialist war." On June 22, 1941 German armies invaded Russia. Thereafter the Communists denounced fascism and gave their whole-hearted support to the American war effort in what they called "the people's war." The leader of the American Communist party, Mr. Earl Browder, now defended American "big business" against criticism from liberal groups, and in his book *Teheran* (International Publishers, 1944), he pledged the support of the Communists to the capitalistic system in the United States: "We declare in advance our understanding that the democratic-progressive camp to which we adhere will adopt the defence of 'free enterprise,' that we understand this term as a synonym for capitalism as it exists in our country, and that we will not oppose it nor put forth any counter-slogans."

In 1946 the American Communists attacked the leaders of the United States and its capitalistic system, denouncing them as the enemies of mankind.

Questions:

1. Which hypothesis would you suggest as the best explanation for the twistings and turnings or the "divergations and tergiversations" of the policies of the American Communist party during these years? How probable do you regard your hypothesis? Can you suggest a second hypothesis which would also explain the known facts?
2. Can the method of prediction be used in problems such as this one?
3. Can a problem such as this one be explained by the theory of "economic determinism," which holds that all political decisions are based upon economic factors? Can this theory predict an event before it occurs?

H. *The Problem of Relevant Evidence in Historical Problems*

If you were interested in finding the answers to the following questions, what types of evidence would you consider relevant?

1. Did Moses write the Pentateuch (the first five books of the Old Testament)?

2. Was Jesus a historical character?
3. Did Homer write the *Iliad* and the *Odyssey?*
4. Was Abraham Lincoln assassinated by John Wilkes Booth?
5. Is Hitler alive?

I. Prove the following propositions by using the Reductio ad Absurdum method:

1. The earth has the shape of a spheroid.
2. The interests of capital and labor are not identical.
3. The rule, "Thou shalt not lie," should not be followed without any exceptions whatsoever.
4. Wealthy taxpayers do not dictate income tax legislation.

Chapter 16

Cause and Effect: the "Experimental Methods"

Section I: The Significance of Causal Analysis

When the ancient poet Virgil said, "Happy is he who knows the causes of things," he was in agreement with the more modern Sir Francis Bacon who proclaimed that "Knowledge is power." For, in large measure, man's power and control over nature has its origin in man's understanding of the causal connections of natural events. It is unnecessary to catalogue the achievements of modern science, including nuclear fission, to prove the importance of knowing the causes of things. Suffice it to say that our knowledge that germs are a cause of diseases has enabled us to come near to eliminating diseases such as tuberculosis and that it is through knowing causes that we can often produce at will such effects as we consider desirable. Our search for that better world that will meet the heart's desire depends in great part on our knowing the appropriate causal patterns. When we learn the causes of cancer and business depressions, we shall make progress in eliminating these evils.

So much for the importance of understanding the causal relation. Before we proceed, let us consider a basic question: Do all things have causes? If a motorist should suddenly hear an unfamiliar ticking sound in the motor of his car while cruising on a highway, his immediate response would be that something is wrong, that *something is responsible* for the unfamiliar noise. Our motorist has made the assumption that there is a cause of the noise. Now, this assumption, that nothing happens without a cause, is a basic assumption of rational thinking. We assume the existence of a world in which invariant order prevails, in which things "don't just happen by themselves." We say that

397

there must be a reason for everything; even though we don't know what the reason is. Science does not know the cause of cancer, but that there is some cause for cancer is beyond doubt. We may despair of ever unravelling the causes of such a complex event as war, but even when we despair of finding an explanation we are certain that such causes must be present.

We assume then, that something is responsible for every event in experience, that nothing happens without a reason. But it was not always thus. The Greeks did not assume that every event has a cause. Aristotle believed that Nature's laws were not uniform, that some things occurred by mere "chance," that Nature acted in a certain way only "for the most part." A. N. Whitehead, in *Science and the Modern World,* proposes the interesting thesis that our modern scientific view of universal causation and invariant law is due to the influence of mediaeval theology. The theologians believed that there was a sufficient reason for every smallest detail in the universe, since an omniscient, omnipresent, and omnipotent God would let nothing happen—not even the fall of a sparrow—except in accordance with His Will. Whitehead argues that science adapted the theological view that all things have meaning and significance into the scientific assumption that there are natural causes for all events. But however the matter may be explained, modern science accepts the principle of "universal determinism." The scientist assumes that everything that happens is determined by a necessary chain of causation, that every occurrence has a cause, that every change in nature occurs because of some previous happening, in accordance with invariant laws. "Chance" and "luck" are not regarded as objective aspects of the world which is pictured by science. It is not "luck" whether the coin falls heads or tails; its fall depends entirely on the velocity with which it is spun, the pressure of the air, etc. The word "chance" is simply a name for our ignorance of the precise conditions which are present.*

A distinction between two types of causes may be noted

* Some contemporary physicists have questioned the principle of determinism, but the doctrine as stated is still the prevailing view. Many philosophers have also questioned the applicability of the principle to human choice, raising the problem of "free will." The scientific psychologist, however, assumes that human conduct is determined by causes.

here. In Plato's *Phaedo*, which describes the last hours of Socrates in his prison cell, Socrates discusses (among other matters) the problem of causation. For example, what was the cause of his sitting in his cell at that particular moment? Some philosophers, Socrates tells his friends, would say,

> that I am now sitting here because my body is made up of bones and muscles . . . that I am able to lift my bones at the joints by the contraction or relaxation of the muscles, and this is why I am sitting here with my legs bent. They would have a similar explanation of my talking to you, in terms of air, sound and hearing . . . forgetting the real cause, which is that the Athenians saw fit to condemn me, and that I have thought it best to remain here and undergo my sentence. It may be said, indeed, that without bones and muscles and the other parts of the body, I cannot execute my purposes. But to say that I do as I do because of them, and that this is the way in which mind acts, and not from the choice of the best, is a very careless and idle mode of speaking. I wonder that they cannot distinguish the cause from the condition.

Socrates is here distinguishing between physical causes and purpose-as-cause. Aristotle used the term "final cause" for purpose-as-cause. Why are you wherever you are now? Because your muscles contracted in a certain manner? Or because a purpose brought you here? That is the distinction which Socrates makes. This distinction warns us that when we are concerned with finding the causes of human conduct we should not limit our search to some particular kind of cause and exclude all others.

Section II: The Definition of "Cause" and "Condition"

Exactly what do we mean when we say that alcohol causes intoxication? We mean that there exists an invariant relationship between the alcohol and intoxication such that, upon the occurrence of imbibing the alcohol (under specified conditions and in appropriate quantities) intoxication will invariably follow.

To begin with, we shall distinguish the term "condition" from that of "cause." There are two types of conditions: necessary and sufficient. A necessary condition is an event or circumstance which must be present in order to get a certain result or effect, but which is not sufficient in itself to "produce" the result. A lighted cigarette or match is thrown into a bush by a camper. A forest fire results. Was the match the cause? But suppose that the leaves had been damp because of a recent rain. There would then have been no fire. The dryness of the leaves, we say, was a *necessary condition* for the fire; but dry leaves are not a *sufficient* condition, by which we mean "sufficient to produce the result." But was the match sufficient to produce the result, since it required dry leaves in order to act as the cause? And what shall we say of oxygen in the air, which is also a necessary condition for combustibility? These questions indicate the importance of distinguishing conditions from causes. Let us now define these terms more precisely.

a. Necessary conditions

A necessary condition (symbolized by N) is a condition without which the effect (symbolized by E) cannot occur. N is indispensable to the occurrence of E: Without N, no E. A certain kind of virus is a necessary condition of our having a catarrhal affection of the respiratory tract, commonly called a "cold." But this virus is not a *sufficient* condition of our having a "cold," since it is presumably present in many persons all of the time, without their having colds. There are four ways of showing the relationship of N to E: *

(1) If N is present, E may or may not occur.   (N . . . E?)
(2) If N is not present, E will not occur.   ($\sim$N . . . $\sim$E)
(3) If E occurs, N must be present.   (E . . . N)
(4) If E does not occur, N may or may not be present.
                                        ($\sim$E . . . N?)

b. Sufficient conditions

A sufficient condition (symbolized by S) is one which can, by itself, produce the result or effect, but which need not be present for the effect to occur. Thus, a specified quantity of

---

* Note that the relation of a necessary condition to an effect is identical with that of the antecedent to the consequent in an exclusive proposition: Only if N, then E. This converts into, If E, then N. E is the superimplicant; N, the subimplicant.

cyanide of potassium is sufficient to produce death, but death may be produced by other causes, such as drowning.* In tabular form:

(1) If S is present, E occurs.   (S . . . . E)
(2) If S is absent, E may or may not occur.   (~S . . . . E?)
(3) If E occurs, S may or may not have occurred.   (E . . . . . . S?)
(4) If E does not occur, S did not occur.   (~E . . . ~S)

There is a certain vagueness in the notion of a "sufficient" condition. We usually assume the presence of certain necessary conditions when we speak of sufficient conditions. Further, this notion leads to the concept of the "plurality of causes," i.e., that a given effect may have more than one cause, as when we say that death may have been caused by poison, or drowning, or many other things, but that any one of these things is sufficient to produce death. But this is perhaps a somewhat loose way of speaking, since the effect produced by poison is not identical with that produced by drowning. Instead of describing the effect (death) in both cases by "D," should we not say "D^p" and "D^d"? Certainly a coroner finds different kinds of evidence in the two cases. In other words, the plurality of causes will hold only when we analyze the effect in a general rather than in a precise manner.

c. Necessary and sufficient conditions

To fully satisfy our notion of the causal relationship we need a combination of necessary and sufficient conditions, so that we may say, "If C then E, and if E then C," or "If and only if C, then E." "C," in other words, stands for *necessary and sufficient conditions*. When C occurs, the effect will always follow, and where we find the effect we can be sure that C was present, viz.:

(1)   C . . . . E
(2) ~C . . . . ~E
(3)   E C
(4) ~E . . . . ~C

---

* S implies E, but not vice versa. E is now the subimplicant.

There are now no cases where C is present and E absent, or vice versa. When two events have this relationship, then C is the cause of E.

For illustration, let us return to the match and the forest fire. Was the match the cause? Can we say "If a match is thrown into underbrush, then a forest fire will always occur?" Obviously not. Without the necessary conditions of dry leaves, and certain atmospheric conditions, there would be no fire. The cause of the fire is the total combination of various factors and conditions, so that we should say, "A forest fire is caused by the igniting of dry leaves under specified meteorological conditions."

In practice, however, scientists are often satisfied with less than the "ideal" statement of the cause as just outlined. Practical considerations generally determine how far research will be carried on, and frequently it is quite sufficient to know either the necessary or the sufficient condition. The goal of the research may be a controlling consideration, i.e., it may be "production" or "prevention." If scientists are given the task of producing something new, such as a specific to cure a disease, a synthetic rubber, or a stimulus to business activity, they need only know the sufficient conditions of these effects. If they wish to prevent or eliminate an effect, such as a disease, it is enough if they know the necessary conditions without which the disease cannot occur.

In popular speech the word "cause" is also used in a looser, though quite adequate, manner. This is illustrated in the concept of legal responsibility, which would hold the careless camper responsible for the forest fire, since he "caused" it with his lighted match. Such statements presuppose, without making the presuppositions explicit, that all of the necessary conditions were present. Further, his act was one under human control; it was a sudden and dramatic change in the situation which existed prior to the fire, and it initiated the sequence of events which led to the occurrence of the fire.

One further point concerns the distinction between "proximate" and "remote" causes. A stone falls from a building under construction and kills a passer-by below. What was the cause of his death? The stone? Gravitation? The strong wind which blew the stone off a ledge? Or a careless workman who left it there?

The contractor who hired this careless workman? The architect who hired the contractor? The wife of the man who ordered the building in order to satisfy her social ambitions? The parents of the wife for bringing her into the world? This analysis, which reminds us of the old verses, "For the want of a horeshoe the battle was lost," points to the earlier conditions which are responsible for the present conditions, so that ultimately we must go back to the beginning of things for a complete causal explanation. In practice, however, we consider the proximate causes. We do not seek for the total set of conditions which lead to the effect, but only for those which, when present, will always bring the effect into existence.

Section III: The Discovery and Testing of Hypotheses of Causal Connection

The logician's primary interest is in the study of scientific techniques for *testing* hypotheses of causal connection, rather than in methods for *discovering* the causes of things. Scientific discovery always requires imagination and sometimes requires genius, but testing is more a matter of applying rules. The application of rules, it should be obvious, will not enable us to *find* the cause of cancer, for the best scientific brains in the biological sciences are baffled by this problem. But by applying rules we can *test* hypotheses of causal connection, and say that certain factors probably are or are not the causes.

When the problem is one of discovering a causal connection, previous knowledge is a necessary condition for the suggestion of appropriate hypotheses. Thus only a trained physiologist can suggest a likely cause of cancer. But knowledge is not a sufficient condition. The great scientist may be likened to a great poet in his ability to see new analogies and connections in things supposedly unlike, for this ability is also the secret spring of the poet's metaphors. Thus, it took imagination to suspect that the pollen of ragweed was the cause of hay fever, that the "child-bed fever" of the mothers of new-born infants was due to germs brought to them by physicians who had just come from sick patients, and that the presence of germs in previously sterile liquids came from the dust of the outside air. Rules cannot substitute for the flash of insight of the scientific imagination.

In the instances cited, imagination was required to find the cause in order to remove it, and thus eliminate the effect. But the scientist also needs imagination to discover the causal relations which will *produce* a desired effect. Here, also, hypotheses of causal relations are required. During the last war American and European physicists learned how to produce the atomic bomb. Edison worked painstakingly for a long period of time to find the proper filament for his incandescent bulb. Or scientists may seek for serums to combat diseases. Ehrlich tried out hundreds of hypotheses in search of his "magic bullet," a cure which would kill certain deadly microbes called trypanosomes. The six-hundred-and-sixth hypothesis worked, and "606" became the effective cure for the "disease of sin," syphilis. Ehrlich seems to have used the trial-and-error method, but imagination was also required in order to try out dioxy-diamino-arsenobenzol-dihydro-chloride from among the enormous number of substances the world contains.

We have drawn a distinction between the *discovery* and the *testing* of hypotheses of causal connection. The formulation of a hypothesis is a problem requiring "discovery." After the hypothesis has been formulated we deduce its implications and then test it.

The problem of discovery is: What is the cause? In the typical problem of discovery we find that various hypotheses will be suggested: H, H', H'', or H'''. We then have a testing problem. We must eliminate the false hypotheses. If we eliminate all but one, this establishes some probability that it is the cause, but the formulation of the alternative hypotheses is distinct from the testing procedure.

One further point before we turn to the "experimental methods." A cause in the strict sense, i.e., the necessary and sufficient condition, gives us the relations: CE, $\sim$C$\sim$E, EC, and $\sim$E$\sim$C.* The formula states a causal *law,* i.e., a generalized and invariant relationship between C and E. But in practice we usually find causal relationships in particular instances. Thus, a man frequently suffers from a temporary swelling of his upper lip. His physician assures him that his lip is not infected, and tells him to watch his diet, since he may be allergic to certain

---

* This is from the table shown on p. 401.

foods. Subsequently his lip swells again. He thinks back to determine what he ate just prior to the swelling. It was X, he thinks. But he is not sure. On a later occasion he again eats X and awaits the swelling. It appears. He then avoids X, and the swelling does not recur. His hypothesis was verified by a confirmed prediction. But may he *generalize* the causal relationship between X and "swelling of the lip"? Does this rule apply only to himself, or to others as well? Does it apply to himself under certain conditions or under all conditions? The problem of generalizing such connections involves the problem of "inductions," or generalizations, to be studied in the next chapter.

Section IV: The "Experimental Methods"

By "experimental methods" we mean certain rules for *testing* hypotheses of causal connection, or more generally, of any statements of invariant connections. "Experimental" here does not necessarily refer to laboratory experiments but to deliberate observations in testing hypotheses. Our discussion will be based upon the formulation of the experimental methods in John Stuart Mill's classic *System of Logic*. Mill worked out the "canons" of five methods, which he called the Methods of Agreement, Difference, Joint Method of Agreement and Difference, Concomitant Variations, and Residues. We shall follow Mill's titles, except for the Joint Method, but we will restate his definitions and his treatment of the canons.

The basic form of the reasoning involved in these canons may be stated as follows: After a hypothesis of causal connection has been suggested, such as "C is the cause of E," we formulate the hypothetical proposition: If C is the cause of E, then we will find the basic relations CE, $\sim$C$\sim$E, EC, and $\sim$E$\sim$C. The tests are designed to determine whether these relations are present or not. If they are, it is probable that C is the cause of E; if not, we may eliminate C as a possible cause.

1. The Method of Agreement

The following case will illustrate this method. An epidemic of typhoid fever occurs in a small town. Among the individuals stricken are A, B, C, D, and E. The Public Health authorities wish to discover the cause, and investigate the relevant events which took place just prior to the occurrence of the disease.

Such events, or conditions under which the effect occurred, and among which we may find the causal condition, will be called the "antecedent factors," symbolized by lower case letters. The following information was gathered:

ANTECEDENT FACTORS

INSTANCES	WATER	MILK	VEGETABLES	OYSTERS	EFFECT(E) (TYPHOID)
Case A	Tap (t)	Dairy (d)	Yes (v)	Yes (o)	E...Occurred
Case B	Tap (t)	Dairy (d)	None	Yes (o)	E...Occurred
Case C	Bottled (b)	Condensed (c)	Yes (v)	Yes (o)	E...Occurred
Case D	Bottled (b)	Dairy (d)	Yes (v)	Yes (o)	E...Occurred
Case E	Tap (t)	None	Yes (v)	Yes (o)	E...Occurred

To simplify our discussion of this case we shall gather the symbols in the table:

$$A.\ t\ d\ v\ o \ldots \ldots E$$
$$B.\ t\ d\quad o \ldots \ldots E$$
$$C.\ b\ c\ v\ o \ldots \ldots E$$
$$D.\ b\ d\ v\ o \ldots \ldots E$$
$$E.\ t\quad v\ o \ldots \ldots E$$

(The *effect* also occurs in a contextual situation, but we shall ignore such elements in order to simplify the problem.)

Note that previous knowledge (and imagination) were necessary for the gathering of the items classified in the table, i.e., that the cause of the typhoid might be found in factors such as t, b, c, d, v, or o. No cognizance was taken of the types of clothing worn by these individuals, nor of their occupations, since these items are known to be irrelevant. A preliminary hypothesis, that the source of typhoid will be found in liquids or substances in contact with liquids, is an indispensable requirement for the gathering of this *relevant* data. The range of possible culprits thus becomes greatly narrowed. This ground work is necessary before we can apply the rules.

The rules, once again, will test each of the antecedent factors in order to determine whether any one of them is the cause. If any factor fulfills our definition of a cause, it probably is the cause; if not, we will eliminate it. The rules thus have two aspects, negative and positive. Negatively, we seek to eliminate false causes, and positively, to identify the true cause. After we eliminate a number of factors we assume that the cause will be found among the remaining factors. If we eliminate all but one, it is probably the cause. We shall begin with the negative aspect of the rule.

a. The Negative Method of Agreement

Our first task is to *eliminate* factors which *cannot* be the cause, using the rule, "No factor can be the cause in whose absence the effect occurs." For example, let us consider the possibility that tap-water (t) was the cause of the typhoid. We immediately reject t as the cause since the effect occurred in the absence of t (cases C and D). If t were the cause, E would always occur when t is present, by our previous definition of a cause. Similarly, using this principle we can eliminate b, since the effect occurred in cases A, B, and E in b's absence, and so on with all the other factors except o. Note that the negative method never tells us what the cause is, but only what it is not.

b. The Positive Method of Agreement

We now examine the factor or factors not eliminated. The positive formulation tells us what the cause *is*, by the following rule, "If, in two or more cases where an effect occurs, we find that one and only one of the antecedent factors is common to all of the collections of antecedents, then that factor is probably the cause." * We find that only o is common to all the sets of conditions preceding the effect, so o is probably the cause. The instances *agree* in possessing this factor alone.

Our illustration is, of course, a highly simplified case. It would be advisable to take a laboratory analysis of the oysters before drawing any conclusions, for it should be obvious that oysters as such are not the cause of typhoid, but rather the cause is the presence of a bacillus in the oysters. This is an important point, and it teaches us that the Method of Agreement is open to the possibility of careless analyses. There may be some unknown factor in the probable or ostensible cause, and this unknown factor may be the true cause. Search for such un-

---

* Or an indispensable part of the cause. This qualification will apply throughout the following discussions.

known factors begins when an exception to a previous generalization is discovered; e.g., it may have been believed at one time that oysters were the cause of typhoid and then a case of typhoid occurred in which no oysters had been eaten. Progress in science comes through the discovery of exceptions to such generalizations.

Another point: If our laboratory analysis shows that the oysters are not contaminated, our conclusion that the instances "agree" only in *o* must be rejected, and we must then reanalyze the known factors or search for additional antecedents. On reanalysis we may now find that the tap water was the cause, for the vegetables in cases C and D may have been washed in tap water.

2. The Method of Difference

We begin again with an illustration. Susan suffers from a skin irritation and inflammation of her face. This irritation occurs after she uses face powder. We assume that the powder is the cause, but Susan wishes to use face powder, and she desires an analysis of the powder in order to determine whether some one ingredient in it is the true cause of the irritation. A chemist friend finds that the powder contains six ingredients: talc, kaolin, magnesium carbonate, zinc oxide, ochre (for coloring), and perfume. The chemist suspects that the perfume is the cause, and performs an experiment. He prepares a batch of face powder containing only the first five elements. He then divides this batch into two parts, to one of which he adds perfume. Susan now tries the face powder without the perfume (Batch 1) and finds no after-effects. She then tries powder with the perfume added (Batch 2) and finds that the irritation recurs. She concludes that the perfume is the cause of the irritation.

Let us now set up this experiment in schematic form:

Instances	Antecedent Factors						Effect(E)
Batch 1	talc(t)	kaolin(k)	mag. carb.(m)	zinc oxide(z)	ochre(o)		No irritation
Batch 2	talc(t)	kaolin(k)	mag. carb.(m)	zinc oxide(z)	ochre(o)	perfume(p)	Irritation occurs

Gathering the symbols, we have:

Batch 1: t, k, m, z, o   ..... no E
Batch 2: t, k, m, z, o, p ...... E

Let us now see how the rules apply to this case.

a. The Negative Method of Difference

We wish to eliminate the non-causal antecedents. We apply a new negative rule, "No factor can be the cause in whose presence the effect fails to occur." We know that t cannot be the cause, for the effect failed to occur when it was present. Here also we apply our definition of a cause, which tells us that if t were the cause, then E would not fail to occur in its presence. In the same manner we may eliminate all of the other factors in Batch 1. The factors t, k, m, z and o must also be eliminated from Batch 2. Only p cannot be eliminated. Note how this new rule differs from the Negative Method of Agreement. There we worked with cases in each of which E occurred. Here we have two cases, in one of which E did not occur. But in both types of negative methods we are told what the cause is not, rather than what it is.

b. The Positive Method of Difference

The reader should refer to the symbols in reading the positive rule, "If a case in which an effect occurs, and one in which it does not occur, are exactly alike except for the presence or absence of a single factor, the effect occurring when that factor is present, and not occurring when it is absent, then that factor is probably the cause."

The rule tells us that p is the cause. This was a successful case of proof, but we did have a good hypothesis to work with. Our conclusion, however, is only probable. It is possible that Susan is allergic only to some kinds of perfumes, i.e., those which contain a particular ingredient, and that it is really this ingredient which causes the irritation. But this method of testing is a very efficient one, precise and convincing, especially in a laboratory, where all of the relevant factors can be strictly controlled. It is aptly called the "laboratory method," or the method of "control experiment"; i.e., one of the two situations is the "control," so that we may determine the precise effect which follows from varying or adding a single factor in the other.

Many simple examples will illustrate the method. A drop of iodine is added to a glass of water. We say the iodine is the cause of the brown color, because all of the factors in "water uncolored" and "water colored" were the same except for the introduction of the drop of iodine. Another: a man is shot through the heart and dies. The only significant difference between the man alive at 3:15 A.M. and dead an instant later is the bullet in his heart.

It is extremely important to note the factor of relevance in applying the positive rule, since no two situations are ever *exactly* the same. Time has elapsed, for one thing. But only relevant factors need be considered. Also note that the factor identified as the cause may not be a completely sufficient condition, but may require the presence of other factors as necessary conditions.

3. The Joint Method

Our discussion of the Joint Method departs considerably from Mill's treatment. We shall use this title to indicate how the Negative Method of Difference may help to locate the cause when we cannot strictly comply with the requirements of the Positive Method of Agreement.

Let us assume that in the typhoid example of the Method of Agreement there were two factors, rather than one factor, common to all cases—e.g., individuals A, B, C, D and E had all been to the circus where they had all drunk pink lemonade in addition to having eaten oysters. Assume, too, that no laboratory analyses are available. We cannot then say whether the oysters or the pink lemonade is the cause. The problem now is to eliminate either the oysters or the lemonade, since our hypothesis has become, "Either oysters or lemonade is the cause." We should then seek for additional cases to determine whether there were other individuals who had drunk the circus lemonade or eaten the oysters and suffered no ill effects. If we find such we can eliminate one of these factors by the Negative Method of Difference, and this leaves the other as the sole cause.

4. The Method of Concomitant Variations

A manufacturer of cosmetics uses newspaper advertising to sell his products. He wishes to test the hypothesis that larger ads sell more goods. He had previously used a 400-line ad. He now runs a larger one in different cities, keeping all factors constant except the size. These constant factors are such things as similarity of newspaper coverage, the use of pictures, written material, and composition. As a check on the effectiveness of the advertising he includes within each ad a coupon asking the reader to send it in for a free sample. The results:

City A: 400-line ad brought in 500 coupons
"   B: 500-line "   "   " 580   "
"   C: 600-line "   "   " 640   "
"   D: 700-line "   "   " 695   "
"   E: 800-line "   "   " 725   "

The manufacturer concludes that within certain limits he will get increased sales with an increase in the size of the ads.

Let us now set up our example in symbols, using n for newspaper coverage, p for pictures, w for written material, c for composition, ls for lines, and E for coupons:

City A: n p w c 400 ls........500 E
"   B: n p w c 500 ls........580 E
"   C: n p w c 600 ls........640 E
"   D: n p w c 700 ls........695 E
"   E: n p w c 800 ls........725 E

This example illustrates the principle of "concomitant variations"; i.e., when the factor of advertising lineage varies by increase in size, the effect (numbers of coupons) varies by increase in number. The canon: If we find that a certain factor varies in concomitance with variations in the effect, then that factor is probably the cause of the variations in the effect.

The great value of this method as compared with the others lies in its ability to handle *degrees*. In the methods of Agreement and Difference, typhoid and skin-irritation were either present or absent; by the method of variations we can determine just *how much* of a variation in the cause will produce a given variation in the effect. Another of its values is that it may be usable in instances where no other method is applicable. If we wished to test the hypothesis that the moon is the cause of the tides, it would be impossible to use the positive method of difference, since that method requires that we use two situations in one of which the causal factor does not occur. The moon cannot be removed. But the variations show the causal relationships: The closer the moon to the seas, the higher the daily tides, and vice versa.

Concomitant variations may be either direct or inverse. By direct variation we mean the type we have illustrated, where an *increase* in the cause is accompanied by an *increase* in the effect, and vice versa. In inverse variation, an *increase* in the factor is accompanied by a *decrease* in the effect, and a *decrease* by an *increase,* as in, "The larger the production of goods, the smaller the unit-cost of the items produced (within limits)," and vice versa.

Direct and inverse variation will now be illustrated by symbols, in which the plus signs refer to larger amounts of the factor or the effect; the minus signs to lesser amounts. A letter shown without a plus or minus sign refers to the amount which is taken as "standard," i.e., some established measure of quantity, viz.:

Direct variation	Inverse variation
a b c−.... E−	a b c−.... E+
a b c .... E	a b c .... E
a b c+.... E+	a b c+.... E−

The examples we have used represent ideal situations in that all other factors have remained constant. But the method may also be applied in an unideal situation, as in the following:

$$a \quad b- \quad c- \quad d \quad e \quad ..... \ E+$$
$$a- \quad c++ \quad e \quad f \quad b+ ..... \ E--$$
$$m \quad f+ \quad b- \quad a- \quad c+ ..... \ E-$$

Only *c* varies concomitantly with E.

We shall add a brief comment on the relation of the Method of Concomitant Variations to the "functional" method. A function, as used in mathematics, means a quantity whose value is dependent upon some other quantity, illustrated by the relation of the circumference of a circle to its radius. If we know either, we can compute the other. The ancient philosopher Pythagoras discovered that the pitch of a plucked string on a musical instrument is a function of its length; thus the length of the string on middle C of a piano is twice as long as that of the octave above and half as long as the one below. These are examples of perfect "concomitant variations," where the variations are in exact and proportionate correspondence. But these functions do not state causal connections. Thus, some concomitant variations indicate causal connections whereas others do not. A causal connection involves an asymmetrical sequence of events in time, in which the cause *precedes* the effect. There is no such temporal sequence in some functions. We may call such non-causal functions "pure functions."

Modern science, in its search for invariant relations, finds non-functional causal laws, functional causal laws, and non-causal or purely functional laws. An example of the latter is Newton's law of gravitation: "Every particle of matter attracts every other particle of matter with a force directly proportional to the product of their masses and inversely proportional to the square of the distance between them."

5. The Method of Residues

Let us assume that a European educator visited the United States after World War II. He was puzzled by the enormous enrollments in American colleges and universities. He studied the causes of college attendance, such as the desire to get ahead in life (g), to acquire knowledge and cultural background (k), to train the mind (m), to acquire friends (e), and to have a good time (t). But these reasons also existed before the war and did not account for the much larger post-war attendance. He also noted that the caliber of the faculties (f), the laboratory equipment (l), and the campus attractions (c) were substantially the same as they were before the war. There must therefore have been some additional and as yet unknown factor which accounted for the very large enrollment.

The European educator began with a knowledge of the causes of a "normal" enrollment, and found that he could eliminate these as the causes of the excess attendance, so he had to seek for the unknown factor which was the cause of the excess. A more thorough examination of all relevant factors was required. He found that business conditions (b) had improved, but this accounted for only a small part of the excess. The European educator then discovered the existence of Public Law 346, the so-called "GI Bill of Rights" (GI). He assumed that he had taken account of all generally known factors; he knew that all of the factors except the GI bill accounted only for an approximately normal enrollment, and he concluded that the remaining factor accounted for the excess.

In summary form, using E for "enrollment" and 100E for "total enrollment":

> The effect to be accounted for: 100E (normal: 50E).
> The known factors (g,k,m,e,t,f,l,c,b) account for: 55E.
> Some unknown factor must account for 45E.
> The only other factor is GI.
> Therefore, GI accounts for 45E.

This is an application of the Method of Residues. Mill stated the canon as follows: "Subduct from any phenomenon such part as is known by previous inductions to be the effect of certain antecedents, and the residue of the phenomenon is the effect of the remaining antecedents."

The method is a useful one, though it is, strictly speaking, only an application of deductive reasoning. We assume a knowledge of the causes of the "normal" to begin with, and then apply a kind of logical arithmetic. The same method is used in the following simple example: The candy in a box weighs one pound, fourteen ounces, but the box of candy weighs two pounds. Some other factor accounts for the two ounces, namely, the box. We assume that there are no other relevant factors. Of course, the method itself does not suggest which factors are relevant.

An example from the history of science is the Curie discovery that radium is the cause of the high radioactivity of pitchblende. In the early stages of the investigations into radioactivity, it was found that the radioactive emissions of substances were proportional to the amount of uranium present in them. Let us use the symbol "r" for a "radioactive unit." In terms of this unit, a gram of uranium oxide (88 per cent uranium) gave off 88r, and a gram of uranium nitrate (47 per cent uranium) gave off 47r. It was assumed that uranium in pure form would give off a maximum emission of 100 units.

The Curies then found that a gram of pitchblende emitted radioactive units in the neighborhood of 10,000 units, or several thousand times as much as uranium oxide and uranium nitrate. The Curies knew that pitchblende contained the following components: U(uranium), Th(thorium), Pb(lead), and

O(oxygen). They also knew that only uranium among the elements listed could produce radioactivity, and, since it constituted only 5 per cent of pitchblende, it could account for only 5r. They therefore sought the cause of the high radioactivity in some element hitherto unknown, but which must be present as its cause. They then discovered radium(Ra), which constituted only .0001 per cent of pitchblende, but which was responsible for its high radioactivity.

The method of residues was applied as follows: Pitchblende is the cause of 10,000r. (Our figures are of course approximations.) The known factors, U, Th, Pb, O, can account for only 5r, so some unknown factor must account for the remainder. After further analysis we find the presence of an additional factor in pitchblende: Ra. Ra accounts for the remainder.

Section V: Causality in the Social Sciences

In our discussion of the uses of the experimental methods we have touched on some of the difficulties which arise in their application. Most of our illustrations have been drawn from the physical and biological sciences. These difficulties are multiplied enormously when we seek for causes in the psychological and social sciences. This is because human behavior, the subject matter of these sciences, is vastly more complex than is the career of a germ. Human actions are not indefinitely repeatable, and the variables involved are exceedingly large.* Consider the difficulties, for example, in using the Method of Difference in the search for the cause of juvenile delinquency. We must isolate one factor and trace the results when this factor is absent and present. But can we find two individuals, one a delinquent and one a good junior citizen, in whom all characteristics except one are alike?

These are the difficulties, and they appear insuperable to some social scientists. These scientists argue that social science should abandon the search for causes, and limit itself to a search for statistical "tendencies" or "correlations." ** As an example of this method, let us assume that we find that the rate of de-

* It may be argued that there are other differences, too, such as "human freedom." This problem, however, raises issues of a metaphysical nature, and cannot be discussed here.

** These terms will be defined and discussed in chapter 18.

linquency is greater in the slums and in "broken" families than it is in the "better" residential areas and in "whole" families. This will indicate a "tendency" for children living under these conditions to turn to crime. This does not mean, we are warned, that these factors are the cause of juvenile crime, nor even an indispensable part of the cause. But such knowledge is useful insofar as it indicates that certain sociological, psychological, and economic conditions may furnish a favorable environment for delinquency.

Is it impossible to find the causes of human behavior? Shall we agree with the criminologist who said, "Sociologists know nothing whatsoever concerning the cause of crime, and probably never will"? Is it futile to hope that we will some day find the cause of wars, since it is "inconceivable" that we shall ever find a cause "C" such that, whenever it is present war will follow, and never in its absence? The answers to these questions should not be prejudged. It requires an excessive boldness to assert that social scientists will *never* discover the causes of human behavior. And certainly only on the assumption that there are such causes will we ever find them, if they exist.

In any case, the experimental methods and their tests should be applied to hypotheses of social causation. Statements of "tendencies," moreover, are simply modest ways of indicating causal hypotheses. The experimental methods, of course, give us the ideal relations, and it is too much to expect that this ideal should be exemplified when we test hypotheses of social causation, but it is always useful to know just how far short of the ideal we have fallen. The cautious social scientist will be careful not to out-talk his knowledge and to assume that he has found the cause where none is known. The negative tests will also be useful to the social scientist in helping him to eliminate *false* hypotheses. Thus, we know that fiendish torture is *not* an efficient way of eliminating crimes of passion. Such negative knowledge concerning causes is also of value.

Section VI: The Fallacies of Causal Analysis

A fallacy is an error of reasoning in an argument which claims to be valid. In this section we shall discuss some typical fallacies which arise in the application of the experimental methods. Though all such fallacies involve improper analysis of the factors in the given situation, we shall classify the errors into special types.

1. The "Post Hoc" Fallacy

A cause always precedes its effect in time. But mere temporal succession is no proof of a causal relation. "Post hoc" is an abbreviation of the Latin expression *post hoc, ergo propter hoc* (after this, therefore because of this). Its form: "X occurred, then Y occurred; therefore, X is the cause of Y." The error consists in assuming that X is the cause of Y merely because X precedes Y in time. Some examples: In 1940, during the presidential campaign, Wendell Willkie charged that the New Deal was destroying the greatness of the United States, since the birth rate was considerably lower in 1938 than it was in 1932, when the New Deal took over. Another: "Hoover was elected president in 1928. In 1929 we had the worst stock-market crash in our history. Just put those two facts together." But the mere fact that one event follows another is no proof that there is any causal connection between them.

The fallacy is not always so easily detected. Thus, in 1947 the coal miners went out on strike, and the next day the newspapers reported that a number of steel-making furnaces had been shut down. The public assumed that the strike was the cause of this shut-down. But steel furnaces are shut down regularly for cleaning and repairs. The fact of temporal priority does not prove causal connection.

The Post Hoc lies at the basis of many superstitious beliefs. A baseball team wins on a day when the manager neglects to shave. He refuses to shave the next day and thereafter as long as the winning streak lasts. Thirteen people sit down to dinner. One of them is killed. Ergo, the number 13 is unlucky, and barber shops skip the number on their chairs, apartment hotels call the thirteenth floor "No. 14," etc. An old story ascribes the superstitious injunction against "three on a match" to the fact that three soldiers once lighted their cigarettes on one match, and thereupon the third man was killed by an enemy sniper.

2. Identifying a Necessary Condition with the Cause

The cause of an event is often confused with one of its necessary conditions. Thus, a young man desires economic security. He learns that surgeons enjoy good incomes, so he becomes a surgeon. Can we say that his desire for a good income was the cause of his becoming a surgeon? But other young men who also know the facts concerning surgeons become accountants, or lawyers, or civil servants. A good income may be a *necessary condition* before some persons will enter a given profession, but it is not the cause which explains why any given individual enters any specific profession.

3. The Fallacy of Emphasizing Irrelevant Factors

This title covers a very broad area, but we shall note only two typical forms. This fallacy results from applying the rules of the experimental methods without considering the importance of relevance and usually occurs in connection with the Methods of Agreement and Variations.

When we apply the Positive Method of Agreement we should beware of assuming that the "single common factor" is the cause unless we are sure that it is a relevant factor, i.e., likely to be the cause. What may happen when this warning is neglected is illustrated by the case of the man who made a study of the conditions antecedent to his getting drunk at various parties which he attended. He found that he had been drinking bourbon and soda, scotch and soda, rye and soda, gin and soda, rum and soda, brandy and soda, and vodka and soda. Since soda was the only factor common to all of the antecedents, he concluded that he had found the cause of his intoxication, and at the next party insisted on drinking his whiskey straight.

Another form of this error will be found in applying the Method of Concomitant Variations. Though the fact that two things vary concomitantly lends some probability to the existence of a causal connection between them (or that some third factor may be the cause of both), such variation is not proof. Thus we might find that the rise and fall of bank deposits in New York banks is in precise variation with the rise and fall in the number of semicolons on the editorial page of the *New York Times*. The concomitant variation is irrelevant. In general, we should not assume that variation proves a causal connection unless there is some reason, independent of the variation, to suspect this relationship.

4. The Fallacy of Neglecting Negative Instances

This error frequently occurs when we use the Method of Agreement. We may find many instances of the occurrence of an effect where the antecedents all have a possibly relevant common factor. But we may err by failing to observe instances in which this common factor is not followed by the effect. In other words, we fail to apply the negative rule that no factor can be the cause in whose presence the effect fails to occur. Thus, we may point to many well-adjusted persons who had religious training and fail to note instances where religious training does not produce this result.

5. The Fallacy of Neglecting Differences

In applying the Method of Difference we must compare two situations all of whose relevant factors are identical except for one element. We sometimes overlook the fact that other factors are not identical. Typically this happens when we note some striking difference between two situations, A and B, and note that a given effect occurred in A and not in B. We assume that the striking difference was the cause in A. Thus, Frederick Hayek argues, in *The Road to Serfdom,* that a striking difference in the early twentieth century histories of the United States and Germany was that government planning was practiced on a large scale in Germany. Fascism was the result in Germany, he continues, so government planning was the cause of fascism. He draws the inference that if we have planning in the United States we too will be on the "road to serfdom." This argument is by no means completely devoid of merit, but it overlooks the fact that the conditions and people of the United States differ very greatly from the conditions and people of Germany.

6. The Reversing of Cause and Effect

This may be called the "putting the cart before the horse" fallacy. What appears to be the cause may be the effect, and vice versa. Consider the following argument: "When we consider the major subjects of students who rank high scholastically we find that all of the mathematics majors rank in this group. This is conclusive proof that the study of mathematics improves the mind." But it may be that only students with high scholastic aptitudes will choose mathematics as their major.

It is also important to note cases of "reciprocal" or "interdependent" causation. Thus, it is argued that TV programs are the cause of the low cultural taste of the public. The broadcasters retort that they merely give the public what it wants, so that the public's low taste is responsible for the programs. Which is cause, which effect? The factors are in reciprocal relation, mutually affecting each other. Thus the programs may further debase a public taste that was already low. Our example is an illustration of a "vicious circle." But this vicious circle also has its opposite in what Gunnar Myrdal has called "the beneficial circle." If the programs improve, the public taste will improve, and the programs will then become still better.

Exercises

A. Symbolical Statements

The following exercises illustrate the experimental methods. Explain your answers to the questions, and formulate your statements in the language of the appropriate method.

1. Apply the Positive Method of Agreement to the following group of six collections of antecedents of the effect (E). Which factor among these antecedents is probably the cause of E? Why?

```
(1)  a  b  c  d  e  f  .  .  .  .  .  .  E
(2)  b  c  d  e  f  g  .  .  .  .  .  .  E
(3)  c  d  e  f  g  h  .  .  .  .  .  .  E
(4)  d  e  f  g  h  i  .  .  .  .  .  .  E
(5)  e  f  g  h  i  j  .  .  .  .  .  .  E
(6)  f  g  h  i  j  k  .  .  .  .  .  .  E
```

2. Why can the cause not be identified in the following group, in terms of the same method?

```
(1)  a  b  c  d  e  f  .  .  .  .  .  .  E
(2)  b  c  d  e  f  g  .  .  .  .  .  .  E
(3)  c  d  e  f  g  h  .  .  .  .  .  .  E
(4)  d  e  f  g  h  i  .  .  .  .  .  .  E
(5)  e  f  g  h  i  j  .  .  .  .  .  .  E
```

3. Now apply the Negative Method of Agreement to Groups 1 and 2. Show how you can eliminate each factor which cannot be the cause, in these two groups.

4. Apply the Positive Method of Difference to the following group. What is the probable cause? Why?

(1) y p w t g r a x h   . .   ~E
(2) a g h t x w r p n y . .   E

5. Why is the Positive Method of Difference inapplicable to the following?

(1) a h t o y v r s p x g b m w . . .   ~E
(2) a g h t x w b p n y r s m o . . .   E

6. Apply the Negative Method of Difference to Groups 4 and 5. Show how you can eliminate each factor which cannot be the cause.

7. Explain why the Negative Method of Difference cannot be used in connection with Group 1 and why the Negative Method of Agreement cannot be used in connection with Group 4.

8. Which factors can be eliminated in Group 5? Which negative method did you use? Which factor cannot be eliminated?

9. Explain why the following additional information would be useful in connection with Group 2, using the Joint Method.

(6) b c d f a . . . . . . ~E
(7) g d c b f . . . . . . ~E

10. Use the Method of Concomitant Variations to find the probable cause in the following "unideal" situation. Is the variation direct or inverse? Why?

(1)	a	b	c	d	e	f	. . .	E
(2)	a—	b	c+	d+	e	f	. . .	E+
(3)	a+	b	c—	d—	e	f—	. . .	E—
(4)	a++	b	c++	d+	e	f++	. . .	E++
(5)	a+	b—	c—	d—	e—	f	. . .	E—

11. Which factor is the cause of what, in the following?
      a b c d and e account for 100 E.
   (a accounts for 13E, b for 17E, d for 19E, and e for 21E.)

B. Examples of the Use of the Experimental Methods

Analyze the reasoning in the following examples and exhibit the structures of the arguments in the appropriate schematic forms.

1. In the previous chapter we analyzed Goldberger's discovery that pellagra was a consequence of a lack of milk and fresh meat in the diet. But many scientists believed that his proof was inconclusive, and they inclined to the microbe theory. Goldberger then established further proofs of his hypothesis by the use of the experimental methods. He was granted permission to try out a dietary experiment at one of the state's prison farms with convicts who volunteered for this purpose. Twelve convicts lived on a diet chosen by him for six months, after which time they were given their freedom. These men were isolated from the others and fed almost nothing but white bread, corn pone, grits, sweet potatoes, salt pork, cane syrup, and cabbage for six months, beginning in April, 1915. After several months of this diet these men became listless; they began to develop severe abdominal pains, and they finally developed skin eruptions of the pellagra type. The other convicts on the farm, who received normal diets, did not suffer from these disorders.

But many cautious scientists were still not satisfied. Perhaps the convicts did not really have pellagra, they said. Or perhaps they suffered a recurrence of former cases of pellagra. Perhaps chance microbes had gotten into these men alone. And despite the fact that persons in contact with the sufferers did not catch the disease, the fact remained that the victims *always were in contact* with other victims. So perhaps the disease was caused by a microbe after all. Goldberger decided to put the microbe hypothesis to a conclusive test. He and his assistants injected the blood of pellagra victims into themselves, and even ate small portions of the excreta of these diseased persons. They suffered no ill results except for a temporary discomfort. He had now satisfactorily proved that the disease was not caused by microbes.

Goldberger had discovered the cause of the disease and how to eliminate it. His final problem was to find an inexpensive cure, for not every sufferer can be fed the comparatively expensive diet of milk and fresh meat. By chance, in experimenting with dogs, he discovered that two ounces of yeast per day will constitute a satisfactory substitute for milk and meat in pellagra treatment. (Show how the first paragraph illustrates the Positive Method of Difference; the second, the Negative Method of Difference.)

2. The planet Neptune was discovered in September, 1846, by two astronomers, the Englishman, J. C. Adams, and the Frenchman, U. J. J. Leverrier. Working independently of each other, these astronomers were sure that the actual orbit of the planet Uranus, supposedly the outermost planet in the solar system, could not be accounted for by the gravitational attraction of the known heavenly bodies. Its orbit was not what it should have been on the assumption that the sun and the inner planets were the only forces influencing its motion. These astronomers formulated the hypothesis that the actual motion could be accounted for only on the assumption that Uranus was being attracted by another planet whose orbit was exterior to its own. Leverrier then estimated the probable position of this unknown planet in terms of the force which it presumably exerted on Uranus, and the stars in this region were then carefully searched with a telescope. Star-charts then showed that one of the "stars" changed its position from night to night. A new planet had been discovered. (Method of Residues.)

3. The French scientist, Louis Pasteur, laid the foundations of the modern science of bacteriology. He had proved that liquids containing organic matter, called "putrescible liquids," will never show the presence of micro-organisms if they are completely protected from the outside air after being sterilized by intense heat. He then wished to prove that the presence of organisms in such liquids is due to exposure to the dusts of the outside air, rather than to the air as such. (He believed that the invisible organisms in the outside air cling to dust particles.) To prove his hypothesis he arranged an ingenious experiment. He used two flasks, both of which had open ends to permit entrance of the air, but he curved the neck of one of these flasks downward, after sterilizing the fluid within it. The liquid in this flask remained pure. He also performed other experiments. He exposed ordinary flasks to the air in various places, in laboratory cellars, in the streets of Paris, in the country, and in the high Alps. These experiments showed that as the air was freer of dusts, the less was the degree of putrescence in his liquids. (Positive Method of Difference, Method of Concomitant Variations.)

4. Pliny the Elder, the ancient Roman author of the *Natural History*, disproved the claims of the astrologers in the following manner: "If a man's destiny is caused by the star under which he is born, then all men born under that star should have the same fortune. But masters and slaves, and kings and beggars are born under the same star at the same time." (Negative Method of Difference.)

5. "You say that the capitalistic system is the cause of imperialism, which you define as the desire to extend the territory of one's country. But I can cite some noncapitalistic countries which are imperialistic in this sense, so capitalism cannot be the cause." (Negative Method of Agreement.)

6. Ignaz Phillipp Semmelweiss (1818–1865) is one of the chief originators of antiseptic surgery. His great achievement was his discovery of the cause of puerperal (child-bed) fever, an affliction of women, originating at childbirth. Semmelweiss was attached to the Vienna General Hospital as assistant professor in charge of the maternity ward. This ward had two divisions. In one, the First Division, the medical students were instructed. In the Second Division women were trained to become midwives. During the six-year period prior to 1846 the average deaths per thousand births was 99 in the First Division, 33 in the Second. Why this difference? Semmelweiss set to work on this problem.

Various suggestions were made. Such factors as climate, overcrowding, and the fact that unmarried women came to these charity wards were suggested. But these were obviously not the cause, since these conditions prevailed in both divisions. It was then suggested that the fear which women had of coming into the First Division was responsible for the high rate in that division. But Semmelweiss argued that their fear was an effect, not the cause, since the high mortality preceded the fear. Could it be the difference in sex of the attendants? This was absurd. Could it be the fact that women in the First Division were delivered on their backs; the women in the Second Division on their sides? He tried out this hypothesis, and ordered side deliveries in the First Division, with no change in the death rate.

Then one day one of his colleagues received a wound on a finger from the knife of a student who had come from the dissecting room. The colleague sickened and died. Semmelweiss noted that his symptoms were very much like those of puerperal fever. The hypothesis occurred to him that child-bed fever is wound infection or blood-poisoning, that the women were infected by the hands of the students who attended deliveries after coming from the dissecting room. Though these students washed their hands in soap and water, he was sure that some of the germs must remain on their hands. He ordered the students to wash their hands in chlorinated lime water. Just prior to the institution of this practice, the mortality rate was 122 per thousand. Before the end of the year it had fallen to 30, and at the end of two years it was 12. The rate of deaths in the Second Division remained unchanged. (Negative Method of Agreement [two examples], Positive Method of Difference.)

C. Problems in the Application of the Experimental Methods

1. On a radio program an ex-convict described how unpleasant his boyhood homelife had been, so that he ran away from home and was thus led into a life of crime. Do you think that this man's unhappy childhood was largely responsible for his becoming a criminal? Why or why not?

2. Farmer Brown had poor crops last year, though his neighbors had fairly good crops. His neighbors say that the cause of his poor crops was his failure to attend church regularly. How would you test this hypothesis?

3. Galen, the ancient Greek physician, anticipated the methods of the lie-detector tests. One day, when he was feeling the pulse of a female patient, a visitor entered and remarked that he had just come from seeing Pylades, the famous dancer. Galen noticed that the patient's pulse quickened. Galen suspected that she was in love with Pylades. The next time she came in he had a friend come in to say that he had seen another dancer perform, and on a third occasion, a different dancer was mentioned. No quickening of the pulse occurred. On her fourth visit the name of Pylades was mentioned again, and again her pulse quickened. (Wolf.) What had Galen proved? By what method?

4. In 1926 E. Haldeman Julius, publisher of the "Little Blue Books," published a translation of Victor Hugo's play *Le Roi s'Amuse,* under the title *The King Enjoys Himself.* Eight thousand copies were sold in that year. In 1927 the title was changed to *The Lustful King Enjoys Himself,* and 38,000 copies were sold. (Clarke.) Which hypothesis do you suggest to explain the remarkable increase in sales? Which method will you use in testing your hypothesis?

5. A scientist wished to test two hypotheses concerning the cause of the "flavor" which tobacco has; namely, (1) it is due to the sense of taste, and (2) it is due to the sense of smell. The scientist smoked a cigarette, keeping his nostrils closed while he did so. He found that the cigarette had no taste. What had he proved? By what method?

6. In a psychological experiment described by T. G. Andrews in his *Methods of Psychology* (J. Wiley, 1948), it was desired to test the hypothesis that practice in memorizing increases the ability to memorize. This hypothesis was too general to permit of a specific test, and so it was modified into the more precise question: Does practice in memorizing certain prose passages increase one's ability to memorize certain lines of poetry?

    A group of subjects was chosen for the experiment. The following principles were used in selecting these subjects. (1) The group was a homogeneous one (all were college students). (2) All were given a preliminary test to determine their ability to memorize certain lines of poetry. (3) The group was then divided into two subgroups, each with the same average ability as determined by the pretest and with equal variability in each subgroup.

    One subgroup, the experimental group, was then given practice in memorizing prose passages. The control subgroup received no practice. Both groups were then given the same test to determine their abilities in memorizing certain lines of verse. The results:

	Preliminary test	*Practice*	*Poetry test*
Experimental group:	Grade 62	Yes	79
Control group:	62	No	66

Which method was used in this experiment? Why were the three principles of selection necessary?

7. In his essay "Some Psychological Postulates for Peace" (in Harrison, Mander and Engle, *If Men Want Peace*, The Macmillan Co., 1946) Edwin R. Guthrie discusses the problem: What causes wars? He raises the question as to whether there are conditions which make nations prone to war, just as there are conditions in a forest which make the forest prone to fires, such as the dryness of the wood. He then suggests

that we shift the problem to the causes of belligerency, and continues:

There is one widespread notion of the causes of belligerency that a psychologist must regard as silly and mistaken. This is the belief that nations are prone to war when they are driven by hunger or need. But hungry men are not belligerent. It is hard to interest them in glory or in conquest, or even in revolt. They will listen attentively only to talk of food. And they will not exert themselves particularly even to get food. Outside the walls of a Chinese city there encamped, according to one account, some two hundred thousand starving peasants. Into the city, which was on a trade route, came large shipments of grain on their way to a more distant market. The starving thousands died quietly and without violence. During the great Irish famine, families lost members by starvation though the proprietor's share of the potato crop was in the cabin untouched. During the Russian famine, starving folk lined the banks of the Volga, occasionally in the presence of a Red soldier who was adequate to guard a storehouse of grain which was government property. The French revolution, often misunderstood because of Marie Antoinette's famous "Why don't they eat cake?" was a revolution of the best-fed peasants in Europe. They were not hungry. They were full of the fighting energy that only food and freedom from want can give. . . .

An economy of plenty is one of the conditions of belligerency, (but) it is only one feature of the situation that makes nations ripe for war. There are other and more complex determiners. . . . The second requirement of belligerency lies . . . in the existence of a large body of youth for whom the culture can easily provide food and shelter but for whom there are open no adult roles. These youth provide the manpower, the energy, the enthusiasm for conquest, invasion, political revolution, adventure, and colonization . . .

Something more than the pressure of a new generation on a static state of occupation is required. That something more lies in the possession of a military tradition. Military roles must be part of the literature and song of a nation. In Germany, Hitler could not have created these out of whole cloth. He could only cultivate intensely what already had familiar expression in German tradition.

Which hypothesis concerning war does the author seek to disprove? Which does he attempt to prove? How successful do you consider his argument?

D. *The Fallacies of Causal Analysis*

We noted six types of fallacies under this heading, but discussed two forms of Type 3, making seven in all:

(1) The "Post Hoc."
(2) Identifying a Necessary Condition with the Cause.
(3) The Fallacy of Emphasizing Irrelevant Factors.
   a. The Irrelevant Common Factor.
   b. Irrelevant Concomitant Variations.
(4) The Fallacy of Neglecting Negative Instances.
(5) The Fallacy of Neglecting Differences.
(6) The Reversing of Cause and Effect.

The following group contains one example of each type. Note the fallacy or subfallacy in each case, and explain your answer.

1. The height of the hem-line of women's dresses is caused by general business conditions. You will find that the dresses are short during periods of prosperity and long during depressions. Thus, the 1920's was the period of short dresses and prosperity. During the depression of 1932 dresses were long. During World War II and in the postwar prosperity they were short. The "New Look" of long dresses came in with the recession of 1949. As the stock market reaches new highs in 1959 dresses are beginning to shorten again.

2. Samuel Grafton in the *New York Post,* replying to a campaign speech by Mr. Thomas E. Dewey in Cheyenne, Wyoming, in 1940, pointed out that the latter "abounds in quaint comparisons between what it cost the government to do so-and-so in 1938 and what it cost in 1802 . . ."; and then pointed out that, according to Valentine's Manual of the Common Council of the City of New York for 1864, there were only two rape cases during the year. "But for the year 1939, with Mr. Dewey as prosecutor, there were 73 rape cases in the courts. Why this appalling increase in rape under the administration of Mr. Dewey?" (As quoted in H. A. Larrabee, *Reliable Knowledge,* Houghton, Mifflin Co., 1945.)

3. A farmer wished to test the agricultural value of lime. He plowed up two plots of ground, applied a coat of lime to one

and planted corn in both plots. In the lime plot he planted yellow corn; in the other, red corn. He cultivated the lime plot five times after the corn was up; the other three times. The lime plot yielded ten bushels per acre more than the other.

4. To which error is Sir Francis Bacon calling attention in Aphorism 45 of his *Novum Organum?*

And therefore it was a good answer that was made by one who, when they showed him hanging in a temple a picture of those who had paid their vows as having escaped shipwreck, and would have him say whether he did not now acknowledge the power of the gods—"Aye," asked he again, "but where are they painted that were drowned after their vows?" And such is the way of all superstition, whether in astrology, dreams, omens, divine judgments, or the like; wherein men, having a delight in such vanities, mark the events where they are fulfilled, but where they fail, though this happens much oftener, neglect and pass them by.

5. In every great war the onset of hostilities finds the belligerent nations fully armed. Wars cannot be fought without great armaments. We may therefore conclude that great armaments are the cause of wars, and there would be no wars if we limited armaments.

6. In the Semmelweiss case, some doctors suggested that the hysterical fears of many expectant mothers was the cause of their acquiring child-bed fever.

7. In his early years, H. L. Mencken attended Professor Knapp's Institute. He reports that the professor had a great contempt for the public schools.

Every time there was a hanging at the city jail . . . he referred to the departed, not by his crime but by his education, which was invariably in the public schools. No authentic graduate of F. Knapp's Institute, he let it be known, had ever finished on the gallows. (H. L. Mencken, *The Days of H. L. Mencken,* A. A. Knopf, 1947.)

E. *The Fallacies of Causal Analysis: Miscellaneous Examples*

Analyze this group as before. Explain your answer in each case.

1. I felt miserable before I took those pink pills. But now I feel fine.

2. In the early years of the twentieth century it was argued that wages in the United States were higher than they were

in England because the United States had a protective tariff, whereas England had no system of "protection."

3. "My men were in the trenches when they saw a fearsome sight. The dreaded green-colored gas came rolling toward them. Soldiers were running about in the gas and falling. I said to my men: 'There is no use in trying to escape. Let us sing a hymn.' We stood up and sang 'Abide With Me.' The poison gas disappeared, and not one of my men was harmed."

4. Corruption in the police force is due to the fact that so many so-called "good citizens" offer bribes to the police in order to escape the just penalties of the laws.

5. Old man Jones recently celebrated his ninetieth birthday. He ascribed his longevity to the fact that he drank a pint of beer every day.

6. All of the students in a logic class did consistently well on four tests. On the fifth test everyone failed. A student sought the cause of the failures. He found that some students had prepared for this test by studying in solitude; others had studied in groups. Some had studied in silent rooms; others had studied with the radios on. But in all cases he found that the students had studied until 1:00 A.M. He concluded that the common factor, studying until 1:00 A.M. was the cause of the failures.

7. Certainly I believe in magic. I saw a magician operating with an empty hat. He said "abracadabra," and a rabbit appeared. I carefully noted that the only difference between the hat empty and the hat filled with a rabbit was the utterance of the magic formula.

8. I have found that only students who study conscientiously get A's. It is therefore obvious that high grades are the result of hard work.

9. An investigator found that the rise and fall of the stork population of Sweden varied with the rise and fall of the birth rate of human beings in the United States.

10. An English writer noted that those among the English poor who had cows were the most industrious, so he argued that the way to make the others industrious was to give them cows.

11. Henry Ford: "If you will study the history of almost any criminal, you will find that he is an inveterate cigarette smoker."

12. A Chicago newspaper in 1936: "In 1928 there was a total of $5 billions in new financing of domestic operations. In 1929 there was $8 billions, and in 1930 there was $5 billions. In 1933 the New Deal established the Securities Exchange Commission and what was the result? In that year there was only $161 millions, not billions. Abolish the SEC and we shall again have financing in the billions."

13. John and Jim grew up together and were graduated from the same high school. John went to college and was graduated with honors, while Jim became a salesman. Today Jim earns $10,000 per year while John, who has become a high school teacher, earns $6,000. This proves that a college education is not a good investment.

14. It was during the middle of my freshman year at high school that I noticed my grades in the weekly "exams" took a sudden drop. Study as hard as I might, I could not raise my low average. I could not account for this drop, for I studied just as hard as ever. Now I am not what you might call a superstitious fool; but I could not help going backward in my mind and searching for some recent event or change of habit that could possibly coincide with the beginning of my change from the high to a low grade. It was not long before I discovered the desired coincidence. I had, up to the date of my 'drop,' been riding to school by the subway train. But on the very Friday I had received my first low grade I had met a friend with whom I had ridden to school on a surface car. As I found this route shorter and more convenient I continued to use it, and was still using it at the time of this strange discovery. On the very next day I returned to the subway route and the very next Friday my grade rose from a "50" of the previous week to a "90." A foolish coincidence, you will say; but it has influenced my actions in spite of myself. Every day I go out determined to try the surface cars just for the fun of it, but some unseen instinctive force impels me to seek the subway route. Even now, while attending the University, I walk every day a distance of almost half a mile to get a subway train, rather than take the surface car which runs right by my house. But every now and then I meet some friends, who also attend the same college and live on the same street; and I am compelled for companionship's sake to ride with them when they take the surface car. Invariably on such a day I have poor luck in all my work. For instance, I often

upset apparatus in my chemistry laboratory when I ride on the subway; but the damage is never so great as when I use the surface route. What would you call such a coincidence? (A. M. Tozzer, *Social Origins and Social Continuities*, pp. 254–5. Copyright 1926 by The Macmillan Company and used with their permission.)

Chapter 17

The Nature of Induetive Reasoning

Section I: The Meaning of Generalizations

A generalization is a statement to the effect that something is always the case; in the simplest form, "All A's are B's," or "All crows are black." Generalizations are indispensable in everyday matters as well as in science. We guide ourselves in our daily activities by generalizations, and we would find it difficult to move a single step without them. When we are hungry, we eat food because we know that food is nourishing and that it will satisfy hunger. We know that fire will heat, that it will burn, and that it will boil water. We know that alcohol intoxicates. The scientist, of course, would require that these generalizations be stated more precisely and with the proper qualifications before asserting them as true. Thus, only some kinds of food are nourishing. And even such a generalization as "Water boils at 212° F." requires the qualification: "under certain conditions of atmospheric pressure."

In our previous discussions we frequently noted the important role which generalizations play in our reasoning. Generalizations typically form the major premises of our syllogisms: "All men are mortal," "If P, then Q," etc. Causal laws, which tell us that X is the cause of Y, and functional laws, which tell us that X is a function of Y, are also generalizations.

Before we proceed further, an important qualification to our definition of generalizations must be noted. A statement in the form "All A's are B's" is a generalization only when all of the A's have *not been observed*. "All crows are black," is a genuine generalization, for it refers to the unobserved as well as to the observed crows. A generalization, then, is based upon an incomplete observation of the facts of experience. Generalizations in this sense are called "inductions" by logicians, but the two words are usually used interchangeably. Let us now look at a different type of statement in the form "All A's are B's": "All the chairs in this classroom are brown." If this statement is based upon our observation of each and every chair in the room, then it is not a genuine generalization. It is merely a *description* of things which have been observed. Though cast in the form "All A's are B's," we shall call such statements "quasi-generalizations." Aristotle used the expression "perfect inductions" for these quasi-generalizations, but in our terminology they are not genuine generalizations or inductions.

Three fundamental questions concerning generalizations or inductions are: (1) By what process do we arrive at generalizations? (2) Is the process of reasoning valid? (3) Are generalizations true? Let us look at these questions:

(1) We begin with a simple example. I visit the Brookfield Zoo near Chicago and see a panda. I note that he has rings around his eyes. I then visit the New York zoo and find other pandas with rings. I then visit Tibet and China and see more pandas, all with rings around their eyes. I then generalize: "All pandas have rings." The reasoning proceeds as follows: "All the observed cases of pandas (p1, p2, p3, p4, . . . pn) have rings, . . . Therefore, all pandas have rings." Note that we conclude that all pandas have rings on the evidence that all the observed cases have rings. The jump from the *observed cases* to the generalization concerning *both* the *observed* and all of the *unobserved cases* is called the "inductive leap." We shall use the symbol → for this inductive leap. Our reasoning may thus be represented by: "All the observed P's are R's → All P's are R's."

(2) Is our reasoning valid? Obviously not. "All of the observed cases" represent only a fraction of all cases, past, present, and future. We have therefore drawn a conclusion concerning *all* on the evidence of *some*. This is a violation of the fundamental rule that we cannot distribute an undistributed term. Note again that the sentence "All the chairs in this room are brown" does not involve an inductive leap, since it is not a generalization.

(3) Is our generalization concerning the pandas *true?* All observed cases have rings, and no cases without rings have been observed. It is true so far as we know. But this does not guarantee that all future pandas will be found to have rings around their eyes. Nor that all existing pandas have such rings. Nevertheless, our generalization may be said to have a measure of probability, the degree of probability depending upon factors which we shall presently examine.

Induction differs from deduction in that the former process seeks to establish true statements about the facts of experience, whereas deduction merely exfoliates the logical consequences of what is already known. Insofar as induction is a method of proof or inference, however, it too involves some aspects of deductive reasoning. John Stuart Mill, for example, argued that every inductive inference can be cast into syllogistic form, in which the uniformity of nature is the ultimate major premise: "The induction, 'John, Peter, etc., are mortal, therefore, all mankind are mortal,' may . . . be thrown into a syllogism by prefixing as a major premise . . . that what is true of John, Peter, etc., is true of all mankind."

The "ultimate ground" of inductive reasoning is a matter of controversy among logicians. We shall merely note here that the major premise stated by Mill can never be known to be true, and so an inductive generalization can never have more than probability. The specific problem of induction, then, is to determine on what basis we are warranted in asserting the probability of a generalization. Stated in another way, what are the principles which permit us to generalize concerning a population on the basis of a sample of that population?

Section II: The Truth or Probability of Generalizations

The process of induction involves a generalization from some to all, from the observed cases to all cases (the observed and the unobserved). The inductive leap is a "leap in the dark" to the unobserved cases of the present, future, and past. The observed cases are regarded as a sample of all the cases. A buyer of cloth takes a sample from a bolt, and the sample is regarded as a fair or representative sample of the whole (or of the unobserved portions). Similarly a buyer of wheat takes sample handfuls from a carload. The induction can be relied on if the sample is a fair one. The big problem, then, is to assess the fairness of the sample. If the sample is fair or representative, then the generalization will be highly probable; if not, not.

But before we discuss the probability of inductions, we must note certain distinctions in the types of inductions. Inductions may be classified in two ways: as referring, on the one hand, to *indeterminate* groups of things, or to *determinate* groups; and in a second classification we shall divide inductions into the *uniform* and *statistical*. We shall now examine these two distinctions.

Every induction goes from some to all, from the observed sample to the whole collection. The generalization concerning the pandas makes an assertion concerning an *indeterminate* group, by which we shall mean a group whose membership is indefinite, or "infinite," in size. There are no known limits to the total membership of the panda group, for pandas have existed since time immemorial, we have observed only a fraction of those existing today, and there are pandas yet to come. But compare the induction when we take a sample of wheat from a carload. Here we generalize concerning *this* carload, a *determinate* group whose membership has definite limits. But this case also represents genuine induction, since here, too, we find the inductive leap from some to all. We say, "The observed grains have X characteristics → all the grains have the same characteristics (in this carload)."

Our second distinction refers to *uniform* and *statistical* inductions. On the one hand we may find a uniformity in the sample. *All* of the observed pandas have rings.* We then generalize and say, "All without exception" have rings. In a statistical induction, on the other hand, we find that a certain *proportion* in our sample has a certain characteristic. We study 1000 cases of childbirths, and find that 52 per cent of the children are males. This fact does not constitute a generalization in itself, since it is merely a description of what has been observed in a sample collection of cases. But if we should make further observations, studying other collections of cases under different conditions, and at different times and places, and should find

---

* One exception will destroy a uniform generalization. The exception does *not* "prove the rule," at least in this sense. For other meanings of this expression, see H. W. Fowler, *Dictionary of Modern English Usage.*

that our percentage is confirmed under any and all conditions, we may generalize and say, "52 per cent of all births are males." We have now made the inductive leap from some to all, but instead of finding that all of the observed cases have a certain uniform characteristic, we find that all of the observed collections of cases (or the one large varied group) show that a certain proportion of individuals have a given characteristic. Our generalization then asserts that all as yet unobserved collections of cases will show the same proportion.

We may also combine our two distinctions. Uniform generalizations may be made for indeterminate or determinate groups (the pandas and the wheat), and we may make statistical generalizations which deal with indeterminate or determinate groups. The generalization concerning childbirths is a statistical generalization which refers to an indeterminate group. A statistical induction dealing with a determinate group is illustrated by a poll of public opinion, such as the Gallup poll, which examines the opinions of a sample group of individuals, usually about 3,000 persons. The pollsters find a certain division of opinion in the sample, then generalize and tell us that the opinions of all adult Americans (75,000,000 persons) will divide as the sample did. In this case we deal with a determinate group, the American people existing at a specific time. The childbirth generalization concerns an indeterminate number of children existing anywhere or at any time. But in all of the various types of genuine generalizations, be it noted, we find the inductive leap from the *observed* cases to *all* cases. In this chapter we shall be concerned primarily with uniform generalizations. Statistical generalizations will be considered further in the next chapter.

We now return to the problem of the probability of generalizations. We shall consider such generalizations as the following: Pandas have rings; water is composed of H_2O; all men are mortal; typhoid fever is caused by the typhus bacillus; the volume of a gas is a function of the temperature and the pressure; and every particle of matter attracts every other particle of matter with a force proportional to the product of their masses and inversely proportional to the square of their distances. How probable are such generalizations, and on what principles do we assess their probabilities?

The important question concerning the probability of an induction involves the dependability of the sample. Is it fair? Is it representative of the whole collection of cases we are considering? Can we be sure that all cases yet to be examined will be like those we have examined? A number of factors will influence our judgment of the fairness of a sample and hence of the probability of an induction:

1. The number of cases

Other things being equal, the number of cases on which the generalization is based will affect its probability. The generalization that all pandas have rings will be less probable if our sample consists of 10 cases than if it is based upon 100 cases, and similarly with all generalizations. The enumeration of cases is basic in all induction.

But the number of cases is only one of the factors which determine the fairness of a sample and hence of the degree of probability of a generalization. When a generalization is based upon enumeration *alone,* i.e., on nothing more than that all of the observed cases have a characteristic in common, we shall say that such a generalization is based upon "simple enumeration." Simple enumeration is the weakest type of evidence for a generalization. Its weaknesses were noted by Sir Francis Bacon:

> The induction which proceeds by simple enumeration is childish; its conclusions are precarious, and exposed to peril from a contradictory instance; and it generally decides on too small a number of facts, and on those only which are to hand.

This condemnation is perhaps too sweeping, but the weakness of such generalizations is generally recognized. Our lack of confidence in inductions based on simple enumeration may be illustrated by an imaginary case. If, on our next visit to Tibet, we should find a panda without rings around his eyes, we would be surprised, but we should not consider the instance incredible. We would immediately revise our generalization and say, "Most pandas have rings around their eyes." But, as we shall see in a moment, we are less ready to abandon inductions based on grounds other than simple enumeration.

2. The homogeneity of the cases examined

When we take a sample of a carload of wheat, we are confident that the quality of the whole will be like that of the sample. But if we should take a sample carton of cherries from a carload our assurance would not be so high. Why is this? Because cherries differ from each other in quality much more than do grains of wheat. Grains of wheat are known to be more homogeneous when taken from a given area than are cherries, with respect to the qualities important for commercial uses. The homogeneity of the individuals in a collection, then, appears to answer our question as to how we determine whether a sample is a fair one. If we *know* that a class of things is homogeneous, then we can be sure that our sample is a fair one.

But, the reader may ask, is this not circular reasoning, since we *assume* that a whole class is homogeneous, and this is something we can never be sure of so long as there are unexamined cases? We must admit that the use of the principle of homogeneity does require this assumption. Nevertheless, homogeneity is a factor in induction, and the assumption will be more or less probable depending upon our past experiences with the class in question. Some characteristics are probably homogeneous, others not. Thus, on a visit to Mexico we note in the first cases examined, that Mexicans are dark-complexioned and that they drive their cars recklessly. We regard the complexion as a more homogeneous characteristic than driving habits and we will be more confident that all will be dark-complexioned than that all Mexicans drive recklessly. But these inferences can be no more than probable.

3. The careful analysis of the cases

When we compare the examples of inductions we have examined thus far with those in the exact sciences, we are struck by a great contrast. It is certainly a safer induction to say that the speed of a falling body increases in direct ratio to the time it falls than it is to say that all pandas have rings. Newton's law of gravitation is an induction with a much higher probability than that all crows are black. If we found a ringless panda in Tibet, as noted, we should be surprised and interested in our discovery. But if we should find that unsupported objects do not fall to the earth in Tibet, we should doubt our senses. Why is this? Why are the inductions of the exact sciences more probable than those concerning the blackness of crows or the spottiness of leopards and panthers? Our third factor gives us an answer: such inductions involve a careful analysis of the cases examined. When we use the experimental methods, for example, we carefully examine the instances. When we use the Positive Method of Agreement, we must not only find the uniform presence of a certain antecedent, but we must find this to be the case no matter how the other surrounding factors are varied, under any and all conditions. In a control experiment (Method of Difference) the relevant factors are carefully analyzed.

Thus a chemist may justifiably affirm that he has discovered a new law of nature on the basis of a few experiments (or samples), whereas thousands of instances will give a much lesser probability to inductions concerning leopards and their spots. Furthermore, the chemist can produce the effect he desires at will, or prevent the effect at will. When the cause is present, the effect occurs; when not, not. Thus the methods of experimentation studied in the previous chapter furnish us with inductions with a very high probability. But there is yet another factor affecting the probability of inductions, viz.:

4. The systematic organization of knowledge

The aim of science is not the mere accumulation of true propositions concerning reality. Its ultimate aim, rather, is to find an explanation of the entire "system of nature" and of the structure of the universe. The ideal of science is to integrate all known truths into a system of truths in the form of a deductive system, in which all subsidiary laws and their applications can be deduced from a few simple basic laws. The science of mechanics is such a system. With Newton's law as the basis for the system, we can deduce the other laws of mechanics in exact mathematical terms. The different parts of Nature's jig-saw puzzle are seen to fit together in a beautiful harmony. The over-all system explains the particular laws, and the parts of the system support the whole. In the social sciences, of course, this ideal is as yet only a remote vision, except, perhaps, in economics. Classical economics assumes certain basic axioms (concerning human behavior) and then deduces the consequences which will follow *if* these axioms are actualized in reality. It seeks to organize all of the principles of economics into a deductive system.*

The systematic organization of the laws of the exact sciences furnishes additional evidence to support new inductions in these sciences. For when a chemist discovers a new compound, his induction is supported not only by the evidence which he has before him, but he knows that his discovery can also be deduced from the general laws of chemistry. He experiments along lines suggested by the general laws and his results are deducible from them. Myriads of experiments support these general laws. Their authority now lends great weight to generalizations deducible from them.

Let us look at a simple illustration of the principle of systematic organization: We know that all machines wear out in time. This principle is based upon the enumeration of cases, the homogeneity of the cases examined, and the careful analyses of cases.

Now, consider the generalization that "All men are mortal," or, more precisely, that men will die before they reach a certain anniversary of their births. We can do more than point to the enumeration of cases, homogeneity, and careful analysis. There is additional support for this generalization. We also know that the human body is a machine and that all machines must eventually wear out because of friction. In a similar manner the law concerning machines may be deduced from higher generalizations, and so on. Such generalizations give mutual support to each other and increase the probability of any induction within the system.

We shall distinguish, then, between two types of generalizations, which we shall call "isolated" and "integrated." An isolated generalization is one which stands alone, without receiving the support of others. Pandas and their rings are an example. There are no laws of nature which require that pandas should have rings. An integrated generalization, on the other

---

* When predictions are made on the basis of deductions from postulates, however, the probability of these predictions will depend upon the extent to which the actual situation corresponds to the ideal situation assumed by the postulates. Thus in *applied*, as distinguished from *pure*, economics we have no assurance that we have taken account of all the ways in which an actual economic situation may depart from the system assumed by the postulates.

hand, is one which is supported by other generalizations and which in turn supports them. This explains why we should be so shocked if we found that a basic law of physics, such as gravitation, did not hold in Tibet. For we should then have to discard not merely that particular law (for one exception is sufficient to overthrow a law), but we should also have to discard a host of other laws which are integrally associated with that one. Our structure of knowledge would topple into ruins. This is the basic reason why scientists are sceptical concerning reports of miracles.

We have noted some of the factors which determine the "fairness of a sample" and which explain why some generalizations have a much higher probability than others. But in the end, it is the evidence of experience which controls our judgments of the probability of inductions, and experience always comes back to the enumeration of cases. We always go from the evidence that X has happened in *some* cases to the generalization that it will happen in *all*. Though we use the systematic organization principle to support inductions, the basic inductions of the "system" also go back to the enumeration of cases, and rest upon supporting generalizations which also use that principle. In practice, however, the generalization which is based upon the four factors will have a higher probability than one based upon enumeration alone, or upon what we call "simple" enumeration.

Section III: The Justification of Inductions

The probability of a specific induction depends upon the number of cases examined, the homogeneity of the instances, the varying times and places in which we have observed the instances, the careful analysis of the observed cases, and the supporting generalizations. Underlying our belief in the probability of any specific induction, however, is the principle of the "uniformity of nature." Whenever we say that an induction is probable, or make a prediction concerning the future, we assume this principle. We assume that the future will be like the past, that similar causes will have similar effects, and that the structure of the world will remain unaltered in certain fundamental respects.

Note that the principle of the uniformity of nature does

not tell us that any specific induction is true. It merely tells us that some inductions are true, i.e., that there *are* uniformities in nature to which no exceptions will ever be found. This obviously cannot be proven. The principle is simply accepted as an unproved assumption, or postulate, by all scientists.

But, it may be asked, though the principle is not certain, is it not highly *probable* since there are myriads of inductions to which no exceptions have been discovered? This justification for the principle involves circular reasoning. It uses the principle in the very act of seeking to justify it, for the concept of "probability" assumes that nature is uniform. The principle, then, cannot be proved. It is simply accepted as an unproved assumption or postulate of science.

Though the principle of the uniformity of nature is only a postulate, this does not mean that there is any reason to reject it. The following remarks of Hans Reichenbach indicate the attitude of the scientist towards his assumption:

> To renounce the assumption of induction would be necessary only if we knew that the assumption is *false*. But that is not the case—we *do not know* if it is true or false. And that is quite another matter! Without believing that the assumption is true or false, we are still justified in defending it in the sense in which we make a wager. We want to forsee the future, and we can do it if the assumption of induction is justified—and so we wager on this assumption. If it is false, well, then our efforts are in vain; but if we use the principle of induction, we have at least a chance of success.
>
> We are in the same situation as a man who wants to fish in an unchartered place of the sea. There is nobody to tell him whether or not there are fish in this place. Shall he cast his net? Well, if he wants to fish, I would advise him to cast his net, at least to take the chance. It is preferable to try even in uncertainty than not to try and be certain of getting nothing. [*Journal of Philosophy*, Vol. XXXIII (1936), p. 157.]

The principle of the uniformity of nature is also assumed, be it noted, whenever we seek to explain the events of prehistory, or of any events not observed by human beings. We might be able to *describe* the past without this principle, but we would not be able to *explain* it. For whenever we seek to *explain* past events, we assume that what is today was also then.

We assume the regularity of nature: that the uniformities of today prevailed in the past. When we find a tree with one hundred rings we infer that it is one hundred years old; when we find ancient rocks of the Paleozoic Age we assume that they were formed as rocks are formed today. We believe that the earth is millions of years old on the basis of such reasoning. Limestone is built up at the bottom of the ocean floor by slow processes today, and we assume that the limestone of the past was also built up by the deposits of foraminifera on the ocean's floor. We then compute the length of time it must have taken to build up the rock crust of the earth. Though these explanations cannot be demonstrated conclusively, we regard them as highly probable because of our postulate that nature is uniform in many respects.

Section IV: Analogy and Scientific Method

In this section we shall examine a method of inference which is closely related to induction. This is the method of analogical reasoning which, like induction, draws inferences concerning unobserved entities on the basis of what has been observed. Both involve the "inductive leap." Analogical reasoning, however, uses a type of analysis which differs from that used in induction. Let us look at an example taken from Thomas Reid, the eighteenth-century Scotch philosopher:

> We may observe a very great similitude between this earth which we inhabit, and the other planets, Saturn, Jupiter, Mars, Venus, and Mercury. They all revolve around the sun, as the earth does, although at different distances, and in different periods. They borrow all their light from the sun, as the earth does. Several of them are known to revolve around their axes like the earth, and, by that means, must have a like succession of day and night. Some of them have moons, that serve to give light in the absence of the sun, as our moon does to us. They are all in their motions, subject to the same law of gravitation, as the earth is. From all this similitude, it is not unreasonable to think that these planets may, like our earth, be the habitation of living creatures. There is some probability in this conclusion from analogy.

We shall criticize this argument in due course. But first let us note its structure. To simplify the argument, let us restrict the discussion to the comparison between the earth and Mars. Reid finds that both revolve around the sun (r), both borrow their light from the sun (b), both revolve around their axes (a), both have moons (m), and both are subject to the law of gravitation (g). Now, he continues, the earth also has life (l); therefore, it is probable that Mars also has life.

We shall now exhibit the structure of this argument in symbolic form. We note that a thing or situation (A) has characteristics r, b, a, m, g, and l. We then find a thing or situation (B) which has r, b, a, m, and g. B thus resembles A in five characteristics. A also has a sixth characteristic, l. We infer that B will also have the sixth characteristic. This is reasoning by analogy. "B resembles A in certain observed respects; therefore it will also resemble A in the as yet unobserved respects." Such reasoning involves a process similar to the inductive leap, and the conclusion can be only probable at best. We move from similarity in *some* respects to similarity in *all* respects.

The distinction between analogy and induction has been well stated by the English logician, W. E. Johnson: "Induction is understood to depend primarily upon the number of instances known to be characterized by a certain adjective; while the force of analogy depends upon the number of adjectives which are known to characterize a certain instance." This means that in induction we observe a number of instances, i.e., individuals such as pandas, and "leap" from a finding concerning the observed instances to an inference concerning the unobserved instances. Thus:

Panda$_1$ has rings.
Panda$_2$ has rings.   →   All pandas have rings.
Panda$_3$ has rings.
Etc.

In analogical reasoning, on the other hand, we deal with two things or situations having adjectives in common. One of these things has an additional observed adjective. We infer that the other will have the additional adjective though it has not been observed, thus:

Earth has r, b, a, m, g, and l.
Mars has r, b, a, m, g.   →   Mars also has l.

The distinction between the two methods may be illustrated by simple examples: When we reason from the fact that all of the honeydew melons we have eaten had a certain flavor, to the conclusion that *all* have the same flavor, we reason inductively. (From the fact that a number of instances were characterized by a certain adjective, we infer that all will be so characterized.) In analogical reasoning, on the other hand, we reason as follows: "Honeydew melon A has a certain shape, color, odor, and flavor. B resembles A in its shape, color, and odor. Therefore, B will resemble A in flavor." (From the fact that A and B have a certain number of adjectives in common, we infer that they will have another adjective in common.) The two methods are also interrelated, for an induction will be strengthened when its instances are highly analogous, and an analogy will be strengthened by a number of previous instances in which the inference was justified. But the two methods are logically distinct.

The problem of determining the probability of an analogical argument is similar to that of determining the probability of an induction. The four criteria we studied earlier will be applicable here, in approximately the same manner. Thus, the probability of analogical argument will depend in part upon the number of resembling characteristics. Other things being equal, the greater the number of resembling characteristics, the stronger the inference. Similarly, criteria such as homogeneity, careful analysis, and the relation to a deductive system of knowledge will also determine the probability of the analogy. Most important of all in these arguments, however, is the absence of significant "negative analogies," i.e., respects in which B is dissimilar to A. Thus, the following situation would not justify the inference:

$$A \text{ has } v, w, x, y, \quad \text{and } z.$$
$$B \text{ has } v, w, x, y, n \rightarrow z.$$

The presence of the dissimilar negative characteristic n may destroy the possibility of B also having z. This is also the crucial weakness of Reid's analogical argument. He pointed to several resembling features between the earth and five planets, but there is a significant negative analogy which he does not mention: On all of the planets except Mars, the temperatures are such that life, as we know it, would be impossible. With respect to Mars, however, the argument undoubtedly has some probability, the degree of probability depending upon many other factors which Reid did not consider.

Section V: Analogy and Argumentation

Analogies play an important role in scientific reasoning, but they also have many other uses. They are coins of intellectual currency in everyday argumentation, where we frequently encounter the "argument from analogy." They are also useful in non-argumentative discourse when we seek to prove nothing, but only to describe or illustrate. We shall comment briefly on these two latter uses before considering the use of analogy in argumentation.

Analogy is widely used in literary discourse when a vivid description is desired. The use of similes and metaphors involves comparisons, and every comparison is an analogy. In a simile the comparison is explicit: "Life, like a dome of many-colored glass, stains the white radiance of eternity." In a metaphor the comparison is implicit, as in speaking of "the raging sea," or "the ship of state." Historians frequently use analogies for descriptive purposes. An ancient event becomes more vivid when we can liken it to a contemporary one: "When Demosthenes warned the Athenians to prepare for war and not to believe that concessions to King Philip of Macedonia would divert him from his aggressive designs, he was doing what Winston Churchill did in warning the British people against appeasing Hitler." This is not an argument; the analogy is not used as proof. Descriptive analogies are also used in writings which seek to popularize the explanation of scientific concepts for the layman. Thus E. N. daC. Andrade, the English physicist, explains the differences between a solid, liquid, and gas by picturing the different motions of the molecules in each:

> In a solid, the molecules can be pictured as a crowd of men all doing physical exercises—"the daily dozen"—without moving from the spot where they stand. . . . In a liquid the molecules can be pictured as a swarm of men gathered together in a hall at a crowded reception; they are tightly wedged, but each one works his way through the others, with many a push and apology. . . . For a gas we have to think of a large open space

on which men are walking without looking where they are going; each man continues in a straight line until he bumps into
someone else, when he abruptly starts off again in a different
direction. (E. N. daC. Andrade, *What is the Atom?* Harper and
Brothers, 1926.)

These illustrations show the use of analogies in non-argumentative forms, where no proofs are attempted. But note that
an analogy which is used for description or illustration may subsequently be used in an argument. We might use the Demos-
thenes-Churchill analogy in trying to prove that it was just as
wrong for the British to appease Hitler as it was for the Athenians to appease Philip.

We shall now examine the "argument from analogy." This
argument may use the simpler types of analogies which we
studied in the previous section, but it may also involve the use
of analogies between *relations.* The remainder of this section
will be devoted to the analysis of "relational analogies." Let us
illustrate by an example which also shows the context in which
one such argument might originate: A legislature, let us say, is
considering the question as to whether the private communications between a priest and penitent should be "privileged" in a
law court, so that a priest may not be compelled to testify as to
communications made to him in confidence. The legislature
finds that communications made as between husband and wife,
doctor and patient, lawyer and client, are granted this immu-
nity. An argument from analogy may then be constructed, as
follows: The priest-penitent relation resembles the doctor-patient relation in the following respects: The communications
are made in the expectation that they will be held in the strict-
est confidence (c); it is socially desirable that the communicators
should have trust in the communicatees (t). The doctor-patient
relation is entitled to "privilege" (p). Therefore, the priest-
penitent relation is entitled to "privilege."

The structure of a relational analogy is thus exactly like
that of an analogy between two things, except that instead of
saying, "X is like Y in some respects, therefore:—," we say, "The
relation of A to B is like the relation of C to D in some respects;
therefore:—." In the example given we say that the relation of a
priest to his penitent is like the relation of a doctor to his patient in two respects; therefore, it resembles it (or should re-

semble it) in a third. In other words: The doctor-patient relation has *c* and *s* and *p*. The priest-penitent relation has *c* and *s;* therefore, it also has *p*.

We shall now present a detailed five-step analysis of a relational analogy as a model for analyzing such arguments by analogy. The purpose of this analysis is to exhibit the structure of the analogy so that we may be better able to judge its merits as an *argument*. The argument to be analyzed runs as follows:

> The colonial system is a boon and not a curse to mankind. It is right and proper for advanced nations to control undeveloped nations until the latter become more advanced. Will not everyone agree that it is right for parents to control their children until the latter reach the age of discretion, which we call maturity or adulthood?

The argument obviously seeks to prove that it is morally right for advanced nations to control undeveloped nations.

The five-step analysis:

(1.) The argument should first be stated as clearly and simply as possible in hypothetical form, omitting all rhetoric and irrelevancies: "If it is morally right for parents to control their children until they mature, then, by analogy, it is right for advanced nations to control undeveloped nations until the latter mature."

The argument assumes that a certain characteristic attaches to a given relationship, i.e., the characteristic of moral rightness is attached to the parental control of children. This assumption is stated as the antecedent or premise of the argument. The consequent (or conclusion) asserts that moral rightness also characterizes the analogous relationship between advanced and undeveloped nations.

(2.) (a) Symbolize the two pairs of terms whose relations are regarded as analogous. We shall symbolize "Parents : Children" by "P : C" and "Advanced Nations : Undeveloped Nations" by A : U. The analogy states that A is to U as P is to C, or A: U :: P : C. This may also be shown as $\dfrac{A}{U} : \dfrac{P}{C}$

(b) Symbolize the characteristic possessed by P : C and alleged to hold for A : U by "*r*" (moral rightness).

(c) Now restate the original argument symbolically: The

P : C relation has *r;* therefore, the A : U relation has *r.*

(3.) We should now seek to find the adjectives or characteristics which are alleged to be common to both relations. One common characteristic is stated explicitly: the relation of an adult or mature entity to an immature one. A second characteristic is implied: the relation of a superior to an inferior with respect to power. We shall symbolize these relations by *m* and *s,* respectively.

(4.) We are now prepared to symbolize the full intended argument:

> The **P** : C relation is characterized by *s* and *m* and also by *r.*
>
> The A : U relation is characterized by *s* and *m.* Therefore, also by *r.*

(5.) Look for "negative analogies." After stating the argument in the manner of Step 4 its structure is clear and its weaknesses, if any, will be exposed. The chief basis for criticism of analogical arguments is the finding of significant differences or negative analogies between two relations. There may be similarities between two relations, but if the differences outweigh the similarities, the argument from analogy has little or no worth. Now, does our illustration have any significant negative analogy? It does. In the parent-child relation, the control is exercised for the benefit of the child, rather than for the parents. In the colonial system the advanced nation has been typically concerned with its own interests, rather than with the interests of the colony. There are honorable exceptions, but this is the general rule. (Another weakness of this argument lies in its equivocal use of "mature," as applied to individuals and nations.)

Our example, then, contains a negative analogy (*n*), and the argument fails. Self-interest (*n*) characterizes the A : U relationship, so that the two relations are not similar in all significant respects.

When we analyze analogical arguments in everyday discourse, it almost goes without saying, we are not concerned with scientific proof. But one such argument will be more reasonable than another, depending upon the absence of known significant negative analogies.

Section VI: Miscellaneous Fallacies

In this section we shall comment on some fallacies related to the inductive process, and we shall also note a number of fallacies which, though unrelated to this process, involve errors with respect to "generalities," i.e., general assumptions which lack precision and clarity.

1. Hasty Generalization

Francis Bacon, in his strictures against induction by simple enumeration, said that this method was apt to decide "on too small a number of facts, and on those only which are to hand." He was warning against "hasty generalizing," which he elsewhere described as an "Idol of the Tribe," an error common to all mankind.

Most of us generalize too much. We generalize on the basis of insufficient evidence and neglect to note negative instances. We jump to conclusions, e.g., "All women are poor drivers," "All Californians drive recklessly." Such generalizations are usually based on a few instances without noting negative cases. A tourist speaks to two or three Frenchmen who dislike the United States and comes back to report that "All Frenchmen (or all Europeans) hate us."

Prejudice is a chief cause of hasty generalizing, since it leads us to stress the few instances that confirm our prejudices and to ignore all exceptions. Thus the prejudiced person notes that a few union officials were found guilty of embezzling pension funds entrusted to their care. The conclusion he draws is that "Labor unions are nothing but rackets." Minority groups suffer from this tendency of the prejudiced to magnify the exceptional and unfavorable behavior of some of their members. Another reason for this error is the desire to attract attention to oneself by exaggeration, a not-too-subtle form of exhibitionism. If one were to say that some politicians are crooks, no one would pay any attention to him, since it is well known that politicians are not saints. But the statement that "All politicians are crooks" immediately attracts notice. Goethe once said that it is easy to be brilliant if one respects nothing, not even truth.

A careful thinker will not generalize unless his evidence is sufficient to do so and his generalizations will be limited in scope to the precise characteristics he is investigating. There is one error above all that a careful thinker will not commit. This is to go from the fact that some generalizations are bad to the conclusion that all are bad. Generalizations based on adequate samples and safeguarded by careful analysis are the very foundations of our knowledge.

2. Composition

Composition is a fallacy which occurs when we argue that a group must have the same qualities or characteristics as its members. An example: Each of the football players on the All-Star team is the best player in his position in the entire country. Therefore, the All-Star team is the best team in the entire country.

This kind of reasoning must be carefully distinguished from induction. In induction we go from "Some individual A's have the characteristic x" to "All individual A's have x." In the composition fallacy we reason that if each individual member of a group (or parts of a whole) have certain characteristics, then the group as a collective whole must have the same characteristics. But this inference does not follow. The individuals may have qualities not possessed by the group as such, and the group *as a group* may possess characteristics which its members do not possess. A group may be an "organic whole" in which the interrelationship of the parts is responsible for its character. An operatic production may have the greatest stars, but a cast made up of male and female prima donnas may show a deplorable lack of teamwork, and the production may not be as good as many in which the lesser stars work harmoniously.

3. Division

The fallacy of division is the reverse of the fallacy of composition. Here we go from the group to the member, or from the whole to the parts. An example: The Montreal Canadiens are the best hockey team in the world. Therefore its goalie must be the best goalie in the world. The fact that a whole has a certain characteristic does not justify us in concluding that its parts will have the same characteristic.

We have discussed composition and division in their purest forms. These fallacies also occur in subtler ways. Thus, we may argue that because it would be undesirable for everyone to be educated until the age of thirty it is therefore undesirable for a particular individual (division), or we may argue that because it would be desirable for an individual to possess something (such as a doubled income) it would be similarly desirable if everyone possessed it (composition).

An error resembling division occurs on a more philosophical level when we argue that a physical thing is "nothing but" the atoms that compose it. This ignores the organizational structure and the relations of the atoms to each other. Similarly, water is "something more" than hydrogen and oxygen combined.

4. The Use of "Generalities"

Under this heading we shall discuss errors which result from assumptions that lack precision and clarity. These errors are not inductive fallacies, nor related to the inductive process.

There are many principles which state what is true in general, or desirable in general, but they should not be applied to particular cases without the proper qualifications. We should be sure that there are no important countervailing considerations. What is true *ceteris paribus*, (other things being equal) should not be applied when other things are not equal. "Every man has a right to keep his own property" is true in general but this principle does not prevent the state from "condemning" his property for public purposes, and taking it from him upon payment of a reasonable price therefor, under its right of "eminent domain." "It is wrong to tell a lie" and "Thou shalt not kill" are basic moral principles, but they should not be interpreted to mean that it is necessarily immoral to tell a lie to a person who has an incurable disease, or to kill in order to defend one's country in war.

This type of error was referred to as the "Fallacy of Accident" by traditional logicians. By "accident" they meant "the nonessential." A favorite illustration used in the twelfth century (and since) is the following: "You ate today what you bought yesterday. You bought raw meat yesterday, so you ate raw meat today." The basis of the error lies in taking the general statement, "You ate today what you bought yesterday" as meaning that you ate it *in the same state*. The rawness of the meat is an accidental circumstance not implied by the general rule.

Exercises

A. (1) Classify the following items (a) as inductions or descriptions, (b) as uniform or statistical. (2) Where you find the "inductive leap," state whether the leap is made to a determinate or to an indeterminate group.

1. Exactly 90 per cent of the members of our student council disapprove of dating on school nights.
2. Accepting the facts as stated above, I would guess that 90 per cent of the students at this university disapprove of dating on school nights.
3. I have read this book and examined every page, so I am safe in asserting the generalization: "All the pages in this book are white."
4. In all of the observed cases, the volume of a gas is a function of the temperature and pressure, so we may assert this function as a law.
5. All of the students in this class are hard workers, so I assume that all the students in this college are hard workers.
6. About 51 per cent of the babies born in our city are boys. The same ratio has probably held throughout the history of the human race.

B. Make a rough estimate of the probabilities of the inductions in Group A. Explain your standards of evaluation.

C. How would you answer Mill's question, from his *A System of Logic*, Vol. I, page 363? "Why is a single instance, in some cases, sufficient for a complete induction, while in others, myriads of concurring instances, without a single exception known or presumed, go such a very little way towards establishing a universal proposition? Whoever can answer this question knows more of the philosophy of logic than the wisest of the ancients, and has solved the problem of induction."

D. Is the following analogy usable both as illustration and argument? Explain.

> Bacon: "He that hath wife and children hath given hostages to fortune; for they are impediments to great enterprises, either of virtue or mischief."

E. Distinguish the induction from the analogical arguments in the following and show how the "inductive leap" is involved in each:

1. I enjoyed Arthur Koestler's last novel. The reviews say that his new one also deals with a significant current issue and shows philosophical insight, so I am sure that I will enjoy it too.

2. I enjoyed Koestler's first four novels so I am sure that I will enjoy his fifth.

3. An agnostic visited the laboratory of an astronomer and became interested in a mechanical model of the solar system which he saw there. The machine was so contrived that it showed how the various planets moved in their orbits around the sun. "Who made this ingeniously contrived mechanism?" he asked the astronomer. "No one made it," was the answer. "But that is impossible," said the agnostic, "for a machine must have a maker." "Well, then," was the astronomer's reply, "how can you assert that this gigantic machine which we call the universe, did not have a Maker?"

F. The following analogical arguments should be analyzed in terms of the 5-step procedure as used in the example on pages 449–50. We shall summarize the procedure used in the text:

(1) State the argument in the form of a hypothetical proposition, with the assumed relation and its special characteristic as the antecedent, and the inferred relation-characteristic as the consequent.

(2) Symbolize the argument as given:

(a) Symbolize the two pairs of terms whose relations are regarded as analogous, and state the analogy symbolically.

(b) Symbolize the characteristic possessed by the assumed relation and alleged to be possessed by the other.

(c) Restate the given argument symbolically.

(3) Find the common adjectives or characteristics in the two relations.

(4) Symbolize the full intended argument.

(5) Check for negative analogies, symbolized by "n."

1. Democratic elections are foolish. Are children capable of selecting their own teachers?

2. If a doctor is justified in deceiving a sick patient, if there is no harm in telling the children about Santa Claus, if a stage manager in case of fire behind the scenes ought to deceive the audience so as to avert a panic, it is only logical to conclude that there is no wrong in cribbing at an exam. (Castell)

3. A determinist argued that it was absurd to show moral indignation toward our fellow human beings because of

their cruelty, their injustice, their pride and self-love, and their callousness. Like the lower animals and inanimate objects, he said, human beings follow the law of their natures. They are what they are because of the environmental causes which make them what they are. To be angry with them, then, is like being angry with the stone for falling or with the flame for rising.

4. Henry George: "We would hold it a crime if a transatlantic liner were not brought to a stop by a signal of distress from a mere fishing smack. Yet a miner is entombed alive, a painter falls from a scaffold, a brakeman is crushed in coupling cars, a merchant faces financial ruin, and organized society leaves widow and child to bitter want or degradation."

5. Plato, *Republic*: "Are dogs divided into hes and shes, or do they both share equally in hunting and in keeping watch, and in the other duties of dogs? Do we entrust to the males the entire and exclusive care of the flocks, while we leave the females at home, under the idea that the bearing and suckling of their puppies is labor enough for them? No, they share alike in the various duties, the only difference being one of strength. Then, since the difference between men and women consists only in the fact that men beget and women bear children, women ought to follow the same pursuits which men follow, and they ought to receive the same education and training."

6. Bacon, *The True Greatness of Kingdoms:* Nobody can be healthful without exercise, neither natural body nor politic: and, certainly, to a kingdom or estate, a just and honorable war is the true exercise. A civil war, indeed, is like the heat of a fever; but a foreign war is like the heat of exercise, and serveth to keep the body in health; for in a slothful peace, both courages will effeminate and manners corrupt."

7. Newell Dwight Hillis: "The canvas Raphael painted has endured for three centuries. But has God ordained that the canvas shall be preserved while the artist has fallen into dust? Is 'In Memoriam' more than Tennyson? Is St. Paul's Cathedral more than Sir Christopher Wren, its architect? Is the leaf to live, while the tree dies? Reason and conscience whisper, 'It cannot be. If thoughts live, the thinker cannot die. To suppose that death ends all is intellectually as absurd as it is morally monstrous.'"
(Cited by Castell.)

G. We noted three fallacies of induction: Hasty Generalization, Composition, Division, and the error of "Generalities" (the Fallacy of Accident). In the group below you will find one example of each:

1. Thrift, since it enriches the individual, can hardly fail to benefit the community.
2. You are inconsistent. You say that you enjoy jokes, but now, when the joke is on you, you say that you do not enjoy it.
3. Three times during the past month I have read about paroled convicts who committed new crimes. This proves that "once a criminal, always a criminal."
4. Every nation seeks to perpetuate its existence, so that it is unthinkable that any statesman would sacrifice his country's existence for the welfare of others. It is therefore unthinkable that any individual can sacrifice his own existence for the welfare of others.

H. Miscellaneous Fallacies of Induction and Accident

1. Whatever is the cause of evil is itself an evil. Religion has caused much evil in the world, such as wars and persecution. So religion is an evil thing.
2. You should not major in philosophy, for then you may become a philosopher, and what kind of world would we have if everyone was a philosopher? Who would do the menial jobs?
3. I have talked with a number of Chinese laundrymen, and they do not seem to be men of high culture. So I conclude that the Chinese people do not have much culture.
4. Since unemployment is an evil, anything that creates a demand for labor is a social blessing. We should therefore welcome wars, earthquakes, tornadoes, hurricanes, fires, and sabotage, for all these create a great deal of work.
5. You say that you believe in socialism, and if socialism means anything at all, it means equality of wealth. You have more wealth than the average. Why don't you begin by giving it away until you are down to the average?
6. Napoleon got along on only five hours of sleep, so that is all the sleep anyone really needs. (Show how this example may illustrate two of the fallacies.)
7. Whatever you have not lost you still have. You have not lost your horns. Therefore you still have them.
8. The steelworkers will benefit from an increase in their wages. So will the automobile workers. So will the bricklayers and everybody else. So we could easily have universal prosperity if a wage increase were given to everybody.

9. I have noted that Edison, Ford, and other successful men did not have college educations. Evidently most famous men did not go to college.

10. You are not what I am. I am a human being. Therefore, you are not a human being.

11. There are exceptions to every rule. But this statement is itself a rule, so there must be exceptions to it. So if the rule is true it must also be false.

12. All generalizations are false, including this one.

13. Epimenides, the Cretan, said, "All Cretans are liars." If this were true, then Epimenides was also a liar, since he was a Cretan. If he was a liar, then his statement is a lie, so we may conclude that Cretans are not liars. If they are not liars, then we may believe Epimenides. Then it must be true that all Cretans are liars. But if so, then Epimenides is also a liar, etc.

14. All Indians walk single file. How do I know that? I once saw an Indian walk that way.

Chapter 18

Statistics

Section I: The Need for Statistics

Is the divorce rate high in the movie colony in Hollywood? The reader will probably answer this question with an emphatic Yes, but let us now ask a second question: How does the reader know? By what he has read in the newspapers concerning the breaking-up of alliances among the stars and starlets? It is well to remember, however, that items concerning prominent persons receive a disproportionate amount of publicity and that judgments based upon "what everybody knows" may be snap judgments. If the reader is really interested in knowing the answer to our first question, then he should consult the statistics concerning the divorce rate per thousand of population in Hollywood, the rate for the rest of the United States, and he should then compare these rates with each other. "High" is a relative term, and means high in terms of some standard. Does the United States as a whole have a high divorce rate? In relation to which standard? In comparison with the rest of the world? With the rate in the United States 100 years ago? In any case, only the statistics can give us answers which are something more than mere guesses.

A college administration is interested in establishing admission standards in order to limit admission to students who will have a fair chance to succeed. One of the deans proposes that an entrance examination be given to all applicants. Applicants in the lowest percentiles of those who take such a test, he contends, are highly unlikely to pass their freshman courses. A few will pass, he admits, but the great majority will not. How does he know this? He cites the fact that colleges which use such examinations have found a high *correlation* between a student's success on the examination and his subsequent success in his college work. To say that a correlation exists does not mean that every student who does well on the entrance test will do well in his college work, and vice versa. It does not mean that there is a "one-to-one" relationship, or an exact correspondence between the two variables, but only that in a large group there is a definite *tendency* for students who do well in one variable to do well in the other. In general, the better a student does in his entrance examination, the better he will do in his college work. A correlation also establishes a definite probability that any student who gets a certain score on the entrance examination will have a given chance of success.

Our illustrations point to the frequent need for numerical information concerning groups. Statistics is the science that deals with the collection, classification, and evaluation of large masses of numerical or quantitative facts concerning groups. Statistical information is indispensable in such varied fields as market research, economic trends, insurance rates, opinion polls, education, population trends, and many others. Statistics is a very complex and highly developed science, but we shall touch on only a minute portion of its principles and problems.

Our primary concern will be to clarify the logical principles used in statistics, in particular, the use of the inductive process. Our discussion in this chapter will deal, accordingly, with two aspects of our subject matter. We shall first explain the nature of a *statistical description,* i.e., the techniques used by statisticians to describe large masses of data, whether by averages or correlations. We shall then discuss *statistical inductions,* which draw generalizations by making an "inductive leap," from statistical descriptions or samples.

Section II: Statistical Descriptions

We shall now consider some aspects of statistical descriptions. A broad division will be made between two types of statistical descriptions. As an example of one type, assume that we desire a "picture" of the yearly incomes of Americans. We know that Americans receive different incomes, but there is an enormous amount of "raw data" here, and we would like to know how these incomes break down into various classifications so that we may have a clear picture of the distribution of such incomes. How many receive less than $2,500 per year? How many between $2,500 and $5,000, etc.? The statistician's "frequency tables" give us this type of information. He may also give us a convenient *summary* of this classified material in the form of "averages" or statements of "central tendencies."

In our example, the description involved only one characteristic, namely, incomes. But we may also desire a description which shows the relationship of two or more characteristics to each other, as in our illustration of the relationship between entrance examinations and college grades. We desire to know whether the extremes in one case are the same as the extremes in the other, and whether those falling in the middle of one group are the same as those in the middle of the other. Such descriptions deal with more than one variable.

Our discussion of statistical descriptions will thus divide into two parts, into descriptions which deal with one characteristic or variable, and those which deal with more than one. We shall devote special attention to one example of each type: averages, which deal with one variable, and correlations, which deal with more than one. Averages, or statements of "central tendencies," will be discussed in Section III. In Section IV we shall discuss "measures of dispersion," which indicate the variation of the items in connection with averages. Correlations will be examined in Section V.

Before we go on to discuss these special types of statistical descriptions we shall note some of the preliminary aspects of a statistical investigation, i.e., the manner in which such an investigation begins. When confronted with a large mass of unassembled data, the first important task is that of classification and definition. Some of the special features involved in this task may be conveniently set forth in terms of the criteria to which a good classification should conform.

a. The terms should be clearly defined

If we are gathering statistics on unemployment, the term "unemployed" should be clearly defined. Does it mean wholly or partially unemployed? Is a worker in a seasonal industry, such as canning, "unemployed" during the slack season? Does a temporary lay-off constitute unemployment? Should an individual who does not desire steady work be called unemployed? Are workers on strike unemployed? Our statistics will have little value without such careful definitions.

b. There should be sufficient classes to cover all of the data

The classification should be exhaustive of all of the classes involved, i.e., all data should be included. To illustrate: A classification of religious denominations in the United States into Protestant, Roman Catholic, and Jewish, would violate this rule, for it omits Eastern Orthodox, Christian Science, Mormon, etc. When the class of "All others" or "Miscellaneous" is used, this designation should not cover important classes.

c. Only one principle of classification should be used

A classification of college students into majors in the physical sciences, biological sciences, social sciences, humanities, and summer-school students would violate this rule, for "summer school" is not a type of major. Controversies may also arise over subtle violations of this rule. A classification of Christian religious denominations into Methodist, Episcopalian, Presbyterian, Baptist, Lutheran, Roman Catholic, etc., would indicate that the Roman Catholics were the largest religious group. This classification would ignore the bonds that unite all sects within the "Protestant Church."

d. The classes should not overlap

The classes should be mutually exclusive of each other. Our classification of students above would also involve overlapping, since various types of majors who go to summer school would be counted twice. Working students, classified into those who work by day and those who work by night might also involve overlapping for those who work both afternoons and nights. Librarians often find it difficult to avoid this error in classifying books. Should a history of politics be classified as history or political science? Henry James, J. M. Whistler, and T. S. Eliot may be classified under the headings of American or English writers, painters, and poets, since they were American by birth and English by adoption.

After our data have been properly classified and grouped, they may be arranged more systematically in a number of ways.

We shall not describe the various methods used in presenting material, as by graphs, tables, and so on, except to note that a typical form of classification is found in the "frequency tables," or "frequency distributions," which classify numerical data according to size, i.e., with respect to the number of individuals who have a given characteristic. A simple example is a list of grades in an examination:

Number of students	Grades
5	91–100
12	81– 90
26	71– 80
7	61– 70
3	0– 60

This material may also be exhibited by bars, or pictograms, or other devices.

We shall now discuss the nature of averages, or statistical descriptions which deal with a single characteristic or variable.

Section III: Statistical Averages

College students are interested in many kinds of averages. They are interested in the batting averages of professional baseball players. They are also interested in the average earnings of doctors and lawyers and engineers, and perhaps in what an "average day" in the consular service is like. But just what is meant by "average"? By "average" the statistician means a statement, in summary form, of the "central tendency" in a group of items. By means of such statements of central tendencies, the numerical characteristics of groups may be compared with each other. The statistician uses three types of averages, i.e., three ways in which central tendencies are exhibited: the arithmetic mean, the mode, and the median. Each of these averages states the central tendency in a different way, and we shall find that each has its own peculiar usefulness and limitations. Each is appropriate for some groups and inappropriate for others. We shall discuss each in turn.

1. The arithmetic mean

The arithmetic mean, which is what most persons have in mind when they speak of "the average," is derived by adding the items and dividing by the number of cases. Thus, if we had a series of items such as 4, 5, 6, 7, 8, 12, the additive total is 42. We then divide by 6 (the number of items) and we have the arithmetic mean: 7. Note that the average does not describe any particular individual in the group, except coincidentally, but gives us only the central tendency in the group as a whole.

In taking the mean, each item should be properly "weighted." Consider the following case. We wish to determine the average grades (the mean) of the students who take an elementary accounting course in a college. We find that the average in Section A is 72. This section has forty students. The average in Section B with twenty students is 82, and it is 92 in Section C with ten students. Shall we add these averages together and divide by three? The mean, if we do this, would be shown as 82 (246/3). But this would be incorrect, for the items are not properly weighted. Each class average should be multiplied, or weighted, by the number of students in the class, and the total divided by the total number of students. We shall then find that our fraction is 5440/70, and that the average is 77.7. The same result, of course, would have been obtained by taking each individual's score, adding all together, and dividing by 70; but it is often more convenient to classify the items before taking the mean.

An average of the kind just described is called a "weighted mean." In a very strict sense, of course, all averages are weighted, since the "simple" mean, illustrated by our first example, is one in which each item has a weight of *one*. In each of the accounting classes each student had a weight of one, so that the total of the grades for each class would be divided by the number of students. A simple mean is one in which each item is multiplied by one, in entering into the average. In general, however, "weighted average" is reserved for cases in which we multiply by numbers other than one.

The use of the weighted mean is particularly important in averages such as the Consumer's Price Index (or "cost-of-living" index) regularly compiled by the Bureau of Labor Statistics of the U. S. Department of Labor. The Bureau takes a typical expenditure for an average family, in a period chosen as standard, and then computes the changing costs of the same items at regular intervals. But some of these items are more important than others, and so the items are given different "weights." In the following tables we find the percentage weights given to different items in the general Consumer's Price Index (December, 1957) and the weighting of the items which go into the food index:

Consumer's price index		*Food index*	
Food	28.6	Cereals and bakery products	3.2
Housing	32.9	Meats, poultry, and fish	6.8
Apparel	9.	Dairy products	4.
Transportation	11.5	Fruits and vegetables	4.2
Medical care	5.3	Other foods at home	5.6
Personal care	2.2	Food away from home:	
Reading and recreation	5.3	restaurant meals	4.8
Others goods and services	5.2		
	100.		28.6

Thus a rise in the price of one item will not influence the average as much as a rise in the price of another. Each cost is multiplied by its percentage in the whole group, and the total divided by 100, since we multiply by percentages here, and not by a given number of items as in the example of the accounting students.

A warning is required concerning the sometimes illusory appearance of mathematical accuracy in statistics, particularly when we use the arithmetic mean. Let us assume that we wish to know the average number of hours a student devotes to his studies each day. He tells us that he put in the following hours each day in a given week: 3, 4, 5½, 4, 3, 2. The total is 21½; divided by 6, we find that the mean is 3.5833. The "accuracy" of this mean figured to the fourth decimal point, is misleading, since the student probably made a rough guess as to the approximate time he studied each day. The accuracy of the mean would then be grotesque as compared with the carelessness with which the data was compiled.

The chief limitation of the mean as an "average" is that the mean may be misleading as an exhibition of the central tendency in a particular group. This will occur when there is an extremely wide range between the extremes in a group. There is then a wide "dispersion," or "deviation," of many items from the mean. For example, the mean of the following group is 35:

3, 19, 31, 97, 25. Four out of the five items are below the mean because of the wide range and the extreme dispersion of the items from the mean. The mean, in this case, is a misleading "average." The extent of the range is also a very important consideration when we wish to compare two groups with respect to their central tendencies. To illustrate: In Factory A, nine individuals receive $5,000 per year, and one man receives $33,000. In Factory B, eight individuals receive $7,500 each; one receives $8,000, and one receives $10,000. The mean is exactly the same for both ($7,800) but the arithmetic mean is a rather meaningless "average" when applied to the first group. It is because of such limitations that statisticians use other types of averages.

2. The mode

The mode is "the average" in the sense that it is the most typical case, i.e., the item which occurs most frequently. In Factory A the mode was $5,000; in B it was $7,500. In popular language, when we speak of the "average American girl" we mean the modal girl, the type who occurs most frequently or is most frequently encountered. The term "mode" is also used for "style," meaning what is in fashion or use.

The mode is more reliable than the mean in one important respect: it is not influenced by extreme variations, and may thus be a better indicator when we wish to compare two groups, such as the two factories. But the mode also suffers from a serious limitation, as when it is used to describe the central tendency of an array of items such as the following: 9, 8, 7, 6, 3, 2, 2, 2, 1, 1. The mode is 2, but the mean (4.1) is certainly more indicative of the central tendency here. Note also that it is sometimes impossible to state the mode, as when no item occurs more than once.

3. The median

In a report of the Census Bureau concerning the incomes of the American people for the year 1946, just before the postwar inflation got under way, the "median" income for all American families was stated as being $2,378. This meant that half the nation's 40,075,000 families received more than that amount and that half received less. The median, in other words, is the value of the middle item in a series of items arranged in the order of magnitude from the lowest number to the highest number. Thus, in the following series of items: 2, 2, 3, 3, 4, 4, 4, 5, 5, 6, 6, 6, 8, 8, 8, 9, 9, 9, 9, 9, 9, the underlined number is the median, since there are 21 items, of which there are 10 below this item and 10 above in the order of the series. When the number of items is an even number, the median is the arithmetic mean of the two middle items. In the series: 2, 5, 6, 8, 15, 29, the median is 7. The number of these items is even (6 items). 6 and 8 are the middle numbers, and 7 is the mean of these numbers.

The median, unlike the mean, is not influenced by wide variations, but may be misleading as a measure of central tendency when we have a peculiar range such as the following: 2, 2, 2, 2, 2, 2, 2, 2, 58, 76. The median here is 2, the same as the mode. The mean would also be misleading here. This illustrates the need for supplementary information when an average is stated, whether it be the mean, mode, or median.

We shall now sum up our discussion of averages. (1) There are three ways whereby the average, or central tendency of a group may be exhibited: the mean, the mode, and the median. It is generally useful to know all three, though for some purposes, and depending upon the nature of the array, one of the three averages may give us more useful information than the others. (2) We should always remember that when the range of variations among the items is very large, the three averages may give us quite different results, and each may be misleading in different ways. When the range of variations within the group is small, all three averages will give us approximately the same results, as in the following: 3, 4, 5, 6, 6, 7, 8, 9. The mean is approximately 7; the mode and median are 6 each. But the average alone will not tell us how widely the items deviate from each other, nor what the range is. In order to furnish us with this necessary supplementary information, statisticians have devised methods for indicating the range or dispersion of the items. We shall now turn our attention to these measures of dispersion, which will indicate the extent of the fluctuations of a given series or array of items.

Section IV: Measures of Dispersion

By "measure of dispersion" is meant a number which indicates the extent to which the items differ in size from the average. We have seen that the average may be unreliable as a picture of the central tendency within a group; thus it becomes necessary to know how closely most of the items resemble the average. The devices used here are called dispersion or deviation numbers. We shall examine a few of the important ones.

1. The range

The range is the numerical difference between the lowest and the highest number in the group plus 1. If grades in a class run from 43 to 92, the range is 49 plus 1, or 50. "The mean is 77; the range, 50" gives us the average and the extent to which the items are scattered. It is obvious that the same average may be found among different ranges. The same range may also be found among different averages, as in the following two groups: (A) 1, 7, 8, 9, 10, and (B) 1, 1, 2, 2, 10. The ranges are the same but the averages quite different. The range is a satisfactory measure for some purposes, but does not tell us what the probabilities are that a given individual's score will fall within a certain part of the range, nor the probable percentage of cases which will fall within a certain distance from the mean. Devices for indicating such information will now be considered.

2. The mean deviation

In the series of grades: 90, 84, 80, 70, 66, the mean is 78. The "mean deviation" states the average (mean) deviation of the items from the mean. To compute it we find the numerical difference between each item and the mean, always subtracting the lower number from the higher. When the item is higher than the mean, subtract the mean from it; when the mean is higher, do the reverse. Plus and minus signs are ignored in taking the mean of these items, for otherwise the result would be zero. We then add the deviations, and divide by the number of items. In the series of grades above, the deviations from the mean are 12, 6, 2, 8, 12. The mean of these numbers is 8; so the "mean deviation" is 8. This item is sometimes called the "average deviation" or "average error" (which does *not* mean "mistake"). The mean deviation may also be computed for the mode and the median, when these are used as averages.

The value of the mean deviation is that it informs us that it is probable that most items will fall within the range of 78 ± 8, or between 86 and 70; i.e., most individual scores will fall within these limits. It lacks a high degree of accuracy as a guide, however, since the same relative importance is given to large deviations from the mean as is given to small ones. A large deviation, however, makes the mean less representative of the central tendency than would be the case if all of the deviations were small. A mean deviation does not adequately reflect the importance of large deviations. In order to correct this fault statisticians use the next measure.

3. The standard deviation

This is the most widely used measure, for it corrects the last-mentioned inadequacy of the mean deviation. It does this by squaring the deviations from the mean before their sum is taken; then it finds the mean of the sum of the squared deviations, and then takes the square root of this mean. We may thus define the standard deviation as the square root of the mean of the sum of the squares of the deviations. In our example above, we would first square each deviation as follows: 144, 36, 4, 64, 144. The sum of these is 392. We then divide by the number of items (5), and we find that the mean of the squares is 78.4. The square root of 78.4 is 8.85, the standard deviation. This is .85 higher than the mean deviation, and tells us that the scattering was greater than was indicated by the mean deviation. The formula for the standard deviation, symbolized by "σ" (sigma) or "S.D." is $\sqrt{\dfrac{\Sigma d^2}{n}}$, in which Σ stands for "summation," or "sum of," "d" for the deviations, and "n" for the number of the items.

Statisticians estimate that there is a probability that approximately two-thirds of the items will fall within the range of the mean, plus or minus the standard deviation. In our previous example, this means that two-thirds of the items will fall within the range of 78 ± 8.85. This probability, however, will hold only when the items are distributed in approximate accordance with the curve of "normal probability." The so-called "normal probability curve" refers to a symmetrical distribution around the mean, as in the following distribution: 95, 90, 85, 80, 75, 70, 65, 60, 55. This is a symmetrical distribution around the mean of 75. Another popular measure used in this connection is the "probable error" (an ambiguous expression used in different senses by statisticians), which usually refers to ".6745 of the standard deviation." Thus, when we know the mean and the "probable error," we know that approximately 50 per cent of the items will fall within the limits of the mean, plus or minus the probable error.

Section V: Correlations

We are now ready to discuss statistical descriptions which show the relationship of two or more characteristics to each other. Our discussion will be limited to the relations of two characteristics or variables. Let us say that we suspect that there is a definite relationship between the I.Q.'s of students and their grades, and wish to determine whether they are correlated, and if so, to what degree. Two variables are said to be correlated when in groups of corresponding instances, an increase or decrease in one variable is accompanied by an increase or decrease in the other, whether in the same or in the opposite direction. This is the common core of meaning in all usages of this term, but some writers limit the use of "correlations" to relationships which are less than uniform and use the term "function" for uniform relationships. It will be recalled that we previously used the term "function" for uniform correlations, illustrated by Galileo's discovery that the speed of a falling body is a function of the time of its fall. In what follows we shall call a function a "perfect correlation," but we shall be primarily concerned, in our discussions, with connections which are less than uniform, i.e., with groups which show conflicting trends.

Before proceeding to discuss the more technical forms of correlations we shall examine an allied method, called "statistical associations," for noting the association or connection between two characteristics.

Consider a simple problem: Are red-heads hot-tempered? We require statistical information to answer this question. But first, the question should be rephrased to make its problem clearer: Is there a greater tendency for red-heads to be hot-tempered than for non-red-heads? The statement that a certain percentage of red-heads are hot-tempered would be ambiguous with respect to significance unless we knew how the percentage compared with that of other groups. Our problem, then, is to determine whether there is some special connection between red-heads and hot-tempers. Is there a greater tendency for red-heads to be hot-tempered than for non-red-heads? Is the probability greater that a red-head will be hot-tempered than that others will be?

A statistical association should furnish us with the following data: (1) the number of A's which are B's, (2) the number of A's which are ~B's, (3) the number of ~A's which are B's, and (4) the number of ~A's which are ~B's. Using the symbols "R" for red-heads, "~R" for non-red-heads, "T" for hot-tempered persons, and "~T" for persons who lack hot tempers, we shall study a sample group of 1,000 persons and classify our data as above. (The figures we use will be purely imaginary.) Let us assume that we find that 200 persons in our sample group are R's, that 800 are ~R's, that 80 of the R's are T's, and that 200 of the ~R's are T's. We then assemble our data in a chart such as the following:

	T's	~T's
200 R's	80	120
800 ~R's	200	600
(1,000)	(280 T's)	(720 ~T's) = (1,000)

Our table indicates that 280 persons in 1,000 are hot-tempered, or 28 per cent. We also find that among the 200 red-heads, 80 or 40 per cent are hot-tempered, and that among the 800 non-red-heads, 200 or 25 per cent, are hot-tempered. This indicates that there is a greater tendency for red-heads than for non-red-heads to be hot-tempered. Similar procedures may be used in many other problems, such as whether there is a special tendency for quartz miners to contract silicosis, etc.

The method of statistical associations, however, is powerless to answer a question such as the following: What is the relationship between the height and weight of individuals? For here we cannot divide our categories into mutually exclusive pairs, but must deal with indefinitely large series of degrees in our variables. The relationship of the two variables, height and weight, will be found to fluctuate in different degrees, and for such problems we need the more precise mathematical method of correlations.

Correlations are expressed in numbers, running from +1.00 to −1.00. A *positive* invariant correlation is expressed by +1.00, which means that an increase in one variable is invariably accompanied by a corresponding increase in the other variable. An *inverse* invariant correlation expressed by −1.00 means that an increase in one variable is invariably accompanied by a decrease in the other. A correlation of 0 (zero) expresses the notion of a complete absence of connection or correlation, and corresponds to the concept of 50 per cent in probabilities. When we toss a coin, there is an even chance that it will fall heads or tails; there is thus no correlation between its fallings heads and the fact that it is tossed. But a correlation of +.5 means that there is a definite tendency toward positive correlation, and has no similarity to the concept of .5 in probabilities.

Let us now examine a very simple problem of correlation. Let us imagine that we are seeking to determine the relationship between the height and weight of the warriors in a primitive tribe. Assume that we collect the following data:

Individual	Height	Weight
A	5′ 6″	150
B	5′ 7″	155
C	5′ 8″	160
D	5′ 9″	165
E	5′ 10″	170
F	5′ 11″	175
G	6′	180

These highly unlikely data may be assembled and diagrammed as in the "scatter plot" shown below. We draw a diagram, marked off as follows: The vertical line, called the "ordinate," indicates the varying heights; the horizontal line, called the *abscissa* indicates the varying weights. We then draw points, representing each individual, on the intersections of the two series, and complete our diagram by connecting the dots by a line:

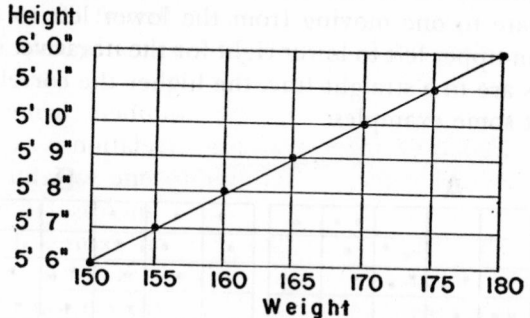

This example represents a case of perfect positive correlation. An increase in one variable is accompanied by an increase in the other. Note the "correlation picture" which the line represents. A straight line moving from the lower left to the upper right indicates a perfect positive correlation.

If the correlation were a perfect negative one, the line would move from the upper left to the lower right. Example: Let us assume that you are on a Cub plane flying home from a distance of 600 miles at the uniform speed of 100 miles per hour. You decide to keep a record of your distance from your destination in terms of the two variables, "time elapsed" and "miles to go." As the number of "elapsed hours" increases (moving upward along the ordinate), the "distance to go" decreases, so that the higher the point on the ordinate, the lower the point on the abscissa, viz.:

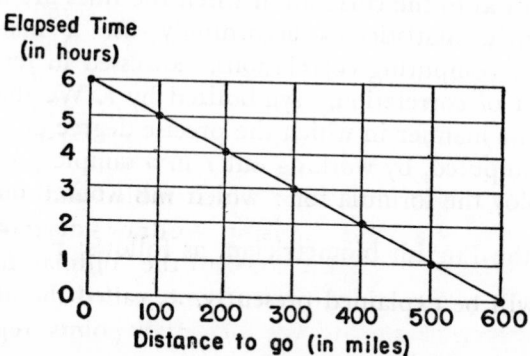

When the correlation is imperfect, but definite or "high," the "line" will tend to approximate to one of the two lines we have described. When the correlation is positive, the line will approximate to one moving from the lower left to the upper right; from upper left to lower right for the negative. The closer the points are to a straight line, the higher the correlation. Let us look at some examples:

The dots in A indicate a higher positive correlation than the negative correlation in B. When there is little or no correlation, the dots will be scattered with no semblance of a line, as in C:

The scatter plots, however, give us only a general and imperfect idea as to the correlation when the lines are only fairly well defined. Statisticians accordingly use a mathematical method for computing correlations, expressed in terms of the "coefficient of correlation," symbolized by r. We shall shortly examine the manner in which the precise degree of correlation may be computed, by working out r in a sample problem. We shall employ the formula for r which was worked out by Karl Pearson, the English biometrician, as follows: $r = \dfrac{\Sigma xy}{n\sigma_x\sigma_y}$. This formula will be explained presently.

Our task, let us say, is to determine the correlation between the scores received by students on an imaginary entrance examination and their subsequent grades in their college work. We shall deal with an oversimplified problem, using a small number of cases for simplicity in exposition, with the warning, however, that a small number of cases is usually an unreliable basis for judgment. We gather our data into two tables, distributing the items in the two variables:

Student	Entrance Grade	College Average
A	94	84
B	88	82
C	86	88
D	84	86
E	78	80
F	74	68
G	70	72
H	66	68

We see at a glance that the correlation is not a perfect one, but nevertheless there does appear to be a real connection. We shall now determine its precise degree by working out r. We assemble our data in a chart such as the following:

1	2	3	4	5	6	7
Entrance Examination	College Average	Deviation of Entrance Exam. from Mean (x)	Deviation of College Averages from Mean (y)	x^2	y^2	xy
94	84	14	5	196	25	70
88	82	8	3	64	9	24
86	88	6	9	36	81	54
84	86	4	7	16	49	28
78	80	—2	1	4	1	—2
74	70	—6	—9	36	81	54
70	72	—10	—7	100	49	70
66	68	—14	—11	196	121	154
Mean: 80	Mean: 78.75			648 (Σx^2)	416 (Σy^2)	452 (Σxy)

We shall now explain this chart. The first two columns simply give us our tables. The mean of each is shown at the bottom of these columns. The mean of the first is 80 (obtained by dividing the sum of the items by the number of items), and the mean of the second column is 78.75. The third column tells us how each item in Column 1 deviates from the mean of 80. These are called the x deviations. Column 4 does the same for the deviations in Column 2, and gives us the y deviations. In Column 5, headed by "x^2" we find the x's squared, and at the bottom of the column we find their sum, 648. In Column 6 we find the y's squared, also the sum, and in Column 7 "xy" means "the x deviation times the y deviation." On the top lines of Columns 3 and 4 the x item was 14, the y item 5; their product 70, as shown on the top line of Column 7. Note that one of the items in the last column has a minus sign before it. Minus numbers must always be subtracted from the total of the plus items.

The Pearson formula: $r = \dfrac{\Sigma xy}{n\sigma_x\sigma_y}$ worked out for this problem tells us that the coefficient of correlation is $+.87$. This formula is interpreted as follows:

1. Σxy refers to the number 452 in the last column, or the sum of the xy's.

2. In the denominator we find n, which stands for the number of items found in the two sets of variables, i.e., 8.

3. The symbol σ stands for "Standard Deviation." Thus, σ_x stands for the standard deviation in the x column (Column 3) and σ_y for the standard deviation in the y column (Column 4). The formula for the standard deviation, as noted earlier, is $\sqrt{\dfrac{\Sigma d^2}{n}}$. To work this out for the x variable, we proceed as follows: Σd^2 refers to the sum of the squares of all of the deviations found in Column 3, since d stands for deviation. The sum of these deviations is 648 (Column 5). We now divide by n, or 8, and we get 81. We must now find the square root of this number. It is 9. The standard deviation for x, or σ_x is thus 9. The standard deviation for y is worked out in exactly the same manner. We must first find Σd^2 for y. Σy^2 is 416. Divide by 8 and we

get 52. The square root of 52 is the standard deviation for y, or 7.21.*

Our standard deviations for x and y are 9 and 7.21 respectively. We are now ready for the final step, in which we give specific values to the symbols in the Pearson formula:

$$r = \frac{\Sigma xy(452)}{n(8)\sigma_x(9)\sigma_y(7.21)} = \frac{452}{519.12} = +.87$$

The interpretation of the "coefficient of correlation," or r, requires some comment. Statisticians interpret r as an indicator of the dependence between a variable A and another variable, B. When r, for example, has a value of .5, this is said to indicate a "37 per cent dependence" between the two variables. This means that among all of the factors which determine the amount of B, the variable A will account for 37 per cent of its amount. When the coefficient of correlation is .95 the degree of dependence is 75 per cent; when .99, 88 per cent. Thus, as remarked earlier, a coefficient of correlation of .87 does not mean "a probability of 87 per cent." The higher the coefficient, however, the higher the degree of association between the two variables, and the higher the probability that a change in one variable will be accompanied by a corresponding positive or inverse change in the other.

The degree of association or dependence is often interpreted in accordance with R. E. Chaddock's classification, in his *Principles and Methods of Statistics*. Correlations of less than .3

---

* The manner in which this square root was derived is shown in this footnote for the benefit of those readers who have *forgotten* the process:

7.21
$\sqrt{52.0000}$... (Add 0's according to need)

  49   ... Find the largest number which, when squared, will go into 52. This is 7. (7 × 7 is 49.) Place 7 above the top line, and subtract 49 from 52.

 3.00 ... Bring down two 0's and place a decimal point to the right of 7.

 2.84 ... The number 2.84 is derived as follows: Double the first number at the top: 2 × 7 is 14. Now find the number which, when placed at the right of 14, and then multiplied by that number, will come closest to 3.00. We try a 2 after 14: 142, and then multiply by 2, and we get 2.84. (141 × 1 would be too small; 143 × 3 too large). Now place a 2 after the 7 above the top line.

  1600
  1441 ...We now double 72: 144. We place a 1 at the right of 144 and multiply by 1. Now place the 1 at the right of 7.2, etc.

indicate a low degree of association and are of little significance, especially when the number of related items is small, though this proviso applies in all cases. A correlation of .3 or more, but less than .5, indicates a "moderate" degree of association; .5 and less than .7, "marked" association; .7 and less than .9, "high"; and .9 and over indicates a "very close" association and a high degree of dependence between the variables.

The reader may be interested in a few examples of actual correlations based upon adequate sampling. The following items are from R. S. Woodworth's *Psychology*: The coefficient of correlation between the I.Q.'s of identical twins is +.9, i.e., there is a very close association between them, so that if we find that the I.Q. of one is high, it is very likely that the I.Q. of the other will be high also. In fraternal twins, the coefficient is +.7. The coefficient of correlation between the I.Q.'s and grades in a group of college students is +.6. The correlation between the I.Q.'s of parents and children is +.3. The coefficient of correlation between the height of the forehead and intelligence is .00.

Section VI: Statistical Inductions and Sampling Procedures

We have completed our discussion of statistical descriptions, and will now turn our attention to *statistical inductions*. The principles of inductive logic studied in the previous chapter are relevant here. An induction, as we already know, involves the inductive leap from "some" to "all." Statistical inductions are no exception to this rule. They simply generalize from statistical samples. Two basic points to keep in mind in this discussion are (1) the distinction between a statistical description and a statistical induction, and (2) the precise nature of the inference that is made when we generalize from a statistical sample.

Two earlier distinctions will be helpful. One is the distinction between a "perfect induction" and a genuine generalization. In the former we merely describe each and every member of a collection. No inference is involved in such descriptions. Similarly, a statistical description which describes each and every item in a group, in the form of a complete tabulation, involves no inference. A second distinction is that between groups or populations that are determinate or definite in number, and those that are indeterminate or indefinite in number. Inductions may be made with respect to both kinds of groups.

Statistical inductions, then, involve generalizations made on the basis of statistical samples, and the leap may be made to a determinate or to an indeterminate group. Thus, if we were to desire a statistical picture of the transportation habits of Chicagoans, we would take a sample, instead of interviewing everybody in a city of 4 millions. The description in the sample would then be generalized, and we would have an induction concerning a determinate group. On the other hand, we generalize to an indeterminate group if we take a sample of the workers in quartz mining, find that a certain proportion contract silicosis (under certain conditions), and then infer that what holds for the sample will hold for any group of individuals who work in this industry.

Note that a correlation is not necessarily a generalization. A correlation may be a mere description, like a "perfect induction," when it simply describes the correlation which holds for a given population. An example would be a study of the correlation between I.Q.'s and grades at a given college, if based upon the record of each and every student. No induction here. But if we were to use our study as a *sample* and generalize from it to the statement, "All college student groups will show the coefficient of correlation, r, between I.Q.'s and grades," we would have an example of statistical induction, albeit a bad one. In this induction we referred to an indeterminate group, but we may also use a correlation as a sample for a determinate group. For example, instead of examining the I.Q.'s and grades of all of the students at a college, we might take a sampling of these items, find the correlation in the sample, and then generalize to *all* of the students at the *same* college.

The probability of statistical inductions is of course determined by the same considerations we discussed earlier. A statistical induction which uses simple enumeration can be no more probable than any other induction which uses that method, despite the complicated mathematical computations involved in the description of the sample. The reliability of statistical inductions, will depend, as usual, upon the fairness or representativeness of the sample. Unless the sample is a fair one, the leap from it will be into the realm of guesswork. Since the sample is of such great importance in determining the validity of the inference, we shall now discuss some of the aspects of good sampling procedure.

The sample should be taken at random. It should be chosen without bias. When we select a sample to prove a predetermined thesis we mislead, but we do not inform. A simple example of a random sample is illustrated by the procedure used in sampling wheat from a carload. Handfuls are taken from both ends and from the center.

A random selection means that each entity in the collection or population has an equal chance of being included in the sample. Statisticians regard the following as an ideal form of random sampling: Let us suppose that we have a barrel containing 10,000 marbles of various colors. We wish to take a sampling of 100 marbles in order to determine the colors of the marbles in the barrel. We shake the barrel thoroughly, take out a marble, note its color, replace the marble, shake thoroughly again, take out another marble, replace it, and so on. But random sampling need not take this "ideal" form. The method described can obviously not be used in taking a sample of a human population.

If we wish to sample a human population for some characteristic, such as opinion about a public issue, we might check off every nth name on a census list, and then interview these individuals. This is a random selection, and it is generally a reliable method. It can yield accurate results, provided that the sample is sufficiently large. But statisticians have also developed various devices to make the human sample more truly representative of the population. One such device is called "stratified" sampling. This technique is used by the Gallup, Roper, and other polls of public opinion. We shall describe the method as used in a national election.

A sample of 3,000 individuals may be taken, apportioned with respect to attributes that are regarded as significant in an election. The whole population is classified into subgroups: by geographical regions; by rural or urban residence; and by economic status, age, education, and declared politics. The 3,000 interviews are distributed so that each geographical area and each educational and economic group will be represented in its appropriate numerical strength. "Quotas" are then assigned to interviewers on the basis of these classifications, and individuals are then interviewed "at random" within each subgroup. When the tabulation of the interviews is completed, the result is a statistical description of the sample. The pollsters then generalize from the sample to the entire population and expect that the vote at the election will show the same proportions as the sample. Each interviewee thus represents 25,000 individuals, since there are approximately 75,000,000 voters.

This method gives us a fairer sample than does random sampling of the whole group. It guarantees that the source of the sample will be properly varied, i.e., that all of the chief classes will be represented in their due proportions.

The alert thinker will of course check carefully on the methods used in sampling before he accepts an induction concerning 75 million persons on the basis of a sample of one in 25,000. In general, the care used in seeking a representative sample will count for more than mere size, though size is also an important factor. The ill-famed and ill-fated *Literary Digest* poll used a sample consisting of millions of voters, but failed by an extremely wide margin in predicting the election of 1936. This was because its sample was not taken at random in the strict sense. The pre-election ballots were sent to names taken at random from telephone directories and lists of automobile owners, thus ignoring the large numbers of voters who were in the lower-income brackets. This, of course, was unconscious bias. The fiasco of the pollsters in the election of 1948, however, cannot be explained in this manner for they used more sophisticated methods of sampling. In that year all of the national public opinion polls predicted that Dewey would defeat Truman by a substantial margin. They erred about 10 per cent too high for Dewey and 10 per cent too low for Truman. In election forecasts between 1936 and 1948, on the other hand, the polls had never erred by more than 4 per cent. The Social Science Research Council, in analyzing the 1948 disaster, found three major errors: The pollsters stopped polling too soon and did not discover a last-minute swing to Truman; the "undecided" vote leaned toward Truman rather than Dewey; and the polltakers did not adhere strictly to the rules of stratification: they neglected the poorer districts.

On the whole, however, the polls have had an excellent forecasting record, not only in elections but in market research, as in predicting the sales of new products. The accuracy of such forecasts is established by empirical verification. Election predictions can be checked by the actual vote. This kind of verification, however, cannot be used to check the accuracy of public opinion polls on current political issues or radio and television "ratings," based on telephone calls made to homes chosen at random, with the inquiry: "Are you now 'tuned in' to TV, and if so, to which program?" In any case, it is important to remember that there is an inductive leap involved in *all* statistical inferences so that our conclusions can be no more than probable. Nevertheless, with a certain margin of error, such statistical sampling gives us predictions that are far more reliable than guesses based on personal "impressions."

There are many other aspects of good sampling procedure, but we shall note only two more. In some cases, the time at which a sample is taken may be crucial. A typical period should be used. In 1942, after the United States entered World War II, the federal government instituted "excess profits" taxes. Excess profits were defined as those in excess of average profits earned in the years 1935–39. This was regarded as a fair period, since it included good as well as bad business conditions. Finally, in taking a sample, we should know whether or not it is a good index as to the character of the whole. Thus, the military strength of the armed forces of the great powers cannot be compared by noting only one of the components of each. Each of the powers may put its chief reliance on different components, such as stockpiles of atomic bombs, rockets and missiles, or size of armies.

Section VII: Fallacies in the Use of Statistics

Statistics reduces large masses of data to understandable form and finds precise statements of tendencies or associations among variables. But statistics is not a new logical method of proof. Insofar as we draw inferences from statistical samples we use the logical principles of induction. Thus we shall find no new logical fallacies in this field. When we generalize too hastily from a sample, whether it be uniform or statistical, we commit the fallacy of hasty generalization. Nevertheless, the field of statistics affords its own sources of error, and these will be examined in this section.

Errors of inference are frequently overlooked in statistics because of the presence of mathematical figures and computations. Many persons are awed when confronted with numbers. We are also influenced by the prestige of the exact sciences such as physics and chemistry, whose impressive contributions to knowledge have come through the use of mathematical methods. The fact that statistics also uses mathematical language may lead us to assume that its findings are similarly demonstrable. The formal fallacy in such reasoning is of course obvious. An induction is never more probable merely because it is stated in mathematical form; everything depends upon the careful analysis of the facts on which such inductions are based. Statistics, of course, gives us a tool for the precise description of many facts, but its inferences are not more probable because they are in mathematical form.

The spell which numbers weave often results in our failing to see the unsoundness of arguments whose weaknesses would be palpable when not clothed in statistical garb. Special pleaders can reach opposite conclusions from any given set of statistical data. This accounts for jibes such as, "Figures don't lie, but liars figure," and, "There are three kinds of lies: ordinary lies, damnable lies, and statistics." But these cynical remarks should not be taken as criticisms of statistics. The fault never lies with the figures, or with the science, but with their careless use. It is simply not the case that "you can prove anything with figures" (or statistics), just as it is not the case that "you can prove anything by logic." It just seems that you can, to the uninitiated.

We shall now take note of some of the special sources of error to which statistical descriptions and inferences are prone.

1. First, let us summarize some of the main points already discussed in this chapter, in the form of useful admonitions. (a) We should classify our data properly, and define our terms properly and consistently. Thus, an increase in yearly incomes is meaningless unless money income is defined in relation to the cost of living. (b) When averages are used we should beware of giving an illusory impression of accuracy when the data are imprecise, as in the case of the student who studied 3.5833 hours each day. (c) Remember that a statement such as "Red-heads are

hot-tempered" is infected with the "ambiguity of significance" unless it is supported by a "statistical association." (d) In sampling procedures, we must avoid bias and choose our samples at random. We must guard against taking the sample at the wrong time, or place, or with the wrong components. Samples must also be of an adequate minimum size. A school advertised that "33 per cent of the stenographers who enrolled in our 'marriage' course married their employers." Three stenographers in all had taken the course. (e) We should note that an average or a correlation does not describe any given individual within a group. If we know the average of a group, then, for any individual taken at random from the group, we can estimate the a priori probability that he will resemble the average. But this is quite different from saying that the individual actually does have the characteristics of the average. Finally, (f) we should remember that correlations do not necessarily prove a causal connection between two variables. John Maynard Keynes has said that "sensible investigators only employ 'r' to test or confirm conclusions at which they have arrived on other grounds." (*A Treatise on Probability.*) The fact that two variables are correlated may be a wholly fortuitous matter. It was once discovered that expenditures for the British navy were correlated with the growing consumption of bananas, but this proves nothing concerning their connection. A high correlation may indicate a connection, and it justifies an initial expectation that a connection exists, but in itself it does not prove one.

2. Statisticians may find what is called a "trend line" in a "time-series." For example, the rate of industrial production may be increasing over a period of several years, and the rising trend may be projected into the future. This type of projection is the basis of all forecasting. But such forecasts are predictions based on samples and can be only probable, at best. Some forecasts based on long-run trends, as that the "gross national product" will increase on an average of 3 to 4 per cent annually over the long term, will have a high degree of probability, but the intermediate trends are much less probable. They may begin to reverse themselves on the day after a forecast is made. Intermediate trends are based on the assumption *ceteris paribus*. But the causes of business conditions are so various that no one knows all of them, and there can be no guarantee that an up-

ward (or downward) trend will continue upward (or downward) in the next few years. Similarly, we can have very little assurance when we forecast the behavior of the stock market on the basis of its performance in the recent past. The "Dow theory" of market behavior forecasts trends on the basis of "bull" and "bear" markets, but the only trend we can be sure of is in the past, and where the variables are exceedingly large, little confidence can be placed in stock-market predictions concerning the near future.

Statistical trends, then, will have higher or lower probability depending upon whether they are based on more or less stable factors. Above all, we should not regard statistical predictions with a fatalistic attitude. This attitude seems to pervade our expectation that a large number of fatal accidents will occur on a Fourth of July weekend because similar numbers of accidents have occurred in past years. Such predictions have a high degree of probability, for human patterns of careless behavior are relatively constant; but we should not think of a holiday weekend as "claiming" a certain number of victims. Safety campaigns may some day modify our behavior. In any case, there is no unvarying cause which necessarily results in a given number of accidents.

3. The improper interpretation of statistical information is especially important in correlations and statistical associations. All the relevant factors should be analyzed with care. An interesting illustration of improper interpretation is found in the following, quoted by L. S. Stebbing from an English publication: "Vaccination doesn't prevent smallpox or render it milder when contracted. More young children die from vaccination than smallpox, according to the Registrar-General's returns." We may grant the facts cited and deny or doubt the conclusion. There are several statistical situations which may be constructed on the basis of the known facts. The following situation would make the quoted conclusion false: Assume that 20 millions were vaccinated and that one million were not. Assume further that 30 vaccinated persons die of vaccination, and that three vaccinated persons and 20 non-vaccinated persons die of smallpox. Thus more people die of vaccination than of smallpox. But this does not prove that vaccination doesn't prevent smallpox, or that the cure is worse than the disease. Let us

assume that one per cent in each group were exposed to infection. Then 200,000 vaccinated persons were exposed to smallpox, of whom three died. Ten thousand unvaccinated persons were exposed, and 20 of these died. In the same proportion 400 of the vaccinated persons would have died if they had not been vaccinated.

Exercises

1. Which rules are violated in the following classifications?
   a. American political parties in 1948: Republican, Democratic, Progressive, Socialist, and Communist.
   b. American political parties in 1956: Democratic, Republican, Progressive, and radical.
   c. Schools: technical, professional, public, private, and liberal arts.
   d. Religions: Christian, Jewish, Moslem, and miscellaneous.
   e. Criminals: born, habitual, professional, occasional, and emotional.
2. State the mean, the mode, and the median in the following series:

$$1, 2, 3, 3, 4, 5, 6, 6, 6, 7, 8, 9$$

3. A factory employs 100 workers. Wage increases are given as follows: 80 employees received 5¢ per hour, 5 received 7¢, 10 received 9¢, and 5 received 15¢. What was the average (mean) wage increase?
4. Two factories report their wage schedules as follows:

Factory A			Factory B	
7 employees	....	3,500. per annum	5.......	3,500.
6 "	....	4,000. " "	6.......	4,500.
5 "	....	5,500. " "	4.......	6,000.
1 "	....	12,000. " "	5.......	6,500.
1 "	....	14,000. " "		

   a. Which factory has the higher mean? higher mode? higher median?
   b. Which wage schedule shows the greater dispersion?
5. Which average would you consider most useful in stating "the average" in the following?
   a. The annual earnings of employees in the radio industry.
   b. The weights in the "line" of a football team.

   c. The earnings of union members in the oil industry.

   d. The income of the average family in the United States.

6. State (1) the range, (2) the average deviation, and (3) the standard deviation for the following series:

1, 3, 3, 5, 6, 7, 7, 7, 8, 9, 10, 49, 67

7. Work out the statistical association for the relationship between baldness and desk jobs. A population of 10,000 male adults is studied, of whom 4,000 were bald. 1,500 of these had desk jobs. Of the non-bald individuals, 2,300 had desk jobs.

8. Interpret the following statistical information for the association between happiness in marriage and age at marriage, for girls under 19, and 19 and over.

	Happy	Unhappy
Below 19	68	12
19 and over	812	108

9. Work out the coefficient of correlation for the following problem concerning the connection between entrance grades and college averages:

Student	Entrance Grades	College Averages
A	90	84
B	84	76
C	80	78
D	70	74
E	66	72

10. Draw a scatter plot for the above.

11. Interpret the following plot which represents Boyle's law applied to an "ideal" gas, i.e., one which acts in exact correspondence with the law. Explain why it illustrates an inverse functional relationship:

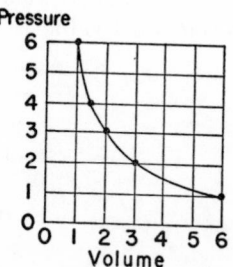

12. What kinds of additional information would you desire in the following?
   a. "A is a better teacher than B, for 95 per cent of A's students pass, but only 85 per cent of B's do."
   b. "Lawyer Z has the enviable record of 100 per cent success in all cases he has tried."
   c. "Poll A tells us that 90 per cent of the people are in favor of sending military supplies to Europe, but Poll B says that 75 per cent of the people are opposed."
   d. "The fluctuations in the amount of electrical disturbances in the sun is in precise correlation with the fluctuations in the average prices of stocks on the New York Stock Exchange."

13. A study was made of 100 children to determine the degree of correlation, if any, between the number of toys possessed by these children and the number of times they nagged their mothers. Discuss the following questions:
   a. Is this a suitable subject for a correlations study?
   b. Assuming that a coefficient of correlation of $+ .32$ was found, would this be an example of "illusory accuracy"?
   c. Ignoring the question of the accuracy of "r" in 2, would this finding be an example of a statistical induction?

14. The book *Sexual Behavior in the Human Female,* by Alfred Kinsey and his staff, was based on interviews with 5,940 white American females. Data obtained from these interviews were tabulated and classified. Most of the interviews were taken in Illinois, Florida, and California. The results showed that 75 per cent of the subjects had gone to college, as compared with a national average of 13 per cent. A larger than average number were from middle and upper economic groups, and there was almost no representation of Roman Catholics and Orthodox Jews.
   a. Kinsey asserted that he did not draw any generalizations from his findings. Is this consistent with the title of the book?
   b. If the data are regarded as a sample, how would you criticize its composition? Do the statistical weaknesses mean that his findings have no statistical value?

Chapter 19

Logic and Evaluations

Section I: "Statements of Fact" and Evaluations

Consider the following pairs of sentences:

(1) A: Nero reigned during the years 54-68 A.D.
B: Nero was a wicked man.

(2) A: It is illegal to serve liquor to women at bars in the state of Indiana.
B: Women ought not to sit at bars.

(3) A: The Tribune Tower in Chicago is higher than the Leaning Tower of Pisa.
B: The Tribune Tower is more beautiful than the Leaning Tower.

The reader will note a fundamental distinction between the A's and the B's above. The A's are typical "statements of fact," i.e., statements concerning existences in space and time, and verifiable by the methods we have examined throughout Part Three. We can readily prove the truth or falsity of these statements. The B's, on the other hand, are "evaluations," or value judgments which, though they *refer* to *facts*, also do *something more* than that. Evaluations, such as the B's, assert that something does or does not possess a certain value, or disvalue. By "values" we refer to objects or situations or activities which are liked, or desired, or approved by human beings. Disvalue, the antonym of value, refers to things which are disliked, held in aversion, and disapproved. Personal attitudes and preferences are important in evaluations, but not in statements of facts. Food and drink, love and companionship, music and poetry, courage, wisdom, and justice are a few among the many things which are valued. In our subsequent discussion, how-

489

ever, we shall be primarily concerned not with all types of values, but with moral and aesthetic evaluations, chiefly the former. By moral evaluations we shall refer to judgments that certain forms of conduct are right or wrong from an ethical standpoint; by aesthetic evaluations we shall mean judgments that something is either beautiful or ugly. The specific logical problem which we shall consider in this chapter is whether moral and aesthetic evaluations are capable of verification by scientific methods, or, stated in another way, whether it is possible to prove that such evaluations are true or false.

A prevalent view concerning values is that "value-judgments" (or evaluations) are neither provable nor disprovable since they are matters of taste or "opinion." * They are thought to be based on "subjective" experiences involving purely personal preferences and individual notions as to what is desirable. The terms "true" and "false" are regarded as inapplicable to evaluations. If this view is correct, then it follows that the three evaluations listed below are mere matters of taste or opinion, and that "one man's opinion is as good as another's":

(4) The most beautiful sight on this earth is a pile of dishes on the sink.

(5) Caruso was not the worst tenor of all time.

(6) A teacher ought not to flunk a student merely because the student disagrees with some of his opinions.

Does the reader feel that he could *agree or disagree* with these statements with equal "justification," since no justification of them is possible? Or does he believe that (4) is false and that (5) and (6) are true? Let us explore the problem of the logic of evaluations.

Section II: Values as Expressions of Preferences or Attitudes

Before we can judge the truth of any statement, we must understand its meaning. Our first problem, then, is a semantical

---

* "Opinion" is a word whose meaning is vague. To say, "In my opinion, most Americans eat a balanced diet" simply expresses the speaker's feeling that he cannot prove his statement, but he believes the statement to be *true*. Opinions, then, are true or false, but we usually qualify our statements in this way when we are doubtful or when we have no proof. In the sense in which the word was used in the paragraph, however, it appears to mean "something which *cannot* be proved," or "a matter of personal taste." This is a dubious usage and it begs the question which we are now discussing.

one, to determine the meaning of an evaluation. In this section we shall consider two interpretations of the meaning of evaluations: (1) They express personal preferences, or likes and dislikes, in short that they are matters of "taste," and (2) they express group preferences, or the approval or disapproval of groups. Each of these theories denies that evaluations can be true or false. A corollary of these positions is that it is not possible to engage in genuine disputes concerning values.

1. Values as expressions of personal likes and dislikes

Consider the following pairs of sentences:

(1) A: I like Picasso's "Guernica."
    B: I don't like Picasso's "Guernica."

(2) C: "Guernica" is a beautiful painting.
    D: "Guernica" is not a beautiful painting.

In the first group we find no dispute between A and B. Each asserts his feelings concerning the "Guernica." B has not said that A was mistaken. In the second pair, however, there appears to be a dispute. D seems to disagree with C; he appears to say that C is wrong. But as we learned earlier, an apparent dispute may not be a real or actual dispute, as when two parties use the same symbols to designate different referents. Perhaps C and D have different meanings in mind when they speak of "beautiful paintings." There is also another possibility. Perhaps C means merely that he likes the painting, and D means that he does not like it. If this is the case, then again there is no real dispute.

The first theory is concerned with the language of evaluations and presents a kind of definition of values, namely, that all statements of value can be translated into statements of liking and disliking. Evaluations, it is alleged, are not arguable, but merely indicate personal feelings or attitudes. Our example above concerned "aesthetic" values; the following pairs of sentences make the same type of translations for "moral" values:

(3) A: Hitler was a wicked man.
    B: Hitler was not a wicked man

may be translated, according to this theory, into

(4) A': I dislike Hitler.
    B': I don't dislike Hitler.

This theory gives us a valuable insight into evaluations in that it correctly emphasizes two important characteristics of value-judgments: that our evaluations do express our preferences and that evaluations are admittedly not merely factual statements. But if the type of translation noted above is *all that can be said* about evaluations, then we shall be forced to accept the rather startling conclusion that there has never been a genuine argument over values in the entire history of mankind. Every time men thought that they were disputing over values, i.e., whether a painting was beautiful, or whether a singer had a good voice, or whether it was right or wrong for the United States to use the atomic bomb, they were engaging in verbal disputes and talking at cross purposes, since each person was merely asserting his personal likes or dislikes. For there is never a real dispute when one man asserts that *he* likes something, and another answers that *he,* for his part, does not like it. This brings all values into the realm of mere tastes, and of tastes, as the proverb has it, there is no disputing. These are some of the implications of the first theory. Can we accept these conclusions?

We are dealing with a problem of definition here and seeking for what we regard as an adequate meaning. The first theory would appear to be inadequate as an analysis of the meaning of evaluations. It holds that human beings have suffered from self-delusion through the ages. But this has not been established. For liking and valuing are not identical. There is a difference between saying "I prefer the music of Brahms to that of Tchaikowsky" and asserting that "Brahms is a better composer than Tchaikowsky." The second statement claims objectivity: the first does not. Similarly, there is a difference between disliking Hitler and saying that he is a wicked man. It is possible to like a wicked person, knowing that he is wicked. It is possible to dislike a just man, to admire the bravery of an enemy, and to enjoy a work of art which we consider second-rate. When we say that a painting is beautiful or that a man is just, we usually also like these things, but we do not *mean* merely that we like these things; we mean that the object or conduct has certain qualities or relations which fulfill or do not fulfill certain standards. The first theory stresses the truth that human beings express their preferences in their value judgments, but it ignores the fact that they also mean something more than this.

2. Values as expressions of group approval or disapproval

This theory is a "collectivistic" variation of the first, except that its scope is generally limited to the field of moral values. This theory holds that moral values are based on *group* preferences and attitudes, expressed in the form of approval or disapproval. Thus, if A (a Southerner) says that General Sherman was wicked and B (a Northerner) says he was not, their statements, this theory holds, may be translated as follows:

A: My group disapproved of General Sherman.
B: My group approved of General Sherman.

Thus the original conflict of opinion is declared to be an apparent rather than a real dispute. The parties, it is said, were not actually in disagreement over anything. Disputes might arise, of course, over whether the groups actually did approve or disapprove, but this is not a problem of value, but one of fact.

The approval theory is based on the insight that human beings do get most of their basic notions of right or wrong from their communities, and these notions vary from community to community. We also find changes in group attitudes within a given country, as toward the institution of slavery. It is the approval of the group, this theory holds, which puts the stamp of moral rightness on some customs and not on others. From this it follows that when we say that justice is a moral good we mean that our group approves of justice; when we say murder is wrong, we mean that our group disapproves.

But is this an adequate translation of our meaning? We shall consider a number of criticisms which may be advanced against the group-approval theory. We note, in the first place, that the term "group" is a vague term, and this vagueness will be found to have some paradoxical consequences. Let us apply this theory to a particular problem, such as that of race segregation in some Southern communities in the United States. The group-approval theorist is committed to the position that segregation is morally right in these Southern communities, since these groups approve of this institution. But there are also Southerners who regard segregation as a moral crime. Are these individuals immoral in their communities since they refuse to accept the prevailing "morality"? The question points to a fatal vagueness in the word "group." The whole American people also constitute a group. Shall we say that segregation is wrong in the United States as a whole, including the South, if we find that a majority of the American people are opposed to segregation? But the Southern states also constitute a distinct group. Shall we then say that segregation is morally right in the South? If the latter, then we find that some Southern states are exceptions to the rule. Is segregation immoral in those states? Can segregation be moral in a county and immoral in the rest of the state? Immoral in a township and moral in the rest of the county? Can the Hatfields and the McCoys constitute their own groups? Can a group, like a class, have a membership of only one person?

A second criticism is that the theory makes the vote of the majority the source of all moral judgments. But "This has the vote of the majority" seems different from "This is morally right," just as "You are stronger than I am" does not mean "You are right and I am wrong." Legality is not identical with morality. The theory makes it nonsensical to say: "I think this action is wrong, but I am in a minority," for what meaning can "wrong" have if the majority vote *makes* it right? Is it not possible, however, for the majority to be wrong?

Finally, let us grant that some individuals regard all of the customs of their own group as right. But are these not perhaps uncritical and unreflective persons? Reflective individuals examine the customs of their own groups in a critical manner to determine whether they are right. If they believe that these customs are not right, they may seek to correct them by discussion and persuasion. But as already noted, the group-approval position makes it impossible to carry on discussion or argument concerning moral values. The sole question in each case is, does the group approve? The man who conforms is always the moral man; the dissenter is always in the wrong. He cannot logically try to convince the majority that they follow wrongful practices, for the mere fact that they approve of these practices is proof that they are moral.

Section III: Standards of Value—Ends and Means

Let us pause for a moment to see where we stand. We have agreed that evaluations involve our preferences and approvals and that they are not mere statements of fact. Nevertheless we found the personal preference and group-approval theories unsatisfactory, for these theories deny the possibility of genuine disagreements concerning values, though such disputes do occur. We shall now examine a different type of approach to the meaning of value judgments, an approach which has the merit of making genuine disagreements intelligible.

Let us consider a problem in social ethics. Ought we to legalize gambling? Your first response to this question may be, "Yes, I don't see why not. Let people gamble if they wish to," or it may be, "No, gambling is wrong." But there is a counterpart of the "law of rationality" in the field of values. The law of rationality tells us that we ought to base our beliefs on evidence and reasons. Similarly, if we are reflective persons we will seek to make our value judgments reasoned judgments. We will think of our reasons for being in favor of or against legalized gambling instead of being content with saying, "I like (or dislike) gambling," or, "My community approves (or disapproves) of gambling." We ought to consider the logical consequences of saying either that we ought to or that we ought not to legalize gambling.

Our thinking may proceed along the following lines: "It is impossible to suppress the human desire to gamble. If this desire is denied a legal outlet it will find an illegal one. Illegal gambling funnels vast sums of money into the hands of undesirable elements in the community and gives these elements great power. They corrupt the police force and may even control the political machines in our great cities." These considerations make us tend toward legalization. Then we consider the other side: "If we legalize gambling, it will become more respectable to gamble, and many more people will take to this vice, including many who can ill afford to. Undesirable elements usually manage to obtain control of legalized gambling, etc."

We have indicated how it is possible to support a value-judgment by an argument. When we utter a "because" we appeal to a reason. This reason may be an assumption or premise which expresses a value-standard. A value-standard is a generalized value judgment which states a general principle of value, such as, "The corruption of law-enforcement agencies is a great evil," or, "an accused person ought not to be required to testify against himself," etc. The American colonists objected to the tea tax on the ground that taxation without representation was wrong.

Many value discussions proceed in this way. We assume a general principle, or general value standard, and apply it to a particular case. Our reasoning takes a syllogistic form: "Whatever is so-and-so is right (or wrong). This is so-and-so. Therefore it is right (or wrong)." As a rule there are more disagreements over the application than over the principles.

Now, every value conclusion must rest on value premises. The "ought-to-be" can be deduced only from another "ought-to-be," and never from a mere "is" or statement of fact. A premise that merely states that something is or is not the case cannot yield a value conclusion.

Some value principles are of greater generality than others. Some are "higher" in a logical sense, i.e., they are more "basic" which simply means that they are assumed in order to establish the less basic standards. The less basic standard is deduced from the more basic one. Thus we might ask, "Why is taxation without representation wrong?" and we might answer that it violates the principle of justice or fair treatment. Justice, then, is more basic than the taxation principle. Justice, on the other hand, may not be deducible from a higher standard. It may be an ultimate principle. We shall postpone discussion of ultimate principles for the time being and go on to discuss another type of justification of particular value judgments.

Our thinking about values often takes a means-end relationship into account. The relationship of means to ends is a familiar one. Reduction of calorie intake is a means toward the goal of losing weight; hard work is a means to success. In social problems we have certain ends, or goals, or objectives, and we seek to find the appropriate means to bring these objectives into being. Similarly we may set up a value objective, such as civil peace, the elimination of war, or the stability of the family; and we may seek to find the means to achieve these goals. Means and ends are often inextricably intertwined with each other, and John Dewey has warned us against sharply divorcing means from ends, but the distinction is nevertheless a useful one.

We often justify a value-judgment on the ground that it is a means to (i.e., it results in) a desirable goal. In our thinking about social-ethical problems we often set up a basic goal conceived of as the "general welfare," or the general good of society. John Stuart Mill, in his *Essay on Liberty,* argues that free speech for dissenters ought to be allowed on the ground that such freedom is beneficial to society. In our previous illustration it might be argued that corruption of law-enforcement agencies or the encouragement of gambling is detrimental to society.*

A means-end problem is essentially a technical one, and thus capable of being verified by scientific methods of proof. Will swift and sure punishment deter the commission of criminal acts? This is a factual question. Similarly, if we can agree on the definition of "general welfare," we can judge the efficacy of proposed methods for the achievement of this goal. We shall judge some methods as successful, others as not. The difficulties of proof will of course be very great, since we are dealing with vague terms and extremely complex factual relations, but the difficulties are not theoretically insurmountable. It is thus possible to "prove" whether or not free speech and legalized gambling are beneficial to society.

Now, when we consider that two persons may accept the same value standard, or the same value objective, but disagree only with respect to the application of the standard or with respect to the efficacy of the means to be employed in reaching the agreed-upon goal, then genuine discussions concerning the rightness or wrongness of an act become possible.

But now comes the more difficult problem. Suppose that there is no agreement on the goal. Is it possible to prove to others that they ought to accept our goals—or can they prove that we ought to accept their goals? If this cannot be done, we

---

* This is not the only possible kind of justification we can give of social-ethical value judgments. Some philosophers have claimed that freedom of speech is a "natural right" of man and that no consideration of public policy justifies any government in limiting this freedom. It is not our purpose to attempt to find the "correct" basis for value-judgments, however, but only to show the possibilities of rational-scientific discussion concerning values.

seem forced back to personal preference or the approval of our groups as the ultimate basis for our value-judgments.

Goals, of course, are like standards, in that some are more basic than others. Any goal short of the "ultimate" can be justified by a more basic goal. But a truly ultimate standard or goal cannot be justified by logic, for a proof requires a premise—in this case a value premise—and "ultimate" means "nothing more basic."

It would appear then, that we must simply "accept" an ultimate basis for our evaluations. Our ultimate values rest on ultimate decisions as to the kinds of lives we wish to live. We simply choose to be certain kinds of persons. We thus seem to have come full circle to the notion that personal preference is really the basis of our evaluations. But even if this is so, we shall nevertheless have to modify the original statement of the preference theory. For we now see that it is only the truly ultimate standards or ends which are beyond the scope of logic and scientific evidence. For many evaluations are subject to the criteria of logical proof.

Further, disagreements with respect to ultimate values are not the rule, most disputes being concerned with difference of means. It is of course true that some differences over means may be so deep-seated as to be equivalent to differences in ultimate ends.

But there is another consideration to be noted here. In practice the "ultimate" end is never fixed so long as human beings are capable of reflection and deliberation. A reflective person constantly re-examines his goals, even his supposedly "ultimate" ones, and he sometimes finds that he does not really want to be the kind of person he thought he wanted to be. He may have achieved a new insight into the values which life offers. Thus even our "ultimate" ends are subject to the possibility that they are not really ultimate and that they may be the wrong means to some "higher" end. Our conclusion here is that we should always assume that rational discussion will be useful where men appeal to ends or standards as a justification of their evaluations.

Section IV: Are Morals "Relative"?

It is a corollary of the group approval theory that moral values are relative to the group that approves them. Group-approval means group-relativism. An outstanding representative of this view is the American sociologist, W. G. Sumner, whose *Folkways* forcefully argues the position that moral values are based upon the "mores," or customs considered socially important by a group of human beings. Sumner and the anthropologists have shown us that there exists a multitudinous variety of customs in different parts of the world, and everywhere men think that their customs are morally right. All are actually justified in so believing, the group relativist adds. "The mores," said Sumner, "can make anything right." There is no higher standard than group approval in judging such matters, for there are no independent judges who can compare and judge the different codes and customs. Every judge will be inside a particular group and must therefore judge in accordance with the standards of that group. Thus, no group can legitimately criticize the standards of a different group since each group uses a standard which is valid only within its own region. To say, then, that an action is right or wrong simply means that a group approves or disapproves.

This theory has an appealing plausibility. The relativist widens our mental horizons and shows us that what we may regard as an absolute standard may in truth be a very provincial one. Indeed, a good deal of nonsense has passed muster under the guise of "morality." In many communities, for example, smoking by professional people such as ministers and school teachers is regarded as immoral. Another reason for the popularity of the group-relativist view is that it may be regarded as the sole alternative to a forbidding absolutism, which, holding fast to certain narrow dogmas, is intolerant of diversity and is responsible for much bigotry. The attitude of narrow absolutism is illustrated in a story told about the German philosopher, Fichte, who said that a lie could never be morally justified. When asked whether he would not deceive a sick wife concerning her illness if the truth might cause her death, he replied, "If my wife must die by the truth, then let her die!" But let us not assume that group-relativism is the sole alternative to this kind of thinking.

The relativist teaches us that differences in customs are not necessarily differences in right or wrong. This lesson would be of great value if it taught us to take a more critical attitude toward our own standards in order to determine whether these standards are really adequate. But the relativist destroys the value of the wider outlook he has attempted to give us when he tells us that even reflection can find no other standard than the approval of a group.

We shall examine the relativistic view in some detail presently, pausing to note two points at this juncture. One concerns an implication of the view that the mere fact of group approval establishes the moral rightness of any action whatsoever. This means that cannibalism is morally right in the Solomon Islands, and, if the Germans approved of gassing millions of innocent victims, then such action was morally right in Germany. A second point to be noted is that the mere recognition of the diversity of moral customs in different parts of the world is not in itself sufficient to prove that moral values are relative to the approval of groups. The mere fact that a difference of moral opinion exists is not, *in itself,* sufficient to prove that each opinion is justified, any more than the fact that there have been different opinions concerning the shape of the earth in different times and places proves that the earth's shape is relative to group opinions. Similarly, it is *logically possible* that some groups may be wrong in their moral evaluations by approving the wrong things.

The mere fact that customs differ, then, does not establish the relativity theory. Let us now consider how the problem of "different customs" is seen through the "value-standard" theory, and contrast this treatment with that of the approval-relativity theory. A social group establishes moral rules and imperatives which it regards as the means necessary to achieve the "general welfare" of the members of the group. Among these moral rules is the sanctioning of a certain kind of marriage relationship. Thus, disregarding religious considerations, Americans regard monogamy as the ideal form of the marriage relation because they believe that it best attains certain social and personal values. But another group, say the Indonesians, may have the same basic goals and yet differ with respect to the choice of means. They may believe that polygyny is the ideal form of the marriage relation. In this hypothetical illustration both groups have the same ends but differ with respect to the nature of the appropriate means. The illustrations are, of course, oversimplifications, but this has been done deliberately, in order to exhibit the logical structure of the problem as clearly as possible.

We have noted that different means, e.g., customs, may be employed to achieve the same ends. The fact that different marriage customs are found in the United States and Indonesia may reflect legitimate differences of opinion concerning the facts in the matter, and as to the probable effects of different kinds of customs. On the other hand, such differences may indicate that one nation is ignorant of the consequences which flow from its own customs. Or, what is perhaps more often the case, differing customs may be due to differences in the conditions under which people live. Under one set of conditions custom A may achieve the general welfare; under different conditions, custom B may do this. Time, place, and circumstance must always be determining factors in our choice of means. Thus, it may be that monogamy achieves the general welfare in the United States because of the character of the people and the special conditions under which they live, and it may be that polygyny will achieve the general welfare in Indonesia because of their differing circumstances of life. But these differences are logically compatible with the acceptance of exactly the *same goals* in each country. Similarly, there is one rule for good health in respect to diet: One's foods should be well-balanced. But this does not require that all shall eat the same foods, for human beings live in the Arctic and in the tropics; they differ in their physiques. One man's food may be another man's poison. Different means, again, achieve the same end.

The group relativist emphasizes the existence of different customs, but he ignores the fact that the *general principle,* or standard, may transcend group boundaries. The means-end analysis differs from that of group relativism in that it does not hold that polygyny is the right system for the Indonesians merely because they approve of it. Perhaps, if they knew better, they would find that monogamy is the better method for achieving the well-being and dignity of their people, if this is what they desire. Polygyny may make the attainment of this goal impossible. Thus the choice of the means is not an arbitrary matter. By the same token, if monogamy is a means to an end, then it is not guaranteed to be the best system merely because Americans approve of it. The question is: How does this or that custom bring about the end we desire? An adequate answer to this question will require a vast amount of knowledge, including the experiences of human history and the findings of the social sciences. This is an enormously complex problem, and human beings will, in general, accept a system which has worked well in their own history, for experiment in such matters can be very dangerous. But peoples do criticize their own customs and those of others, and when they do, the logical basis of their criticism will be found in assumptions similar to those which we have indicated.

The relativist makes intercultural dialogue impossible; for him, the bare fact of approval is the final touchstone. The basic weakness of group relativism, however, is that it fails to take account of the distinction between particular value-judgments, as evidenced perhaps by customs on the one hand, and value standards on the other. Or the relativist may fail to distinguish between intermediate and more basic standards. But though different groups may have different customs and intermediate standards, they may share the same basic standards.

If we look for what is common to all human groups instead of for differences, we shall indeed find what appear to be the elements of a "universal morality" among the peoples of the world. All the great religions of mankind, such as Buddhism, Christianity, Confucianism, Hinduism, Islam, Jainism, Judaism, Sikhism, and Taoism emphasize the Golden Rule as the essence of morality. Though this agreement is with respect to a formal principle, rather than with respect to specific goals, it suggests that discussion may result in finding a basis of agreement on specific goals. The issues which divide men may thus be based upon differences of opinion concerning the efficacy of means rather than on ultimately different ends. And if this is so, then logic and scientific method may contribute not only to the enlightenment of the human mind concerning nature and its laws, but also to the understanding of the basic conditions which will result in the satisfaction of the heart's desire.

Section V: Conclusion

We began with a basic distinction between statements of fact and evaluations. Scientific methods of proof can be used only with respect to statements of fact. We found that these methods can be used when the question is one of the efficacy of means to achieve an agreed-upon end. When common standards or ends are accepted, discussion of means is fruitful and may lead to the ironing out of differences in evaluations.

Ultimate standards or ends cannot be proved to be "true" in terms of scientific methods of inquiry and proof. But we also noted that we can never be certain that we have actually reached the "ultimate" so that inquiry is justifiable to determine whether the accepted "ultimate" may not be a means to a yet higher end. The great American philosopher C. S. Peirce once admonished us never to put obstacles in the way of inquiry, and this advice is relevant in our discussion concerning values. Let us now sum up by noting four ways in which logical analysis may be helpful in discussions concerning values:

1. Logic helps us to clarify the meaning of evaluation.

2. Logic helps us to determine whether our means make sense in terms of our ends, by working out the consequences that follow from our choices. This is an ever-present problem for legislators. After a wave of kidnappings, for example, the public may demand the death penalty for kidnappers. But legislators who work out the consequences of this kind of legislation know that it defeats its own purposes. There should be some inducement to make the kidnapper preserve the life of his victim, and it is also evident that juries will be reluctant to find a verdict of guilty when the victim's life has not been taken.

3. Logical analysis may show us that we are striving for the wrong goals; that our immediate goals will defeat the attainment of more important goals. Thus many socialists discovered that the abolition of private property in the U.S.S.R. did not bring about the elimination of cruelty and oppression.

4. Logical analysis may also reveal inconsistencies in our thinking. Few of us, perhaps, are as inconsistent as was the Mexican Society for the Prevention of Cruelty to Animals when it raised funds for its propaganda by staging a benefit perform-

ance at the bull-ring, but all of us sometimes fail to practice what we preach.

Logic, then, is relevant in all human problems, in problems of value as well as in those of a scientific nature. Reason is opposed to dogmatism, fanaticism, and obscurantism. The rational individual will recognize the complexities of human problems, and the difficulties in proving one side or the other in controversial issues. But he will not assume that any human problem is inherently insoluble. Many years ago Socrates taught that "the unexamined life is not worth living." The life that is not scrutinized by intelligence is a life not fit for a human being. Logic is an indispensable tool in achieving the enlightenment of the human mind.

Exercises

A. Factual Statements and Evaluations

In the following group, distinguish the factual statements from the evaluations. If a statement is ambiguous, interpret it in accordance with its different possible meanings. Also note whether any of these statements are moral or aesthetic evaluations.

1. Some Americans say that race discrimination is morally wrong.
2. It is proper to indent quotations.
3. The optimum population of the world is 2 billion persons.
4. Unemployment will be our most important problem six months hence.
5. This commemorative stamp is in perfect condition.
6. It is sinful to commit murder.

B. Ends and Means

The economic system of the United States is one of "free-competition." In the Soviet Union the system is one of state-ownership and control. In answering the following questions, state your value standards, and also indicate which types of factual evidence would be relevant to the problem:

1. Do you believe that it would be desirable for the Soviet Union to adopt the free-competition system?
2. Do you believe that it would be desirable for the United States to adopt the system of state-ownership?

3. Do you believe that the free-competition system is best for the United States, and state-ownership for the Soviet Union?

4. Is it possible that both countries ought to abandon their present systems?

Some Problems for Discussion

1. "If I say, 'Birth control is morally wrong,' that is my opinion and not an assertion of fact. It can't be proved. It can't be disproved. So, there's no use in arguing about it."

2. Can the disputes between communists and anti-communists be settled by an appeal to the facts? Do these disputes involve different ultimate evaluations?

3. You have a friend who is not interested in classical music and who says that he has no desire to be interested. Is it possible for you to prove to him that he ought to be interested?

4. Are there any socially approved customs which you consider to be wrong? On what basis do you make your decision? Do you think that you could prove that these customs are wrong to one who accepts them?

5. Show how standards are used in passing judgment on a work of art (or a performer). Do you find any important differences between the use of the "means-end analysis" in the fields of ethics and aesthetics?

6. Do professional interior decorators have better taste with respect to home furnishing than the average housewife?

7. "The history of evolution shows us that those among the lower animals who cooperated with each other were able to survive, whereas those who failed to cooperate perished. This indicates that the moral obligation to cooperate is established on the basis of scientific evidence."

8. In the following, on what bases would the speakers justify their assertions, if challenged?

   a. A "taste" theorist asserted that convicting accused persons without a fair trial is a "monstrously immoral" practice.

   b. A "group-approval" theorist stated that it was wrong for churches to exclude members of certain "minority" groups.

9. Is the author of the following inconsistent in his reference to tolerance as a desirable trait?

I think that ethical writers are often inclined to overrate the influence of moral theory upon moral practice, but if there is any influence at all, it seems to me that ethical subjectivism, instead of being a danger to, is more likely to be an advantage to morality. Could it be brought home to people that there is no absolute standard in morality, they would perhaps be on the one hand more tolerant, and on the other more critical in their judgments. (E. Westermarck, *Ethical Relativity,* Harcourt, Brace and Co., 1932, p. 59.)

D. *Discuss the following quotations:*

1. Three degrees of latitude reverse all jurisprudence; a meridian decides the truth. Fundamental laws change after a few years of possession; right has its epochs; the entry of Saturn into the Lion marks to us the origin of such and such a crime. A strange justice that is bounded by a river! Truth on this side of the Pyrenees, error on the other side. (Blaise Pascal.)

2. Deep-seated preferences are not to be argued about—you cannot argue a man into liking a glass of beer—and, therefore, when differences are sufficiently far-reaching, we try to kill the other man rather than let him have his way. But that is perfectly consistent with admitting that, so far as appears, his grounds are as good ours. (Justice O. W. Holmes)

3. Every dispute is based upon someone's ignorance. (Justice Louis D. Brandeis.)

4. A vast number of the apparent differences between the dictates of our own and the primitive conscience thus represent nothing but differences in conceptions of the effects of actions, and, as such, afford no evidence for the existence of a diversity of moral standards. Many others, again, are due to actual differences in particular situations, in consequence of which a standard that among ourselves calls for one concrete mode of conduct, as the care and support of our aged parents, may elsewhere require, or appear to require, the abandonment of the aged to their fate. (F. C. Sharp, *Ethics,* D. Appleton-Century-Crofts, 1928, p. 177.)

5. To say that something is enjoyed is to make a statement about a fact . . . ; it is not to judge the value of that fact. There is no difference between such a proposition and one which says that something is sweet or sour, red or black. . . . But to call an object a value is to assert that it satisfies or fulfills certain conditions. . . . Only a child . . . thinks to settle the question of desirability by reiterated proclamation: "I want it, I want it, I want it." . . . To say that something satisfies is to report something as an isolated finality. To assert that it is *satisfactory* is to define it in its connections and

interactions. . . . That it is satisfying is the content of a proposition of fact; that it is satisfactory is a judgment, an estimate, an appraisal. (John Dewey, *The Quest for Certainty*, Minton, Balch and Co., 1929, pp. 260–1.)

6. It is certainly undesirable for men of science to restrict their thinking to what is and will be, leaving to propagandists and reformers and talkers the decisions about what ought to be. Is any group of thinkers qualified to study the wants of mankind, the consequences of acts and events, and the improvement of human valuations without reliance on the facts and methods of anthropology, psychology, sociology, economics, government, and other sciences of man? Can science avoid trying what impartial curiosity and honest work can accomplish in this field of controversy and prejudice? (E. L. Thorndike, "Science and Values," in *Science*, Jan. 3, 1936.)

The Venn Diagrams

In our discussion of the diagramming of syllogisms we used the method invented by Euler. We shall now explain an alternative method developed by the English logician John Venn.

The Euler method as applied to syllogisms is most useful in exhibiting the invalidity of syllogisms that are already known to be invalid. The Euler diagrams, as we saw, often required much ingenuity on the part of the investigator. The Venn diagrams, on the other hand, furnish us with an "automatic" method for exhibiting validity or invalidity. These diagrams, however, require a new way of stating the A-E-I-O forms, in the form of algebraic equations, and it is to these equations that we must first turn our attention.

Section I. The Venn Diagrams for Categorical Propositions

In his *Algebra of Logic* the English logician and mathematician George Boole introduced an algebraic interpretation of the A-E-I-O forms. To illustrate: Let S and P stand for the classes "spars" and "painted things." The things which are members of both classes (painted spars) will be symbolized by SP. SP is the "product" of the two classes, i.e., of the things which are both S and P. Another example: If the class of "men" is represented by A and the class of "tall things" by B the class of "tall men" will be designated by AB.

A line above a symbol, called a "bar" stands for the "negation" of that symbol. Thus, the class of "things which are not painted" is shown by $\bar{P}$, read as "bar-P," or "non-P." The product of the classes of "spars" and "things which are not painted" is shown by $S\bar{P}$. This is read as "spars which are not painted" or "spars which are outside the class of painted things."

Let us now look at the A-E-I-O forms stated algebraically in the form of equations:

A-form	All S is P	$S\bar{P} = O$
E-form	No S is P	$SP = O$
I-form	Some S is P	$SP \neq O$
O-form	Some S is not P	$S\bar{P} \neq O$

The "O" stands for the "null class," i.e., a class that has no members. The symbol " $=$ " is read as "is equal to," and " $\neq$ " as "is not equal to." Thus $S\bar{P} = O$ (the A-form) is read as "the class of things that are S and non-P equals zero." This equation asserts that $S\bar{P}$ has no members, i.e., "there are no spars that are unpainted." The last statement is equivalent to "All spars are painted." The negative formulation in the equation, however, is a matter of great importance, as we shall soon see.

The E-form: $SP = O$ tells us that the S's which are P's are non-existent, i.e., the product of both classes is without membership. This is to say: No S is P.

The I-form, $SP \neq O$ tells us that the product of the two classes is *not* equal to zero. This means that it does have members. In other words, there are an unspecified number of things that are in the product of both classes and this is to say: Some S is P.

Note the important difference between the two universals (A and E) and the particular I with respect to existence.* The universals state that there are no existing members of the class products designated and assert nothing concerning the existence of any members of S or of P or of $\bar{P}$. The I-form, however, asserts that there *are* existing members of the class SP. This distinction concerning "existential import" has a significant bearing on the validity of syllogisms in the Boolean-Venn interpretation, as we shall note presently.

The O-form $S\bar{P} \neq O$ states that there are existing members of the class of things which are in the product of the two

---

* For a previous discussion of "existential import" the student may refer back to Chapter II, Section IV.

classes S and $\bar{P}$. Some things, in other words are S's and non-P's, i.e., some S's are not P's.

We shall now examine the Venn way of diagramming the A-E-I-O forms. The basic model is seen in the following intersecting circles for S and P:

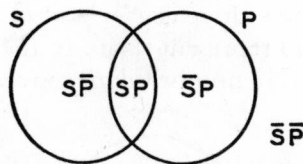

The middle portion marked SP indicates the product of the two classes S and P. On the left we find $S\bar{P}$, or the part of S that is outside of P, and on the right $\bar{S}P$, the part of P that is outside of S. Outside the two circles the symbols $\bar{S}\bar{P}$ indicate the area that is neither S nor P. This area will be ignored in our discussions.

The A-E-I-O forms are diagrammed as follows:

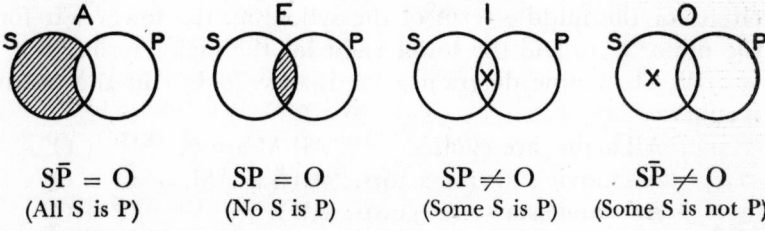

A	E	I	O
$S\bar{P} = O$	$SP = O$	$SP \neq O$	$S\bar{P} \neq O$
(All S is P)	(No S is P)	(Some S is P)	(Some S is not P)

Let us begin with the A-form. The shaded portion indicates that the $S\bar{P}$ area is non-existent, i.e., $S\bar{P} = O$. This means that there is no part of S that is outside of P, or, No S is non-P. The E-form, we note, shows the SP portion shaded. This area of non-existence shows that SP is equal to zero, i.e., the product of classes S and P has no members.

The I-form tells us that there *are* members of the product of the two classes. This is shown by "x." The O-form indicates that there are existing members of $S\bar{P}$, i.e., S's that are not P's.

Note that the shaded portions give us definite information, to wit, that the shaded area is a null class. An "x" also definitely tells us that there are existing members of the class-product. But a blank area tells us nothing: it does not tell us that there are, nor that there are not, members of the class. There may be or there may not be, but this is left uncertain.

Section II. The Venn Diagrams for Syllogisms

Syllogisms involve three classes, and so we shall need three intersecting circles to represent them. In the diagram below the seven compartments are numbered for convenience in reference:

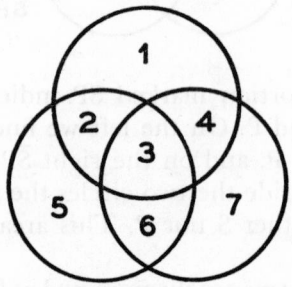

In diagramming syllogisms we shall reserve the upper circle for the middle term of the syllogism, the lower left for the minor term and the lower right for the major term.

We shall now diagram a familiar syllogism in the Venn manner:

All actors are egoists.	All M are P.	$M\bar{P} = O$
All movie stars are actors.	All S are M.	$S\bar{M} = O$
All movie stars are egoists.	All S are P.	$S\bar{P} = O$

The first step is to draw three intersecting circles, marking them M, S, and P. The next step is to diagram the major premise by shading M outside of P:

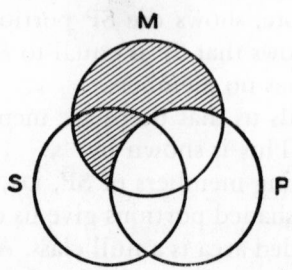

We now diagram the minor premise, shading the area of S outside of M:

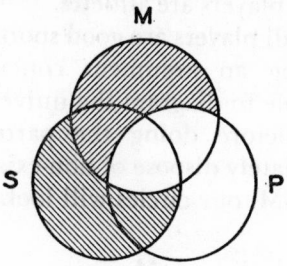

Our diagram is completed. We check, now, to determine whether the syllogism is valid or invalid. If the diagrams of the premises also show the correct diagram for the conclusion, then the argument is valid. The conclusion was $S\bar{P} = O$. The completed drawing shows that the part of S that is outside of P is shaded. The syllogism is valid.

Another example:

All Socialists are integrationists.	$M\bar{P} = O$
No Democrats are Socialists.	$SM = O$
No Democrats are integrationists.	$SP = O$

We shade compartments 1 and 2 to diagram the major premise, and then find that we need shade only compartment 3 to diagram the minor premise:

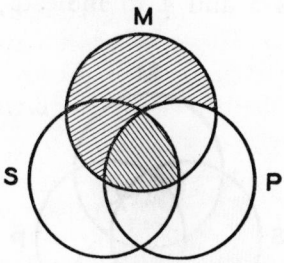

The conclusion states that the product of S and P is nonexistent. This should be shown by shading in compartments 3 and 6, where S and P intersect. But number 6 is unshaded, so that our conclusion is not shown by the diagrams for the premises. The syllogism is invalid.

Our next example involves particular propositions:

Some athletes are good sports.	$M P \neq O$
All baseball players are athletes.	$S \bar{M} = O$
Some baseball players are good sports.	$S P \neq O$

In diagramming an argument containing a particular premise it is advisable to diagram the universal premise (which requires shading) before doing the particular premise, for shading will immediately dispose of non-existent compartments. When we diagram $S \bar{M}$, our circles will look like this:

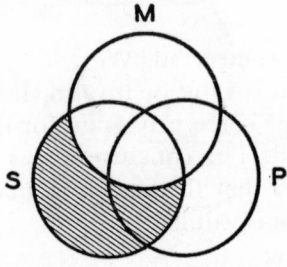

We must now add the diagram for $M P \neq O$. This requires that we place an "x" in the intersection between the M and P circles. The area of intersection is represented by compartments 3 and 4. It is obviously not a matter of indifference where we place the "x" since 3 is *inside* S and 4 is *outside* S. Since no definite instructions are given we write the "x" on the line between compartments 3 and 4 to indicate that it may be in either one:

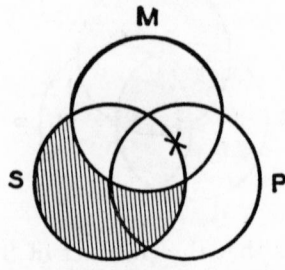

We check for validity. The conclusion requires an "x" in the intersection of S and P (compartment 3). This is not shown, so the syllogism is invalid.

For our final example we shall examine a syllogism valid under the Euler diagrams (and the Aristotelian rules) and invalid by the Venn circles:

All mortals are sinners.	$M\bar{P} = O$
All human beings are mortals.	$S\bar{M} = O$
Some human beings are sinners.	$SP \neq O$

Diagrammed, we have:

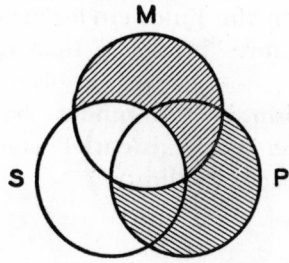

The conclusion requires that we have an "x" in compartment 3 but obviously no "x" can be drawn if both premises are universals, and the syllogism is thus invalid under the Venn method. In other words, it is impossible to derive an existential conclusion from non-existential premises, and the Boolean-Venn algebraic formulas require this as a sixth rule of the syllogism. The syllogism, of course, is valid under the Aristotelian rules which permit a term distributed in the premises to be undistributed in the conclusion. The older logic did not formulate universal propositions in a non-existential manner. For further discussion of this subject see Chapter 11, Section IV.

To sum up: The Venn diagrams offer a simpler method of testing the validity of syllogisms than do the Euler circles since the method is more or less "automatic," whereas the Euler method requires the exercise of ingenuity on the part of the tester. The Euler method requires us to *find* the "picture" which shows the premises true and the conclusion false in invalid arguments.

Another important difference between the two methods is that the Venn diagrams indicate *validity* as well as invalidity. The conclusion must be exhibited in a positive manner;

if it is not so exhibited, the argument is invalid. The Euler drawings, on the other hand, may lead us astray on this score, so that their use should be restricted to the visual demonstration of the invalidity of arguments that are already known to be invalid. Thus the Venn diagrams give us an alternative method for testing the validity of syllogisms. Diagramming, however, is never necessary for the determination of the validity of syllogisms: the rules are sufficient for that purpose. And if the chief value of the diagrams is to show that the rules accord with "real" situations, then the Euler circles may be said to give us visual proof that is more "intuitive" than that given us by the Venn diagrams.

When a syllogism is valid under the Aristotelian rules and invalid under the new "existential" convention, we should note this double aspect of validity.

Exercises

Diagram the ten syllogisms on pages 189–90 by the Venn method. Indicate validity or invalidity under both the Aristotelian and Venn analyses and explain why the Venn diagram supports your conclusion.

Index

517